A PLUME BOOK

REVOLUTION OF HOPE

VICENTE FOX was born in Mexico in 1942. Before his election as president, he was a rancher, boot maker, truck driver, Coca-Cola executive, democracy activist, congressman, and governor of the state of Guanajuato. He now lives at the farm his immigrant Ohio grandfather pioneered a century ago. Rancho San Cristobal is now home to Mexico's first presidential library, the Centro Fox academic think tank for global democracy, and the antipoverty foundation Vamos Mexico, which the president founded with his first lady, Marta.

ROB ALLYN is an author, TV commentator, and political consultant who has advised campaigns in the United States, Latin America, Asia, the Middle East, and the Caribbean. He has worked closely with President Fox for a decade and lives in Dallas, Texas.

Praise for *Revolution of Hope*

"Well-written and well-researched."

—*U.S. News & World Report*

"[Fox] poured out his heart in this book . . . thank you for writing it."

—Wolf Blitzer, CNN

REVOLUTION OF HOPE

THE LIFE, FAITH, AND DREAMS OF A MEXICAN PRESIDENT

REVOLUTION OF HOPE

VICENTE FOX

AND ROB ALLYN

A PLUME BOOK

PLUME
Published by the Penguin Group
Penguin Group (USA) Inc., 375 Hudson Street, New York, New York 10014, U.S.A. • Penguin Group (Canada), 90 Eglinton Avenue East, Suite 700, Toronto, Ontario, Canada M4P 2Y3 (a division of Pearson Penguin Canada Inc.) • Penguin Books Ltd., 80 Strand, London WC2R 0RL, England • Penguin Ireland, 25 St. Stephen's Green, Dublin 2, Ireland (a division of Penguin Books Ltd.) • Penguin Group (Australia), 250 Camberwell Road, Camberwell, Victoria 3124, Australia (a division of Pearson Australia Group Pty. Ltd.) • Penguin Books India Pvt. Ltd., 11 Community Centre, Panchsheel Park, New Delhi – 110 017, India • Penguin Group (NZ), 67 Apollo Drive, Rosedale, North Shore 0632, New Zealand (a division of Pearson New Zealand Ltd.) • Penguin Books (South Africa) (Pty.) Ltd., 24 Sturdee Avenue, Rosebank, Johannesburg 2196, South Africa

Penguin Books Ltd., Registered Offices: 80 Strand, London WC2R 0RL, England

Published by Plume, a member of Penguin Group (USA) Inc. Previously published in a Viking edition.

First Plume Printing, October 2008
10 9 8 7 6 5 4 3 2 1

Photograph credits appear on page 375.

Ⓟ REGISTERED TRADEMARK—MARCA REGISTRADA

The Library of Congress has catalogued the Viking edition as follows:
Fox Quesada, Vicente.
Revolution of hope : the life, faith, and dreams of a Mexican president / Vicente Fox and Rob Allyn.
p. cm.
Includes bibliographical references and index.
ISBN 978-0-670-01839-0 (hc.)
ISBN 978-0-452-28993-2 (pbk.)
1. Fox Quesada, Vicente. 2. Presidents—Mexico—Biography. I. Allyn, Rob. II. Title.
F1236.9.F69A3 2007
972.08'41092—dc22 2007021284
[B]

Printed in the United States of America
Original hardcover design by Carla Bolte

To the people of Mexico, with love

CONTENTS

INTRODUCTION

THE YEAR OF HIDALGO

Rancho San Cristóbal
December 4, 2006

In Latin America, presidents generally do not retire to the farm to write their memoirs. Most flee abroad, to escape extradition. More than one has lived in house arrest.

Former chief executives of Mexico did not build presidential libraries, crusade against hunger, or run the United Nations. They generally caught the first plane to Europe, turning over power to a designated successor by pointing the *dedazo,* the "finger." The traditional cycle of our six-year presidential term, the *sexenio,* worked like this: A president used his first five years to spend the nation deep into debt. In his sixth year, known as the "Year of Hidalgo," he cut off the flow of money to the economy and diverted hundreds of millions of dollars from Mexico's oil revenues to fund the campaign of his successor. Then the incumbent handed the sash to the man to whom he'd "given the finger" and got the hell out of the country, before the economic crisis kicked in.

Memoirs would have been a bad idea. They might have been used as evidence.

With the advent of real democracy in Latin America, our part of the world is no longer the sole province of dictators, demagogues, and deadbeats. Now we have peacemakers like Nobel Prize winner Oscar Arias of Costa Rica; democratic socialists like Ricardo Lagos of Chile, Alejandro Toledo of Peru, and Fernando Henrique Cardoso of Brazil. My own predecessor, Ernesto Zedillo, who steered our country's transition to democracy and now teaches at Yale, made a bit of history himself: a Mexican ex-president so honest that he actually needed to work for a living.

Typically, Mexico's former presidents exiled themselves to Ireland, drew on their Swiss bank accounts, and hid from the world in walled suburban villas. The presidential palace of Los Pinos used to be the place where you couldn't go home again: If a former Mexican chief of state went out to a taco stand in his native village, people would boo and hiss. Our leaders were famous for spending their last year in the presidential palace systematically looting the building, taking with them furniture, paintings, antiques, even doorknobs and light fixtures. Imagine the president in his imperial sash, sneaking down the gilt-railed staircase with a malachite bedside clock in one hand and a Flemish tapestry rolled under his arm, like a hotel guest ducking the bill while stealing the shampoo bottles.

A Mexican president's final year in office is called the "Year of Hidalgo" to honor Miguel Hidalgo, the great priest who fought for Mexico's independence from Spain. But a century and a half of authoritarian rule turned the sixth year of our presidents into a sad old joke: *¡En el año de Hidalgo, chingue a su madre, el que deje algo!* This translates politely as, "In the final year, the son of a bitch won't leave a thing!"

THREE DAYS AGO, at the stroke of midnight, I handed the green, red, and white presidential sash of Mexico to my successor, Felipe Calderón. A brilliant and courageous young reformer, President Calderón defeated a dangerous ally of Hugo Chávez named Andrés Manuel López Obrador, known as AMLO, winning a razor-thin upset in the closest election in our nation's history. The mood was tense. AMLO had held our nation's capital hostage for months to defy the vote of the people in a contest hailed by international observers as one of the cleanest, fairest, and most accurate elections ever conducted in Latin America. The swearing-in of Felipe Calderón was a historic moment: the first time in Mexico's history that one freely elected president turned over power to another, officially bringing democracy to the land ruled for nearly a century by what Peruvian novelist Mario Vargas Llosa called "the perfect dictatorship."

When I left Los Pinos, I took very little, determined to change Mexico's *sexenio* pattern of cronyism, corruption, and crisis. The first lady and I packed up my blue jeans and the vaquero belts with the big silver FOX buckle I wore on the campaign trail. We boxed them up with the proper suits and ties a president must wear to the United Nations, the White House, and the Vatican (in case anyone invites me back). For the mantel of my farmhouse, we brought a few photographs from my own inauguration day: Nelson Mandela and Lech Walesa, personal heroes of democracy; Bill Gates and Fidel Castro, two of the more fascinating dinner companions of a life in the global village; my daughter Paulina, holding aloft the banner of the Virgin of Guadalupe that caused such a stir in the secular world. For the presidential library that my first lady and I are building here at the ranch, I kept a copy of Mexico's first Freedom of Information Act; a thank-you note from a schoolboy in Chiapas, written on one of the computers that now connect every schoolhouse in Mexico to the Internet; a pottery bowl in vivid Mayan red and ocher, spun by the elderly hands of an indigenous woman in Chiapas with a loan from our microlending bank, inspired by Nobel Peace Prize winner Dr. Muhammad Yunus.

Then I went home to the farm of my immigrant forefathers, who came to Mexico from Ohio and Spain in search of their American dream, to tell you the story of mine.

I SIT HERE in the morning sun of our ranch near the exact geographic center of Mexico, literally confined to a rocking chair because I was struck by a bull last weekend; the doctors say the hairline fissure in my back will heal only if I stay very still.

This is difficult for me, this business of sitting still. The son and grandson of restless pioneers, I've spent my life in constant motion: striving, competing, fighting, changing, sometimes losing, sometimes winning, but, like any son of immigrants, always on the *move*. My American grandfather, who despite half a century in Mexico spoke only English until the day he died, used to growl, "Vicente, you have a bug up your ass!"

My late mother, whom I loved above anyone I've ever known, would have cringed to see these earthy words in the first pages of my book. Scandalous! But Doña Mercedes was an elegant Spanish merchant's daughter from Colonia Roma and always was shocked by our coarse language on the farm, as were so many of the people I later encountered in public life. Once, after being called to account by the press for using a barnyard epithet, I began a speech warning parents in the audience, "Mothers and fathers, please cover the ears of your children! The governor of Guanajuato is about to speak."

It seems like I have been on the move since I was a boy. Racing my brothers to the barn to see who could lift the heaviest bale of wheat (I won, and if José wants to tell you different, then he can write his own book). Driving Coca-Cola trucks pell-mell across the Chihuahuan desert to deliver more cartons of Coke than our competitors (we won, making Coca-Cola number one again in what is now the world's largest per capita soft drink market). Leading mass protests for democracy at the golden Angel of Independence amid the blaring traffic of the Paseo de la Reforma in the second-largest metropolis on the planet. Riding in campaign caravans through the moonlit mesas of Sonora, the jaguar jungles of Yucatán, the fertile fields of Morelos. Until yesterday my life was a whirlwind of bumpy helicopter rides into the mountainous south to open a hospital for *indígenas;* bounding up to the stage in a crowded *zócalo* to fire up the crowd in the plaza; the smooth familiar lift of the *Benito Juarez* as the Mexican presidential 737 headed to the Forbidden City of Beijing; Number 10 Downing Street; Crawford, Texas; and the Kremlin (Putin kept me waiting the longest, as though the KGB had briefed him on my restlessness).

In Mexico, people say, "God has nothing but time, yet Fox is always in a hurry." Even now, just forty-eight hours out of office, I am ready to move on to my next challenge, my next dream for the Americas.

It is right to tell you my story here at San Cristóbal, surrounded by the half-timbered, white-plastered walls of the house I started drawing as a child with visions of becoming an architect. Sons and daughters of the Americas are like that, sketching the floor plan of the dream house on the kitchen table of the tenement, scribbling a business plan on the back of the envelope in the lunch box: always moving, dreaming, building, hoping. During my years at Coca-Cola, I collected old stones from ruined cathedrals and the oaken beams of demolished houses in Mexico City. Then I lugged them here in an old Ford pickup to plant this house at the far corner of my grandfather's farm, down the tree-lined lane from the two-hundred-year-old Spanish-style hacienda where I have eaten Sunday dinners as long as I can remember.

It is still a surprise to look down the table and realize that my mother is no longer there. It was Doña Mercedes who pointed out to me that my life was an unfinished book of five chapters. Chapter 1, farm boy and student. Chapter 2, Coca-Cola truck driver and corporate executive. Chapter 3, farmer and boot maker. Then my latest chapter, fifteen years in politics as democracy activist, opposition congressman, governor, president.

"What will you do with the next chapter, Vicente?" she asked not long before she died, her bright green eyes shining with hope. "Become a priest?"

As much as I admire the Jesuits, I think my first lady might object.

I went to mass yesterday and lit a candle for Doña Mercedes in the church whose steeple I can see from my front door. Then I walked to the town square to look my neighbors squarely in the eyes, knowing that I led my country with clean hands. This is perhaps because these hands were slapped hard and often by the wooden rulers of the priests as they schooled me to be a "man for others" like St. Ignatius Loyola. This, too, was my mother's teaching: that the highest calling was to serve your neighbors.

One night when I was ten, I watched her gentle hands press tight over the bubbling crimson of a ranch worker's bullet wound, as Doña Mercedes in turn watched me out of the corner of one eye to make sure I didn't pass out from the sight of blood. A well-loved woman of San Cristóbal, my mother tended the sick, educated the children of poor campesinos, and stood strong when pistol-waving invaders came to seize our farm. The people whose lives she touched sit now in pews beside me, boyhood friends grown to fathers and grandfathers, freshly scrubbed in their best Sunday suits after a rough week in the fields.

They, too, deserve to find their American dreams.

So do all of the poor and the hardworking, the restless and striving people of the inner cities and rural valleys and jungle plantations and native villages, from Coahuila to Canada, and from Harlem to Haiti. The American dream is not just the dream of wealthy and successful people of the United States. It is the dream of my campesino neighbors, of all people of the Americas, North and South.

Remember, America is more than the name the United States gives to itself. It is a fact little known around the world, but it drives people in Latin America, Canada and the Caribbean quietly mad when people in the United States, Europe, or Asia refer to the United States as "America," thus claiming for U.S. citizens the sole title of "Americans." South of the Rio Grande, which we call the Río Bravo, *we consider the entire hemisphere to be the Americas.* America is the New World, where ancient civilizations like the Maya and the Aztec mingled with the bold and the enslaved and the desperate from Europe, Arabia, and Asia. In this sense we are *all*

Americans, and from Canada's Yukon to Argentina's Tierra del Fuego we all share the dream of a better life.

They also dream who live in the back alleys of Asia and the sands of sub-Saharan Africa. The poor and the sick and the hardworking of every continent yearn for the prosperity my grandparents found in the Americas. They are the simple dreams of every family: a home of your own, a doctor for your sick, a school for your children, a good job—perhaps, if you work very hard, a piece of land or a corner store. This dream of the Americas is the hope we all share, born of poor people who crossed oceans, deserts, and prairies with heads full of big ideas and nothing in their pockets but courage.

Some, the remarkable few, are the visionary pioneers, the Andrew Carnegies who stowed away in the holds of stinking ships, and they are still coming even today, from Mexico, China, Pakistan, Vietnam. Some—like Andrew Grove, the Hungarian-born founder of Intel Corporation, or Russian-born Sergey Brin, cofounder of Google—will found empires, heal millions, direct Hollywood movies, invent new cures.

But most are humbler people, like my family—and perhaps yours. They come to new lands even today, from Mexico to the United States, from Guatemala to Mexico, from Africa to Italy, from Cambodia to Australia: hungry and desperate, seeking refuge from disease, war, persecution, and poverty, the four horsemen of desperation who drive immigrants to the gates of hope. Their dreams belong to all of us, because needs that basic, values that common, and a hope that divine simply cannot be limited by borders. America is in this way not so much a country but an ideal. And with all its faults, this dream of the Americas remains the last, best hope of mankind on earth.

WHILE I LOVE my own country and will always be Mexican to the toes of my boots, I save a special place in my heart for the United States, the place where I was briefly exiled as a schoolboy to learn that America is a land of opportunity, where every child is raised to achieve anything he or she will earn, to say anything he or she believes, and pray to any god who will answer his or her brightest hopes. I believe that the dreams of the Americas are universal, not just because I witnessed them in the United States but because in my own life I have seen the same revolution of hope in Mexico.

The ambitions of my German Irish American grandfather, who came from Ohio on horseback to marry the daughter of a French soldier and an *indígena* peasant, then worked his way up as a factory night watchman to buy the ranch where I tell you this story: These are American dreams.

The faith of my Catholic parents, who grew up among the bloody *Cristero* wars after the Mexican Revolution unleashed a wave of persecution against the church, a time when sacraments were forbidden, baptism meant jail, priests were murdered, and the Fox family worshipped at the chapel outside their front door: These are American dreams.

The hope of a Mexican farm boy to rise from truck driver to CEO of Coca-Cola Mexico, then topple the longest-running dictatorship of the twentieth century and become the first president of a true Mexican democracy: This was an American dream.

So, too, is my dream of a creating a great Union of the Americas to rival the European Union and the economic tigers of Asia, harnessing the power of the world's largest economy to lift people out of the shadowy borders of poverty and into the bright light of promise. This is my American dream. An America of bridges, not walls. An America where gates of love once again welcome those caught in the barbed wire of hate. An America of open hearts and open arms, where today, we find too many closed minds.

THE WORLD NEEDS this dream of the Americas, now as never before. From Oaxaca to the South Bronx, from teeming Pakistan to the trouble spots of Darfur and Gaza, the world hungers for the original promise of the Americas: a New World of freedom, prosperity, and opportunity. Most of all we pray for a revolution of hope to restore the founding spirit of our hemisphere, where the Statue of Liberty once welcomed the eager dreams of the poorest, bravest, and most desperate people of the earth.

It was in this spirit that my family came from Europe and the United States to build our own earthly paradise here at Rancho San Cristóbal, with the sweat of our brows and God's hands on our aching shoulders, guided by the hope of a better life. Think about it: In the Americas almost every one of us—unless your ancestors were all truly indigenous, like my great-grandmother—are descended from immigrants. If we would stop fearing each other for a moment and remember the stories of our own family albums, we could join hands across our borders to restore the vision of our ancestors. Such a revolution of hope could help heal the north-south continental divide between the haves and the have-nots, between America and the rest of the world.

As president, I traveled the world to promote Mexico's new democracy. I watched fireworks on the White House lawn and wore the wrong shoes to see the king of Spain. I made dozens of state visits to Europe, Africa, Latin America, and Asia, in and out of the United Nations and the Vatican, slums and presidential palaces, Castro's dining room, Tony Blair's fireside, the modest Houghton offices of Nelson Mandela. I've talked about the dream of the Americas to Chinese farmers, to Russian helicopter pilots, to Arab leftists, to an African woman threatened with death by stoning for her adultery.

And I am convinced that the naysayers are wrong. The world doesn't hate America. We love America. All around the planet, people admire the ideals of the Founding Fathers, the Statue of Liberty. We seek the revolution of hope that America once held up with that torch. And despite all that has happened, we still hold our breath in the hope that America will return to that promise. It is in this spirit that I write this book, because it is in this spirit that the world still looks to America to lead.

As a farm boy, I was an indifferent student, more interested in baling hay than studying mathematics. But history I loved, drinking in the stories of the great heroes of Mexico's struggle for independence, our revolution and the Cristero Rebellion, told to me around the fire by men who had fought for freedom in the early 1900s. I ignored my textbooks of grammar and science but devoured biographies of Napoleon and Genghis Khan, George Washington and El Cid. And if history proves nothing else, it is this:

Walls don't work.

The Great Wall of China didn't work. The Berlin Wall didn't work. The West Bank Barrier won't work. Walls *never* work. Walls are a medieval solution to a twenty-first-century problem. Mongols invade them. Escapees tunnel under them. Television beams over them. Palestinian car bombs explode them. Immigrants crawl through their barbed wire in the night, in search of a better life.

Today, as National Guard troops patrol the rivers from Arizona to Iraq, the United States isn't building a wall.

It is building a prison.

A wall of troops around the United States would suffocate the American dream. Inside the gilded cage of this new American hacienda envisioned by the isolationists, in a gated community surrounded by video cameras and guard dogs, the dream of the Americas would be forever hostage to fear, hate, greed, and indifference.

The America I love, the America of my grandfather, could never build that wall.

Instead we should return together to the spirit of San Cristóbal, the 2001 summit held here at our family's ranch, where George W. Bush came to meet my mother and made history by honoring Mexico with his first trip abroad. Now that Mexico is a democracy that puts computers in its schools and buys more products from the United States than all the greatest nations of Europe combined—a country with the rule of law, that retires its presidents to the farm to write books instead of letting them steal the silver—we should stop building walls between us and build a united continent instead.

IF THE NOTION of bringing our countries closer together unsettles North Americans, the idea is controversial here in Mexico, too. Our yanqui-go-home intellectual class resists ties with the United States and Canada, fearful of domination by the superpower that once took one third of our nation's territory in the U.S.–Mexico War. (The 1848 defeat of my presidential predecessor, the traitorous General Santa Anna, by the U.S. occupation forces resulted in the Treaty of Guadalupe Hidalgo, which handed over undisputed control of Texas, California, Nevada, Utah, and large parts of Arizona, Colorado, and New Mexico, to the U.S. government for $15 million. I would not have made that deal.) In Mexico the idea of foreign invasion is not a fantasy of xenophobes—yes, we have them, too—but the reality of our history, from the Spanish conquest of our ancient Aztecs and Mayans to the U.S. invasion of the 1840s, during which a young lieutenant named Ulysses S. Grant charged up Mexico City's Chapultepec Hill. In the 1860s the French invaded Mexico again and put the Austrian emperor Maximilian in Chapultepec Palace. During World War I, despite Mexico's rejection of German overtures in a famous telegram known as the Zimmermann Note, Woodrow Wilson drew up war plans to blockade Mexico's ports and send 250,000 U.S. troops to occupy our five northern states of Nuevo León, Tamaulipas, Chihuahua, Sonora, and Coahuila. Then the United States invaded Mexico twice again, within this past century, in my grandfather's time. In 1914, U.S. Marines occupied our largest seaport of Veracruz when our revolution threatened the interests of U.S. oil companies. In 1916, General John "Black Jack" Pershing invaded Mexico with an expeditionary force of three brigades of the U.S. Army, along with a squadron of airplanes and a young lieutenant named George S. Patton. They spent more than a year chasing the elusive Pancho Villa, the bandit-general hero of our revolution.

Little wonder that two nations who share the world's longest and most active land border (more than a million people cross it every day) seem perpetually at odds. Leaders on both sides, from our Congressional Palace of San Lázaro to Washington's Capitol Hill, can be expected to reject out of hand any vision of a united continent. Driven by fear or experience, hatred or history, common wisdom or common sense, politicians at the extremes in both countries will always seek to keep us forever "distant neighbors"—no matter how much we need each other.

But if my life proves anything, it is that we are not prisoners to our past.

Mexico was a dictatorship, it had always been a dictatorship, and it seemed that Mexico would always be a dictatorship—until people of courage stood up to change that. I think of the 1968 student demonstrators massacred by our government during that year of the Mexico City Olympic Games—of my hero Manuel Clouthier, who went on a hunger strike in 1988 to challenge the electoral fraud of Carlos Salinas—of the freedom fighters who stood beside me when the PRI men stuck a pistol in my belly and demanded a ballot box that was stuffed full of their forgeries. (I gave them back. We also burned a few.)

Mine is a good American story. There are love stories of hardy pioneers and defiant ranch women, rifle-toting bandits, elegant Latin beauties. As with any cowboy story, there are fistfights, gunfights, bullfights—even a football game. And like the best American stories, mine offers the hope that any farm boy can grow up to be president of a great democracy.

It is a dream that happens . . . only in the Americas.

REVOLUTION OF HOPE

CHAPTER 1

THE NIGHT WATCHMAN

THE STARS AND STRIPES fluttered in the hot summer breeze that Fourth of July. Joseph Fox stooped low beneath the minaret of the cool, dank tower, peering out the eight-inch rifle slit in the thick pink stone. A bullet ricocheted off the squat *torreón,* whose Moorish cupola commanded a view for miles over the central Mexican plain. Unfazed, my grandfather groped in his waistcoat for his pocketwatch, a habit from long nights on duty at the horse-carriage factory in Irapuato.

Three o'clock. Lunch hour in Mexico. Villa's men were right on time.

In 1916, the Mexican Revolution was in its final throes. Joseph Louis Fox had arrived in Mexico on horseback nearly three decades earlier, in the late 1890s. A German American whose ancestors came to Ohio from the Alsatian town of Strasbourg (then part of imperial Germany, now in France), Joseph was sent by doctors in his native Cincinnati to the mountains of central Mexico's Bajío region for its clean, dry air, to cure his asthma. He was born on the day Abraham Lincoln was shot at Ford's Theatre, and he set out for Mexico in the spirit of freedom of the Founding Fathers. Like many pioneers and adventurers, drifters and dreamers who came south to Mexico seeking fortune or fancy, rest or refuge, Joseph rode thousands of miles through swamps, deserts, and prairies, over the mountains of Tennessee and down into the piney woods of Texas, across the deserts of Sonora and past the rugged mesas of the Bajío.

Then suddenly, penniless and weary and for no apparent reason, he stopped. Was it hunger? A pretty girl? A Help Wanted sign? All we know is that the lanky young American tied his mount to a rail and went inside to apply for a job.

Like the dispossessed Mexicans he passed going the other way, Joseph was hungry. It would be more glamorous to style my grandfather an explorer like Lewis or Clark, but Joseph was more like the economic refugees who still head north today, crawling across the muddy Rio Grande to work as busboys in the United States. Like the bandits of Villa who were now shooting their rifles at him above the buttressed stone walls of Rancho San Cristóbal, Joseph Fox had come to Mexico in the late 1890s seeking not a fortune but a steady meal.

He took the first job he could find, as a night watchman at the Irapuato Horse Carriage Factory. Despite poor health he worked around the clock, watching the hours as they ticked by on the pocketwatch he had carried with him all the way from Ohio. With each hour he saved a bit more; eventually Joseph worked his way up to become foreman of the factory, sleeping in a loft above it to save enough pesos so that one day he had enough to buy the carriage factory from its wealthy absentee owners.

Like Joseph, the entire continent was on the move in those days, from New York to Baja California, so carriage sales were good. In the yanqui tradition, Fox was tight-fisted with a dollar. After a few years running the factory, he had saved enough to buy ten thousand acres from the local Mexican grandees. They were wastrels who had inherited the parcel, the smallest farm among their two hundred thousand acres scattered around the nation. As far as anyone recalls, they never bothered to visit, preferring the grandeur of their mansion on Mexico City's elegant Paseo de la Reforma.

Joseph worked the land with his own hands, toiling side by side with campesinos who were born and lived and died on the former hacienda, digging wells, milking cows, scything hay. It was dirty, backbreaking work; no self-respecting local don would be caught dead soiling his hands like this. But Fox was a gringo, and they had strange ways.

The fresh air and the hard work did Joseph good. Before long his asthma was gone and the crumbling walls of the former hacienda, a small fortresslike structure that dated back to the conquistadores, had been patched and strengthened.

But by the Fourth of July of 1916, as revolution ravaged Mexico, the refurbished walls had been pockmarked here and there with bullet holes from Pancho Villa's men. Looking out at the bandits through the turret's rifle slit, Joseph breathed deep and counted to ten, stilling his anger. The horses of the bandit gang were gaunt, bedraggled, sagging with malnutrition under ragged men who looked filthy, angry, hopeless. The desperadoes always came at lunchtime, in bands of a dozen or so; lately their numbers had been growing. Today Joseph counted at least twenty-five.

Their chests, bravely crisscrossed with trademark bandoliers of ammunition, were sunken and hollow. They were meant to look dark and whiskery and fierce, but mostly, my grandfather thought, they looked hungry.

"Hey, gringo, give us your chickens!" The cry came over the walls in Spanish from the man who appeared to be their leader. Belligerent and most likely drunk, he took wobbly aim with his pistol at the U.S. flag my grandfather had raised, in orneriness and defiance of the bandits, to celebrate the Fourth of July.

"What's he saying?" asked Joseph, who understood neither the Spanish language nor the feckless insolence of these bandits who had invaded his home. "This is American territory!" shouted my grandfather. "Go raise your own chickens!"

"Eggs!" demanded the *bandido,* firing at the tower. "Corn! Beans! *¡Viva Villa! ¡Viva la revolución!*" The bandit's swaybacked mount backed uncertainly, and the pistol shot went wild.

A baby's wail drifted up from the walled courtyard, where Joseph's pregnant wife huddled at the kitchen door among the wives and children of the ranch hands. My grandfather's men crowded beside him in the little stone watchtower, anxiously awaiting his orders. In the galleried arches surrounding the cattle pens below, loyal campesinos stood at rifle slits staggered along the walls of the former hacienda. Their weapons were oiled and cocked, ready to defend their food and their families. Though they didn't own the farm, the men depended on Rancho San Cristóbal to feed their children, and they would fight for their chickens.

My grandfather sighed and fingered his pocketwatch. This was a waste of time.

"Corn and beans," Joseph rasped, his eyes flinty and cold as he gave way reluctantly, again. He was a man of few words. "But no chickens!"

They came nearly every week to San Cristóbal in those days, *villistas, maderistas, carrancistas,* even a few who held themselves out as *zapatistas.* They represented themselves as revolutionary soldiers of the northern bandit-guerrilla Pancho Villa or the democrat farmer-spiritualist Francisco Madero, the rebel general Venustiano Carranza or the southern land reformer Emiliano Zapata. But really they were just hungry men, the unemployed and the alcoholic, the dispossessed and the drifters. Desperadoes.

It was this desperation running through it all that made Joseph Fox relent and negotiate, the bandits' hunger and the threat they posed to his wife and infant children and to the families of the men and women who worked the ranch. He pitied the desperadoes more than he despised them, not only for their poverty but also for their lack of industry, their violence and indiscipline. But Joseph never resorted to violence in return, preferring the pragmatic solution of the Yankee businessman: He made a deal. Joseph figured that what he spent giving away corn and beans, he saved in blood and time. In this way the contrarian gringo was becoming fully Mexican: He had the courage to face the guns of Villa's men, but he preferred charity to defiance, family to victory, and peace and calm above all things.

To this day I wonder at my grandfather's maturity and restraint, when everything he loved lay helpless before the guns of Villa's men. He was barely into his forties then. It was not until I reached the presidency in my sixties that I fully grasped his wisdom.

When I first got into politics, I was the bull in the ring. Like the angry five-hundred-pound beasts I faced in the ring as a young toreador, I charged straight at my opponents in the belief that I could bowl them over with the force of my convictions, stampeding into the bright red cape of the perfect dictatorship. Six years in Los Pinos taught me that in a democracy a president must be the matador and use the cape to wave the bull aside.

My grandfather adapted more quickly. When armed men came to San Cristóbal in the uniform of the soldiers of the revolutionary government in Mexico City, Joseph Fox flew the Mexican flag above the turret. Below the green and red stripes with the eagle and serpent in the white center, Joseph learned to be more generous, throwing in a chicken or two, or a side of bacon from the hogs he kept in the rose-colored brick pen within the fortress walls. Joseph raised his children to be proud Mexican rancheros, devout Catholics like their mother, Spanish-speaking like their neighbors, but still driven by the pioneer thrift of Joseph's example.

Flush with the success of the newly renamed Fox Horse Carriage Factory, Joseph married Madame Elena Pont, the daughter of a French soldier of the armies of Napoleon III. On May 18, 1864, the French had landed an invading army at Veracruz to place the Austrian Hapsburg emperor Maximilian on the throne of Mexico. The empire lasted just three years in the face of resistance from Mexico's liberals and our first indigenous president, Benito Juárez. During his ill-fated reign, Maximilian and his empress set up residence in imperial grandeur at Chapultepec Castle on a hill above Mexico City, where they could supervise the construction of the Parisian-style boulevard of the Paseo de la Reforma through the center of the capital. Initially Maximilian upheld the land reforms, religious freedom, and voting privileges instituted by Benito Juárez. But when the native Mexican president Juárez refused to swear allegiance to the new emperor, Maximilian ordered his supporters rounded up and shot. Benito Juárez took to his horse carriage, running a revolutionary government from the open road. After the end of the U.S. Civil War, the United States began supplying arms and money to the Juárez republicans. Soon Maximilian was besieged. In 1867, despite pleas for his life by Victor Hugo and the Italian revolutionary Garibaldi, the emperor was executed at Querétaro, at the gateway to our Bajío region of Mexico, which is so rich with our nation's history, and its blood.

Stranded behind, my French great-grandfather Pont traveled north in search of land and sanctuary. There, like so many European immigrants before him, he fell in love and married an indigenous peasant girl, who gave birth to my grandmother, Elena Pont. Like the majority of us Mexicans today, she was a mestiza, a person of "mixed" blood, and thus so am I. Elegant, cultured, and French-speaking, Elena had first married an Englishman named Jones, who achieved local fame for riding his horse into the dining room of the country club he'd founded, trying to add some culture to the rough, rural Bajío. After Jones's death, Elena married my grandfather and became Elena Pont de Fox. (In Mexico we have two last names: A woman is born with the last name of her father, followed by that of her mother; when she marries, a wife keeps her maiden name and appends her husband's last name to the end; her children carry both the last name of their father, then their mother's maiden name. If this seems confusing, at least it explains why I am Vicente Fox Quesada, to honor both my father and my mother—in this way at least, we notoriously macho Mexicans were good feminists long before the era of Hillary Rodham Clinton.)

As a home for this half-French, half-*indígena* widow of an English aristocrat, Joseph Fox pledged his earnings from the horse-carriage factory to buy a ten thousand-acre farm at San Cristóbal from one Joaquín Ederra, scion of one of the great *hacendado* families of Mexico. The Ederras owned at least seven haciendas, of which San Cristóbal was the smallest. There is no evidence that the landlords ever lifted a shovel or set foot in the tower, no doubt preferring lengthy steamship journeys to the cultured salons of Paris, Madrid, or London.

Much like the United States in those days, where 99 percent of the country's assets were owned by just 1 percent of the U.S. population, Mexico of the early twentieth century was a place of fabulously concentrated wealth, much more so than it is today: Mexican robber barons before 1910 made sure that there was virtually no middle class. Unlike the thrifty, upwardly mobile business classes of the United States and Britain, whose entrepreneurs invented machines and spawned an industrial revolution, Mexican tycoons of the Gilded Age were not hard-driving Vanderbilts and Carnegies, Edisons and Bells. Our country was run by an old Spanish class of absentee landlords who looked down on commerce, industry, and thrift. My ambitious grandfather Fox was only too glad to take advantage of what he saw as the Latin indolence of these wastrels. Joseph raised his son—José Luis Fox—and three daughters—Marta, Ana, and Bertha—in his spartan tradition: severe, frugal, hardworking, demanding, results-oriented, spiritually clean-cut. The Fox creed was this odd yet enormously successful Saxon culture that is simultaneously materialistic yet disapproving of worldly luxury: My aunt Bertha was sent back to Ohio as a girl to become a nun. She still lives there today at age ninety-six, cloistered away from worldly comforts in a Cincinnati convent.

MY GRANDFATHER did not understand the Mexican Revolution. But I do. This is not only because I became a peaceful revolutionary of sorts myself and have the benefit of twenty-first-century democratic hindsight. The real difference is that Joseph Fox was a son of the United States, and I am a Mexican. My grandfather's view was that of the classic American: If these men were hungry, why didn't they grow food? If they were ignorant, why not study late at night by dim candles, improving themselves with Yankee ingenuity? If they had no land, why not go someplace where they could earn themselves a piece of the American dream?

In fact, many of Joseph's new neighbors from the Bajío were doing exactly that. The first great wave of Mexican immigration to the United States began in Guanajuato at the turn of the century, as landless peasants fled poverty and despair to head north to the former Mexican lands of Texas and California. As we say in Mexico, we don't cross the border, the border crossed us.

These people my grandfather respected; they were, like him, pioneers. But to my grandfather, the desperadoes who came to his gates in the name of the revolutionary heroes of my school days—Villa, Zapata, the great farmer-democrat Francisco Madero—were simply armed thugs who killed, raped, and stole from decent, hardworking farmers.

Many of these pistoleros were in fact criminals. Despite the glossy romantic portraits painted later by the textbooks authorized by the Institutional Revolutionary Party, the PRI, the plain truth is that some of our revolutionary heroes were crooks, gangsters, murderers, and thieves. For example, there is Pancho Villa himself. No one knows the whole truth behind the cinematic legend of how Villa turned outlaw at age sixteen, after fighting to protect his sister from the *hacendado*'s advances. But Villa was no Robin Hood: He immediately began robbing, murdering, and abducting women for his own pleasure. His first big score was the gang robbery of a wealthy miner; Villa's share came to fifty thousand pesos, 150 times the annual income of a peasant in Chihuahua. The historians tell us he blew it in less than a year on high living. If Villa ever gave any money away, it was in bribes to local authorities and payments to local peasants for food and a place to hide out. It was a trick he had learned from his first mentor, Ignacio Parra, the gangster "King of the Mountains" in Durango: If you paid in hard cash and let your men loot freely in your name, your network would protect you.

If my strict Calvinist grandfather disapproved of Villa's men, he frowned equally on the *hacendados,* the lazy landowning class of the crooked *porfiriato*, the cruel crony-capitalist dictatorship that had ruled Mexico since 1876 and had driven these desperate men to join Villa and Zapata. By the time the bandits came calling at Joseph's gate, Mexico had been ruled for over thirty years by Porfirio Díaz, the demagogue-general who was our country's nineteenth-century prototype of Francisco Franco, Augusto Pinochet, or Hugo Chávez. If anyone complained, Porfirio kept rebels in line with the rule of *pan o palo,* "the bread or the stick": The dictator's friends were given the bread, and the peasants felt the stick. The *porfiriato* was like the lyric of the American country-western song: The *hacendados* got the gold mine, and Mexico got the shaft.

According to the historian Frank McLynn, by 1910 just three thousand rich families owned fully half of Mexico's land. Only seventeen of them controlled one fifth of Mexico, a land area larger than Japan. Four families controlled 30 million acres in Baja California. One single family in Pancho Villa's Chihuahua owned 17 million acres, a private estate larger than the state of West Virginia.

Even after Santa Anna had lost fully a third of Mexico's territory to the United States, Mexico was still the thirteenth-biggest country in the world, a massive continental empire stretching from coast to coast. Porfirio Díaz seemed determined to give it all away to his friends. Ironically, although Díaz was a Mixtec Indian who had made his name fighting foreign invaders as a hero of the war against Emperor Maximilian (Díaz was twice wounded and three times imprisoned by the French), he handed out mining concessions, oil rights, land and businesses left and right to foreigners. These were big U.S., British, and European companies, with names like Hearst, Guggenheim, McCormick, Rockefeller, Anaconda Copper, and U.S. Steel.

Mexico by then was second only to the United States in oil production (even today we still rank fifth in the world, well ahead of Iraq, Venezuela, or Kuwait). But during the *porfiriato* more than half of Mexico's oil fields were owned by U.S. companies—tax-free. Three fourths of our country's vast mineral wealth was owned by foreign investors—again with no taxes paid to Mexico. By 1910 the United States had more than $1 billion of equity in Mexico—more than the total amount owned by Mexicans, mostly Porfirio's cronies. The joke in those days, according to the historian McLynn, was that "only *gringos* and bullfighters get justice in Porfirio's courts."

The foreigners repaid the favor. Andrew Carnegie called Porfirio "the Moses and Joshua of his people." Theodore Roosevelt paid Díaz his highest compliment, calling the Mexican president "bully." Cecil Rhodes hailed his *porfiriato* as a "beacon of civilization."

It was not. Some 75 percent of Mexico's population worked as peasant farmhands, campesinos who lived in grinding poverty and debt peonage on the great haciendas, with no hope of escape. Ranchos like my grandfather's, where the owner worked his land side by side with his workers, paying them in corn, beans, and a little cash, were the exception. With their Latin disdain for business and hard work, the great *hacendados* looked down on mere rancheros like my grandfather, who dirtied their hands with stoop labor. The landlords left the farm work to the campesinos and the management of money to the thousands of brutal Spanish overseers, the *gachupines,* who had been coming to Mexico from the time of the Conquest; their Mexican-born Creole and mestizo descendants often were even crueler. The job of these overseers was to keep the books and whip the peasants into line, beggaring them into debt so deep that they could never leave the landowner's estate. So campesinos lived from generation to generation on the same farm, bound to the land not by love or pride of ownership but as peons hopelessly mired in debt to the great haciendas, ignorant and sick, at the knife edge of starvation, with barely enough to buy from the landlord's hirelings the food they grew themselves. This accounts for the extreme xenophobia of agrarian revolutionaries like Emiliano Zapata, who hated Spain as much as he did the United States. To unite the campesinos against the overseers, Zapata's revolutionaries of 1910–17 echoed Father Hidalgo's rallying cry from our war of independence against Spain in the early 1800s: "Death to the *gachupines*!"

The cost of staples had doubled in Mexico in the decade prior to the revolution. By 1909, famine began to spread through the country. The average peasant earned just fifty centavos a day, but he could easily be four hundred pesos in debt. By the time he married and had children of his own in a little shack owned by the *hacendado,* the average adult male peasant owed three years of wages to his landlord. Schooling, health care, water, and sewage were virtually nonexistent (McLynn reports that Porfirio Díaz spent more on his eightieth-birthday gala than Mexico's entire 1910 national education budget).

Those few teachers who did exist were forbidden to teach the campesino children any arithmetic, for fear they would be able to calculate what they really owed. Peasants were bought and sold like slaves. Bounty hunters tracked down campesinos who fled their debts, shot fugitives out of hand while "trying to escape" under the unwritten law of the *ley fuga*—or brought the peasants back to the overseer's bastinado, a uniquely cruel whipping with the dried penis of a bull. As late as Villa's time, some lords of the manor still exercised medeival droit du seigneur, forcing virgins to give them the first "taste" before marriage. Some say this may have been what turned Pancho Villa outlaw, as he fled execution for shooting the landlord's son to protect the virtue of Pancho's sister Martina.

As Villa's desperadoes began looting the haciendas and ranchos of 1910, Díaz was preparing a lavish celebration in Mexico City. The dictator's birthday coincided with the centennial of Mexican independence, when Father Hidalgo made his famous cry from the church tower for freedom from Spain. Porfirio Díaz reveled like the Cuban dictator Fulgencio Batista in the presidential palace on New Year's Eve 1958, where Batista feasted with cronies and foreign capitalists while Castro's guerrillas were emerging from the capital into the outskirts of Havana.

Our own revolution was similarly swift. Within months of Porfirio's birthday party, the little goateed farmer-spirtualist Francisco Madero would occupy the presidency. Díaz was forced to flee onto the yacht of his British crony Weetman Pearson, later Lord Cowdray. Then, like so many Mexican presidents before and since, Díaz escaped with his booty to Europe.

Ironically, the dictator's friendship with foreigners like Lord Cowdray may have helped cost Porfirio the presidency. In 1910 the British still controlled 55 percent of all foreign investment in Latin America but only 29 percent of international holdings in Mexico. Lord Cowdray's Pearson companies had built New York's East River Tunnel and railway bridges in Mexico, but the English aristocrat was anxious to get a bigger share of the pie in Mexico. This put the British at odds with rivals in the United States. In 1909 the future Lord Cowdray set out to wrest control of the Tuxpan oilfields from John D. Rockefeller's Standard Oil. Díaz favored his friend Lord Cowdray over Rockefeller. Only then did U.S. President William Howard Taft agree to harbor the enemies of Díaz in Texas, turning a blind eye to the revolutionaries who were smuggling guns, ammunition, and dynamite across the Rio Grande to troublemakers like Villa. Thanks in part to Lord Cowdray, a few of those bullets remain lodged in the walls of Rancho San Cristóbal.

One of Villa's rebel allies was my personal hero, Mexico's first democratic revolutionary, Francisco I. Madero. Later he was scorned by the PRI's revisionist historians as a weak leader who lacked the steel to punish his enemies: Our nationalist party painted Madero as a feeble president who failed to reward revolutionary troops with land grants and impose a dictatorship of the proletariat. But think about this the next time someone tells you that Hugo Chávez or Fidel Castro has done *some* good for their people: The thing about a dictatorship of the proletariat is, it's still a dictatorship. And the only people who really benefit from a dictatorship are those who are close to the dictator. Madero was determined not to become another Porfirio.

After our own peaceful democratic revolution in 2000, I looked to Madero's example. When advisers urged me to get tough and crack down on supporters of the previous regime and put them in jail, or break heads among the *zapatista* rebels of the pipe-smoking Subcomandante Marcos, or send in the army to subdue violent teacher strikes in Oaxaca, or set police with fire hoses against the leftist demonstrators who seized the streets of the nation's capital to protest the 2006 election on behalf of the losing candidate, Andres Manuel López Obrador, I was guided by the creed of Madero. "I defeated a dictator," he said. "I don't intend to become one."

Like me, Madero was a farmer, a man who detested violence, and a democrat. A weakling as a boy, he strengthened himself through swimming, hard exercise, and an almost monastic life in the spirit of his namesake, St. Francis of Assisi. Like Mexican revolutionary Emiliano Zapata—and my own childhood—Madero was nurtured by the agrarian tradition of St. Francis that "land is the mother who nourishes us all."

As schoolboys we were all captivated by books and movies from Mexico City and Hollywood about the pistol-waving Villa and Zapata. But I always felt a special kinship with Madero, a devout, Jesuit-trained farm boy who abhorred violence. I was a skinny kid who hated the sight of blood (human blood anyway; for us a bullfight is a different thing altogether). I let my big brother, José, fight all my battles for me. Thanks to hard work on the ranch, I grew to ride tall horses and stand six foot five, with the deep booming voice of my father, but inside I am still a man of peace like Francisco Madero.

Mexico's first revolutionary president was a tiny man with a high-pitched, querulous voice and a facial tic, a vegetarian who did not drink or smoke. (This is where we part company—why be a Mexican rancher if you can't eat beef, drink tequila, and smoke cigars?) Unlike me, Madero was from a very rich family, the fifth-wealthiest in Mexico. But he became a revolutionary traitor to the *hacendado* class, deeply inspired, as I was, by the compassionate example of a devout Catholic mother. Francisco's mother was named Mercedes, too, and like my Doña Mercedes she taught her son to make sure the farmhands had clean houses, good health care, an orphanage for homeless children, and proper schooling—unheard-of bolshevism in those hard days of the *porfiriato*.

When Madero's mother died, Francisco sold his wine cellar, began writing strange spiritual exercises featuring visits from a brother who had died in childhood, and authored a book called *The Presidential Succession of 1910*. This book was snapped up by a public hungry for reform; it sold so briskly even in those illiterate times that bookstores couldn't keep it on the shelves.

Madero's slogan called for a *¡Voto efectivo, no reelección!*—"Real vote, not reelection!" To understand why the revolutionary constitution of today's Mexico forbids the reelection of our public officials, from presidents to governors and senators, you must understand Mexico's turbulent and tyrannical past. After independence from Spain in the early nineteenth century, we had more than sixty presidents in about that many years; Santa Anna alone was named president, thrown out of office, and retook power no fewer than eleven different times. Then Porfirio Díaz came to power promising a slogan of "no reelection"—and ruled with an iron fist for more than three decades. Díaz held so-called elections every few years, which he miraculously "won" because he was the only real choice. After the revolution the PRI perfected the art by limiting presidents to a single six-year term, then pointing the *dedazo;* the "fingered" successor won the election by 80 or 90 percent, served his six years, bilked the national treasury, and caught the next ship or plane to Europe.

Porfirio took his own first step toward exile when Madero sent the dictator a copy of his inflammatory book, along with a courteous note that reminded Díaz of his own pledge of thirty-four years before, not to seek reelection. The generalissimo, a bull of a man who even in his seventies rose before dawn to take a cold plunge and lift weights in the military gym, dismissed the little farmer as a crank. Even Madero's own grandfather, the powerful landowner Evaristo Madero, ridiculed Francisco's crusade against Díaz as the battle of a "microbe against an elephant."

Madero responded by retreating into the desert for forty days and forty nights at a remote outpost he called "Australia." But the ascetic Madero had lit a burning bush that spread like wildfire. Followers in his Anti-Reelection Party revered the little farmer like a prophet, reaching up to touch his clothes, comparing his last name to the *madero* (wood) of the cross upon which Christ was crucified—even if they couldn't understand Madero's revolutionary philosophy. The American leftist John Reed once attended a rally where the campesinos cried, *"¡Viva Madero! ¡Viva democracia!"* The Marxist journalist then asked one peasant what *democracia* really meant to him. "I don't know, señor," the peasant said, pointing to the little farmer and his wife on the stage. "I think that must be the fine lady at Dr. Madero's side."

A note to aspiring revolutionaries: You cannot eat democracy. If you want to sell freedom to people, you must explain what it means for their lives and deliver hard results quickly, in terms that people can see, hear, touch, and smell. Corn. Beans. Eggs. Schoolbooks for the young. Houses for their parents. Medicine for their grandparents.

In Mexico before the revolution, a nation of rural farmers, this meant land. "*¡Tierra y libertad!*" became the rallying cry of Madero's revolutionary generals: Zapata the Indian village chief of the south, Villa the bandit king of the north, rebel military men like Victoriano Huerta, who would later betray Madero's presidency and have him shot. But back in 1910, they were all united behind this gentle spiritualist Madero, our own Mexican precursor to Gandhi, King, Walesa, and Mandela, who practiced the civil disobedience that Francisco had learned from reading Henry David Thoreau.

Imprisoned by the *porfiriato* in San Luis Potosí, Madero escaped from his lazy jailers on horseback. He rode across the desert, took a train to Laredo in disguise, then set up a roving series of revolutionary headquarters in San Antonio, New Orleans, and Dallas. There Madero studied the Hindu Mahabharata and used his family fortune to smuggle in several hundred thousand pesos' worth of Mauser rifles, bullets, and dynamite across the Texas border to arm Villa's bandits, wild Yaqui Indian tribesmen and rebel campesinos from Chihuahua. In the fall of 1910, Madero crossed the border at El Paso to Ciudad Juárez and issued his "Plan of San Luis Potosí," Mexico's version of the U.S. Declaration of Independence. The little farmer declared that any reelection of Porfirio in 1910 would be null and void, that Madero would campaign to become Mexico's true and legitimate president, and that Mexicans should rise up in arms to support a free election.

Ironically, in 2006 the leftist demagogue Andrés Manuel López Obrador (or AMLO, as he is known in the press) would attempt to wrap himself in Madero's mantle in a bid to nullify the results of the free and fair election won by my successor, Felipe Calderón. AMLO even draped the green, white, and red presidential sash around his chest in the central square of the nation's capital and declared himself the rightful president of Mexico. López Obrador pronounced that he would ride around the nation leading an "alternative government" with its own system of taxation and laws, like Benito Juárez governing Mexico from his horse-drawn carriage during Emperor Maximilian's reign.

In response to AMLO's antics, I followed the example of the farmer-democrat Madero: to be patient and respect the people's right to decide—and AMLO's right to protest. In this situation AMLO was not the liberal Juárez but the demagogue Díaz, seeking to supplant the will of the people with unilateral rule.

Madero possessed the quality I admire above all things: the spiritual poise of a gentle man who, like King or Gandhi, had the quiet courage to simply stand for what was right and allow the power of the democratic ideal to vanquish the dictatorship. This spiritual strength represents the ability to move souls, and it is stronger than all the Mausers and dynamite, barbed wire and Bradley fighting vehicles in the world.

EVERY REVOLUTION has its military leaders. I grew up devouring books about Napoleon and El Cid, Attila the Hun and Pancho Villa, the "Centaur of the North." Like most ranchero boys, I grew up loving any story of a man on a white horse. I was enthralled by the exploits of Zapata and Villa. Every Mexican schoolboy knows the tale of how Pancho, outnumbered ten to one, set out a line of empty sombreros on a hill to fool the *federales* into believing he had a great army. On the wall of the den of my home in San Cristóbal there are three old black-and-white photos of the "three J's" who were my childhood heroes. The first is my father, José Luis Fox, wearing his pistol, gun belt, and cowboy hat the day that armed men came to take his land away in 1938. Beside this hangs a photo of the anonymous figure we call José Cristero, an unnamed soldier of the Cristero Wars, Mexico's 1920s rebellion for religious freedom; he cockily faces a firing squad minutes before his death, cigarette dangling casually from his lip. The third photo is the American cowboy John Wayne.

But these are childhood heroes; little boys love a gunslinger. The Bible tells us that there is a time to put away childish things. As I grew older, my three J's gave way to three M's: Mahatma, Mandela, Martin. Like Jesus Christ, the original spiritual defiant, Mahatma Gandhi, Nelson Mandela, and Martin Luther King Jr. had the enormous inner strength to face the soldiers and the police dogs, moving millions by the example of their courage and the force of their ideas.

My fourth M would be Madero, who died as do so many spiritual men of peace, gunned down by the men of hate. After Madero won the 1910 election, his generals began the twentieth century's first great and bloody revolution. As so often happens with armed revolutions, what began as a fight for land and liberty soon became a squabble among military men, scrapping over the spoils. (Villa, ironically, later retired to a hacienda of 163,000 acres at Canutillo, until President Obregón, a one-armed fellow general and former comrade-in-arms, paid a team of assassins to execute Villa on the way home from a christening—when Pancho made an unfortunate side trip to visit his mistress, Manuela.)

Indeed, most of the revolution's top leaders ended up being shot by their comrades. But first they decapitated Madero's peaceful democratic vision with a palace coup. The revolutionary generals arrested Madero and shot him "while trying to escape," using the very *ley fuga* they learned from the *hacendados*.

THERE IS A LESSON in Mexico's long and bloody struggle for freedom worth noting today, to those who believe they can bring democracy to the world from the turret of a tank. At the cost of more than a million deaths in the Mexican Revolution, we learned this: When it comes by force, at the price of a bullet to the head, democracy rarely lasts.

In the comfort of today's Rancho San Cristóbal, where a red plastic play set and yellow slide decorate the green lawn and Canada geese come to winter in my little pond, it is almost impossible to imagine the devastation that raged through this land between 1910 and the late 1920s. But my country's experience bears on the trauma the world faces today from the Middle East and Africa to Venezuela and Bosnia.

For Mexico the specter of violent revolution and civil war is not some distant historical event of schoolbooks or a thing we see on TV coverage of Iraq—it is part of our family albums. It happened to our fathers and grandfathers—and our mothers and grandmothers, since despite our tradition of machismo many Mexican women fought as revolutionary soldiers from 1910 to the Cristero Rebellion of the 1920s. (When I think of fierce and proud Latin women like my fearless mother and my outspoken wife, I am quite sure that the sight of a Mexican woman wielding a Mauser must have been enough to strike terror into the heart of any *federal*.)

In any case, the revolution shaped the Mexico of the twentieth century in every respect. First, more than a million deaths—historians put the casualty figures between 1 and 2 million deaths—in a population that was then just 15 million; this is an unimaginable catastrophe, on the order of Europe's losses in the world wars, more wrenching to us than the Civil War was to the United States. This mass murder gave postrevolutionary Mexicans a deep distaste for political discord, disorder, and violence that persists to this day.

After the revolution the PRI used this cultural abhorrence toward unrest to its advantage in establishing its one-party dictatorship. More recently Andrés Manuel López Obrador ignored the Mexican people's distaste for street-fighter tactics—to his peril—in the 2006 election: Voters rejected him, and AMLO sacrificed the democratic ideals of the principled Mexican left on the altar of his personal ambition. Despite the fact that our popular sport of bullfighting ends in a bath of blood, Mexico is a nation whose constitution bans the death penalty and forbids sending troops to fight overseas wars. At a very deep level, Mexicans fear and despise political violence.

We also fear invasion, with good reason. As I mentioned at the outset, in the 1800s we fought off the Spanish, the French, and the U.S. Army. By the 1910–17 revolution, as Mexico traded one military dictator for another, U.S. leaders watched uneasily as the bands of Villa and Zapata rampaged throughout the country and Mexico deteriorated into violence. When the rebel armies threatened the Tampico oil fields owned by the big U.S. corporations, President Woodrow Wilson sent the marines into Veracruz in 1914 to occupy our largest seaport. In 1916 the formerly pro-American Pancho Villa raided across the U.S. border, and Wilson worried about looking weak against the Republicans in the 1916 presidential election. So he sent General John "Black Jack" Pershing and the U.S. Army into northern Mexico on its famous "Punitive Expedition" to chase Villa, by then a great hero of our revolution. These invasions—coupled with the enormous military and economic might of a United States that by 1910 owned more of Mexico than Mexicans did—bred in us a fear of domination by El Norte. This paranoia shaped the PRI's Mexico into the nationalist, isolationist, insular dictatorship that walled off our country from the world for the rest of the twentieth century—where some still resist closer ties between Mexico and the United States today.

MANY PEOPLE outside Mexico do not realize that our revolution was also a war against the power of the church. After 1917, Mexico was led by anti-Catholic Freemasons who tried to evoke the anticlerical spirit of the popular indigenous president Benito Juárez of the mid-1800s. But the military dictators of the 1920s were a more ruthless and savage lot than the liberal Juárez. After Madero's death and the founding of the Institutional Party of the Revolution, a series of anti-Catholic PRI presidents sought to rein in the church, which they saw as keeping Mexico on its knees. From the revolution through the Cristero Rebellion of 1926–29, priests were murdered for attempting to administer the sacraments, church altars were desecrated and sacked by government soldiers, and freedom of religion was forbidden by revolutionary generals. It was the era made famous in books like Graham Greene's *The Power and the Glory* and the Cristero histories that line the bookshelves at the ranch, where I have gathered one of the largest private collections of Cristero literature.

These were the stories of my childhood, told around campfires and kitchen tables by men and women who had lived them. There was of course my grandfather, who had answered revolutionary bullets with corn and beans; the vaqueros and their wives on the ranch, who had ridden for one side or another in the revolution, then served as the soldiers of Christ who declared the free nation of La Cristiada in our part of Mexico from 1926 to 1929. These were the brave men and women who built the great gray fortresslike mountaintop statue of Cristo Rey near our ranch to mark the geographic center of Mexico, a giant 65-foot-tall rebuke to the repressors of religious freedom on the Cerro del Cubilete, the 8,460-foot mountain that pilgrims still climb, inching mile after mile on their knees up the hard cobblestone road to the mountaintop.

Then there were my own parents. My father stood at the gates with his pistol in hand when the perfect dictatorship came to take away his land in 1938. He managed to hang on to a thousand acres when armed men came to take Rancho San Cristóbal away at gunpoint from my brother José and me in the 1970s. In the face of their machetes, my mother swore she would leave our land only in her coffin. I could have warned them: They should have known better than to mess with Doña Mercedes.

CHAPTER 2

MAKING THE AMERICAS

Mercedes Quesada de Fox was an extraordinary woman, a tough and devoutly Catholic Basque born in the crossfire between the Mexican Revolution and the Spanish Civil War. She came to the harsh, lawless lands of Mexico immediately after her birth in the Basque native port town of San Sebastián: Doña Mercedes's pregnant mother had been brought there by my Spanish grandfather, Vicente Quesada, so that my grandmother Catalina could give birth in her hometown.

Vicente Quesada first came to Mexico at the turn of the century, about the same year that my grandfather Joseph Fox crossed the deserts to reach the Bajío. Even before the revolution, Mexico was a dangerous place to bring a young girl from Spain. Our land was rife with gun-toting bandits and fierce Yaqui tribesmen. Apaches still roamed the deserts in my mother's time: Remember that Geronimo's wife and children were killed by Mexicans; the legendary Indian warrior had hated the Mexican people with a passion.

Indeed the rebel separatist tradition of the northern rancheros—which inspired the Cristeros and later gave birth to our center-right political party, the National Action Party (PAN)—grew out of the self-reliant, don't-tread-on-me mentality of Mexico's northern frontier. Like the ranchers of Wyoming or Montana, rancheros learned to depend on themselves. They resented the federal government, which gave them little help as they fought off the bandits, the Miembre Apaches, and the Yaquis, who rose again with Madero during the revolution.

My Spanish grandfather, Vicente, left the Spanish port of Santander around 1900, arriving, like Joseph Fox, without a penny in his pocket. Vicente crawled out of the hold of a ship in Veracruz, the Ellis Island of Mexico, traditional port of entry for the great wave of Spaniards who fled the poverty of postimperial Spain. These were not conquistadores but humble farmhands, fishermen, and grocers' boys. When youngsters like Vicente took ship for the New World, they called it "making the Americas." In Barcelona, Galway, Strasbourg, and Sicily, these desperate boys and girls were just extra mouths to feed. So their families sent them to the Americas in the hope of survival. The emigrant vision was not so much, as popular myth holds, that the bold young pioneers would strike their fortunes on streets paved with gold; mostly it was just a desperate wish that the children could earn enough to keep the family from starving.

So when Vicente Quesada kissed his mother good-bye in Asturias, wiped away her tears, and looked for the last time on all he knew and loved, he didn't say, "I'm going to live in America" or "I'm going to work in America." He said, "*Yo voy a hacer las Americas*"—literally, "I'm going to make the Americas."

THEY DID EXACTLY THAT, these refugee youngsters with their pockets empty of money and their heads full of dreams: They *made* the Americas. Together they built not just a nation but a hemisphere. They arrived by the millions and the tens of millions, Japanese boys and girls who came to Brazil, Lebanese youths to Mexico, Italian kids to Argentina, French children to Quebec. Together they made new lives for their families and new economies for the globe.

In the case of young Vicente Quesada, it was not his family's first try at making the Americas. Vicente's own grandfather—my great-great-grandfather—had gone from Spain to Cuba, where he'd tried and failed to make his fortune, leaving his sons to retreat to the Spanish city of Asturias and then go back again across the Atlantic from Spain to Mexico. As my grandfather Joseph Fox was making his night watchman's rounds at the horse-carriage factory, my other grandfather, Vicente Quesada, was in Puebla, the old colonial city along the route of the conquistadores from Veracruz to Mexico City. Even today Puebla remains the most Spanish city in Mexico, a traditional stopping point for immigrants from Europe.

Vicente found work as a grocer's boy in a local *tienda de abarrotes,* a tiny hole-in-the-wall convenience store of the type that still dot the Mexican landscape today—combination general store, 7-Eleven, and fruit stand. Like Joseph Fox, Vicente Quesada worked around the clock, sixteen or eighteen hours a day, sleeping in the storeroom on bales of grain, with sacks of corn and beans for his pillows.

This was "making the Americas." Soon Vicente had earned enough to start his own tiny corner store in Puebla, importing groceries on the cheap from his native Spain for immigrants who, like today's Mexican immigrants in the United States and Canada, brought with them a nostalgic taste for the food, products, and treats of their youth. With the pesos and centavos that Vicente Quesada scraped from the grain scales, he saved enough to buy a passage back home to the old country to buy more Spanish goods. Vicente got more than he bargained for—a Basque wife.

The Basques are a notoriously stubborn people, and my grandmother Doña Catalina was no exception. As her handsome new husband, Vicente, traveled back and forth to Europe to import groceries, my grandmother Catalina insisted on going with him. To save money for their *changarro* (family business)—which by then was a growing string of mom-and-pop grocery stores—my Quesada grandparents traveled in steerage on smelly grain ships, long seasick journeys of up to forty-five days or two months, from Veracruz to Santander and back, a journey between one bitter civil war and the other: Mexico was in flames, torn by revolution, coups and countercoups, the Cristero Rebellion; soon Spain grew just as dangerous, as the Royalists and Franco's troops battled it out with the Communists and the Republicans.

It was on one of their early trips to the old country, in my grandmother's Basque hometown of San Sebastián, that my mother was born. While she was in many ways my inspiration for entering politics, Doña Mercedes also created a little dilemma for our future democracy movement: Our nation's Constitution requires that both parents of a president must have been born on Mexican soil, giving me my own "Schwarzenegger problem." (My longtime friend Arnold once welcomed me to Sacramento by telling our guests, "Vicente and I have a lot in common. We're both outsiders who came to politics to make a change. We both have trouble saying the word 'California.' Neither of us is allowed to run for president of the United States. And neither of us will ever win an Oscar.")

With the success of the Quesada family business and the birth of their daughter, Vicente and Catalina moved to Mexico City, where they opened a big warehouse on the Calle de Mesones. My grandmother, like most Basques a zealous Catholic, at first misread the sign as the "Street of Freemasons," which might well have worried her: The religious principles of devout Catholics were put to the test in Mexico during the 1920s, as the revolution's Masonic generals cracked down on religious expression. The new government expelled the religious orders, Cristero rebels took to the hills of my native Guanajuato, and thousands of Mexicans gave their lives for religious freedom under the banner that rests now in my ranch house. As my mother grew up, the family traveled back and forth to Spain, where royalists battled under Franco against anti-Catholic leftists of the Popular Front. Soon the streets of Puebla, Veracruz, and Mexico City were full of Spanish refugees from both sides of the conflict, both Republican and Royalist, which made things uncomfortable in the family store. My grandparents' sympathies were with the church, but my grandmother never tired of reminding us that Vicente Quesada had come to Mexico before the Spanish Civil War, so we were immigrants and not refugees; and anyway that she was Basque, so she could stay out of it.

There was no lack of custom for Vicente's stores. As Hitler used the cities and countryside of Spain for his tanks and dive bombers, and broke the shop windows of the Jews on Kristallnacht, the flow of refugees from Europe swelled the holds of ships arriving in Veracruz, which now became Mexico's welcome mat for Jews fleeing the Holocaust. Even when the United States began to curtail immigration from Europe in those dark days, Mexico's Ellis Island kept its doors open. Hungry for new citizens, my country reached out to embrace a great wave of Jewish immigration that helped give Mexico City its rich cultural heritage, many of modern Mexico's most important business leaders, and a tradition of university education that is second to none in Latin America.

They, too, "made the Americas."

I once heard a speech by the Holocaust survivor Elie Wiesel before President Clinton and an august gathering of world leaders, in which the Nobel Prize winner described the ill-fated "Voyage of the Damned" of the *St. Louis.* In 1939 this ill-fated ship headed from Hamburg, its holds crammed with Jewish refugees, bound for Cuba, the United States, Canada—anywhere they could find safe harbor. The *St. Louis* was denied permission to dock and went from port to port, past the Statue of Liberty and finally back to Germany. Three fourths of the ship's passengers died in Nazi concentration camps.

Though Wiesel loves the United States and appreciated the brave sacrifices of the U.S. soldiers who fought their way to Germany and liberated the camps, he has never understood how the America he loved and worshipped, the land of freedom that eventually became his home, could close its doors to the desperate people on that ship. Franklin Roosevelt was a good man, and America was a good country, Wiesel said. Even if for every ship FDR had allowed to dock, ten more shiploads of Jews would have come, did not the Statue of Liberty mean that the world's huddled masses were safe once they reached America's shores? Wiesel described how concentration-camp inmates consoled themselves with the thought that the Allies couldn't possibly know about the conditions in Auschwitz, else how could the America they loved not let the *St. Louis*'s passengers disembark? They could understand the sins of the Nazis, the evils visited upon them by bad people. What they could not imagine was what Wiesel defines as the greatest evil: the indifference of good people.

Years later I became the first Mexican president to visit a Jewish synagogue, and I was overwhelmed by the response. Though I could not understand the Hebrew words, I felt their devotion and bowed my head, covered with a black yarmulke. I felt literally swamped with the love and appreciation of the children of people who had found safe haven in Mexico. I do not mean to draw a parallel between the suffering of the Holocaust and the condition of today's immigrants, or the poor of Latin America or Africa—the suffering of the Jews, Gypsies, gays, Catholic priests, and political prisoners in the concentration camps is too horrible to contemplate, a much greater evil than today's discrimination against our immigrants and the world's poor. But whenever people are persecuted, discriminated against, ignored, abused, arrested, jailed, or deported for no crime other than being what they are, this is a sin against humanity. Even greater is the sin of genocide and ethnic violence in the Balkans or Africa, where still today victims are raped, murdered, or left to starve because of the color of their skin, the faith of their parents, or the spelling of their last name. Even as I write this, too many people in the world are punished harshly merely for being who they are, for having the bad luck to be born in the wrong place at the wrong time with the wrong color skin, for simply trying to live in this world as who they are. And too often the evils visited upon them are met, most painfully, with our indifference.

My Spanish grandparents were not so liberal. The Quesadas would never have set foot in a synagogue or even a Protestant church, not if the president of the United States were at their side. (George W. Bush took me to my first evangelical service during a summit in Quebec in 2001, and I am quite sure I could feel my grandmother Quesada turning over in her grave.)

Flourishing in business by the 1930s, Don Vicente and Doña Catalina bought an elegant home on the Calle de Puebla and sent their daughter to the private school in the Colonia Roma. Despite the sacrifice of martyrs like Father Miguel Agustín Pro of Zacatecas, the Cristero priest who was beatified by Pope John Paul II in 1988, the religious orders were still struggling to restore Catholic education to Mexico. So my grandparents chose the gated confines of the Maddox School as the next-best thing to a convent. Under the steely gaze of the matrons, schoolgirls in their prim starched blouses peeked out the stone-lined windows as the teachers droned on in Latin. No doubt the girls were hoping to catch the eye of a passing caballero. None waited on the cobblestone streets more eagerly than the rancher's son José Luis Fox and his classmates from the Franco-Inglés School. Every afternoon the boys stood vigil in their natty Etonian jackets, peering through the great iron gates at the precise moment they knew that the girls would climb the staircase to prayers.

The Fox family had prospered, too, surviving the ravages of revolution and the Cristero Rebellion to become modestly upper-middle-class rancheros. My grandfather Joseph bought a house in the capital, not so grand as the villas of the *hacendado* nobility along the Paseo de la Reforma, but a pleasant home in the leafy Calle de París, not far from the finer mansion of the Quesada family (and, more important to the future Vicente Fox, the street with the very best ice cream parlor in Mexico City, a place called Chandony). With his American belief in the very best education to help his children get ahead, Joseph packed his own three daughters off to the convent school and sent his Mexican son, José, to the French-English boarding school to learn languages, mathematics, and the classics.

One sunny afternoon in 1938, the schoolboy finally caught the sparkling green eyes of the most beautiful and sought-after Spanish doña in Mexico City. No doubt José clutched his heart, fell to his knees, and proclaimed his love—or perhaps he played it cool and blew her a kiss. In any case my father had invested months at the doorway of the convent school: Now he plunged headlong into an intricate courtship. José was tall and good-looking, with a big thatch of black hair; he'd had many girlfriends back home in Guanajuato. But he was a clumsy farm boy in the presence of this elegant merchant's daughter. How, young José asked himself, can an unknown forestry student from cow country get the attention of this most eligible (and heavily protected) of young ladies?

He tried all the usual techniques of the Mexican courtier, serenading her at windows, besieging her with poetry and flowers. Finally José struck gold: He made friends with Mercedes's big brother, who, conveniently, was dating José's own sister, Ana Fox. Soon it was all in the family: My future Fox aunt and Quesada uncle arranged to visit San Cristóbal, my Fox father got my Fox aunt to invite her Quesada boyfriend's gorgeous Quesada sister. Soon everybody married everybody and became Fox Quesadas and Quesada Foxes, as Doña Mercedes disappointed her many suitors in Mexico City and went off with the tall, handsome ranchero to a dusty ranch smelling of old hay and horse manure.

It must have been quite a comedown, trading the elegant Parisian mansions, brightly lit cafés, and bustling cinemas of Colonia Roma for a little farm twelve hours up the rutted, winding mountain roads of the Bajío. I am sure there were many dark nights when my mother doubted the wisdom of her choice. In the 1930s, Rancho San Cristóbal had no running water, no electricity, no sewage system, and a hand-cranked phone that rarely worked, except for a few scratchy words shouted over the line once every ten days or so, when Mercedes could put a call through to her mother. There were bandits in the hills, snakes in the stock pond, and bats in the barn—not to mention a severe, authoritarian father-in-law who spoke rarely, and then only to bark orders.

It must have been love.

BUT THEN Doña Mercedes was a loving woman, a compassionate Catholic counterweight to my stern Calvinist Grandpa Joseph. Each morning my mother rose early to attend mass; she said her rosary morning, noon, and night, then went forth to help the families of the ranch hands. Like Francisco Madero's mother, Doña Mercedes became a self-taught nurse who kept her own vast medical inventory to treat me and my eight brothers and sisters, along with various aunts and cousins, and the families of 150 campesinos. In those days you could die of everything from snakebites to the common cold, not to mention the hatchet cuts and lesser bullet wounds that my mother stitched and swabbed and bound up by herself. Doctors were a great expense, and far away down muddy roads in the city of León.

Doña Mercedes was a one-woman social program. Among my sharpest memories were those nights when men would come and bang at the door of the main ranch house in a downpour, leading a horse over which was sprawled the groaning, inert body of a campesino who was bleeding or vomiting or howling in pain. Some were prostrate from drinking brackish water from the creeks; others had shotgun wounds to the shoulder or the belly. These were rough and violent times in ranchero country; men would get drunk and quarrel over women or some slight offense, and once every six months or so a man would be shot or killed just for turning his back on a neighbor. There were no police or paramedics. The phones rarely worked. What is today a fifteen-minute drive to León could take hours, or the roads could simply be impassable in the rainy season—many were the times my father had to send the tractor to extract our ancient Ford flatbed truck from the mud.

We had the one vehicle for the nine of us children, our parents and aunts and uncles and cousins, and 150 farmhands and their families. The Ford made one trip every morning to deliver the milk to market and deposit the older Fox kids at the Catholic school. Making an extra midnight trip to León was a major decision: Was the wound serious, or could it wait until the milk run at dawn? My grandfather Fox usually favored the latter. But even his flinty heart could be moved by the compassion of this plucky young Spanish *doña* who would tie tourniquets, administer medicine, use brandy as an anesthetic, and load her patients aboard the old Model T, then climb into the bed of the truck and hold a farmhand's head in her lap on the long, dark, bumpy road to see Dr. Solís.

He was one of those heroic doctors of the old school before technology, in a day when good doctors learned more by listening than some do today from an MRI. My mother made sure that the visits of Dr. Solís to our ranch were greeted by long lines of farmhands waiting to see the doctor. This was my first universal health-insurance program: It was the example of Doña Mercedes that led me to become the first president of Mexico to extend health-care coverage to poor people and ensure that eight out of ten births were attended by qualified medical professionals.

No doubt this vivacious angel of mercy warmed the ranch under my grandfather's Saxon tyranny. Perhaps her best example of Christian compassion is that Doña Mercedes took care of her severe, authoritarian gringo father-in-law even in his final years, after the government had taken most of Joseph Fox's land away and his aging arteries strangled the blood supply to the old man's brain, turning my grandfather into a figure of terror. In his last days, he strode about the ranch swinging his cane wildly in the air, telling all in sight to "Get back to work! Go milk the cows!"

Fans of American movies and television would recognize my mother's character in the westerns we traveled to Mexico City to see when I was young: the elegant Elizabeth Taylor on her husband's ranch in *Giant* or the great matriarch of television's nineteenth-century California, Barbara Stanwyck of *The Big Valley*. But I have always seen my mother as Katy Scarlett O'Hara at Tara. Like Vivien Leigh's character in *Gone with the Wind*, my mother stoutly defended land that she never knew how much she loved—until men with rifles came to take it away.

By 1938 Joseph Fox was over seventy, his blond hair gone steel gray as he climbed again to the minaret-domed turret to defend the hogs and the granaries from the *federal* soldiers. That year, President Cárdenas imposed the *ejido* land reforms that sent armed invaders to take San Cristóbal away from the Fox family.

My grandpa was joined by my father, Don José, lean and mustachioed and strapping a Colt .45. This time the pistoleros at the gate would not be satisfied with corn, beans, or eggs—they wanted the land. Never mind that San Cristóbal was a merely a rancho and not a full-fledged hacienda; the Fox family worked our land, every inch of it. But the president had decreed that all properties over two hundred acres were forfeit. Placing all such lands in public domain, the *ejido* scheme parceled out the rights to farm little ten-to-twelve-acre plots to millions of rural *ejidatarios*, who thus became utterly dependent on the federal government that now owned that *ejido* land, making the *ejidatarios* little more than sharecroppers to President Cárdenas and the PRI. So the *federales* rounded up landless peasants from other states, from drunken ruffians to the genuinely needy, and sent them to storm the gates of farms like San Cristóbal.

One of the sins of the great *hacendados* of Mexico was that they were too lazy to farm more than a tiny portion of their vast holdings. This had been a principal complaint of the *villista* and *zapatista* revolutionaries: If the landlords were too lazy to farm the huge estates, land reform should redistribute those lands to the campesinos.

If my grandfather could not understand the concept of agrarian reform in

Mexico, it was because he was a product of the yeoman-farmer United States, where owning your land was more than a tradition, it was a matter of law. Compare the two nations. A few years before my grandfather was born and General Porfirio Díaz battled Emperor Maximilian for the right to see which dictator would be allowed to hand out landed estates to his generals, the United States passed the Homestead Act of 1862, perhaps the wisest piece of economic legislation in the history of the planet. By granting small, independent farms to millions of penniless, working-class families from around the globe, the Homestead Act dramatically redistributed the economic ownership of the United States—much as the GI Bill would later redistribute educational opportunity after World War II, granting upward mobility to an entire generation of eager young executives, who then conquered the globe for American commerce.

The Homestead Act created a United States of agrarian-entrepreneurial owners like my grandfather, who grew up with the notion of a full incentive in the economy, a true ownership stake in a democracy, and the classic Yankee drive to earn, learn, and improve his lot in life—knowing that if he did, his children would lead a better life.

So the yanqui immigrant Joseph Fox, who had paid his workers in full and milked cows alongside them for thirty years to the contempt of his *hacendado* neighbors, was furious when the soldiers of President Cárdenas came to take away nine thousand acres of his family's land. Finally my grandfather talked his way in to see Lázaro Cárdenas at Los Pinos and reminded the president that there were five Foxes—my grandfather, my dad, and his three sisters. Joseph Fox convinced the president that since each person was allowed two hundred acres, the family should be able to keep a thousand acres of San Cristóbal. To the end of his days, my grandfather still fumed about the nine thousand acres he lost to the federal government and the *ejidatarios,* many of whom he called "foreigners" from Chihuahua and Sonora. A week before he died, my mother had the old man baptized in the Catholic faith, so that he could receive last rites and go to heaven with his family. And so Joseph Louis Fox died, fully Catholic and utterly Mexican—and, no doubt, still angry that the government had taken away his land.

THESE THOUSAND ACRES of Rancho San Cristóbal were my boyhood home. The land nourishes me still, protected by the competitive work ethic of my father, Don José, and the loving care of my mother, Doña

Mercedes. Their twin spirits, Saxon and Latin, rebellious and compassionate, shaped me in the defiant spirit of "El Hijo Desobediente" of Mexican folk song. The "disobedient son" became my label in the family; it also was the rallying cry of our opposition party's campaign for democracy, as millions of disobedient sons and daughters of Mexico fought for the freedom my family had found at San Cristóbal.

My own rebel spirit grew out of the boyhood stories burned into my memory at San Cristóbal: my father standing up to the pistoleros who came to take away his ranch; my mother standing up to my severe gringo grandfather to care for its people. This spirit of San Cristóbal to me is the universal spirit of the Americas, and in their own way Pancho Villa's bandits shared it, too—this hunger of restless souls, always on the move, desperate for a better life. It is this hunger to improve the condition of the poor that *made* the Americas, in both Mexico and the United States, and in Canada and Chile, too—this intense hunger that tells the immigrant he must do anything to get there, just *get* there. It was the competitive spirit of my father, José Luis Fox, always yearning, always striving to improve. He told me, "Be anything you want to be, Vicente, an architect, a street cleaner, but be the very best." I was free to choose any career I liked, he said, as long as I would promise never to be a farmer or a politician, because there was no money in farming and no honor in politics. Of course I did both. *El hijo desobediente.*

AND so it was to this ranch built by the sweat of an American immigrant that George W. Bush came to meet José Fox's rebellious son on February 16, 2001, for the historic San Cristóbal Summit. This had never happened before: A U.S. president had made his first foreign trip to Mexico (the tradition was for a new president to visit Canada first). The world took note. The ranch summit ushered in a new era of harmony between our nations, a spirit of open doors to bring us closer on immigration, free trade, and global democracy. Within seven months I gave a historic address to both houses of the U.S. Congress, the first Mexican president ever to do so. Leaders of both parties thundered their applause for the new partnership of peace and prosperity we had signed here at San Cristóbal.

Five days later terrorists attacked the World Trade Center and the Pentagon, and the door slammed shut on our American dream.

CHAPTER 3

MEN FOR OTHERS

I CAN STILL HEAR my grandfather's voice at five in the morning, echoing along the cold dark stone halls of the old fortress of the hacienda to wake my brothers and me. Like many immigrants, Joseph Fox never learned to speak the language of his neighbors, nor even of his own children and grandchildren; like many Mexican American families in Texas and California today, where the *abuelos* speak Spanish and their grandchildren answer in English, the old spoke to the young in one language, and we answered in ours.

So it was in English that I was first roused from my warm bed, the old man's arm shaking in the air and us wondering if he was reaching for his stick to poke us out of the covers. "Up, up, to work! The cows won't wait! Time to earn your breakfast!"

I was up like a shot. Another three-year-old might have groaned and covered his head, but this was my favorite time of day, working with the men in the barn, moving and striving and competing like my father and grandfather, real men who rose before us to shave and dress in their waistcoats and put in sixteen-hour days nearly to the ends of their lives; they, too, found it difficult to sit still. I remember walking from the brick-arched walls of the former hacienda to the tall, dark barn, where we would tie up the legs of the cows, lift their tails, and get to work in the cool damp. You had to go easy at first, soft and tender to start the milk; then you pulled hard with fingers that soon grew strong and knobby to urge the hot milk into the bucket. Only then could you fill more buckets than your big brother and lug them two and three and four at a time, without sloshing, to the enormous fifty-liter tank at the end of the row. It was 250 cows you had to milk by six in the morning, or no breakfast. But we could do it because eventually there were nine Fox kids, which comes in handy on a farm: my four brothers—José, Cristóbal, Juan Pablo, and Javier—and my four sisters—Mercedes, Martha, Susana, and Cecilia—all born about a year apart from each other, what we Catholics call "Irish twins."

Nothing compares to the smell of tortillas baked fresh on an open fire, not when you come back to the warm kitchen from milking a couple hundred cows with your dad. We men would warm the stiffness from our hands at the fire before we were shooed away by Marquitos—Señora Marcos, the cook, dressed all in black, with her old gray hair pulled back in a bun to keep it out of the fire. It was a big kitchen, with room along the sooty brick walls for Grandfather Fox and my dad, Don José, and my aunts and us kids, plus the foreman and his family and the people who worked in the barn, some twenty or thirty of us crowded around the open fire on the big ceramic-tiled hearth.

There Marquitos worked her magic at the wet corn *molcajete,* the maize dough she had begun kneading before dawn while we were out in the barn, pouring the crushed kernels of the *nixtamal* batter up on the four-legged mortar of lava rock with her strong forearms like big twin pestles, grinding and shaping the dough with loving hands into the big round tortillas she slapped one by one onto the oven hearth, where they inflated on one side with the taste of heaven.

City kids miss *all* of this. I couldn't imagine any other life than getting up to milk cows in the dark, then walking out into the brilliant morning sun of the courtyard and inside, to the close, fire-baked warmth of the kitchen on a family farm. I have never really understood how anyone could live anywhere else.

We had very little contact with the world outside of San Cristóbal. Outside the gates of the ranch, where today stands a *zócalo* with a little park and gazebo surrounded by a cluster of houses and a corner store, in those days there was only the ranch, the church, and the mud. My childhood friends were my brothers and the poor children whose fathers worked on the farm. I slept on the cold dirt floors of their houses, and they slept in the warm rooms of our big farmhouse—to the dismay of my parents: In those days, even if you cared for the poor children of the countryside, as my mother did, or worked side by side milking cows with their parents, like my father and grandfather, there was still a great deal of discrimination against the mestizo poor.

But since the austere Fox family kept its sons perennially short of pocket money—if local boys would get a peso for sweets, my brothers and

I were lucky to get a centavo—one of the blessings of my youth was that we were blissfully unaware of class differences. The campesino boys taught my brothers and me to make spinning tops out of mesquite wood and marbles of fire-hardened adobe. (They end up misshapen and shatter when you strike a rock, and they don't roll as straight as your smooth colored marbles of crystal and agate—but then the dirt of San Cristóbal is rough and uneven, so it all works out.) We tied fishing line to the tails of green and black dragonflies to fly them as airplanes, which might sound cruel but actually doesn't hurt the insects much—or at least they never complained. But unlike flying a kite with its long string, you must run very fast to keep up with a dragonfly.

And hunting, hunting, hunting, because boys are always hungry, whether they are the ranchero's sons who wolf down Marquitos's sumptious eggs, ham, chorizo sausage, and tortillas in the big kitchen—and then ask, "What's for lunch?"—or the truly protein-starved sons of poor ranch hands who are lucky if they can get corn and beans for breakfast. We fashioned slingshots of tree branches to hunt for jackrabbits and doves to eat—even rats, once in a while. I became expert at hitting a duck at twenty paces with enough force to earn dinner by the men's campfire.

We were always competing. How many bee stings can you stand? Who is brave enough to face the ghost in the barn? Ours were the games of machismo, to take one bee after the other by the wings and hold it to your arm and count the stings until you had bested your big brother and your friend, whose campesino father had been a sergeant with Pancho Villa in the revolution, then fought for Father Pro in the Cristero Rebellion.

In Mexico, a land where the Day of the Dead is one of our great religious holidays, we love a good ghost story, and these men told the very best. There was "La Llorona," the weeping lady who waited for us with her white veil at the far end of the granary, whose great cavernous dark spaces so terrified us. By day we would set out a target as the Mexican sun shifted through the barn's rafters, perhaps my grandfather's tattered old flag or the red cape of a bullfighter. Then we returned in the night and dared each other to enter the great barn doors, seven meters wide and terribly tall. We would run like wild horses down the length of the granary, La Llorona hovering and moaning in the wind creaking above our heads, to snatch the banner and return to glory. Somehow my father always caught us escaping out the back door of the ranch house to sleep among the stars and dared us to make it through the night out there alone. My dad was always there to greet us when we slunk back home in the wee hours, cold and scared, perhaps to frighten us in that comfortable way of storytelling fathers, with tales of dead bandits who walked the farm in search of the golden coins my grandfather had buried in Villa's time. (I can tell you that this is fiction, having dug up every inch of the old courtyard.)

THERE CAME the inevitable day when I had to begin day school with the Jesuits in the nearby city of León. The city kids were different, wealthy and sophisticated in their Ivy League haircuts and tasseled loafers. It was my delight to bring my classmates home on weekends to rise with us at dawn and milk the cows, to get their fine shoes muddy. As the Spanish daughter of a wealthy merchant, Doña Mercedes yearned to make me one of these dandies, dressing me in schoolboy short pants and bloused shirts. I was aghast—to this day, no matter the demands of heat or fashion or ambitious mother, no Mexican farm boy will ever be caught dead in short pants. "The other boys will call me *maricón*!" I protested, not wanting to be thought sissy or gay, a fate worse than death in our macho world. I wanted to dress like the campesinos, work with them in the fields, eat tortillas in the fresh air and sunlight among the cattle and the horses—not sit all day under the tyranny of the Jesuits trying to smack the algebra into my head with a ruler.

It was about this time it dawned on me that there was a difference between my friends and me. I went to school; they went to work. I ate beef; they ate corn. I went to the doctor; they waited in line for home remedies from my mother. Little wonder that even the scrawny teenage Vicente Fox could shoulder more hundred-pound hay bales than could the men who worked on the ranch: I was better fed. Little wonder that I went on to be president of Coca-Cola and president of Mexico, while they were forced to emigrate to the United States to pick strawberries: I was better educated.

But when my father sent me away to wash dishes and learn English in the cold, dark winter of Wisconsin, I envied the campesino kids who got to stay behind in the sunny warmth of home and family. They were the only people on earth who understood how life was meant to be lived, these warm and loving people of my halcyon youth. It never occurred to me that Mexico was not so idyllic for them, nor that some of my childhood friends would not be there when I returned.

OF THE MANY MYTHS about Mexican immigration, this is the greatest: People in the United States actually think that everyone here wants to leave all we love—the sunny land of our fathers, the care of our mothers, the church of our priests and the companionship of our friends, the music and food and language and folkways and jokes and dances that are all we know—and seek economic refuge two thousand miles away in what seems, to a boy of fourteen, to be the cold, forbidding land of El Norte.

The enemies of immigration will cite statistics showing that 40 percent of Mexicans would come to the United States if they had a chance. They warn of a "Third World invasion" of swarthy, mustachioed Mexicans who look and talk like me, and the good-hearted, hardworking, dark-skinned indigenous and mestizo kids I grew up with at San Cristóbal. But I have been that exiled farm boy, if only for a year, and then only to go to a Catholic school in Wisconsin with three square meals a day. Even then I can tell you that a Mexican farm boy who crawls across the barbed wire at the Rio Grande desperately loves his homeland and desperately wants to stay. Only the gnawing hunger and low wages on one side of the border, and the golden promise of economic opportunity on the other, lures the young immigrant lad from sunny Guanajuato to a job in a meatpacking plant in the freezing drizzle of Chicago, to pick strawberries in a shantytown of central California, to hang drywall in suburban houses amid the Front Range blizzards of Colorado, far from all he knows and loves, perhaps never to see his home and family again.

These are the desperate young people who still make the trek north today, the Third World invaders of whom Patrick Buchanan and Congressman Tom Tancredo warn. They are not criminals, but innocent farm boys and girls as good of heart and as driven by work, faith, and family as were my boyhood friends. If I have painted them like the rural boys of a Mark Twain novel, it is because they are: A disproportionate number of today's Mexican immigrants come from impoverished rural areas, many of them indigenous; the typical age for emigration is about fourteen. They are just kids, not men and women or entire families, but teenagers mostly, youngsters who leave the warm land they love to "make the Americas" under the cold, gray skies of the north.

Like the Irish in the Potato Famine, the Spaniards of Franco's Civil War, Germans after the 1848 revolution, or Italians of stony Sicily, my boyhood friends left my homeland one by one, many to never come back; despite all our best efforts during my presidency to create more jobs to keep these kids home, our greatest failure is that they are leaving still. Their mothers weep silently, wrap a few pesos and a crucifix in a blanket, and make their children swear to return.

As president my biggest challenge was to create sufficient jobs at good wages to keep these young people home. We made progress, but we did not do enough. Over the last six years, average wages rose 60.3 percent in Mexico, and our unemployment rate dropped below that of the United States. But our people still earn ten times more north of the border. So, sadly, as I write this, the best and bravest boys and girls of the developing world still say good-bye to their families and head for the rich nations of the United States, Canada, and Europe—draining our nations of the talent we need to survive.

When my father told me I would have to go, too, to the Jesuit school in Wisconsin where the priests would teach me English, I cried for a week. I was fourteen, the classic age of real emigrants, but my situation was not so tragic: I was merely going away to prep school. Still, to me that year seemed like a prison sentence. How must it feel to be sent away for life without parole? For the undocumented worker, there is no assurance of job or food at the other end. The police hunt you. You may never see your family again. People in the new land will despise you and call you a "wetback." Today, the reality of immigration lacks the honeyed *Coming to America* glow of films, songs, television, and history books; perhaps it always did.

Of course, I was not a penniless campesino but the schoolboy son of a well-to-do ranchero. Despite the loss of 90 percent of our land to the *ejído* of the 1930s, my father kept my grandfather's traditions, working our remaining thousand acres with discipline and efficiency. The Fox Horse Carriage Factory had wisely made the leap to horseless carriages early in the 1920s. Between this and the milk we sold each day in León, the Fox Quesadas were a prosperous family by Mexican standards, though my father was careful never to let us know it. My family had roots in the upper Midwest of the United States, and now they could afford to banish me there for a year, for my own good.

I had been to the United States before, driving as a boy of twelve and thirteen with my brother José Luis, just one year older. Alone, just the two of us, we frequently made the twenty-four-hour drive to buy American hogs in McAllen, Texas, in our old Ford Model T flatbed. The trek took forty-eight hours on the way back south, with frequent stops to water and feed the hogs and muck out their trailer. Migrant workers have endured far worse discrimination, but you cannot imagine how very unwelcome were two Mexican boys at a motel in McAllen, Texas, in 1955 with a truckful of pigs that squealed and grunted through the night.

I learned many things on these trips. That Milky Way bars were perhaps the most delicious food ever invented. That people on both sides of the Rio Grande Valley, gringos and Mexicans alike, traded freely and went back and forth across the border. That these border people of different cultures went to one another's weddings and funerals and christenings and understood each other, in jumbled Tex-Mex "Spanglish."

And that hogs make an awful lot of noise.

When I arrived in Wisconsin that following year, I found the Midwest much different from McAllen, Texas. In the family tradition of frugality, my dad gave us no money, assuming that we would work our way through school. But everything was terribly expensive—food, clothes, books; to a boy from a poor country where things are cheap, even to breathe seemed to cost money. So I scavenged empty Coca-Cola bottles for the nickel deposits and went to work washing dishes in the cafeteria, another Mexican busboy in the cold dark upper Midwest, looking for my brother José Luis every time my lunch tray was tipped to the floor with an insult about my ancestry.

There were many, because an all-boys' school in Wisconsin of 1956 was not the cosmopolitan Los Angeles or Miami of today, and it sure as hell wasn't San Cristóbal. Grandfather Fox had died when I was very young, so I spoke almost no English by the time I was fourteen. The Wisconsin kids were big and blond and rough, with no interest whatever in the skinny Mexican running out to catch a pass on the high-school football team.

Spic. Beaner. Dirty Mexican.

You heard it all in those days, generally just after the referee's whistle had blown, as the 240-pound Scandinavian linebacker speared you in the gut with his helmet; when winter began, his hockey stick jammed you in the eye; in spring the same boy's elbow slammed into your nose below the basketball hoop. By May there were a few sunny days as you came down the steps and finally began to feel good about yourself, when English was beginning to make sense and even algebra had a certain logic about it, and perhaps there was a girl who might smile kindly on your Latin looks even in this blond land.

This was the moment when the lettermen in school-color varsity jackets tripped you and sent you sprawling down the steps. Their English was clear as a bell: *Get back across the border, greaser.*

This, of course, is why God invented big brothers.

I was good at sports, even American sports, but I always hated physical violence. Give me a bat and a glove, the soccer field and the basketball court; I ran track, hurled the shotput, fought bulls at home in the *corrida*, even played American football. I'm the one you want as your matador or your tight end, whether it means facing a quarter-ton bull or one of those mighty Norwegian linebackers of Prairie du Chien, Wisconsin.

But for a fistfight, there you need José Luis Fox. Later, when things got bad in politics and government soldiers were ready to push me down the stairs of the Mexican Congress, I instinctively looked around for my big brother at my side.

Mexicans do everything in a family group. We eat together, travel together, fistfight together, court girls together. It was the greatest relief in my life to come home to Mexico after this long, cold year in Wisconsin. My brother José Luis and I came back to the ranch along with our younger brothers Cristóbal and Javier, who had joined us in Wisconsin. Now we were proud of our newfound English and our sophisticated gringo ways, the Levi's blue jeans and colored T-shirts with the NFL insignia and the tight, tight sleeves to roll the cigarettes we hid from our parents. We looked cool and American among the faded overalls and white singlets the local farmers still wore in those days. The four of us basked in the sun in the *zócalo* of León, where we went courting on Sundays after we'd gone to mass and done our chores.

Round and round the gazebo you went, as the girls went strolling round in the other direction so you could check them out and they could check you out, round and round twenty or twenty-five Sundays in a row just to get a nod or a smile from the girl of your dreams. Then you put in another twenty-five Sundays to get a handshake in the presence of her parents—a year now you have invested in this one girl, and still not a kiss, nor even a private conversation. Then, if you were very patient and very committed, there was a chance after fifty Sundays that her parents would let their daughter pause in the traditional courtship ritual of the town square. You waited a year for this, just that little hesitation in her step that meant maybe, if your big brother knew her big sister or your mother knew her aunt's second cousin from church, just *maybe* you could sit down with this vision of loveliness on the bench at the extreme edge of the park, under the watchful eyes of her parents still going round, round, round the bandstand in the center of the square.

Her sister sat with you, too, and maybe your big brother, and perhaps after another year of Sundays you might be allowed to invite her out in your car—not the old Model T now, but a much-cherished bright green 1936 Ford we christened "Pichirilo," a secondhand coupe that rasped noisily through the gears but was a great improvement over a Model T milk truck: It had a backseat. You couldn't see the big Hollywood movies in León—to see Cantínflas in *Around the World in Eighty Days* with David Niven, we had to drive twelve hours away to Mexico City (in León we had only the shabby old rustic theaters, which were okay for you and your brothers to watch the old scratchy black-and-white Pancho Villa movies but not much of an attraction for a date). Perhaps you could take the girl for ice cream, properly escorted by a sister or a cousin and a gaggle of other relatives. Perhaps after five years or eight as *novios*, you could marry your girlfriend and have kids of your own. Then, like any good Catholic, you could go round and round the square to protect your own daughter from tall boys in Levi's with colored T-shirts, their hair slicked back like James Dean's in *Giant*.

NOT THAT WE had actually *seen* James Dean. It was a conservative place, this Cristero countryside in the isolated land of the Institutional Revolutionary Party. Between the PRI's temporal power and the moral authority of the Catholic Church, we saw very little of the outside world in Mexico in the 1950s and '60s. They didn't agree on much, the anticlerical PRI and the antifederal church. But both were determined that Vicente Fox not see Marilyn Monroe's skirt blowing in the air above that subway grate.

This was by design: Mexico was deeply walled off from the world through most of the twentieth century. Today León is a city of 1.2 million people with a wide selection of big multiplex movie theatres, but in the 1960s you still drove all day and night to see a film from the outside world—if you had a car, which very few did. Even in the bright lights of

Mexico City, the xenophobic PRI carefully censored films to keep Hollywood from stirring us up with too much good news about life outside the regime's walls. Mostly they allowed us to see the comedies and musicals and westerns, and lots of very fine Mexican films glorifying Emiliano Zapata and Pancho Villa. Meanwhile the Jesuit Club censored the moral content of films and television, so if Rhett Butler kissed Scarlett at Tara or made reference to her petticoats, most people in Mexico never knew it.

All TV and radio licenses in the country were controlled by the official party, some 90 percent of them in the hands of one family, that of Emilio Azcárraga, the legendary "El Tigre" who owned what became the Televisa network. All of this state control mattered little: Campesinos didn't have the money to go to the cinema, and the rest of us didn't have television sets. The first time I ever saw one was peeking through the square stone windows of my Spanish grandfather's living room in Mexico City, where the adults gathered to eat formal dinners on Sunday. Afterward, if we were very polite, we were allowed in to watch the flickering black-and-white images of Spaniards wrestling, the Red Devil and the Masked Man. And for me, of course, the westerns, always the westerns—John Wayne if you could find him, but anything with a horse would do.

In those days you couldn't get much John Wayne in Mexico, much less a hamburger or a pair of Levi's. The protectionist PRI walled off Mexico much as Lou Dobbs and the antiglobal extremists would like to isolate the United States today, barring any product or foreign competition that might threaten the unholy trinity of the nationalist PRI's dominance.

First there were the protected monopolies of the One Hundred, the powerful Mexican family *grupos* that controlled the major domestic industries. There was the Monterrey Group of the Garza Sada clan, which brewed beer, made glass, and later bottled Coca-Cola. The great Chihuahua family the Terrazas were vast landowners who dominated the timber business. In finance, the powerful Legorreta family of Banamex ran the banking industry. Of course, there was the biggest monopoly of all, the federal government, which owned 70 percent of the Mexican economy in those days—all the railroads, telephones, even the movie theaters. The wealthiest men in the country were the politicians themselves, who went into office as unremarkable local party henchmen and came out as millionaire tycoons.

Big *priista* businessmen paid the official party's bills and bribed its politicians—elected officials even bribed one another—to get contracts and permits, erect barriers to competition, and suffocate any entrepreneur from outside the System with red tape. Sold to the public in the name of nationalism, the whole scheme was really about *control*. It was carefully engineered to make sure that the monopolies got no competition—either from young upstarts within Mexico or from outside, from global corporations that produced better products at lower cost, with greater efficiency. Competition from the United States, Europe, and Japan would have lowered prices for the Mexican consumer, just as free trade with Mexico and Asia helps provide lower prices to the U.S. consumer today. But the PRI cared little for the consumer. Its party line was the bottom line: protect the status quo of the oligarchy at all costs.

Then there were the *priista* unions, which the official party used to control the workers who toiled in the mines, poured the concrete, and made the hotel beds. These workers both manufactured and consumed the overpriced and often shoddy goods that were sold at inflated prices by the wealthy politicians and monopolists. Organized labor wanted no competitive threat from workers in the United States, Europe, or Asia, nor did the *priista* unions want foreign companies to show them up by offering Mexican workers better pay and benefits, safety regulations, or product standards. It amuses me when our region's leftist-demagogue critics of globalism accuse Fortune 500 corporations of exploiting the Latin American working class. In reality, U.S. and European companies were the first to treat our employees with dignity, to provide high wages, health-care insurance, and pension plans—indeed, our own government and domestic companies began offering good benefits only when forced to compete with the Fortune 500 for skilled labor.

Finally there was the PRI's political machine itself, which feared U.S. dominance and seditious foreign notions like economic mobility, classless democracy, and freedom of expression. So our nationalist leaders censored the press, bought off reporters, defrauded voters, and set up crippling barriers to keep foreign companies from investing in Mexico. As a result my country was simply left out of the twentieth century, bricked off from the greatest economic boom in the planet's history by towering walls of isolationism and insularity. Like the immigrant bashers and antiglobalists of the Americas today, north and south, the PRI cloaked its motives in patriotism. This is always, in Samuel Johnson's words, "the last refuge of a scoundrel."

Cultures will ever fear diversity, integration, and change, no matter how much people are enriched by them. At Coca-Cola we faced open hostility in Mexico, not from our archrivals at Pepsi but from the federal government, which spoonfed Mexican society nationalist propaganda from birth. Fearful of the global expansion of U.S. products in the 1950s and '60s, the regime indoctrinated Mexicans to fear that Coca-Cola would replace our beloved *aguas frescas,* the delicious "fresh waters" flavored with lime and watermelon, sold hand-bottled by vendors on street corners throughout Mexico.

This irrational fear of "McDonaldization" was worldwide in the postwar years. From Rome and Tokyo to Guadalajara, cultures around the planet feared that hamburgers would replace pasta, sushi, and tacos. Of course the opposite is true. Today they do sell Big Macs in Beijing and León, but you also now find huevos rancheros and chiles rellenos all over Chicago, Toronto, or Charlotte, North Carolina. (This was not so in those dark days of my exile to the United States. There were no Taco Bells in Wisconsin in 1956, so we had to wait for Señora Marcos's tortillas to arrive by slow mail from San Cristóbal).

This cultural isolation extended to new ideas. Foreign ideologies were about as welcome in the PRI's Mexico as they were in Franco's Spain or the Communist Soviet Union. In those days even the leftist Mexican intelligentsia feared competition from Hollywood, which everyone said would bring Mexico a host of trashy, lowbrow films to destroy the once-admired Mexican film industry.

Instead, when we opened up Mexico's culture to the global democracy, the opposite occurred. Yes, today Mexicans can watch *American Pie* or *Dodgeball* in a multiplex theater on Mexico City's Paseo de la Reforma. But we also can see *Hotel Rwanda* or *Syriana* in English. More important for us, Mexican films such as *Like Water for Chocolate* or *Frida* play in shopping malls in Virginia. And a film like *Babel,* whose Oscar-nominated Mexican director Alejandro González Iñárritu shot it in Morocco, California, Mexico, and Japan, appeared on screens from Jacksonville to Johannesburg, Mexico City to Moscow, in a year when Mexican directors were the rage of the Academy Awards.

Because they arose in the era of the Internet and twenty-four-hour cable television, it may be hard for xenophobic talk-show hosts on Fox News Channel or CNN to imagine how limiting it is to live in an isolated, protectionist, closed society. But consider this: As late as the 1970s, a collegiate backpacker could still be arrested for carrying a copy of *Time* magazine into Franco's Spain, which in those days had a state-controlled economy, an isolationist dictatorship, and a per capita income nearly as low as Mexico's. Since then, under the constitutional democracy of King Juan Carlos and a succession of elected governments of socialists from the left and free-marketeers of the center-right, with open competition with the European Union and the genius of artists like filmmaker Pedro Almodóvar, Spain has developed into one of the richest and most culturally diverse nations on earth, with a per capita income three times that of Mexico—and one of the world's very finest film industries. Back in the 1970s, Spaniards were terrified by their authoritarian government not only into believing that Americans and Britons might spread seditious ideas of democracy with their *Newsweek* and BBC, but also that hamburgers and Coca-Cola would replace paella and sangria, that baseball would destroy the bullfight. Of course, there are still paella, sangria, and bullfights in Spain—but now they export the most popular Spanish products to Germany. The difference is that now, thirty years after Franco's death and the opening of Spain's markets to integration with the EU, Spaniards can afford to go to bullfights—and attend World Cup games in Germany, too.

But in the walled-off Mexico of the PRI, a teenager had to drive twelve hours to see a heavily censored American movie; twenty-four hours to McAllen to buy a Hampshire hog, a John Deere tractor, or a pack of bubble gum. In fact, it was on the streets of Texas that I first glimpsed those marvelous glass-domed machines where you inserted a penny and were showered with multicolored gumballs, surely the greatest innovation of the modern age.

THE IRONY of xenophobia is that cultures are so very much stronger than we credit them. Our own traditional values can't be bought so cheaply. In Mexico you find everywhere the strength of the Aztecs and the Mayans, not just in the magnificent stone pyramids and the contributions of these great empires to art, architecture, science, and mathematics (the Mayans invented the concept of zero long before the time of Copernicus or Newton) but also in our culture's patient, enduring work ethic, our intense love of family, the cherishing of spiritual peace, and our special respect for community harmony—indigenous values that still distinguish Mexican society, just as my grandfather's hard-driving Saxon frugality endures in the culture of today's United States or Germany. These core values are stronger than all the consumer buying power of the G-8 nations combined, more influential than all the films of Hollywood, mightier even than all the tanks the National Guard can mass along the border.

Here in Mexico we have survived military, economic, and cultural invasions by Spaniards, Frenchmen, and gringos (a term we always used with respect and affection; it is still said more often with a smile than a curse in Mexico). In fact, a nation's culture does not so much withstand invasion by other cultures as it is enriched by such diversity. America, as the historian Carl Degler has said, is less a melting pot than it is a salad bowl. Each ingredient retains its distinctive flavor, tossed together to create a larger harmonious flavor for the whole.

Immigration, free trade, outsourcing: These are not the threats of a "Third World invasion" of the United States or Canada, but a global phenomenon whose values have enriched—even created—the economies and the cultures of both the richer host countries and the aspiring nations. Spaniards went to work in Germany; the Irish emigrated to the United Kingdom, the United States, Canada, and Australia. Mexicans crossed the deserts to reach the United States, but my American grandfather once met them coming the other way. Even today, people from the United States, Canada, Germany, and China come to Monterrey, São Paulo, and Mexico City. Here in our New World, they realize their own aspirations running microchip factories, rendering legal advice, improving the efficiency of Latin America's agriculture, or investing in the Mexican stock exchange. (I am proud to report that anyone who invested a single dollar on the Mexican bolsa on the day I took office, now, six years later, has $3.50 in his or her pocket.) Today, seniors from the United States and Canada are finding their American dream of retirement in Mexico, in colonial San Miguel de Allende an hour from our family ranch, or in Puerto Vallarta or the beachside communities sprouting up along the Sea of Cortez. With this ceaseless ebb and flow of global immigrants—investors, students, migrant crop pickers, captains of industry, skilled stonemasons, wealthy retirees—people bring not only their skills, dollars, and hard labor but also their cultural values. We should not fear cultural invasion, but embrace it: We might learn something.

In the ruckus over immigration, free trade, and globalism, we hear a lot about the need for assimilation. But what is it to "assimilate" in the Americas, where nations like the United States, Canada, Mexico, and Brazil are not monochromatic walls of flat color but diverse cultural mosaics of a thousand hues? French-speaking natives of Quebec have spent decades fighting the English-speaking majority in Canada, but the answer is not separatism. An independent Quebec would devastate the Canadian economy, threaten the nation's security, and eviscerate the diversity that is one of Canada's greatest assets. If the French language, literature, arts, and cuisine are strong enough to merit the love of Canada's people, they will survive. Those aspects of French culture that the world decides it can do without (the amicability of Gallic waiters, perhaps, or the incessant smoking of long brown cigarettes) will either slowly evolve for the better or perish.

The success of the European Union has proved beyond a doubt that even with untrammeled free trade, immigration, outsourcing, and cultural interchange, the best values of Italian family life, French cuisine, Germanic efficiency, and Spanish architecture have endured and flourished. Meanwhile the weakest aspects of various cultures (Eastern European pollution, the tardiness of Greek ferries, English cooking) have been forced to improve—or face extinction.

To those self-styled "culture warriors" in the United States who raise fears of a "Third World invasion"—who say that Mexicans will turn North America into a continent of Spanish-speaking, tattoo-wearing, drug-dealing East L.A. gangsters—I would ask them to think again about U.S.-Mexico relations in terms of cuisine. No offense, but in Mexico before NAFTA, even the poorest Mexican mother turned up her nose at American fast food. Some 95 percent of Mexican women were housewives in those days; whether wealthy matriarchs or poor indigenous campesinas, they spent hours lovingly preparing simple peasant ingredients of corn, beans, and chili into fantastic concoctions designed for long, loving meals with extended family—indeed, the rural poor women of Mexico were the great culinary craftswomen of all time. Their art was the alchemy of Marquitos working her magic on the lava rock at San Cristóbal, turning rough maize into works of wonder that a Bajío farm boy dreamed about on the wintry nights of his Wisconsin exile. I wouldn't have traded them for all the Big Macs on the planet.

In those days before NAFTA, Mexicans feared that the paper-wrapped hamburgers and hot dogs of El Norte would flood our markets. This "First World invasion" we feared even more than people in the United States feared Ross Perot's "giant sucking sound" of jobs leaving for Mexico. To us the greatest threat from the United States was not economic or military but cultural; like the xenophobes in today's America, the "culture warriors" of the PRI were master demagogues at exploiting this fear of change. We were afraid that our children would lose their Mexican heritage, their devotion to family and to the Catholic Church; that they would grow up eating pizza, listening to rock and roll music, smoking marijuana, and speaking only English. Like the wall-building congressmen and angry talk-radio hosts of today's Southern California, the nationalist *priista* politicians of the 1950s and '60s used this fear as a weapon to rally a frightened people to their cause. In this way they were like the National Socialists of the 1930s, who cemented their hold on Germany with the specter of the economic domination of working people by Jewish bankers, of the cultural contamination of the land of Beethoven by the foreign influence of American jazz music. In this way the PRI used fear to keep us from opening our markets to U.S. goods and investment, telling us that if we opened Mexico's markets, we would all be forced to drink Budweiser instead of Corona, speak the language of Milton Berle instead of Cervantes, that our teenagers might dance to the seductive rhythms of Motown instead of our *norteño*.

Instead now my collegiate son Rodrigo can choose between seventies disco or *norteño* on the radio stations of León—and so can the kids at UC Santa Barbara. He studies English; they study Spanish. U.S. students come here to read *Don Quijote* at the University of Guanajuato; Mexican students read Shakespeare at the University of Texas.

And Perot Systems, no longer afraid of the "giant sucking sound," just opened an impressive new facility in Guadalajara. It employs hundreds of Mexican software engineers, technicians, and executives, led by U.S. managers who earned their own American dreams training experts in India. This outsourcing center sends millions of dollars every year in profits back to Perot Systems headquarters in Dallas, where the company spends those dollars paying U.S. bankers to manage the funds in U.S. investments, U.S. lawyers to supervise Perot Systems contracts to buy U.S. computers, and U.S. home builders who hire our immigrants to build the houses of Perot Systems' bankers, lawyers, and computer executives in the suburbs north of Dallas—where a growing number of the home buyers are Latinos. Meanwhile in Guadalajara, Mexican families use the incomes they earn from the outsourced Perot center to buy local eggs and cheese, build starter homes, and send their kids to college. Yet the Mexican mothers of these children cook huevos rancheros and not frozen Eggo waffles every morning, even if they have to get up earlier to send the kids off to school, say a quick rosary, and make it to work on time at the Perot Systems bilingual call center.

The best values of Mexico—family, church, work, compassion, huevos rancheros—these have survived NAFTA. Our worst traits—corruption, inefficiency, tardiness, lack of ambition, poverty, authoritarianism—these are fast fading into memory. In Mexico, journalists will criticize me for saying this, for airing our own dirty laundry. But the fact that they are free to do so is proof positive of how far we have come.

WALLED-OFF SOCIETIES are not so lucky. When I was coming of age in the 1950s, the total control that the government exerted over commerce, industry, agriculture, church, and family life put everything in its place, where it could be watched, monitored, and maintained in the status quo. This was particularly true of our schools: Like the old *hacendados,* the PRI didn't want people to learn enough arithmetic to calculate how badly they were getting screwed.

Even what meager public education the PRI did provide was unattainable to the typical sons and daughters of the campesinos. Sure, primary school was free (and worth the price). But like the agrarian America of the nineteenth century, in Mexico most farm families—and in Mexico that was still two thirds of the population—couldn't afford to keep their kids in school. Virtually no poor boys stayed in school past the sixth grade, and girls often didn't go to school at all. (After the advent of democracy in 2000, we responded to this need by offering 6.1 million scholarship payments to parents to enable them to keep their daughters and sons in school, more than doubling the number of poor kids who were financially able to attend school.)

Kids like Antonio Valdivia, my childhood friend at Rancho San Cristóbal, finished school at age twelve, barely knowing how to read. Meanwhile I went off to the Jesuit schools in León and Wisconsin so that I could be better prepared with my new high-school English and college-prep calculus to face the global economy.

This, of course, was blatantly unfair, at odds with the compassionate philosophy of our Jesuit teachers and the ideological cant of liberty and equality that the PRI's teachers droned in the public-school classroom. Returning to the ranch to finish high school, I was startled by the inequality of educational opportunity—a gap even greater than our disparity in incomes in Latin America. It was a stark contrast to the compassionate example of my devout Spanish mother and the passionate Yankee faith in education and self-improvement espoused by my Papa Fox. I never saw the difference between the United States and Mexico more clearly than when I came home from Wisconsin. Once I'd gotten over the euphoria of sitting down to my first five-course breakfast of huevos, chiliquillas, tortillas, refried beans, and homemade jam in Marquitos's kitchen, I looked around and realized how different life was for the campesino kids, compared with the astonishing equality of opportunity that kids in Wisconsin seemed to simply take for granted.

For my brothers and me, Mexico was a paradise: a warm and friendly macho world where men milked cows, broke horses and drank tequila straight up, fought bulls in the ring, hunted ducks, and generally ruled the roost. The only mild irritant was that the woman in charge occasionally yanked you out of this halcyon Eden, put you into a uniform, and packed you off to the Jesuit *preparatario* in León—which is where I returned to finish high school.

But when I got back from Wisconsin to the farm, Antonio Valdivia couldn't play marbles anymore. At fifteen he and my other childhood friends were earning the pesos that bought barely enough corn for their families to scrape by, with never enough to pay for a doctor for a grandmother's diabetes or a fine new suit of clothes, much less the tuition fees of the *preparatario* in León. Others had simply vanished, sent off to El Norte to work. They were locked, now, in the failed authoritarian system run by the fathers of the well-connected boys I would later meet in college.

THIS WAS THE BEGINNING of my rebellion as a proud *hijo desobediente,* the disobedient son of the mariachi song. It would be thirty years before I joined the opposition National Action Party, the PAN, but my opposition to the System began the day I came back from Wisconsin to find the gap widening between me and Antonio Valdivia. I watched my boyhood pals leave one by one to wash the windows of cars they could not afford in Mexico City, to build houses their future wives would enter only as maids in Houston, to pave roads they were not legally allowed to drive in Arizona. If they went to wash dishes in Wisconsin, it was not to earn treats at the school commissary but to send money home to purchase frijoles and rice for their family.

This was a sharp contrast to the American dream I had witnessed in Prairie du Chien. From behind my busboy's tray at Campion Jesuit High School outside Lacrosse, I had been astonished by the material wealth of these children. I gawked at the nourishing food they threw away (half-eaten Milky Ways, even), the soda bottles they tossed into the snow without collecting the nickel deposit (a whole nickel or a dime, even, a fortune in the mid-1950s, when that kind of income could keep you rolling in chocolate). And there was the amazing fact that everyone, literally *everyone,* seemed to go all the way through high school, and then they packed up their fine colored varsity jackets and went off to college—not just the sons of the bankers and doctors but farm kids, too, and girls, even blue-collar kids whose fathers worked in the meatpacking plant or at the gas station.

Interestingly, none of those Wisconsin kids ever invited us home—a fact I didn't really notice until thirty years later, when I ran into one of the other Mexican boys who had been with us at the Campion school, Limón Rojas, who went on to become secretary of education under President Zedillo; another Campion classmate, Rivas Mercado, became a successful businessman. But for the entire time we lived in Wisconsin, none of us could remember once setting foot in a single one of those cozy American houses. At vacations the Wisconsin boys went home to the hearths of the blazing fires we imagined inside those big houses. We would stay in the dormitory, dreaming of fresh-baked tortillas, or tackle the Nordic trails, Mexican brothers floundering in the snowdrifts, ever watchful for a return-deposit Coca-Cola bottle.

Not to be taken home by one's schoolmates: This was extraordinary to us Mexicans, who truly believe that no matter how humble, *mi casa es su casa.* Antonio would always share his dirt floor and divvy up half of his mother's tacos as we played cowboys by his back stoop. I could never have imagined failing to invite my high-school friends home from the León *preparatario* to see how we lived. How else could we have passed along to them the valuable inside information that farm kids know long before city boys?

Mexican culture has great values it can share with the world—hospitality, family, community, compassion—but in 1960, high-quality public education wasn't among them. So boys like me were packed off to the Jesuits to prepare us for our college entrance exams. Somehow I got through the calculus and did well enough in history to get into college—with my big brother, of course—at the Iberoamericana University in Mexico City, the Jesuit college I would attend with the natty youths who would soon become Mexico's wealthiest and most powerful men.

Oddly enough, while the Mexican establishment didn't care much about public elementary and secondary schools, the System prized excellence in university education—both public and private. The sons of the rich monopoly capitalists required good institutions of higher education. Even if they were protected against the competitive demands of the world marketplace, the powerful family *grupos* wanted to polish their young men with the business and technical skills to take the greatest possible advantage of an establishment that gave one family a monopoly of cement, another the right to brew the beer, a third the hegemony to forge Mexican steel. The System demanded managers who could make their factories produce the products, even if these sons of the *priista* nobility often showed up late and bleary-eyed after long nights in the nightclubs of Polanco.

These finely dressed *chilangos* of Mexico City with their London-tailored suits and striped old-school ties—theirs was a very different world from mine. These boys had fast sports cars and faster girlfriends; no twenty-five times for them around the *zócalo*, no arriving at the university in the Fox family's 1936 Ford, still wheezing up and down the mountain roads. In 1960 our beloved green Pichirilo deposited us gangly farm boys at the steps of the Iberoamericana University. I can see those city boys still, in their Parisian haircuts with the languid swirl of hair cream above their foreheads, cigarettes dangling from their lips, looking European and very sophisticated. Perhaps there was a bit of color on their cheekbones from a weekend in the Acapulco homes of their fathers to match their glossy shoes, a stark contrast to the mestizo playmates of my youth in their work boots and overalls.

And here comes Vicente Fox in his blue jeans and dusty T-shirt, clomping up the steps of the Ibero at a time when the whole university was in a single house in Avenida Taxqueña. Even then I was aware of being different. I liked it, being the ranchero's son, the guy in the cowboy boots from León-Guanajuato who didn't give a damn what the *chilangos* from Mexico City thought. Oddly enough, being different has always made me feel more secure: I relished this image of the maverick. For the first time, I noticed that after years of my big brother's tutelage round the square of León, finally the girls noticed me, too—that they liked this confidence. And so I stood taller, strong now from a decade lifting the heavy *costales* of grain, playing sports, and yoking the team of oxen my brothers and I used to sharecrop garbanzo beans under my father's harsh discipline. We were proud to be entrepreneurial rancheros, these Fox boys suddenly set down among the indulged sons of the wealthy establishment.

Throughout history this has been the strategy of the Jesuit order, to educate the sons of kings and emperors, financiers and factory owners to become "men for others." The order of St. Ignatius Loyola has molded future world leaders, from the ancient kings, emperors, and popes of Europe to President Bill Clinton (Georgetown University, Class of '68) or Spain's Crown Prince Felipe (Georgetown, Class of '95).

St. Ignatius teaches us that one cannot find real happiness until one brings happiness to others. At the Iberoamericana University, the Jesuits picked up the job of molding me into a "man for others" from the priests in León and Wisconsin, no longer smacking my hand with their rulers but leading me now, as did my mother, by their example of action for social justice. The Jesuits taught us that it wasn't enough to build up our own life projects; the real goal was to improve the lives of those around us. As president I always believed that more world leaders should allow our faiths to guide us. In her book *The Mighty and the Almighty,* former U.S. secretary of state Madeleine Albright argues for "faith-based diplomacy," encouraging world leaders to navigate by their moral compass, regardless of denomination. Would that all the poor nations of the world were led by devout people like President Ellen Johnson-Sirleaf of Liberia, who is tolerant of all the warring factions, clans, and denominations in her troubled land yet really *lives* her faith: Leaders in Ellen's humanist mold are consumed by helping the poor, instead of helping themselves to the treasury. And if more rich nations were led in the spirit of Madeleine Albright, the wealthy nations might become just as concerned with helping their poor neighbors as they are with maintaining their own supremacy.

In a true revolution of hope, perhaps someday the world's many faiths could convene a "spiritual UN" to focus our presidents and prime ministers on the moral imperatives that must begin to guide nations. Whether Muslim or Hindu, Catholic or evangelical, Protestant, Buddhist, or Presbyterian, surely presidents and prime ministers would do better to follow a moral compass than the narrow self-interests of their politics. This view will of course violate the secular world's abhorrence to the public profession of faith by its leaders and further incense the intelligentsia of secular Mexico City. But if God does not guide our actions, what will? Greed? Oil? Power? Public opinion polls?

THE 1960s were the beginning of a great schism in the Jesuit order. This debate pitted the traditional Ignatians—dedicated to educating the future leaders of business, politics, and the intelligentsia to be "men for others"—against a new breed of revolution theologians who considered educating the wastrel sons of the rich to be a colossal waste of time. Historic Jesuit schools like the Instituto Patria in Mexico City closed their doors as priests gave up on the favored sons of the elite and headed to Chiapas, Guatemala, and El Salvador to educate the poor—some to foment political unrest, even armed rebellion.

One of these revolution theologians, a Jesuit seminarian who lived and worked with the guerrillas in El Salvador, became my presidential press secretary, Rubén Aguilar. Another of their disciples is rumored to have been Subcomandante Marcos, the pipe-smoking *zapatista* guerrilla leader in the black ski mask, who may have taken instruction as a priest from the Jesuits. This would fit: The enigmatic Chiapas revolutionary was, like the Jesuits, to me both the source of much frustration and occasional admiration.

The Jesuits who stayed behind at the Ibero to hammer some sense into the thick head of Vicente Fox and his friends had their own share of frustrations. I eked out a living on three pesos a day—carefully rationing the money I'd saved as a teenage sharecropper under my father's regime, I would take a series of three buses to reach the front steps of the old colonial mansion that housed the Ibero. Many days I would walk the hour and a half to save bus fare, crossing what was becoming one of the world's largest cities. (Today Mexico City, with some 20 million inhabitants, is second only to Tokyo; in the United States, only New York ranks in the top ten. Latin America also boasts number four, Brazil's São Paulo. The world is bigger than you think.)

There were distractions along the way for a Bajío farm boy: pretty girls, fancy cars, cinema posters of the new John Wayne movie, domino games with my classmates. Despite a childhood drilled in my grandfather's strange Yankee punctuality—I was the only kid in the state of Guanajuato who was expected to be on time for dinner, or face an empty table—often I never quite reached the inside of Father Schiefler's classroom in time for roll call.

"Torres! Osorio! Hernández!" barked the white-haired Spanish priest, another stubborn Basque bulling through the class roster. "Fox!"

"Presente!" my friend Osorio would answer in a deep rumble from behind his hand, imitating my basso from the back row. We took turns covering for each other, so that whichever freshman was late could horse about on the front steps, making time with young ladies passing by, gambling at cards, wasting the precious gifts of education for which the parents of Mexico's poor—or Wisconsin's middle class—would have sacrificed everything. I flinch to think of it now, but as George Bernard Shaw once observed, "Youth, like education, is wasted on the young."

I CAME face-to-face with Father Schiefler a decade later, at the ten-year anniversary of our college graduation. Ibero alums had by then already acceded to positions of power in the Mexican family *grupos,* government, and Fortune 500 corporations—one of my best friends was Roberto Hernández, who went on to sell his banking empire Banamex to Citibank and become one of the wealthiest men in the world.

Our class reunion spared no expense. We rented out Mexico City's swank University Club, and here we all came, anxious to dazzle our friends and teachers with our success stories, smoking cigars and drinking brandy, with our wives and girlfriends draped in designer clothes and sparkling with jewelry. It seemed a farm boy's American dream, this celebration of my brilliant rise to become the youngest Coca-Cola president in the company's global empire at age thirty-two. Surely this would impress Father Schiefler, who had once thrown me out of college just to get my attention on my grades, a 7.5 on the Mexican 10-point marking system. (Oddly enough, this would be my grade from the Mexican people forty years later, in the job-approval polls at the end of my presidency—a 75 percent rating is a high score in politics, but it's a mediocre grade in college.)

"I am totally disappointed in all of you," the Basque priest told the glittering assembly. "And why?" Above the tight clerical collar's white square and black jacket, he watched our blank grinning faces fall, as they had so often in class, at one of his Jesuit rhetorical questions. "Clearly, I wasted four years of my life on you."

Tears literally ran down the old man's cheeks as he explained, "Listening to your success stories makes me so ashamed of the way I have wasted my gifts. Where did I fail, if my teaching led you to become nothing more than leaders of business, completely consumed with enriching yourselves while the poor suffer in the streets?"

The room had been full of clinking cocktail glasses and laughter as we celebrated our marvelous world. Now you could hear a pin drop. I sat there, stunned. It was a defining moment of my life. Here I was at the pinnacle of my business success, the hotshot president of the world's best-known brand name in the biggest foreign market of the most popular consumer product on the planet. By then I was a prince of the city, with a fine car and a pretty wife, a motorcycle and a camper and a boat. I'd been to Europe and Asia, flown first class to meet with captains of industry in Frankfurt and Tokyo, moved among Madison Avenue ad agencies and London financiers. But inside, there was this great emptiness, and Father Schiefler could see it.

This is because every one of us whom God puts on this earth requires a great crusade, a great canyon of need worthy of pouring in all our capacities, talents, and willpower, our hard work, intelligence, and love. For some this canyon is a child, a business, or a piece of land, and all of these meant something to me. But it wasn't enough, and Father Schiefler knew it. He had trained us to be "men for others." But ten years after our graduation, we were merely men for ourselves.

I thought of all the altruistic people who had seen something in their *hijo desobediente*. My mother, with her love for the poor and the sick of our ranch. Father Pérez Alonso, my Nicaraguan confessor at the university, who opened my eyes to the knowledge that there were people in Nicaragua who considered Mexico a First World economy (he took the time to hear my sins, then gave me a zero on my first ethics exam). Brother Enrique, the burly LaSalle monk who taught me to box out the center in basketball and led us on hikes in his love for God's mountains. Dean Reyes Ponce, Mexico's master of Harvard-style business administration that was all the rage in those days: We fairly worshipped at the altar of delegation, the gospel of time management and the sacred temple of MBO, Management By Objectives.

The concept of delegation I'd already mastered, "making others make things happen," getting Osorio to answer roll call for me. Time management: This I translated as the decision whether to skip class and read the books or skip the books and go to class. But I had missed the point. When the Jesuits brought in Harvard-trained business scholars to teach me Management By Objective, they never intended that the objective of my personal MBO would be a Honda 750 motorcycle.

CHAPTER 4

THE COLA WARS

I HAD FINISHED college in 1964, a decade before that ten-year reunion with the Ibéro's Father Schiefler. The sixties were go-go times for business majors in the Fortune 500, even if they were bad times for Antonio Valdivia's family. Until the priest brought me face-to-face with the shallowness of my success, I was having the time of my life.

I never even took the final exit examinations to get my college diploma (I ended up taking them at age fifty-six, the year before I was elected president—gratefully, I passed). Before the end of my final term, I had sent out applications to the ten largest U.S. companies doing business in Mexico. I'd always been impressed with the U.S. business model—the Henry Fords, the Andrew Carnegies, the A. P. Gianninis. These were the great tycoons who built the milk trucks that Mexican farm boys drove, whose steel mills employed the fathers of future collegians, who founded the Bank of America, where Italian immigrants saved the dollars they earned building the Golden Gate Bridge. This was the great era of corporate capitalism, and the United States led the way. So I sent my neatly typed résumé, filled with my mastery of the boardroom bingo of the 1960s, to the Ford Motor Company. They hired me as a management trainee before graduation day, put me in a business suit, gave me an office and a desk, and assigned me a secretary to take dictation at smoke-filled meetings where we drank lots of coffee, and set our MBO goals for manufacturing and selling automobiles in Mexico.

I was miserable. Outside the window was the bustle of Mexico City, the Sheraton with its fancy shops and restaurants, the shining golden Angel of Independence, lovely girls and cinema posters. Beyond them lay the vast open spaces of Mexico, where a young man could breathe the fresh air of freedom. Instead I was strangling in a coat and tie, with that bug up my ass that my grandfather liked to talk about.

So when a letter came three months later from Coca-Cola asking me if

I'd like to drive a route truck, I jumped at the chance. My friends thought I was crazy. They had office jobs where shoeshine men came to your desk and called you *licenciado* or *ingeniero* (in Mexico we title professionals by such college degrees, which loosely translate as "esquire" or "engineer"). My brothers went back to the farm and did the respectable thing, running the family businesses. When my father heard my plans, he just shrugged and said, "A truck driver? Well, just make sure you are the best truck driver in the company." Here I was, fresh out of university, heir to a former Spanish hacienda, wearing a khaki jumpsuit with its red Coca-Cola logo and my name stitched on the breast pocket, no *licenciado* at all, just VICENTE. From now on, my meetings would be held while wheeling a dolly full of Coke into hole-in-the-wall *changarros* along the remote mountain roads of Michoacán.

I was in heaven.

No one ever loved driving a Coca-Cola truck like I did. I'll never forget arriving at La Soledad, an elegant resort in the old colonial silver city of Morelia, more like a hill town in Tuscany with its ancient vine-covered aqueducts and gracious cathedrals. There was the traditional late lunch at four in the afternoon, where my new bosses at Coca-Cola toasted me in tequila, handed me the keys to the little red-and-white truck, and led me to the bottling plant to load up for my first day. I remember shouldering the cartons, competing again, carrying two cases to every one lifted by the rough, grizzled truck drivers who had been on the routes for twenty years.

I was back on the farm schedule again, up before dawn, shifting gears down the steep jungle-green roads of central Mexico—no hogs in the trailer and no big brother beside me to show me how to use the clutch, but exhilarating all the same. The village of Tacambaro was truly a hidden Eden of the Americas, an oasis with the God-light of sunshine streaming down through the blue skies and puffy white clouds. The blossoms of cherry and apple orchards drifted across the road like pink snowflakes. I laughed aloud in joy to be free of that stuffy office in Mexico City, as I lugged cases into mom-and-pop stores just like the ones my Spanish grandfather owned in Puebla, competing with the Pepsi men to put more bottles on the shelves than the old guys could. Osorio and my college buddies would have laughed themselves silly, but I had the last laugh.

THIS WAS serious business, the front lines of the Great Cola Wars. Mexico was then, and still is today, the number-one per capita soft-drink market in the world. We are a nation of sweet tooths. We add sugar to our bread in the morning, our margaritas in the afternoon, and the coffee we drink with our sugary flan at midnight. Even though Mexico has a far smaller population than China, India, Russia, or Brazil, Mexicans in the 1960s consumed the second-largest total volume of soft drinks after the United States. In Mexico, poor people drank Coke and Pepsi as food. Good nutrition and diet are far down the priority list of working people, who simply want to find the maximum number of calories for their daily intake. (This was decades before Diet Coke, which took forever to penetrate the Mexican market. Few watch their waistlines in a culture where men have machismo and *Real Women Have Curves.*)

Coca-Cola had been in Mexico since 1910. A group of Mexican businessmen came to Georgia to buy the bottling rights, anxious to find the source of this dark, sweet elixir that the Mexican immigrants up north were finding so seductive. They would bring the little six-ounce bottles home with them as Christmas presents—the teetotaling Pancho Villa, a fan of most things American (he even had himself filmed for Hollywood movies), was said to drink Coca-Cola as he raided across the Texas border.

American economic expansion after World War II made Coca-Cola Mexico's brand of choice. The Coca-Cola Company was a darling of the U.S. stock market, its shares doubling three and four times, a stock that split and split again to enrich the portfolios of the Great American Baby Boom as more global consumers outside the United States reached for a Coke.

But by the time I went to work for Coca-Cola in 1964, the company had suffered a severe reversal of fortune. The sixties and seventies were the Pepsi Generation back in the States. Pepsi-Cola was marketed as *cool:* Pepsi's market share boomed on the coasts, connected in the public mind with surfers in California, bikinis, the beach. The enemy's strategy in Mexico was completely different—but just as effective. In Latin America, Pepsi competed as a low-priced discount brand like RC Cola, a sort of Brand X generic soft drink. By the time I hit the road in Michoacán, Pepsi had broken our hold on the little *changarro* stores by offering twelve ounces of Pepsi for the price of one of our little six-and-a-half-ounce bottles.

This was devastating to Coca-Cola in the impoverished Mexico of the 1960s. The mom-and-pop stores, scratching to make ends meet in the boom-and-bust *sexenio* cycles of one distastrous kleptocrat president after another, couldn't pass up the opportunity to buy soda at half price. Two thirds of Mexican consumers were poor and rural; they couldn't possibly remain brand-loyal to Coca-Cola when they could "feed" twice as many children with Pepsi-Cola.

In the 1950s, in the heady early days of U.S. economic expansion, Coke had outsold Pepsi two to one in Mexico. By the 1960s, Pepsi's discount-driven market share skyrocketed to 66 percent of the mammoth Mexican consumer market; Coke had dropped to 34 percent.

Atlanta sent down two new hotshot troubleshooters, my boss and mentor Ted Circuit and a Mexican business guru named Alfredo Martinez Urdal. They designed a two-pronged Harvard Business School–style plan to reconquer Mexico: invest in the human capital of the company with new hires from Mexico's latest crop of college-educated business students, then charge them to "make things happen" by bringing the product within arm's reach of the customer.

I was hired to do more than shift gears and carry crates. I was an experiment: Could a university-trained executive in a khaki jumpsuit help kick-start a comeback at the grassroots level? Soon I was pounding the pavement of León, going door-to-door to ask housewives if they needed three bottles of Coca-Cola to replace the Pepsi in their icebox.

"Aren't you Mercedes's boy Vicente?" the fine matrons would ask, a trifle embarrassed. "Don't I know your mother from church?"

Uh-oh, I thought. *El hijo desobediente.*

The rebel son of Doña Mercedes was as happy in that job as any I've ever had. I am a restless soul. At Los Pinos, I was always ready to escape the endless meetings where politicians talk, talk, talk, and talk but change happens only when you get out of the office and onto the road where the people are, where you can make things *happen.*

This was Ted Circuit's lesson, the credo of America's postwar economic boom: Get out of the damn office in Atlanta or New York and put some boots on the ground out in the marketplace, wherever two or more customers are to be found. I never forgot the lesson, or the people I met on twenty-four hundred Coca-Cola routes down every lonely highway in Mexico.

My first job was to make friends with the old guys, the veterans of the cola wars, who knew every dirty trick in the book to beat the opposition. It was a friendly combat. You drank tequila with the Pepsi drivers in the rough trucker bars until dawn. At 5:00 A.M. you stumbled into the parking lot of a highway strip club and wolfed a quick bolillo, the Spanish version of French bread, hollowed out and then stuffed with hot cheese and chili. Often you drank a Coca-Cola and a raw egg for breakfast, or perhaps just a quick beer if you were hung over. Then you reached into the front seat to grab an ice pick and spiked the tires of the Pepsi truck beside you. Next you jumped into your red-and-white truck and gunned the engine down the road to the *changarros,* because the first guy through the door got to fill the empty icebox with his brand.

I respected the veteran *compañeros* who showed me the ropes, like sergeants breaking in the new lieutenant fresh from the academy. It was war from dawn to midnight, and the old guys knew the ropes. How to let the last few Pepsi bottles in the icebox slip through their hands as they restocked the stores, shattering them quietly on the icebox floor. How to tell the owner that this Pepsi stuff was shit and no one would buy it, that the workers pissed in it at the plant and it made your kids sick to their stomach.

Again I was between two worlds, the road and the office, the classes and the masses: I leave it to you to figure out which was more fun. Though I had no thought of public service back then—schooled in my father's dictum that politics was for crooks—the job of Coca-Cola route salesman was the perfect training ground for a candidate. Between 1964 and the 1970s, I drove every inch of Mexico, from the Apache country of Chihuahua to mining towns at Lázaro Cárdenas, from the rough border towns of Tijuana and Juárez to the tropical jungles of Morelos and Yucatán. It was along these routes that I built the network that would later form the nucleus of Amigos de Fox, the grassroots army that would bring democracy to Mexico in 2000. It was back in my route-truck days, forty years ago, that I came to know the Mexican nation in all its beauty and tragedy and the Mexican people in all their warmth, faith, and compassion.

Mexico is not just the thin slivers of sand at our coastline and border shantytowns that gringos see, touching down in Boeing jets at Cancún or staring across the barbed wire at the slums south of San Diego. Like Russia, Canada, and Brazil, the three countries we rank closest to as one of the dozen or so largest economies on the planet—Mexico is a vast and diverse sprawl of territory. Mexico is a continental empire like the United States, India, or Russia, with twelve different ecosystems, an amazing 1,428 species of animals, and 1,041 types of birds. We are the world's fifth-largest producer of oil, with more foreign visitors than 186 nations of the world and more population than many of the economic tigers of Asia.

We are as diverse ethnically as any immigrant nation, from the blue-eyed Chihuahuans and fair-skinned *chilangos* of European ancestry in Mexico City's swank Polanco district to the indigenous Mayans in Chiapas. There are descendants of African slaves along the Gulf coast, plus the vast mestizo population of mixed ancestry that accounts for people such as me and the majority of our 109 million people. Like Americans, Britons, Canadians, and Europeans, we come in all colors and all faiths. There are some five hundred thousand Jews in Mexico, most descended from the dark days of the *St. Louis,* of which Elie Wiesel so eloquently speaks. Another five hundred thousand Mexicans are of Lebanese-Syrian descent (including the world's wealthiest man, telecommunications tycoon and philanthropist Carlos Slim, whose estimated net worth recently surpassed those of Warren Buffett and Bill Gates). Another twenty thousand Mexicans derive from Chinese, Japanese, and other Asian descent. As in the United States, their forefathers came to build railroads, dig canals, and work mines; now their descendants are successful Mexican business owners, scientists, and teachers.

In fifteen years on the road with Coca-Cola, I met all of these cultures. Francisco Labastida, the man who would be anointed as the PRI candidate in the 2000 presidential election, had not. This made all the difference. Despite the vaunted grassroots machine of the PRI, the leaders of the official party were top-down authoritarians. They had little real contact with the people, outside of staged ribbon cuttings festooned with green and red bunting, where speeches were made and people were paid to applaud. My years at Coca-Cola were more like those a U.S. presidential candidate spends barnstorming from Iowa to New Hampshire. It wasn't just retail politics; it was actual retail, door-to-door. In Mexico the brand of democracy needed a salesman who knew the customer. Thirty years later my résumé would fit the bill.

In the late 1960s, the only people who considered me presidential material were the folks at the Coca-Cola Company. In four years I lived in six different cities as I climbed the corporate ladder—León, Puebla, Tampico, Monterrey, Chihuahua, Culiacán—doing my level best to find a girlfriend in every port. Finally I was promoted to corporate headquarters, where

I sat in my boss's outer office in thrall to his secretary in her hot pants (it was the seventies, man; I had long sideburns and bell-bottoms). Within eight months—record time for a boy who'd grown up pacing patiently around León's town square—I brought Lilián home to meet my mother. Soon we had the traditional dinner with her father, a Pemex engineer, and I asked for her hand in marriage.

We were the model young executive couple of the era, like one of those American television programs we still couldn't get on Televisa, with a twelfth-story apartment overlooking the park in Colonia del Valle where I ran and did chin-ups in the mornings while Lilián walked the dog. We went to nightclubs and the movies (still censored, so we couldn't see *The Graduate*; the raciest thing we saw was a Disney mother who pecked her husband on the cheek). We traveled in a VW camper van from London on the ferries to Ireland, France, and Scandinavia, where reindeer nibbled at the fish we caught and cooked by the campfire, and we swam naked in icy rivers of Norway. High above the Arctic Circle, I was most amazed of all to see that Norwegian gas-station owners went on holiday for weeks at a time in the midnight sun, leaving a collection basket where customers paid their krone for the gasoline—in Mexico they'd have stolen your wallet if you blinked for a second. Was this the result of Scandinavia's extraordinarily flat income distribution—that everyone here was so equal they could afford to be honest? Or was it this Nordic integrity, this culture of the rule of law and exactitude, that helped produce these lands of peace and prosperity?

These were the wonders of the world outside the high walls around Mexico. I traveled the planet in the Coca-Cola years, negotiating with impassive Japanese tycoons who bowed formally over their business cards (the opposite of my 2001 state visit to Prime Minister Koizumi, who would astonish me with his dynamic energy and down-to-earth charisma, much like the effervescent "just call me Tony" Blair). There were sober, correct German businessmen from my great-great-grandfather Fox's astonishingly punctual homeland (but give them a beer or two and they become the heartiest, most persuasive people in the world, as I was to learn when Chancellor Gerhard Schroeder lobbied me to cast Mexico's crucial UN Security Council vote against the invasion of Iraq). And there was the United States, of course, the agency guys at McCann-Erickson, the cocky young fraternity men at corporate headquarters in Atlanta and Miami—

my first introduction to the American postwar M.B.A. culture that produced George W. Bush.

I kept an old Ford pickup with a pop-top camper in McAllen, Texas, where I had once peddled vegetables from the family farm. From there my wife and I drove to Oregon and Vancouver and back the other way all the way down Mexico's coastline to Chiapas and Mazatlán, across the Sea of Cortez in a ferry and back up the Baja desert, camping out and dragging a little inflatable boat with a thirty-horsepower motor. Southern Mexico wasn't really safe in those days: We kept a .22 rifle in my pickup and a pistol in the glove compartment, until the army stopped me in Oaxaca and confiscated them. But it was the 1970s, we didn't have children yet, and we were on the road, Lilián on the back of the Honda as I played the *hijo desobediente* with my rebel sideburns and leather jacket.

Like my Coca-Cola routes, these travels taught me a great deal. First, that my new wife was a really good sport. Second, that it is a long, long, *long* way from McAllen, Texas, to virtually anywhere else, and the first twelve or eighteen hours look flat and hot, pretty much the same as McAllen, until you reach the border of New Mexico. (As the late-night comic Craig Ferguson later said, did Americans ever think, if you didn't want Mexicans to come to New Mexico, that you shouldn't have *called* it that?)

At the vanguard of the postwar economic boom of the 1960s and '70s, Fortune 500 giants like the Coca-Cola Company were the mightiest forces on earth. My trips abroad confirmed what I'd seen in the Wisconsin of 1956: that people in the free-market democracies outside Mexico prospered together in safety, peace, wealth, and efficiency, while the walled-off, protectionist Mexico of the PRI's perfect dictatorship was the great loser of the twentieth century, still living in the feudal *porfiriato* of the 1800s.

These were the heady years of American globalism. The United States led the way in every field: manufacturing, consumer products, marketing, industry, science, technology, democracy, media, energy, film, music, agriculture, heavy machinery, aviation, finance, trade. You name it, Americans built it, bought it, invented it, designed it, refined it, mined it, grew it, improved it, created it, invested in it, sold it. This is the irony of America's lurch toward isolationism: Now that the shoe is on the other foot, and the world is beginning to compete on a U.S. level, the world's chief proponent and primary beneficiary of free trade wants to slam the door shut on the American dream—just when the rest of us are figuring out how it works.

Here's how globalism happened: After World War II and the U.S. economic boom of the 1950s, Fortune 500 corporations had saturated the domestic U.S. market with their goods and services. So they sent forth the "Greatest Generation" to conquer the world for democracy: young veterans who had been shipped off the farm or factory floor to the fields of Normandy and the islands of the Pacific. They were supermen who could do anything, these handsome young veterans in their navy blue suits and narrow ties. Whipping out their slide rules and peering through their horn-rimmed glasses, they drew up projection charts in the supreme confidence that their arrows would always march upward. George W. Bush, like me the first product of business school to serve as his country's president, often strikes me like these trim, grinning, baseball-loving Americans I met on business trips to the United States in the 1960s. When I first met George in the Texas governor's office in 1996, surrounded by Texas Rangers baseball memorabilia, he exuded that enormous self-assurance that some find arrogant but I have always rather liked in Americans. People in the United States simply love to compete, to be the best—in sports, business, drinking games, bar bets, game shows, war. The most popular American TV shows have always featured competition: Who is the best singer, dancer, dieter, millionaire? Who will win a job as Donald Trump's apprentice? Who will survive on the desert island?

In the 1950s, '60s, and '70s, the American empire sent out a crusade of self-confident Knights Templar to compete with the infidels of Third World protectionism, corruption, dictatorship, and poverty. Of course the Americans won: They had better ideas, better products, better resources, better suits, and better educations. Most of all they had the American dream of their immigrant fathers and mothers, the hunger and the drive to convert the heathen to the gospel of the free market. In doing so they remade the Americas—and the world—in their image.

At Coca-Cola in the 1960s, I came face-to-face with these talented Americans who ruled the world with the business degrees they had earned on the GI Bill, and the superior machines and processes they had employed to defeat Hitler and Tojo. The rallying cry of their global crusade was "Competition, competition, competition." Though we weren't ready to compete with the mighty United States, their crusade was in many ways good for countries like Mexico, creating jobs, teaching young people new skills, and generating tax revenues to build factories and roads, hospitals and airports.

Free trade was even better for the people back in Wisconsin and Georgia. The American knights returned home bearing enormous riches, repatriating massive profits back to the United States to help make Americans the wealthiest people on earth. This was not booty stolen by imperialistic looting and exploitation, despite what Hugo Chávez or Evo Morales would have you believe. Our NAFTA association with the United States and Canada has given Mexico the highest per capita income in Latin America; in the last five years alone, multinational corporations helped create 1.5 million jobs in Mexico, often at higher wages than domestic industries paid.

Nor did this globalism simply ship American jobs abroad, as labor-union protectionists and wild-eyed TV pitchmen often claim. Even now, as outsourcing increases, the U.S. unemployment rate has fallen steadily. This is because trade goes both ways: During the 1990s, exports accounted for 25 percent of all U.S. economic growth. Even with all we read and hear about China and India, the United States remains the world's largest beneficiary of free trade. In fact, a 2002 study by the U.S. Senate Joint Economic Committee showed that the United States exported nearly $300 billion in services abroad, while China and India had a combined total of just $62 billion.

I admired nearly everything in Barack Obama's thoughtful and well-written book *The Audacity of Hope*—except his critique of globalism. Writing of his visit to a Maytag factory in Galesburg, Illinois, that was closing down, about to "lose" twelve hundred jobs to a refrigerator-manufacturing plant in Mexico, Obama tells the sad tale of the unemployed former union chief at the plant who worries about losing his health-care coverage. Suddenly, free trade with Mexico is somehow responsible for the fact that Tim Wheeler's son Mark may not get the liver transplant he needs to save his life. This is of course tragic, but misleading. While the right-wing nationalist who wraps himself in the flag is an obvious enemy of global progress, the liberal antiglobalist who wraps himself in compassionate anecdote is not far behind. I admire Barack Obama—he reminds me of Bobby Kennedy—but he is flat wrong about trade with Mexico.

First, U.S. exports of products like Maytag refrigerators still account for a fourth of all jobs in the United States—one out of every five American factory workers depends directly on free trade for that job. And these exporting plants pay U.S. workers 18 percent *more* than factories that *don't* export goods. NAFTA alone has raised the standard of living of the average American family by two thousand dollars a year, just by trading more heavily with Mexico and Canada.

What Barack doesn't tell you about are the jobs that Maytag *saved* in Rust Belt states by having some of the work on its appliances performed in Mexico. Outsourcing protects high-paying jobs at home for American workers, who still do skilled technical and manufacturing jobs and hold middle-management, clerical, and "expertise" positions. But if U.S. manufacturers like General Motors, Ford, General Electric, and Maytag can't produce at least part of their production chain in Mexico, they will go out of business altogether.

I believe that the Illinois senator feels genuine compassion for working families. But surely, Barack, workers in Mexico deserve good jobs and decent health care, too? After five decades in which the First World was the primary beneficiary of free trade, globalism finally has become a win-win deal for workers on both sides of the global divide—for the wealthy investing nations of the United States, Europe, and Japan and for developing countries like Mexico, Malaysia, Brazil, and India. Now India is the world's fourth-largest economy, soon to pass Japan. (Within a generation Mexico will rank number five, thanks to NAFTA.) Free trade has helped Asian countries like Malaysia and Vietnam to grow at rates up to 20 percent in some years, while Brazil has become one of the world's leading makers of cars and airplanes. What the United States needs is *more* free trade, not less—a recent University of Michigan study shows that lowering global-trade barriers by just one third would boost the U.S. economy by a whopping $177 billion.

At Coca-Cola, I was corporate America's most fervent ally. By then our company was earning more from its overseas markets than from the highly competitive and less profitable U.S. domestic soft-drink market. I defended globalism then, and I still do today. Managed properly, with sound market policies infused with socially conscious programs for the education, training, health, and welfare of workers, trade can help heal the global divide between haves and have-nots, north and south.

Here in Mexico we never stopped believing in the free-market dream sold to us by the United States. But suddenly the United States has ceased to believe in itself. America stopped building bridges and starting building walls. As I later told President George W. Bush, just as you convinced us to open our markets, you closed the doors on us. Just as we began to see a gleam at the end of the tunnel, the United States wants to turn out the lights on the American dream.

THE IRONY is that the American emissaries of free trade are still here in the emerging world. You can see these knights-errant from Bank of America, Ford, Coca-Cola, and Microsoft in the conference rooms of Beijing and the government offices of Mexico City, the hotel lobbies of São Paulo and the airport lounges of Mumbai. They ride in bulletproof cars, armored in the steel of free-market capitalism, astride steeds of technologically advanced productivity, holding aloft their banners of globalism. Having won the world, will the rich countries now retreat to the castle and pull up the drawbridge to live in luxury, surrounded by moats and walls?

The United States came to Mexico, convinced us to open our markets, and taught us to compete American style—to make better products at lower prices, to use computers and cell phones, to show up on time, to work through lunch so that we could be more efficient (a horrendous habit that I installed at Los Pinos, to the dismay of my team). We traded some of our lifestyle for this progress, but countries like Mexico learned to make products cheaper, faster, better. So I ask the antiglobalists in the United States: Now that you have won and the world is competing the American way, how can you throw up walls of tariffs, string barbed wire around your borders, and turn back Mexican eighteen-wheelers at the Rio Grande? For decades the wealthiest nations absorbed the profits of globalism. Now, just when we have bought into the dream, is it fair to slam the door shut?

Beyond the moral question, the practical self-interest of wealthy nations dictates a return to the open-door policies that made them rich. We in the emerging world are very good customers for First World products. Today Mexico is one of the three largest trading partners of the United States, bigger than Japan or Germany. In fact, Mexico buys more U.S. products than do France, Germany, Great Britain, and Italy *combined*.

This has been good for Mexican consumers. When I was a young executive in a a country walled off by the nationalistic PRI, you could buy a Ford, a Ford, a Chrysler or a Ford (which was okay with me, because ever since our bright green Pichirilo I have loved Fords). But I could afford this limited selection of high-priced brands; my campesino neighbors in San Cristóbal could not. My colleagues in Atlanta chose from 800 different models in the U.S. market—low-priced Datsuns, family-safe Volvos. But in the old protectionist Mexico, we were limited to 50 brands. Those few Mexicans who could afford cars selected from this narrow band of choice; those who could not, walked.

Today there are 850 models to choose from in free-market Mexico, which now has trade agreements with more countries than any nation on earth. Car ownership went up 33 percent in Mexico in just the last six years. Most of those cars we still import from the United States. (Barack Obama should love Mexico—we buy lots of Maytags, too.) In exchange, nearly all the cars we export from Mexico are sold back to the U.S. market. Trade is a win-win deal for both countries: More than a million Mexicans have jobs in automotive manufacturing (we build more cars than Italy). Millions of autoworkers in the Midwest keep their jobs, because our workers help Ford and GM stay competitive. And consumers on both sides of the border get more choices at lower prices.

Here at Rancho San Cristóbal, where in my childhood hundreds of human beings depended on one old Model T Ford, I now drive a red Jeep Wrangler. My neighbors drive Nissans, Suburbans, Aerostars, Hummers, Yukons, and Chevy trucks—some built just down the road in Guanajuato, others in Indiana, with parts made in Illinois and designs drawn in Detroit, blaring loud *norteño* music on radios made in Germany. Everybody wins: union workers up north, Mexicans who stay home instead of emigrating, the two thirds of the U.S. public who own stock in global corporations, and budget-conscious consumers on both sides of the border, who drive cars their parents would only have dreamed about as they walked to work or rode the bus.

LET'S LOOK at this like businesspeople. With the competitive challenges of Asia and the European Union, America literally cannot afford to wall itself off from the world, as Mexico did during the twentieth century. It would be an act of economic suicide. You *need* us, our increasingly affluent buyers for your products, our hungry young workers for your industries. And we need *you*, your customers for our goods, your technology for our youth, your capital for investment.

To Senator Obama, I would say this: We should be *business partners,* your country and mine. He is a smart man, and I suspect he would agree: Canada, Mexico, and the United States are natural economic allies. If we open the door, the future will come in. Close the door and opportunity will knock elsewhere—China, India, Europe.

Too often the world of public opinion operates from stereotypes, the cheap visual from Fox News Channel of immigrants sneaking across the border, the presidential candidate holding a press conference at the closed factory in New Hampshire, the unsourced statistic cited on the call-in show in San Diego. But if the view is that Mexicans are too lazy to compete, taking our siestas beneath the cactus in the shade of our wide-brimmed sombreros, we will never come together to spark a revolution of hope. If Americans just hold all Mexicans out as crooks, too busy dealing drugs and shooting our guns in the air to be productive citizens of the New World Order, then our hemisphere will fail in the twenty-first century—and so will the American dream.

With the ugly outbreak of antiglobalism in the United States and Europe, the developing world is beginning to wonder: Is this dream only for Americans? If everyone must compete fairly and the best man wins, what happens when that man is Mexican—or a woman who owns a microbusiness in Bangladesh?

Today one in ten native-born Mexicans works in the United States, a tragic loss for us: a powerful statistic in the hands of the anti-immigrant lobby, which uses numbers like these to frighten Americans. Millions more work in the factories and outsourced plants of U.S. companies here in Mexico. The plain fact is, *this huge labor pool of Mexicans is all that stands between the United States and the Asian challenge.*

Without Mexican plants to build auto parts in Aguascalientes, U.S. car manufacturers would go out of business altogether, just as Chrysler nearly did in 1979. The same is true for Mercedes-Benz, Land Rover, even Toyota. Once the United States ran the table; now it needs outsourced labor to compete with Europe and Asia.

The United States has outsourced a total of about 400,000 jobs over the last six years. But over the last decade, even with the economic slowdowns and 9/11, the resulting productivity enabled the United States to create 3.5 *million* jobs every year, according to a McKinsey study. What would happen if government were to decree that U.S. business could no longer use outsourced employees? What would happen if the United States suddenly deported its immigrant workforce, as the Republican-led U.S. House tried to do in 2006?

If you want a good look at how America would fare, watch the brilliant, darkly comic film *A Day Without a Mexican,* which depicts what would happen if all our immigrants in California disappeared in a strange fog. Closing America's doors would be the death knell of the American dream.

The United States will need even *more* of the competitive advantage offered by overseas workers in the years ahead. As their populations age, the superpowers must find more young workers to keep their economies productive—and fund the pensions of their affluent retirees. Today the average Mexican is twenty-five years old, while the average U.S citizen is thirty-six. Mexico's population doubled and tripled during the twentieth century, but it will never do so again; the United States, Japan, and Europe are already leveling off, and Mexico will do so by around 2040. In the meantime a million Mexican youths enter the job force every year, more than our domestic economy currently can absorb. Conversely, the U.S. economy, sixteen times the size of ours, produces many more jobs every year than Americans can possibly fill. Over the next twenty years, immigrants will provide the *entire net labor-force growth of the U.S. economy,* because population experts tell us that the number of native U.S. citizens entering the job market—young people between ages twenty-five to thirty-four—will not grow at all in America's future.

If the United States were to deport every undocumented immigrant, the American economy would take a trillion-dollar hit. Were the United States to lose the competitive advantage of all the outsourced labor it uses around the world, America would suffer its second Great Depression, and the global economy would collapse overnight. Only labor-rich nations like China or India would survive.

So in the coming years, the United States must ask itself, is the American dream only for Americans? And what does it mean to be an American anyway? Is it to be white and blond, college-educated and wealthy? Is Barack Obama an American, since his father was born in Nigeria and young Obama grew up in Indonesia? Is Arnold Schwarzenegger an American? How about Nobel laureate U.S. physicist Tsung-Dao Lee, born in China—or Samuel C. C. Ting, born in Michigan?

If immigrants are not allowed to pick the apples of Washington State and cannot go on creating new technology out of their hunger for the American dream, the fruit of that dream will simply rot on the tree. If Intel cannot produce microchips at competitive costs using Mexicans or Vietnamese workers, whether they live in Palo Alto or Ho Chi Minh City, won't the world simply stop buying into America?

CHAPTER 5

THE IMPERFECT DICTATORS

In 1970, as a corporate warrior for free trade, I ran headlong into the brick wall of protectionism in the form of Luis Echeverría, the perfect dictator for Mexico's perfect isocracy.

Perhaps the worst in the long line of Mexico's kleptopresidents (and it is a fierce competition), Echeverría undoubtedly never knew my name, this obscure Bajío farm boy who was by then the twenty-eight-year-old marketing director of Coca-Cola Mexico. But in 1970, Luis Echeverría sent armed men into the safe, secure bubble of my happy life to take away what was left of our land at Rancho San Cristóbal. Simultaneously he set out to nationalize the rest of my country's industries and declared that the most precious asset of Coca-Cola would henceforth be state property of the Republic of Mexico.

In other words, Echeverría set out to take away everything private citizens had in Mexico. In the process he utterly shattered our nation's fragile economy.

The president had gotten off to a bad start. In 1968, as interior minister under the previous *priista* president Gustavo Díaz Ordaz, Echeverría had been in charge of making sure that Mexico put on its best face to the world during the 1968 Olympic Summer Games—the event that later became so famous when the winners of the gold and bronze medals for the two hundred-meter dash, Tommie Smith and John Carlos, raised their fists in the air in their famous black-power salute. There was Bob Beamon's historic long jump and Alfred Oerter's four gold medals, the warm reception of our music and food, our architecture and culture, our pride as Enriqueta Basilio became the first woman to light the Olympic cauldron. Mexico City was a showplace, and the government was determined to make it the best, safest, happiest venue the Olympics had ever known. It fell to the nation's powerful interior minister, Echeverría, to make sure that things stayed that way.

In Mexico the job of interior minister is nothing like the U.S. cabinet post that looks after national parks, tribal reservations, and litter. Until the advent of democracy in 2000, the interior minister was a dark and shadowy figure in charge of *gobernación,* the government-within-a-government whose police-state powers were the iron fist in the velvet glove of the PRI, sort of a combination between J. Edgar Hoover's FBI, Vladimir Putin's KGB, and a particularly powerful vice president or White House chief of staff. The interior minister was in charge of state security, the crafting of legislation, and the running of government. He told Congress what to do, interpreted the laws that his ministry wrote, controlled the federal police force, and wiretapped the opposition. (Later, during the 2000 presidential campaign, *gobernación* agents would tap my cell-phone calls to Mexico's future first lady, spy on our campaign-strategy meetings, and leave transcripts in the bowels of the interior minister's filing rooms at Bucareli.)

Echeverría took his job seriously, knowing that it was the ticket to his own *dedazo* as presidential successor (only in Mexico do politicians *want* to get the finger). But 1968 was the summer of protest. The worldwide student movement that began in France and the United States against the Vietnam War, racism, and the establishment had spread to the UNAM, the national autonomous university where my father once studied as a forest engineer. Now the UNAM had grown to a mammoth campus of 162,000 students. Many of these young people were on the streets of Mexico City that year, mobilizing for democracy, freedom of speech, and the right to assemble in peaceful protest—like the sit-ins at Berkeley, the Vietnam protests of revolution theologians like Father Berrigan, and the civil-rights marches of Dr. Martin Luther King Jr. None of this got much airplay on state-controlled Televisa.

At the time we were told that the students were just Communists, led by outside agitators from France and the United States, funded by the KGB and Castro—Che Guevara backers with long hair and tie-dyed shirts who would disgrace the Mexican people, ruin the Olympic Games, and endanger our economy and the serenity of our nation's capital, which had spent billions of pesos preparing for the Olympics. They came off without a hitch: The mariachis played gaily, tequila flowed freely, and the government pounded the airwaves day after day with propaganda, hailing the economic success of the games—and building a case for the police to intervene in the student mobilization.

On October 2, 1968, students gathered at the Plaza of Three Cultures at Tlatelolco in the heart of downtown, where Aztec ruins and colonial façades meet below the great modernist structure of the SRE, Mexico's State Department. As at Ohio's Kent State, shots were fired, probably by police and soldiers in windows above the square—most likely Echeverría's men, acting as provocateurs. Some two hundred to three hundred unarmed students, passersby, and children were killed, and many more were injured in one of the darkest and most hidden moments of modern Mexican history.

Later, greatly influenced by the way Nelson Mandela's administration probed into the abuses under apartheid, my government would open the files with a special prosecutor and investigate the 1968 massacre. President Díaz Ordaz was dead by the time democracy came to Mexico, but Echeverría was still alive, and during my presidency he was prosecuted for the murder of the students. The vast cover-up of the 1968 student massacres made it difficult to collect evidence. The courts declared that the statute of limitations had run out. But few in Mexico today believe that Luis Echeverría is innocent. As of this writing, he is no longer under house arrest in Mexico City. But I trust that he will to the end of his life be hounded by fear of the next warrant for allegations of corruption, genocide, embezzlement, or human-rights abuses.

Like most Mexicans (except for those brave enough to lead the student movement and the small opposition factions), I spent 1968 largely unaware of the events in Mexico City and the world around us. I was by then a young Coca-Cola executive, driving up and down my routes with the radio droning out government propaganda. The 1970s that followed were the "Decade of the Disappeared" in Mexico and throughout Latin America. Like the *desaparecidos* in Argentina and Chile, Mexican opponents of the regime simply vanished without a trace. We know now, because our democracy finally investigated those terrible years, that many men were probably tortured and buried in shallow graves outside the capital; women may have been raped, mutilated, and murdered.

But you cannot underestimate the power of a government that can control the free press. Evil things happen, yet you never know it; everyone around you accepts that life is good, that the nation is at peace and the economy has never been better, that a few troublemakers in Mexico City shouldn't get in the way of a great party at the Olympics. The PRI was adept at *tapándole el ojo al macho,* sweeping the dirt under the rug, so that the living room was clean for our guests.

But the sad truth was that Mexico was broken by the time Echeverría got the finger and moved into Los Pinos in 1970. Debilitated by one *sexenio* crisis after another, crooked presidents had bankrupted the country—most recently to build fabulous edifices for the Olympic Games.

But then the well ran completely dry, which is what happens when oil prices are low and your economy is walled off by monopoly protectionism: when you are hostile to foreign investment and you keep your people ill-educated, ill-fed, and ill-prepared to compete in the world. Echeverría's big campaign contributors were doing fine, because they had state-protected monopolies for products that the consumers, the workers, the peasants, and the tiny middle class were forced to buy at state-controlled prices. Like feudal debt peons of the nineteenth-century *porfiriato,* under the PRI we had no other choice but to buy at the company store of Mexican protectionism.

By the 1970s the system was near the brink of collapse. The government could never repay its debt, and the peasants were ready to revolt; Mexicans knew that their pesos were worth less and less, while corn and beans cost more and more, no matter how much propaganda the government put out on the radio. (Even by then hardly any Mexicans yet had TV sets in their homes, which is the way an authoritarian government prefers it.)

Like Hugo Chávez in Venezuela, Echeverría did what any self-respecting Latin American pseudoleftist demagogue does: He went after the landowners and the global corporations and blamed all of Mexico's problems on the United States. This is an old trick in our part of the world: If your money's no good at the foreign bank, you just nationalize the bank. If the peasants are getting restless because they can't afford vegetables, you send out armed thugs to expropriate the vegetable fields. And if you can't repay the money you borrowed from the United States and Europe to keep your economy afloat, you just start shouting, *"Yanqui go home!"*

Once again the pistoleros invaded Rancho San Cristóbal in a ritual that seemed to happen every thirty years or so. Combining the PRI's powerful propaganda machine with his control of the national campesino union,

Echeverría tried to channel the spirit of leftist president Lázaro Cárdenas and his 1938 *ejido,* when armed men had come to take my grandfather's land. They came through the gates, fifty or sixty campesinos from other states, a rough-looking bunch wielding shotguns and rifles, pistols and machetes. They seized the warehouses and the barns, the fields and the old irrigation works where we still watered our crops Aztec style, pulling wooden blocks out of stone dams to flood the fields with the brown waters of the lagoon, leaving patches of mud where my brothers and I grew garbanzo beans under our father's eye.

Now it was my dad's turn to defend the farm. My father, Don José Luis Fox, was nearly sixty, about the same age his father had been when the government came in 1938 to take away Joseph Fox's farm. There was a sprinkling of gray in my father's mustache, but still he stood strong and tall in the turret, watching everything he'd worked for all his life fall under the guns of the *ejidatarios.* Beside him paced his twenty-eight-year-old son, the Coca-Cola marketing director. I had rushed home in my Chrysler Valiant from corporate headquarters, four or five hours' drive now down the new debt-funded-but-never-repaid highway from Mexico City. And over the whole scene loomed my big brother, there as always to do the fighting for rest of the Fox boys.

"Shovels," my brother José ordered, handing out tools to my younger brothers and me. "We need to dig a well."

"Shovels?" we asked incredulously, ready to man the turret with rifles.

"They can't take the land from us if we're working it," my brother explained. "Start digging!"

Echeverría had decreed that squatters could simply move in and take any land that wasn't being farmed. So every weekend that year of the third great invasion of *bandidos* at San Cristóbal, we dug, my brother and I. We shoveled out irrigation trenches and made post holes for fences, sleeping in the mud and keeping vigil over the land of our fathers. In heaven I am sure my grandfather Fox smiled to see so much hard work being done.

Behind us, barricaded in the house, hid José's wife, seven months pregnant. My sister-in-law Lucha wrung her hands in worry for her unborn child; two children clung to the hem of her maternity dress. Outside, the *ejidatarios* from Sonora and Oaxaca waved their machetes and shot pistols in the air, shouting insults at the pregnant lady.

"You should go away from this, all of you," my father advised us one night, tight-lipped with concern as we gathered around the kitchen table. "Lucha is pregnant; you should all go and take Doña Mercedes to safety in the city."

"No one is leaving," my mother stated flatly, to Lucha's tears. "Papa Joseph would never allow it. This is our home. I leave here only in a coffin."

And so we stayed. The invaders grew bored after months of occupation. Their efforts to whip up the local *ejidatario* smallholders came to no avail. San Cristóbal was an armed camp, a local civil war pitting the outsiders who wanted our land against the ranch hands who worked it. In the middle were the men who'd taken Papa Joseph's other nine thousand acres, all tilling their little ten-acre plots from the 1938 edict. They did not own any land—the land belonged to the state, which after 1938 had become one big *hacendado* for all of Mexico. The *ejidatarios* merely farmed their pieces of the federal hacienda as sharecroppers on the world's biggest fiefdom, keeping them utterly dependent on the state's largesse for seed, equipment, markets for their farm products, and continued permission to work their plots of land. By 1970 our *ejidatario* neighbors were in a quandary: They knew my family, that José and his men worked the thousand acres we had left, that my mother spent her days caring for their children. On the other hand, the state—their landlord and master—was telling the *ejidatarios* to take the rest of our land away from us, even to give some of our land to "foreigners" from outside the state. Fortunately, the farmhands of San Cristóbal and our *ejidatario* neighbors were not minded to join the pistoleros drinking, cussing, shooting, and gambling in our yard—there was work to be done on their own *ejidos*.

With the stress, my niece Paula was born to my sister-in-law Lucha two months premature. But she survived, as did Rancho San Cristóbal. I came home every weekend, down the mountains every Friday night to work with my brother in the moonlit fields—digging, digging, always digging, through the nights to Sunday, when I drove back to Mexico City and reported for work at Coca-Cola headquarters, where I was now (finally) back in an office, in a coat and tie. After two years of violent struggle, food shortages, mass protests from the farmers and an outcry from urban consumers, the government finally enforced the law on behalf of small farmers who worked their own land, and the would-be *ejidatarios* gave up waiting for us to finish digging those wells.

Meanwhile Luis Echevarría had moved on to the next phase of his agenda: seizing the assets of all foreign corporations. As we see today in Bolivia and Venezuela, expropriation has long been a favored weapon in the arsenal of the Latin American demagogue. Like my good friend and former foreign minister Jorge Castañeda, himself a recovering leftist, I don't accept the antiglobalist, anticorporate, anti-American rantings of Hugo Chávez or Evo Morales as true-left socialism: *Chavismo* is closer to Nazi state capitalism, an opportunistic populism that pushes the buttons of the common man's anger and then uses nationalism to cheat the poor, directing their frustration at ready-made villains in order to unify the country behind the dictator-demagogue. Whether aimed at Jewish financiers in the Europe of the 1930s or gringo industrialists in the twenty-first century, populist-nationalist demagoguery is a magician's sleight of hand designed to distract the audience's attention from the fact that it is their own government that has failed the people: that the crony capitalism, corruption, and kleptocracy endemic to state-controlled economies will inevitably beggar a developing country. When oil and gas prices come down, when the debts come due and the currency devalues, when the state-protected monopolies cannot possibly compete with world markets for goods and services—this is when the Latin American populist waves the bloody flag and cries, "*Yanqui go home!*"

In an odd way, gringo bashing in Latin America is the mirror image of Mexico bashing in the United States: When politicians are in trouble, they resort to xenophobia. Whatever mistakes a government makes—deficit spending, unpopular wars, corruption, unemployment, inflation, debt—all magically disappear when the politician blames the immigrant, the Jew, the outsourcing corporation, the yanqui imperialist. Demagoguery is demagoguery, whether it comes from the Arizona congressman or the Austrian parliamentarian, the Venezuelan general or the Bolivian coca grower.

In the early 1970s, Luis Echeverría was again trying to revive the spirit of President Lázaro Cárdenas, whose government in 1936–38 had taken over Mexico's oil industry and railroads. But nationalizing Mexico's vast oil and gas reserves, mineral rights, and transportation had some justification, given the backdrop of U.S. invasions just twenty years before to seize the port of Veracruz and the oil fields at Tampico—at a time when the United States, Britain, and Europe owned more of Mexico than Mexicans did.

Echeverría was not so ideological, just a more extreme nationalist looking to rally the people behind the PRI's us-versus-them dialectic. Back then the government already required that new businesses entering the Mexican market had to be 51 percent owned by a Mexican national, a policy that had led to a variety of nonequity "shell partners" of big global corporations—usually family *grupos* with close ties to the PRI. Like those shady late-night infomercials offering you the chance to become a millionaire in real estate with no money down, the 51 percent rule created vast wealth for a lucky few. But Coca-Cola had been in Mexico long before the expropriations of the 1930s; we were exempt from the 51 percent rule.

So Echeverría decided to nationalize the assets of all foreign companies operating in Mexico. He planned to make a state-run company out of every industry, from cinematography to telephones to tobacco. Whether he actually succeeded in expropriating the assets in a manner that benefited the public mattered little to him. The president simply wanted to be *seen* seizing the wealth of the fat-cat gringos and doling it out to his grateful peasantry—and, perhaps, to a select few friends.

One day my boss, Ted Circuit, came by my office. "Hey, Vicente, what are you doing tomorrow?" Ted said breezily. "We've been summoned to see the president!"

"I just saw him in the break room," I said, perplexed. I thought he meant Paul Austin, the president of Coca-Coca USA.

"We've got a noon appointment tomorrow at Los Pinos with President Echeverría," Ted explained, as though addressing a particularly slow child. He looked down at my cowboy boots propped on the desk, still muddy from a weekend digging wells. "Wear some real shoes, Fox."

It's not so easy to find black wing tips in my size, even in Mexico City. But twenty-four hours later I sat in the elegant lobby of Los Pinos, an hour early (as only people from Coca-Cola, or perhaps a *pünktlich* German company like Audi, would be). Our dress shoes were spit-shined, our pinstriped suit coats pulled tight over our shoulders, white shirt cuffs popped just an inch at the sleeves. And there we sat until nearly midnight, twelve hours that first day, another twelve the next week; the same again the next week, and the next. Uniformed officers in the deep army green of Estado Mayor bustled about in their white gloves, bearing messages and bottles of wine for the president's lunch, which took place at about three in the afternoon and lasted for hours. We would smell the tantalizing red snapper served Veracruz style in rich tomato sauce; this let us know we had another six or seven hours to wait until a bureaucrat resplendent in charcoal gray would whisk into the room. Announcing himself as the Subsecretary to the Undersecretary of Commerce's Subsecretary of Foreign Investment's Director of International Affairs, the official would explain courteously that the president had encountered some urgent business, but perhaps we could come back tomorrow?

It is amusing to think of it now, from my comfortable rocking chair at the ranch. But back then it was deadly serious: The president wanted our formula.

The recipe for making Coca-Cola syrup is the most heavily guarded secret of the most popular consumer product on earth. The formula for making Coke was the heart of every Fortune 500 American success story: The Brand. When we got together with the agency guys in Miami to look at storyboards and shoot the new Latin-market commercials, we called the product the "hero," practicing our best Madison Avenue adspeak, insisting that the distinctive red logo be showcased in every shot. But we all knew—as the New Coke disaster later proved—that the real hero of the tale was the classic Coca-Cola formula.

We went to great lengths to protect this formula, not just by suing those who trespassed on our copyrights and by keeping the recipe under lock and key (it was rumored to be guarded in a vault in Atlanta) but also by zealously protecting the quality of our product from tampering, imitation, and adulteration by unscrupulous bottlers. This was a particular problem in foreign markets like Mexico. The PRI's culture of corruption, shoddy work, and complete lack of respect for quality and accuracy—the first by-products of a walled-off, state-controlled economy—meant that some bottlers felt free to make any garbage they pleased, then try to pass it off as Coca-Cola.

There was no real product regulation under the PRI, no Food and Drug Administration, no Federal Trade Commission or U.S. Department of Agriculture or European Food Safety Authority tests. A guy like me, sent out from Coca-Cola headquarters to check quality control, was a one-man FDA, FTC, USDA, and EFSA combined. Cheap sugar, bad sugar, no sugar at all: I saw all manner of unscrupulous practices. We shut down one shady bottler in Chiapas whom I caught pouring flat brown residue into Coca-Cola bottles, then sealing them with Pepsi caps and selling them as the Real Thing.

Echeverría didn't want just to copy or adulterate the formula: The president wanted the Mexican government to own it. Coca-Cola had been in the country for half a century, bottled by Mexican entrepreneurs who had invested their own money to buy into the American dream. We had created thousands of jobs in Mexico, taught job skills to a generation of young salesmen and manufacturing foremen, and invested billions of U.S. dollars in state-of-the-art technology. By 1970 we had schooled a generation of young Mexicans like me—they had even sent me to "Coca-Cola University" at Harvard's Business School, just to handle important business meetings like this one.

But there was no meeting—only the threat of a showdown with the president that repeated over and over again. The Americans looked at me in disbelief as we came to Los Pinos week after week and waited into the evening, only to hear, "Please come back Friday. The president is really looking forward to seeing you!"

"We apologize, but could you possibly return next Monday?"

"I'm sorry, he is just so occupied with the cigarette-company expropriation. Could you please come back on Thursday?"

I had no idea that I would someday live in Los Pinos, that thirty years later I would become a connoisseur of receiving rooms from George Bush's White House to the king of Spain's palace (where once again my boots created a stir), from the glorious czarist splendor of Vladimir Putin's Kremlin (most impressive) to the intimate campaign-headquarters disarray of Tony Blair's Number 10 Downing Street (chummiest). But even then, as a twenty-eight-year-old executive, I could see that the presidential palace of Luis Echeverría was the most disorganized institution one could imagine. We would glimpse the great man himself running to and fro down the hallway to one of four meeting rooms, like a dealer in a roving crap game where he played everyone—teachers' unions and businessmen, Army generals and PRI governors. Some came hat in hand, looking for favors, but with Echeverría you were better advised to hold on to your wallet, because he could take away everything you had.

I sat with my bosses Ted, Alfredo, and Paul, along with Jesús Rodríguez Anaya, head of our Mexican bottlers' association, as we wondered whether ours would be the next heads on the guillotine. Finally a particularly officious bureaucrat strode in to dismiss us. "The president regrets the delay," said Echeverría's chief of staff, without a tinge of remorse. "But he wants to know, how are you coming with the nationalization of Coca-Cola? Have you disclosed your formula to us yet?"

"We can't do that," Alfredo explained. "We would sooner close shop in Mexico, and that would throw eight or ten thousand people out of work."

"Hmmm . . . well, you had better come back and see the president next week."

This time we came bearing gifts, a platter of shrimp from a unique mariculture venture Coca-Cola had started at Puerto Peñasco, a gorgeous wildlife refuge on a desert beach in Sonora. It was the first shrimp farm in the Americas. We were proud of the work we'd done with Dr. Carl Hodges of the University of Arizona, who had shown Mexican peasants how to grow shrimp on barren land. To demonstrate our good corporate citizenship, we also brought an array of Mexican dolls and ceramic plates made by the poor, products we were exporting with the shrimp through Coca-Cola's network—an early version of a microcredit program to foster local entrepreneurs.

After we'd spent three hours in the waiting room, the president whisked by, then paused and retreated a step. "What's that I smell, shrimp?" he said, peering into the reception room.

"Yes, Mr. President," I said proudly. "From our farm in Sonora."

"You mean they're not from the sea?" He walked in and picked one up by the tail, examining it closely. "You grow these in the desert?"

"Yes, sir," said Paul Austin, our president.

"Who are you?" Echeverría demanded, as though affronted by this enigma of sea creatures raised on land.

"Coca-Cola, Mr. President," Alfredo chimed in, anxious to Mexicanize the conversation. "We've been here six times to see you."

The president brushed off the complaint as though it were lint on his immaculate Italian suit. "I still don't understand. Why is Coca-Cola bringing me shrimp and plates with flowers painted on them? Is this your lunch?"

"We wanted to show you how Coca-Cola is helping Mexican shrimp farmers," I said. "And the small handicraft manufacturers. We sell their goods in the United States."

"Young man, you're not telling me that you grow shrimp in the sand?"

"No, sir, in seawater we pump into lagoons," I explained. "Would you like to try a bite?"

"*¡Híjole!*" he cried as he popped the shrimp into his mouth and sucked the meat off the tail. "Look at the size of these bastards! Why don't you bring them into the dining room? We'll have the cook make them for lunch."

So finally we entered the inner sanctum. Echeverría hollered for his wife, "Dear, we have guests, and they've brought the biggest shrimp you've ever seen. Grown on the land!" A fan of Mexican culture, Señora Echeverría always wore hand-embroidered, multicolored indigenous dresses in the style of Frida Kahlo. The first lady loved the handicrafts, the president loved the shrimp, and we never discussed expropriation. We just talked about shrimp and dolls and children and culture. It was the classic Mexican lunch, where the business matter never really comes up but somehow is miraculously resolved by the relationship you have built over a bottle of tequila—and some well-broiled camarones a la veracruzana.

So it was that I met the dictator who later was accused of massacring several hundred students, who tried to take my family's land, and who almost stole the Coca-Cola formula. We agreed to a one-for-one matching program where we sold a dollar's worth of Mexican shrimp or dolls in the United States for every dollar's worth of Coca-Cola profits we earned in Mexico. We also agreed to build a desalinization plant to bring fresh water from the sea to the people of Tijuana. The president never got his hands on our secret formula. And that is how, at Coca-Cola and at Rancho San Cristóbal, we survived Luis Echeverría.

MEXICO'S ECONOMY did not.

By the time the seafood connoisseur left Los Pinos, I was the youngest president in the history of Coca-Cola Mexico. We had recovered our product's two-to-one advantage over Pepsi in the cola wars. I had a pretty wife, a camper, and a motorcycle. Life was good for Vicente Fox, but it was about to get really bad for Mexico. The boom-and-bust cycle of Mexico's *sexenio* was oscillating more wildly every six years. If Echeverría was Hugo Chávez in miniature, our next president, José López Portillo, was the Latin American demagogue writ large. No one ever buckled on the presidential sash with more relish than López Portillo did: Like the Emperor Maximilian's, his was the grandiose dream of Mexican empire.

Like today's Hugo Chávez or Evo Morales in Bolivia, the *priista* presidents of the 1970s took power at a time of Mideast crisis, with rising oil prices and a staggering inflow of foreign petrodollars—and also like Hugo and Evo, they had the bad habit of spending the oil and gas money before it came in. It was the beginning of the Mexican *borrachera,* the drunkenness. Under Echeverría and López Portillo, Mexican economic policy wove an increasingly dangerous path in and out of the lanes of debt and austerity, inflation and crisis, devaluation and unemployment. Mexico was just waiting to crash into the oncoming traffic of economic reality.

For a while Mexico boomed. Under López Portillo we had a 6 to 8 percent growth rate, fueled by the OPEC embargo of the early 1970s. Mexico's oil revenues soared, and López Portillo dreamed of making Mexico the economic superpower of Latin America. He built skyscrapers gaping with vacancies as monuments to his own vanity, airports in cities that few tourists visited, superhighways devoid of automobile traffic—everywhere building, building, building, a presidency of grand ribbon cuttings with local PRI governors and friendly *priista* contractors who always won their bids. Mexico grew, everyone had a job, and the poor got handouts to keep them quiet—until the oil prices dropped, the money ran out, and the debts that López Portillo had run up while building imperial Mexico came due at the bank. It is a sad old story in the petrocracies of Latin America—just wait until Venezuelans get the tab for the decade-long binge of Generalissimo Hugo Chávez.

López Portillo did what any self-respecting Latin American dictator would do when the bankers came like tavernkeepers to the town drunk of the *borrachera,* hemming and hawing and suggesting that perhaps it was time the gentleman paid his bill. For his final 1976 Informe, our version of the State of the Union Address, the president donned the sash, stepped up on the congressional rostrum at San Lázaro, and nationalized the banks.

The markets plummeted: yet another national trauma. The new president, the soft-spoken Miguel de la Madrid, scrambled to undo the damage with temporary austerity measures. But, as usual, the PRI had the party and the Mexican people got the hangover. The economy collapsed, per capita income dropped sharply, unemployment soared, and growth stagnated. Meanwhile the Free World boomed its way through the 1980s.

Mexico, walled off in the perfect dictatorship, missed the good times.

CHAPTER 6

THE HOUSE OF THE CRADLE

It was during López Portillo's oil-fueled spending party of the 1970s that my old professor, the Jesuit priest Father Schiefler, brought me crashing down to earth with his speech at our ten-year college reunion. In 1974, I was named president of Coca-Cola Mexico. The company flourished: Anyone could have sold soft drinks in a Mexican economy growing at 8 percent year on year. As the revenues poured in, I thought about the Jesuit's words, wondering as do so many executives warming up for our midlife crises, *Is this all there is?* At Coca-Cola, I was the man of the hour. But wasn't I supposed to be a "man for others"?

By 1978, Coca-Cola was ready to move me to Miami to become president of the company's vast Latin American empire. It was the chance of a lifetime: The United States was still the capital of the world, and Coca-Cola was the biggest brand name on the planet. "We see big things for you," my boss, Ted Circuit, told me, his big American voice echoing over the phone from Atlanta. "Latin America president at thirty-eight, maybe president of Europe, Asia, North America in your forties. The sky's the limit, Vicente," Ted assured me. "You could run this company worldwide."

This was the dream of my grandfather, my father's reward for all the times he told me to do my best and I would would go far. In their image I had striven to be the best cow milker, the best truck driver, the best soft-drink salesman. But face-to-face with the American dream, I didn't want the Statue of Liberty, the streets paved with gold. After Father Schiefler's harsh words for Mexico's elite at our class reunion, I searched my soul and decided that what I really wanted was to go back home to San Cristóbal.

"*A broccoli farmer?* What are you, nuts?" my mentor Circuit shouted in disbelief when I finally summoned up the courage to quit. "You want to be this 'man for others,' whatever that's supposed to mean. How many thousand guys can you hire building new Coca-Cola plants in Mexico? How many people do we train? You're not the only truck driver we ever brought up into management. How many lives can you change with us?"

Ted was right, of course. The silliest thing about radical-leftist populism is the way the demagogues caricature global businessmen as ruthless exploiters of the poor. The reality is, Fortune 500 CEOs as a class are about as socially committed as any group of people on earth. Few are like Gordon Gekko in Oliver Stone's film *Wall Street,* preaching that "greed is good." In Mexico we've seen much more of the Gates Foundation, the Rockefeller and the Ford foundations, than we ever did of Ken Lay.

But for me corporate philanthropy wouldn't fill the hole. I know it sounds sentimental, but I was drawn back to help the campesinos I had grown up playing marbles with at our family farm, where I felt nourished by the spirit of my grandfathers, my mother and father, my brothers and sisters. It's a hard thing to explain to people from the city, this attraction to a particular piece of land: I don't suppose San Cristóbal looked any different to George Bush's entourage at our first summit than any stretch of highway they'd driven on the campaign bus in Iowa in 2000. But for us it was always the ranch, the land, our neighbors, *home.* I suppose I was just another country boy tired of the big city, spending my weekends at ruined churches and demolition sites of fine old homes in the elegant Polanco neighborhood of Mexico City, picking out darkened oak beams and carting them down to San Cristóbal in the back of my pickup truck.

There I began building a house, a vaguely German-Spanish ranch home overlooking the drained lagoon where I'd grown the garbanzo beans to pay for it. Based on sketches I'd done freehand since my childhood dreams of life as an architect, the house was only half finished when I left Coca-Cola in 1978. But as a Mexican man, I had no compunction about doing what would be unthinkable for a gringo of nearly forty years old who had been a Fortune 500 CEO—I moved home with my mother.

My father was getting older. Lilián and I had no children yet, so we moved into the former hacienda with my folks, within the buttressed walls that protected us from three generations of gun-toting desperadoes. Down the dirt road rose our new home, stick by stick: As my aunt Luisa used to say, "Each in his own house, and God in every one."

I joined my brothers as we switched from corn and beans to more profitable lettuce and broccoli. (How we celebrated in the 1980s, when former President Bush made broccoli famous by saying he detested it; the Bush family literally put the Foxes in the black.) Guided by the border-crossing internationalism of my grandfather, my dad had made the bold decision years before to buy a little home office in McAllen, Texas; now we built a vegetable-freezing plant at home on the ranch to feed the export market.

Like Coca-Cola we diversified—first into the boot business, catching the 1980s *Urban Cowboy* craze with a line of fashion western wear; soon we were making pink leather lady's boots for the boutiques of Paris and London. But even with all this activity at the ranch, surrounded by family and friends, with a new house and a wife and a family business that employed more and more of my childhood friends, there was still this emptiness.

Perhaps it was the fact that we were still childless. Try as we might, Lilián and I could not conceive. We tried the doctors, the treatments, the home remedies from the midwives, the best hospitals in Mexico City and Miami, the adoption lists. It seemed that we were cursed somehow, that it simply was not God's will that we have children. How could this be? We were Mexicans, Catholics, good people, perfect parent material. No one ever loved children as I do; later, in the presidency, I often suspected my staff of planning events in a way that kept me away from interaction with kids, because they knew that would be the end of staying on schedule. As president I would always stray off to play games with the kids (no marbles now, it's all video games), or talk with them about their troubled lives, or kick soccer balls to them (badly, on the front-page photos in *Reforma*). Once, late in my presidency, when I visited a juvenile hall for young offenders, the media had a field day because one of the young people made a rude sign with his fingers above my head—really, this was not much of an insult to a guy with five brothers.

For ten long years, Lilián and I tried to have children. Adoption was not much done in Mexico in those days, and despite my best efforts it is still not as widely accepted as it is elsewhere. The reason is not what you might think—that parents don't want to adopt children in a Catholic culture that encourages you to have your own; that there is prejudice among the lighter-skinned, more affluent couples against the darker skin of the mestizo or indigenous children most likely to be up for adoption; that there aren't many parents who want to adopt the older children and those with health problems; that too many of the adoptable children are taken by rich couples in the United States. None of those factors really exist in Mexico. The fact of our cultural aversion to adoption is far simpler: Mothers here will not give up their babies. Whether or not they can afford to raise the child, whether or not there is a father or a grandmother in the picture to help, whether or not the child will be fed or go hungry—our imperative that mothers must keep their children is so strong that they will rarely give them up to others.

So Lilián and I waited, and waited, and waited. Unless you have experienced this, you have no idea what the pain is like for parents who desperately want a child but cannot have one, in a world where so many kids go unloved, unfed, uneducated, even abused.

We wrote letters. We submitted proposals. We cried. We prayed.

Finally we got a call from Costa Rica and jumped on the next plane—only to find that the shady operation there was selling the babies to the highest bidder. We stormed out, offended at the baseness of a man who could exploit the deepest human desire of parents to share our love with children. Then one day God answered our prayers in the form of Doña Rosario Sada, another of Mexico's sainted ladies. A wealthy woman from the great northern metropolis of Monterrey, Doña Rosario ran a small *casa cuna* (literally, a "house of the cradle") out of her own hip pocket. It was both an orphanage and a shelter for unwed mothers. I will never forget her voice over the line to Rancho San Cristóbal: *We may have a baby for you.*

The phone may be hanging there still, dangling by its cord. We dashed out the door and never looked back, driving pell-mell through the mountains straight through the night, Lilián telling me to drive faster, *faster*—in case some other less suitable, less loving parents would get there first. (This was the night I learned that you absolutely must stop for gasoline, or your Ford will not go any further.) Doña Rosario received us in the early light of dawn, interrogated us with a hundred questions, and then took us to the chapel to pray, which we did most fervently and for two hours. Finally we broke down and asked with hope bright in our eyes, "Where's the baby? Can we see her?"

"Let's go," Doña Rosario said cautiously. "But I'm not sure we have the right child for you."

The moment we walked in, I saw two black eyes staring at me from a crib in the far corner, and I *knew*. I was shocked at how familiar she seemed, but I knew it in my gut. "Doña Rosario, this is our daughter, Ana Cristina," I said. Lilián nodded vigorously.

Doña Rosario shook her head. "But this is not the one. There are others. Look at the beautiful blond child in the corner, the green-eyed boy on the end—"

I never saw the rest of the children. Undoubtedly they were all beautiful, but none of them was my daughter.

"This is Ana Cristina," I said, towering above this warm and wise little woman with her big heart. "You are a gift from God and we thank you, but let's not waste more time. Give me those blankets, and we will get Ana back to the ranch."

"It was important that we take you to this point, so that you are very sure," she said softly. "*Vaya con Dios.*"

If I am able to communicate nothing else in this book—if you disagree with me about immigration or globalism, democracy or the war in Iraq, free trade or social welfare—this I can accept. But please hear my case for adoption: There is no happier moment that can befall a person in this life than the heavenly gift of a child so desperately wanted.

It happened to us four times, and the blessings of all four children were sublime. That first day of parenthood we took Ana Cristina back to the chapel, not wanting to be parted even for a second. There we knelt. It was then that I comprehended the ecstasy of Santa Teresa. In that moment I am quite sure I felt myself, like the saint, literally raised up from the floor in the presence of Christ. When I came back to earth and saw my wife and child beside me, I cried, tears of joy that streamed from my eyes all the way back those twelve hours over the mountains. Surely the Pemex gas-station attendants of the San Luis Potosí thought I was crazy as I hurled the pesos out the window to keep the car moving, but all I wanted was to get home to where I am sitting this minute, to this house that by then was built, but not yet a home.

My joy simply exploded here at San Cristóbal. As I sit here at the ranch today, we are working on raising the fifth generation of our family on this ranch; my second daughter, Paulina, is home from Sydney, expecting her first child; my son Rodrigo comes in, proud with the score he has earned on his college entrance exams, ready to compete with his big brother, Vicente. Each was a miracle from Doña Rosario, and one other *casa cuna* in Veracruz. They were the inspirations for the orphanage I founded, called

Casa Amigo Daniel in honor of my brother's son, who drowned tragically in León. Over the years we repeated this miracle of Santa Teresa again and again for other parents, beginning with Casa Amigo Daniel's first adoption, an indigenous two-year-old from Celaya who spoke no Spanish. Even the presidency would not equal the joy the orphanage brought me over the years, as we lifted a thousand other families to the ecstasy of love.

For a decade this was enough, raising four children and as many small family businesses, running the orphanage, providing a good living for hundreds of neighbors, helping to found a new branch of the Jesuit Iberoamericana University in León, where I served as president. Politics was the furthest thing from my mind: I had broken my father's prohibition on farming and wasn't about to break another by running for office. Besides, politics was the PRI, and by the 1980s it was clear who the bad guys were.

The PRI was destroying Mexico.

Life under the perfect dictatorship was like walking up the down escalator: You took two steps forward and found yourselves three steps back, always striving to rise up, ever falling farther and farther behind—deeper in debt, finding it ever harder to feed your family, to compete with the world. The core of it all was debt and the recurrent *sexenio* crises. Like the government, you owed your debts in dollars but made your money in pesos. When the government defaulted on its debts and devalued the currency, you woke up owing hundreds of thousand of U.S. dollars for the new freezing equipment—for lettuce you were selling in pesos, now valued at half of what they had been worth the day before.

So it was with your land, your business, your home, and your savings, even the coins in your pocket. Imagine waking up in suburban Chicago or London to find that the dollar or euro was now worth fifty cents at the grocery store. Imagine that your fine $500,000 home is now worth $250,000—but you still owe the bank half a million. This was the plight of the Mexican family in the 1980s and '90s.

The hardest hit were the poor. With each peso devaluation and *sexenio* crisis, the middle class lost their life savings, and the working class lost their jobs. But the poor lost the buying power to purchase milk for their babies. They turned for help to the government, which had always been good for a handout as oil soared from $12 to $40 a barrel—but now oil prices were down, and the regime was broke. The typical Mexican might own a modest house worth ten thousand pesos, or about a thousand U.S. dollars. One morning the government devalues the currency; now you owed banks the equivalent of what was thirty thousand or forty thousand pesos the day before.

Whether it is a hole-in-the-wall *changarro,* a tiny boot factory in León, or a restaurant in the Venezuela of Hugo Chávez, to build a small family business in this roller-coaster environment requires an effort nothing short of heroic. You must buy your product and materials in hard cash at the global price of the U.S. dollar or euro, then sell them at the local-currency price. You must work fourteen to sixteen hours a day and lie awake at night, worrying whether your revenues will be worth half their value in the week to come—when you must make payroll in present-value currency, to allow your workers to make ends meet. Banks won't lend money in this climate, because they don't know whether your business can repay them. The rich take their money out of the country to dollar accounts in Miami and safe currencies in Europe, so the pool of available investment cash dries up in capital flight. Foreign investors want no part of the country risk of these veering, drunken economies, where their stake can suddenly be worth a fraction of what they invested. Assets can be seized at any moment by authoritarian governments that do not respect property rights, the rule of law, or the basic priniciples of fiscal discipline.

Money goes where it is treated best. Nowhere was money treated worse than in the Mexico of the 1970's, '80s, and '90s. Echeverría and López Portillo set the country back a century.

On the surface, life in my country was placid, serene. Global policy makers showered praise on Mexico, conferring that absurd adjective which is the highest praise among shortsighted world leaders: "stable." The status quo is the shrine at which the bureaucrats worship. But the next time policy makers in Washington, London, or Tokyo tell you not to worry, that some developing country may be authoritarian and state-controlled and may abuse its people but the economy is *stable,* remember this: People there are suffering. Sooner or later change will come, violently or peacefully, smoothly or bloodily. But people will not forever accept a government with no freedom, no economic mobility, dismal educational opportunities, weak currency, and an uncertain business climate. Throughout the economic turbulence of the 1970's, '80s, and '90s, the pressure cooker of anger built among Mexicans, from middle-class businessmen like me to the campesinos, the urban workers and the poor, always shut out.

On the surface, the state party's propaganda machine said life was good. Mexico loves a party, so we danced to the music the government played. Even as the PRI's vote share began to shrink from its traditional 90 or 95 percent down to the high–70 percent range by 1982, when López Portillo pointed his *dedazo* at Miguel de la Madrid, the PRI kept a lid on this seething unhappiness for seventy-one years, longer than the Communists ran the Soviet Union.

It was the greatest feat of modern authoritarianism. The PRI did it by controlling everything, *everything,* in society. If you wanted to dig a well, you had to go to the PRI for a permit. If you went to the movies, the government censored what you saw. If you were one of the few Mexicans who could afford a television set, you watched PRI-approved news on a government-licensed Televisa station owned by that self-described "soldier of the PRI," Emilio "El Tigre" Azcárraga. If you were one of the 3.5 million *ejidatarios* who had gotten your little plot of land from the PRI's Lázaro Cárdenas or Luis Echeverría, you paid dues to the PRI-controlled CNC farmers' union: On Sundays you had to show up at the PRI rallies to get your party-membership card punched, like a Catholic schoolboy getting his mass ticket punched by the priest. Only then would you receive your allotment of seed from the government; the price of Mexico's oil soared from $5 a barrel to $20 a barrel, so López Portillo could afford to throw around a lot of government grain to keep the peasants happy.

The old PRI was a masterpiece of management control. Harvard Business School should write it up as a case study. Had it been a blatant military dictatorship, we might have rebelled, world opinion might have recoiled, the United States might have invaded; Mexico might have suffered another million deaths in a civil war. But, like a skillful horseman, the regime gave society just enough soft rein to get us moving, then pulled back until the bit cut into our mouths, so that the mount came under control. If you were a businessman and you paid the bribes, you got just enough contracts and permits to keep you barely profitable but remained enmeshed in enough red tape so that you never quite had the economic freedom to stand up against the established order. If you were one of Mexico's 1.5 million teachers, you belonged to a PRI teachers' union and your job was protected:

Whether you showed up drunk on Wednesday, hungover on Thursday, and not at all on Friday, you still kept your job—as long as you also showed up at the governor's ribbon-cutting that Sunday for a new school to be built by a PRI-selected contractor. Whether you did your jobs as teacher or contractor well or poorly was completely beside the point: Both of you were puppets on the string, and if you didn't dance to the PRI's accordion, the government pulled the string, and you felt the jerk and fell back in line.

If you want to understand life in the perfect dictatorship, it is important to make the distinction that these were not for the most part evil people; it was simply an evil system. Many of those within the PRI were very good people—teachers and small businessmen, *ejidatario* farmers and union workers, postmen and shoemakers, even some of the politicians trying to reform the System. In those days the PRI was just Mexico: dysfunctional, changeless, a downtrodden people resigned to the way things were and trying to get by. The greatest evils of a corrupt state economy lie not so much in the sins of its functionaries but in our own indifference to the fact that things never get better.

Our children paid a terrible price for society's complicity in what the advocates of educational reform call "the soft bigotry of low expectations." Take the schools, for example. There certainly were many noble teachers who did their best, but schools were shoddily built and poorly staffed; teachers were not tested, measured, or held to standards for teaching the reading and writing of Spanish, much less English, or calculus. Schools rarely had a computer, a library, or a cafeteria, perhaps not even running water. But *priista* teachers taught *priista* history in classrooms built by a *priista* contractor on land owned by the *priista* mayor, while the *priista* governor got his taste. This almighty *mordida,* or "bite," enriched the union boss and the crony capitalist, while the teacher went ill-paid and ill-trained and the indigenous child went unschooled, unfed, unkempt. And so Mexico went, unchanged.

The same dysfunctional equilibrium ruled our economy. Wages were set by the government. So were prices: corn and beans, lettuce and broccoli, milk and medicine, cars and tractors. No matter that the farmer couldn't afford the government-priced tractor to dig the government-permitted irrigation ditch to water the government-issued seed to earn government-devalued pesos by selling corn at a government-set price; the key was that the System maintained its status quo. The *mordidas* rolled in, the party's friends grew rich, and nothing changed for the poor, the farmer, the worker, the urban middle class.

This was *stability*. And despite the occasional crises, the United States liked Mexico this way, in perfect stasis; so did Europe. The predictable weakness of Mexico's economy as the sick man of North America was something that global financiers could count on: Our backward labor pool produced a steady stream of cheap workers for their economies, and even our poorest consumers bought their products. We may not have been a market for many Audis or IBM computers, but Mexicans would work all day to buy a transistor radio or two six-ounce bottles of Pepsi for the price of one.

Above all, Mexico was *stable*. When the wealthiest superpower shares a border of almost two thousand miles with nearly 100 million people who earn an average of twenty times less than U.S. citizens do—as Mexicans did in the 1970s—stability is no small thing.

Mexico's economy was still growing, fueled by oil revenues and wild debt spending, but the typical Mexican citizen didn't see the money. Averages can be deceptive: Outside of Europe and Japan, where income distribution is fairly even, the focus on the growth of a nation's "average income" often masks huge disparities between the actual conditions faced by that country's richest and poorest citizens. For example, today the average American grows wealthier every year—but the richest 20 percent get 46 percent of U.S. income, while the poorest 20 percent earn just 5 percent of the nation's earnings. In Mexico, inequity is even worse; the top 20 percent earn 57 percent of our national income, while the bottom 20 percent receive just 3.5 percent. Diminutive former Clinton cabinet member Robert Reich once explained distribution of income this way: "I may be only four foot ten, while Wilt Chamberlain stands seven foot one, but on average we are both about six feet tall."

Things were terribly uneven in Mexico back in 1970s. A few "connected" millionaires feasted as our economy grew, but most Mexicans couldn't even reach the food on the table. So how did the regime keep voters from revolting? Were we so submissive, we Catholics down on our knees? Were we so traumatized by the million-plus deaths of the Mexican Revolution that we dared not risk unbridling what we call "*México bronco*"? Certainly culture and history played their parts, but you cannot underestimate the subtle power of the System. If the PRI had been a classic *im*perfect dictatorship, with jackbooted generalissimos marching down the Reforma like Paraguay's Alfredo Stroessner, perhaps they wouldn't have ruled for so long: it was the PRI's puppet show of electioneering, its adherence to the "no reelection" values of our constitution, that gave Mexico's one-party state its veneer of democratic respectability—the quality at which Peruvian novelist Mario Vargos Llosa marveled when he coined the term "perfect dictatorship" to describe the PRI in 1990.

The old guard had dozens of tricks for maintaining power. The nationalist party controlled which politicians would appear on television, which citizens could afford the TV sets to watch them, which journalists would receive bribes to control what was shown.

Once you got to the polls, party officials had a bottomless tool box of devious methods to stack the deck. They stuffed ballot boxes before the polls opened in the morning. At dusk they opened them to see how many more votes were needed to reach their quota. Often this quota was set at 100 percent of the vote, which meant throwing out the ballot of any brave soul who cast a vote for the opposition. *Ejidatarios* arrived with premarked ballots in their pockets and were handed a clean ballot at the door. No one asked for an ID or a photo. (Today, thanks to democracy reforms pushed by the opposition-controlled Congress of the 1990s, Mexico has one of the most advanced voter-identification systems in the world.) Back then farmhands, oil workers, teachers, and mothers would file in to vote under the watchful eyes of many local PRI captains, there to make sure that they dropped the marked ballot in the box and kept the clean ballot as proof they had voted the party line, so they could get their reward: the bag of seed or the new Singer sewing machine that waited for them at the end of the line. Failure to vote for the PRI was a one-way ticket to losing your job at the local school or the Pemex refinery.

As the opposition grew savvier and foreign monitors started showing up from the Carter Center in Atlanta, the old PRI grew subtler. The government subsidized newspapers and TV stations with government-funded advertising before the elections; if media dared to air the opposition candidates, the government simply cut off the funding. Polls often didn't even open until noon in the urban areas, where the disgruntled middle class was beginning to vote for the PAN and urban workers began to flirt with the PRD. But the voting booths were open from dawn to midnight in the

PRI's rural strongholds, all-night polling convenience stores that didn't close until the last customers came in.

There are great lessons in Mexico's struggle for freedom for often well-meaning—but sometimes misguided—leaders in Washington, New York, Brussels, and Geneva working to bring democracy to today's Middle East, Latin America, Asia, and Africa. First, elections in and of themselves do not make a democracy: Freedom is more a matter of changing hearts than changing officeholders. Over the long run, social conditions—economics, cultural values, ethics, religion, education, jobs, health care, a fair distribution of wealth—will have much more to do with public acceptance of democracy than the military force applied behind it. There are better ways to free a society than the Molotov cocktail—or the cruise missile.

The message of Mexico's last century is this: Walled-off, isolationist authoritarian societies make poor allies and worse business partners, no matter how "stable" they might seem on the surface. Before the rich nations cozy up to the next Middle Eastern tyrant or Latin American dictator, they should tabulate the failures of the PRI's Mexico. Authoritarian regimes and pseudodemocracies are the last thing the free world needs today—even if these perfect dictators can win staged elections, even if they vote with the United States in the United Nations.

THE BENIGN FACE of the PRI's caretaker state masked the ugliness beneath. It built huge Pemex hospitals to show off the benevolence of the state-run oil company. But inside, often the beds might be empty; there might not be doctors and nurses to man the wards. After the politicians cut the ribbons and were whisked out of town in their limousines, it was as though the painted façades would topple over in the whoosh of their exhaust pipes, like Hollywood scenery after the director shouts "Cut!" The audience would leave after the show was over; their PRI ticket punched, they could go back to work at the Pemex refinery on Monday.

This was our sad tradition, this submission to the caudillo strongmen of authoritarian government, who peddled the narcotic of an all-powerful, all-caring, all-knowing state until the population grew addicted to the deceptive, dreamlike *somnífero*—Mexicans could take it easy, because someone else would solve our problems. The beauty of it all, the brilliance of the scheme and the horrible truth we're never comfortable acknowledging, was that many people actually *liked* it that way—getting things for free, leaving our woes to a paternalistic state that didn't force us to take too much responsibility.

Above all, the PRI kept things *calm*. Our culture values serenity. Our politicians vie to assure us that they will bring "tranquillity"—versus the United States, where energetic JFK-style politicians vow policies of "vigor" to "get the country moving again." Under the PRI's yoke, we didn't want to move. We just wanted to survive.

Behind the mask of this caretaker state that ordered Mexican lives from cradle to grave, lurked the deeper evil of indifference. According to Reuters, after devastating floods brought cholera and dengue fever to Acapulco and the states of Guerrero and Oaxaca in 1997, stricken residents described how government officials went from house to house like the Angel of Death, handing out hurricane relief only to loyal, card-holding PRI members. Hundreds died and 275,000 Mexicans were left homeless, but those who had not attended the rallies starved and watched their houses wash away, their children bloated with the worms of malnutrition, their senior citizens sickened by rotting sewage.

In contrast, after the 2004 tsunami, the governments of Indonesia and Sri Lanka, respectively, aided the families of Muslim-separatist rebels in Aceh and the Tamil Tigers even though the rebels had been on the other side of long and bloody civil wars. While the Bush administration had its difficulties after Hurricane Katrina, it is hard to imagine the U.S. president ordering the National Guard to go from house to house doling out food and clothing only to card-carrying Republicans.

So morally, which was worse, a nakedly repressive and evil dictatorship like Hussein's Iraq or Pinochet's Chile? Or the callous indifference of the PRI's Mexico, which denied 100 million Mexicans the hope of escaping their misery?

As Elie Wiesel put it so eloquently in his Millenium Lecture "The Perils of Indifference," while the Jews in the concentration camps puzzled over the evil that the Nazis visited upon them, what they found most difficult to accept was indifference, the lack of action from anyone to help them—FDR, the Allies, even God. They could have accepted God's anger or hatred, Wiesel said, but not His indifference. "We felt that to be abandoned by God was worse than to be punished by Him," Wiesel said. Wiesel and his fellow inmates believed that to be ignored by God was more painful than to be punished. "Better an unjust God than an indifferent one," Wiesel told his audience in the Clinton White House. "Man can live far from God—not outside God."

Indifference, Wiesel tells us, is more dangerous than anger and hatred. "Anger can at times be creative," the Holocaust survivor said. Great poetry, music, and art can come from anger and injustice, Wiesel said, but indifference "elicits no response." In Wiesel's view, "Indifference is not a beginning, but an end."

The good people of Mexico endured seventy-one years of the PRI's benign neglect. Like the world today with genocide in Darfur, poverty in Haiti, or AIDS in Africa, many in Mexico knew what was happening. We just did nothing to stop it. In this we proved Wiesel's contention that sin is human, but indifference is inhuman. By the 1980s, Mexico was living testimony to Edmund Burke's view that "the only thing necessary for the triumph of evil is for good men to do nothing."

But where was Vicente Fox in all this? Was I out in the streets with the students in 1968, protesting for democracy? Was I in opposition-party politics, demanding change? No. In the 1980s, I was just another small-time entrepreneur trying to get by, suffering the consequences, struggling alongside my five brothers to keep our family *changarros* afloat. Inside, my anger grew, like that of the Mexican people, but we were all too busy scrambling to keep body and soul together to think of rebellion. Every day at prayer time, the production lines at our little boot factory in conservative Cristero country would cease for our Catholic workers to say their rosary: I would cross myself and sprint over to the vegetable-freezing plant to pay U.S. dollars for equipment—money we could never earn back in devalued pesos. Then I would dash to the bank to beg them to extend the government-approved loan on our land—and pray that the government would let us sell lettuce at the new approved price.

There is a strange triple layer to the rising cake of democratic revolution. At the top there is the middle-class business community, at cocktail bars in Polanco or neighborhood barbecues in Guanajuato. They may grouse privately over tequila that the government is destroying the country, but they are ready to put on their best smile the next day for the government official who decides whether they get the permit to dig a well or the loan for a new leather press at the boot factory. Then there are the working people—the farmhands and the union machinists—and the unemployed poor. They know they are being squeezed out of existence by the System. The class-warfare populists of the state party can turn them against the Americans or the middle class for a while, but eventually working people see through that. The great mass of people feel only hopelessness: They can do nothing, because the state party controls their welfare payments, the rewards for good behavior, the punishments for crossing the regime.

Finally, beneath it all seethes the anger of the true democrats: the students and the intellectuals, the labor activists, the fed-up housewives who take to the picket line. Eventually this third layer finds its voice in a few opposition leaders with the guts and the integrity to stand up against the evils of all this corruption, all this indifference.

This was far from my mind in the 1980s. I was not yet reading Wiesel or Burke, King or Gandhi. I was a disciple of Lee Iacocca, Peter Drucker, and Tom Peters, more interested in *The One-Minute Manager* than "Letter from Birmingham Jail." If anything most infuriated me about the Mexican government, it was its grotesque bureaucratic inefficiency.

My first political act was an act of entrepreneurial mutiny. President de la Madrid had invited some local farmers and León businessmen to discuss government red tape. Everyone was there in fine suits and silver cuff links. But here comes Vicente Fox, clumping up to the podium in his cowboy boots, carrying two volumes of government regulations, each one the size of a small hog. I thumped them down on the table; the president jumped a bit in his chair. "We have to comply with all of the damn rules in these two books just to get an export permit to sell broccoli in McAllen," I complained. "How the hell do you expect us to compete in the U.S. market with all this bullshit?"

I was not invited back.

My brothers and I saw us Fox boys as global visionaries. We were, at least, the biggest international thinkers in León, Guanajuato—too big for the Mexico of the PRI. From the little office my dad had bought years before in McAllen, we sold fresh-frozen quality vegetables for the demanding consumers of the U.S. market. We also launched a line of fashion footwear to meet the rising consumer demand sparked by film trendsetters like Jon Voight in *Midnight Cowboy* and John Travolta in *Urban Cowboy*. Sales were brisk, the American president announced that he didn't like broccoli, and the Fox boys went global. It was about this time that I learned two basic rules of business that they failed to teach me at the Harvard seminars put on by the Coca-Cola Company:

Lesson 1: If you borrow in dollars and get paid in pesos, and the pesos are suddenly worth half what they were the day before, you now owe twice as much as you did yesterday. In other words, you're broke.

Lesson 2: What goes up usually comes down. In the capricious world of high fashion, trends last about two years, at the end of which you're sitting on a large Paris warehouse full of Mexican boots in pink and teal, while the ladies of France have moved on to black Dutch clogs.

This is how Lilián and I came to spend a year and a half living with our baby daughter in Paris. Our friends thought it was terribly romantic, but we weren't dining at Maxim's or painting in a garret on the Left Bank. I was in an industrial warehouse full of $250 designer boots, on the phone all night with my younger brother Cristóbal in Mexico, trying to negotiate another six-month line of credit from the bankers. We owed them $2.5 million for our European inventory, which I was trying to unload on someone so far behind the fashion curve that he might buy our $200 coral lady's cowboy boots with fluffy white fringe. (Eventually I found a buyer in Morocco at five bucks a pair.) My wife and Ana Cristina slept on cots in a loft above the loading dock, eking out a meal or two a day from the little supermarket on the corner. But Paris was still Paris: Thank God for French cheese.

It was at this time, making regular pilgrimages to the sanctuary at Lourdes, praying at mass for the gift of my baby daughter, protection of the family's patrimony, and deliverance from all our worldly troubles, that I discovered what a refuge one finds in religion in hard times—and how curiously secular are the people of Europe, who gave us this great Catholic religion in the first place. The magnificent cathedrals of Paris were empty, even on Sundays—just a suddenly impoverished Mexican boot maker and his wife and child, along with perhaps two or three elderly ladies in black shawls and the priest's voice echoing the mass. And everywhere around us this silence: not like churches in Mexico, which even today rustle with worshippers all day, from dawn to midnight.

Paris is also where I learned the enormous advantage of Mexico's physical proximity to the United States—one of my best arguments for a continental Common Market of North America to compete with the growing power of Asia and the European Union. Whether it was high-fashion boots or fresh vegetables, from Mexico we could ship our product to retail shelves in the United States in a matter of hours or days, up the roads and railways of what is now the NAFTA corridor before the succotash could spoil or the cowboy boots go out of style. But for Mexican or North American products to reach faraway European markets—this is much more difficult. It is even harder for our distant competitors in Asia to get time-sensitive products to New York or Paris. This gives Mexico, the United States, and Canada huge competitive advantages when we trade with one another, as opposed to the Asian or European manufacturer who must carry large inventories and transport them across the oceans. All things being equal, Mexico can serve the U.S. market more profitably than can an outsourced operation in India or Malaysia; the United States and Canada can sell products more profitably to buyers in Mexico than in Europe or Asia. Now that all three nations of North America are free-market democracies, if we used the same currency values, with uniform customs rules and regulations, there is no limit to how successful an EU-style North American Union could be in the twenty-first century.

Even from our cot above the boot warehouse in Paris, I could see the results of the great European economic integration of the 1980s. Back in the early 1970s, when I had traveled around Europe as a young Coca-Cola executive, the continent was divided—like our hemisphere today—into two different groups of countries: rich nations like Britain, Germany, France, and the Netherlands and poor nations like Spain, Ireland, Italy, Greece, and Portugal. As in today's United States, per capita incomes in rich countries like Germany or the United Kingdom in 1975 were much higher than those of poor countries like Spain or Ireland. Back then Spain and Ireland had per capita incomes roughly equal to those in Mexico, with the average worker earning just $3,000 to $4,500 a year.

As the economies of Europe integrated in the last quarter of the twentieth century, the wealthier EU nations imported agricultural products, raw materials, outsourced manufacturing, and immigrants from their poorer neighbors. By the mid-1970s, more than 8 million foreigners lived and worked in affluent northwestern Europe. By the 1980s the United Kingdom had more than a million Irish immigrants: France had nearly 650,000 Spanish workers and more than 600,000 from Italy; 300,000 Spaniards worked in Germany. The wealthy nations of Europe gained from the work of poor immigrants in their fields and factories and grew even richer from selling goods to their poor neighbors. Northern Europe also profited from the finance and management of huge investments in their southern neighbors, as German, French, and British companies located outsourced operations in Spain, Ireland, and Italy.

The poor nations gained, too. Because they started much further behind, the benefits of continental integration to countries like Ireland, Spain, and Italy were nothing short of an economic miracle. Consider what a guest worker does for his home country: Contrary to the myth of the lazy Mexican or the drunken, feckless Irishman, immigrants are hungry, hardworking, highly productive revenue generators with low social-welfare costs and high savings rates. Whether they were barely literate seasonal Spanish and Italian agriculture workers picking berries in the Black Forest or well-educated Irish workers laser-fitting contact lenses in the UK, EU immigrants sent home billions of marks, pounds, and francs to their families in the poor nations. Many of these Spanish, Italian, and Irish guest workers then returned home, repatriating the greatest gift for a "have-not" nation: human capital. They brought back job skills, new languages, and business savvy—along with the financial wherewithal to put these skills to work at home.

In one generation per capita incomes in Spain rose from around $4,500 a year in 1975 to more than $25,000 today—a fivefold increase in just one generation. Today Spain is one of the world's wealthiest nations, a financial superpower whose banks, hotel chains, and telecom entrepreneurs are flexing their muscles throughout Europe and Latin America. Italy is now an economic giant, the seventh-largest economy on the planet.

Or take the case of Ireland, which just a generation ago was one of the poorest countries in Europe—with a per capita income of roughly $3,000 a year, about the same as Mexico's in 1975. Now Ireland is one of the world's richest countries, with a per capita income well over $40,000—about the same as that in the United States. In the single decade of the 1990s, Ireland tripled its per capita economic output, transforming itself from a poor nation of emigration to a rich nation of immigration. Ireland now imports hundreds of thousands of foreign workers: Poles, Romanians, Bosnians.

Most of Ireland's success came from multinational corporations, which accounted for a third of its gross domestic product in the 1990s. Try telling the Irish that globalism doesn't help the poor: Multinationals produced 60 percent of the nation's growth in the last decade and nearly 90 percent of Ireland's exports. Thanks to continental integration and one of the world's great educational systems, Ireland now produces much more for the world than Guinness stout and hardworking emigrants. Today the Irish stay home, and the Emerald Isle is one of the great economic miracles of the twentieth century.

As free trade blossomed across the EU, Spain, Italy, Portugal, and Greece became not just cheap, sunny places for Brits and Germans to vacation but also good business partners for the "have" nations. Newly affluent consumers in formerly poor nations began to buy more British, German, French, and Dutch products. Immigration from countries like Spain and Ireland tailed off as more assembly plants, hotels, wineries, and automobile factories were built in the former "have-not" nations—financed and managed at first by the British, German, French, and Dutch, then by the Italians, Spaniards, and Irish.

Free trade is not a zero-sum game. The entire European pie grew over the last thirty years. So even as integration transformed the economies of Spain and Ireland, the EU also boosted the economies of the wealthy immigrant-receiving, product-exporting nations like Germany and the UK. The European Union today has a larger total economy than that of the United States but manages a trade deficit that is only about a third of the United States staggering $763.6 billion trade gap. As U.S. exports lag further and further behind what it must import from abroad, America gets deeper and deeper in debt to cover the difference—which is bad news for all the nations of our hemisphere, rich and poor. In a global economy, the only answer for our nations—haves and have-nots alike—is trade, trade, and more trade. The Americas simply must have our own answer to the European Union and the mighty economic tigers of Asia.

Two decades after my time in that Paris warehouse, after my election as president, I proposed a "NAFTA Plus" plan to President Bush and Canada's Prime Minister Jean Chrétien to move us toward a single continental economic union, modeled on the European example. This would raise incomes in Mexico, making us richer customers for U.S. and Canadian products; boost the standard of living north of the border; and make all three of our nations stronger allies in the fights against crime and terrorism.

Bush shot the idea down. The White House sent word that life would be easier if this Mexican cowboy would stop raising hackles with his talk of a North American Union. Of course, it is a radical notion and now runs completely counter to the wall-building isolationism that swept the U.S. after the tragic events of September 11, 2001.

But I haven't given up. As a lifelong admirer of the ideals of democracy and free enterprise that the United States holds out to the world, I feel compelled to ask once again: Is the dream of prosperity just for Americans, or can it be shared with the rest of us?

Now that Mexico is a democracy, I believe that we could, within our lifetimes, build one great union of the Americas that one day might stretch from Canada to Chile. This would not be a one-world government but a strong American Common Market, linking the economies of the United States, Canada, and Mexico into a New World economic union that would eventually include all of Latin America and the Caribbean.

Consider the benefits of Mexico as a business partner. According to Goldman Sachs, by the year 2040, Mexico will have the fifth-largest economy on earth. We already rank as the third-largest trading partner of the United States. (Canada, not China, is number one.) Even with all the EU's success, Mexico still buys more U.S. products than the four largest economies of Europe *combined*. If we joined into one continental economic union, this SuperNAFTA would create a North American Common Market larger than the European Union or the Asian giants. In the new world of fierce global competition and the Internet, this may be the key to "making the Americas" in the twenty-first century.

I CANNOT PRETEND that I envisioned all this from my cot in the attic of a Parisian boot warehouse in the 1980s, nibbling on French bread and Spanish sausage as we shipped the last of our pink Mexican boots to North Africa. The biggest lesson I took from our family's time of trouble was the immigrant rule of my grandfathers: You can overcome any challenge if you just keep moving.

So I came back to the ranch to take over the vegetable-freezing plant, with no idea that just fourteen years later I would walk along the lettuce rows with George W. Bush, trying to convince him to unite our nations in a continental trade union. I worked in the freezing plant, paid taxes, adopted three more children, and moved the orphanage to León, where the needs grew ever greater. With the 1990s, Mexico's economic crises deepened, and the results became more acute—more mothers who couldn't feed their babies, more neighbors out of work, more fourteen-year-old farm boys crossing the deserts to the cold and forbidding *norte,* more beggars wiping car windows in the cities with sooty rags, more little boys and girls with painted clown faces dodging through the busy traffic of Paseo de la Reforma, juggling for pesos so they could eat that night. All this I saw, and I did what little I could: some homespun philanthropy at our *casa cuna* and the church, our family scholarship program, my Jesuit alma mater. Beneath the surface, my anger was always building and building, like the resentful dismay of the people in the streets—a seething, silent rebellion against the injustice of this wicked System that had beggared our country. But politics was still the furthest thing from my mind. I had my home, a beautiful wife, four wonderful children, and a quarter horse to ride on Sundays. Besides, we all knew it was pointless. The PRI had always run Mexico, and the PRI would always run Mexico. Those who bucked the system seemed like crazy, deranged, self-destructive, kooky idealists, tilting at windmills.

Then Don Quijote came to town, and I decided to join his crusade.

CHAPTER 7

GUNS IN THE BELLY

MANUEL CLOUTHIER was a farmer from Sinaloa, a bearded bull of a man who had run a noble but impossible campaign for governor the previous year as the candidate of the center-right opposition party, PAN, the Partido Acción Nacionál. Clouthier had carried the PAN's blue and orange banners bravely against the regime in his drug-infested northern desert state, but Sinaloa was a stronghold of the ruling party. (Sinaloa would later engender Governor Francisco Labastida, the PRI presidential candidate we defeated in 2000.) In Mexico, opposition parties were used to defeat, of course, and Clouthier had taken it in stride. By late 1987 the burly farmer was gearing up to run as the presidential candidate of the PAN against the balding, big-eared economist who was in line to get the presidential "finger" in 1988: Carlos Salinas de Gortari.

Until Clouthier's arrival on the political scene, the PAN was primarily a regional party of the north: the Cristero country, where pioneer farmers had learned to depend on themselves, where many distrusted the federal government and rebel roots ran deep. Culturally conservative and devoutly Catholic, the PAN was the party of people like my family, rancheros of the working middle class whose mothers said the rosary and went to mass every day, small businessmen who were unhappy with state-controlled economy and wanted free-market reform, democrats who believed in human liberty and could no longer live with the government's ruthless repression. But we were not really card-carrying *panistas* yet in the Fox family. A working farmer or small-time boot maker in those days needed to stay on decent terms with the government just to sell lettuce or buy leather at the market price. The family dictum passed down by my father was to avoid tainting oneself with the dirty business of politics—keep your nose clean and tend to the farm. This is what I did until Manuel Clouthier invited me to breakfast.

I knew Manuel from my Coca-Cola days, when Cloutheir had headed the business association of Mexico's agricultural producers, the guys who grew the sugar for our soft drinks. When Clouthier asked me to join him at the La Estancia Hotel for eggs and chorizo, my brothers went through the roof.

"You can't be seen with him in public!" José shouted.

"It's a private meeting," I explained nervously across the kitchen table, wondering what I'd gotten myself into. "Besides, I already told him I would come."

"There's no such thing as a private meeting in Mexico," my brothers groused in unison. It was common knowledge: The PRI sent *gobernación* spies to every opposition political meeting. Citizens who attended them were put on a blacklist for reprisals.

"It's just a business meeting," I protested. "Fifty or sixty friends from the chamber of commerce, that's all." I could feel the disapproval of my father radiating across the table. Graying and semiretired, the old man was still our most valuable business counselor. His silence spoke volumes.

So here comes Vicente Fox striding into the La Estancia Hotel, ready to hear the pitch of this angry farmer from Sinaloa who had stood up against the imperial president López Portillo and his disastrous nationalization of Mexico's banks. As I walked into the hotel lobby, I looked around for my fellow León business leaders so we could go in together—safety in numbers—past the eyes of the PRI agents loitering in the foyer. No friends in sight. I went into the room Clouthier had booked for the breakfast. It was nearly empty, a handful of local businessmen and PAN aides, perhaps five or six fellows among a sea of a hundred bare plates. I spotted a fellow bootmaker, Felipe Pablo Martínez, who hastened to tell me he was there not to join the PAN but in his official capacity as head of the local chamber. I nodded and agreed. The meeting was a bust.

But Clouthier was magnificent: a *toro* charging straight at the matador no matter the danger, railing against the PRI's economic failures and corruption, the repression of the authoritarian government that had walled Mexico off in poverty, crisis, and despair. I was so moved that on the way out I barely noticed the flashbulbs of the *gobernación* agents in the hotel lobby, snapping away with their cameras. The five of us agreed to come back that night to the *zócalo* of the big city to hear Clouthier address the crowds in the square of León, where once my brother and I had circled round and round in pursuit of beauty.

"Are you crazy?" José Luis thundered that afternoon in the freezing plant. "You can't go back to hear him in public. It will kill us. And then *I* will kill *you*!"

From my big brother, this was a credible threat. But I had promised Manuel. At eight o'clock that evening, I drove my pickup back to León and parked behind the plaza, wondering who might be watching. Usually bustling with brisk evening business after the traditional Mexican late lunch, the *zócalo* was now oddly deserted. Clouthier stood at the microphone in the glare of a handheld spotlight wielded by the *panista* aides who had been at breakfast that morning. Otherwise the square was dark, empty.

"Psst!" a voice whispered from *los arcos,* the big galleried arches surrounding the colonial Spanish square. "Vicente! Over here!"

It was my friend, the shoemaker Felipe Pablo, hiding in the shadow of a big stone column. I must admit that I didn't see him at first because I was hiding behind the next column. Together we watched as the bull of Sinaloa challenged the System to punish us.

"I am sure there are agents of *gobernación* here in the square, writing down names in their little notebooks!" Clouthier shouted. *Christ,* I thought, *I sure hope not.* A few shoppers slowed down to see what all the fuss was about as Clouthier addressed the government spies, who looked back at him blankly as they took down every word. "Go ahead, write my name down at the head of your list!" Clouthier demanded. "Tell the secretary of interior and his corrupt cronies that we are ready to have our lands taken away. We are ready to lose our homes and our jobs, the seed they give us for our fields, all the little lollipops the government hands out as though we are children, so easily kept happy. We stand here proud and defiant in the PAN! Who will stand with me?"

Felipe Pablo left early. I stood transfixed as Manuel preached to the small crowd. "How long are you going to keep taking the taco?" he cried, railing against the ruling party's practice of giving out food and favors in return for votes. "Don't you understand that there is nothing inside the wrapper?" Now a few dozen people had gathered in the square, and some chanted with him the PAN's cunning slogan, *Acepta lo que te dan, pero vota por el PAN!*—"Accept what they give you, but vote for the PAN!"

It was the moment I mentally crossed the line. I was sick of watching my neighbors take the taco. My frustration, like theirs, had reached a boiling point. Finally here was a man and a cause I could believe in. *I'm voting for the PAN,* I thought. *Let's throw these guys out of Los Pinos and make Mexico a democracy.* It was love at first sight between me and the PAN. All the anger built up inside me had at last met the perfect expression of my discontent. Here was a leader and a party that said everything I believed but had never heard anyone say out loud.

At this point I had it in mind to be to be a follower of the PAN, not a leader. I was still behind the column, not shouting in the square. I would vote for this humanist center-right party, this brave rebel in the *zócalo* with the courage to stand up to the government—but I would keep my head down, so that I wouldn't get the family in trouble.

Clouthier had other plans. Felipe Pablo and his wife had asked me to dinner late that night to chew over the day's events. When I arrived in their dining room, there stood Manuel Clouthier. "We need you, Vicente," he said urgently, over forkfuls of a savory queso fundido of melted cheese and local mushrooms. "I want you to run for Congress."

"Congress?" I cried. "We can't even run a business in this economy. If I got into politics, the PRI would cancel our permits and call our loans. We could lose the farm!"

"Not if we keep moving," said Manuel, echoing my immigrant grandfathers. "If the wolves can't catch you, they can't eat you."

This began a year of angry debate among the Fox boys at San Cristóbal.

"Don't do this, Vicente," my big brother urged the next day. "I'm struggling with the farm, we can't make the notes on the freezing plant, and the government can shut us down at any moment. We're lucky they haven't done it already, after you playing footsie with Clouthier and the PAN."

"Dad always taught us not to get involved," said my younger brother Cristóbal, who was working man-killing hours at the boot factory. "José is right. You can't do this to us."

At Christmas dinner we finally heard from my mother, protector of the family, caretaker of the ranch—the proud pioneer woman who had pumped water and tended the sick, braved the guns of the 1970 squatters, faced down the men with their machete blades. I braced myself: This woman had sworn she would leave only in a coffin the land that her husband's family had defended against Pancho Villa's bandits. Surely she wouldn't risk it to her son's political foolishness.

"You should do it," she said fiercely, her green eyes shining with anger. "These men are destroying the country."

"Mom!" José countered. "We have so much to lose!"

"We will lose it anyway, if things don't change," Doña Mercedes said firmly. "Vicente, it's your turn. You have everything a man could want. Now it's time for you to help your neighbors. You decide. But know that I will support you and your family in whatever decision you make."

At midnight on New Year's Eve 1987, I joined the National Action Party (PAN) and filed as an opposition candidate for Congress. I didn't know it then, but my happy life as a rancher and family businessman was about to fall apart.

In 1988, I was still a happily married man. Over the six months of that first congressional election, I adapted my campaign to the needs of my wife, my four wonderful children, and a struggling family business—shaking hands on the assembly lines in the leather factories of León on weekdays, taking my daughters along on my shoulders to the campaign rallies, holding impromptu strategy sessions among the rows of broccoli at the Farm, talking to housewives in the vegetable markets at daybreak before it was time to take the kids to school. In Mexico this idea of campaigning on weekdays was itself revolutionary, or at least innovative; politics has always been a Sunday sport in our country. The big *zócalo* rallies, ribbon cuttings, and speeches of the PRI were always a weekend carnival, festive events with free T-shirts and mariachis playing, burritos and tamales wrapped in the green, white, and red PRI logo. However, when the music stopped and you unwrapped the free food, there was nothing but crumbs left for the Mexican people.

By 1988 they sensed this swindle, and the PRI's vote share began to edge slowly downward. The worse things got in the economy, the larger the crowds that gathered to hear the two main opposition presidential candidates: Clouthier in the *panista* north and rural central Mexico; in the big cities among the urban workers it was Cuauhtemoc Cárdenas, son of former President Lázaro Cárdenas, who had bolted the party to form the leftist democratic alliance that would later become the opposition PRD.

The poor, the students, and the urban workers responded to Cárdenas as the leftist called for democracy in defiance of the regime. Clouthier, too, was building a national following, reaching beyond the PAN's traditional base in the north as middle-class consumers, farmers, and Catholics from Baja to Yucatán grew frustrated with the PRI's failures. People rallied in droves to hear these two fiery, principled opponents of Salinas.

My first political speech wasn't quite so persuasive.

On New Year's Day of 1988, I went to that same downtown plaza in León to launch my twelve-hour-old candidacy. By this point I had attracted quite a following, maybe ten idlers in the square and two dogs who barked incessantly as I hemmed and hawed at the microphone, wondering what I'd gotten myself into.

"What the hell have you done?" José demanded when I returned home that afternoon. He had already heard: I was a total flop. "This will ruin us, Vicente."

Sure enough, by February the government had shut down the vegetable plant. Suddenly the inspectors were finding "sanitation issues" at the cleanest state-of-the-art freezing operation in Mexico. Our permits were mysteriously revoked. Our loans were called ahead of time at the bank. There were no more agricultural lines of credit for San Cristóbal to buy seed.

In March, the Fox Boot Company experienced its first workers' strike. For seventy years my family had employed hundreds of local workers, from the days when Joseph Fox built the first horseless carriages to the factory where we worked side by side with the boot makers, eating together, praying together, never a hint of labor trouble. But word went out from the PRI-controlled leather workers' union: Fox is against the System; he needs to be punished. The workers shrugged and obeyed. This was the way things worked. The hotheaded Fox knew the risks, and now he must pay the price. But they winked at me on their way out the door. *Acepta lo que te dan, pero vota por el PAN.*

I called Clouthier. "What have you done to me!" I demanded. "These guys are squeezing us to death. What do I do now?"

"*¡Duro, duro, duro!*" Clouthier cried, which is to say, persist, endure, hang tough. "Are you a man or a mouse? Never show fear!" The bearded presidential candidate advised me to get more aggressive in my campaign speeches, not less. "Denounce them! Get in their faces! They can't take your land and hurt your family if you shine a light on them. These are bullies, Vicente, and bullies are cowards. If you hit back, they will respect you. It's the only way out now—you just have to fight, and win."

Ironically, the government had given me the two things I really needed: more time to campaign and the anger to do it right. No one was buying our broccoli; the freezing plant was sealed shut with government tape; the boot factory was shuttered. I had the daylight hours free to visit the other plants, and evenings and weekends free for Lilián and the kids. Now I took to the stump with Clouthier's words ringing in my ears, coming out of my shell in a blaze of indignation. I insulted President de la Madrid, Carlos Salinas, and the powerful interior minister, calling out the big *priista* gangsters by name and challenging them to come and get me. I've never been a fan of physical violence—my idea of how to win a fight was to go find my brother. But in the contest of ideas, I discovered I was willing to fight to the end. Like my grandfather in his turret, I flew the flag of defiance, daring the enemy to take my land away. Like Clouthier, I pointed out the *gobernación* agents to the crowd and demanded that they give our names to the authorities. Like my mother, I did this for my neighbors, the frustrated campesinos and anxious housewives whose anger was rising to the surface.

People responded to this indignation in me. As Elie Wiesel said in his great speech, anger can be a creative emotion, piercing through the evils of indifference. The crowds grew. Soon hundreds were gathering in the square, then thousands, until forty thousand cheering voters packed the *zócalo* for our last big rally.

There were ugly moments along the way to Election Day that July. Our family's business woes became the gossip of every rally. "They are going bankrupt!" said the *priista* leaders, who were masters of the mudslinging campaign, tougher than any American spin doctor. "Vicente Fox can't even run a cauliflower plant. How can he serve in Congress?"

They threw everything at me but the kitchen sink. But when you are doing the right thing, an angel sits on your shoulders. We scrambled to keep the family businesses afloat, got the boot factory reopened, and sold it to pay off notes at the farm. The Servitje family, owners of Mexico's massive Bimbo bakery empire, bought 80 percent of the vegetable-freezing operation. We used the proceeds to pay off our debts, and I sold out my interests to my brothers. From that point forward, they paid me a modest income from the family businesses, which is how my children and I have lived ever since. So I was free to focus all my energy on the fight for democracy.

Starting with Father Hidalgo's cry for independence from Spain, to the revolution of 1910–17, to the Cristero Rebellion of the late 1920s, Guanajuato had always been the heartland of Mexican resistance. My state is home to our Lexington and Concord, where Father Hidalgo made his version of Paul Revere's ride to independence, then led his men to burn the Alhóndiga de Granaditas, the great gray stone prison where the Spanish royalists were holed up. It looms still above a city that is now a UN World Heritage Site, overlooking the amphitheaters, aqueducts, and buttressed mining walls of the state capital. In 1988, I took to the stage with our hero Manuel Clouthier and fifty thousand rebels standing strong in the town square, calling on the campesinos to rise again. "There are still more Alhóndigas to burn!" I cried, tears streaming down my cheeks, waving the banner of the Virgin of Guadalupe in the hot July sun as I shouted the Cristero rallying cry: "If I advance, follow me! If I stop, push me! If I retreat, kill me!"

It was this anger that people responded to, this righteous indignation rising up from nearly a century of repression. That July the people of León got up early to make sure the polls opened on time, then bulled their way past the nose counters of the PRI. I marvel as I think of the courage of the people who risked what little they had to vote for me and and two other *panista* rebels on the ballot for Congress. Thanks to their courage, we won—three *panistas* became the first opposition candidates in Mexican history to win our area's three congressional seats.

Nationwide, the two opposition parties rolled up record numbers, Manuel Clouthier and the center-right PAN and especially Cuauhtémoc Cárdenas on the left. Running as the candidate of a loose federation of left-leaning parties called the National Democratic Front, Cárdenas attracted huge numbers of voters in Mexico City and the urban centers. As Election Night on July 6, 1988, wore on, Salinas and his team grew increasingly worried. The PRI's national vote count had plummeted, hovering at the 50 percent mark. By eight o'clock that evening, the vote counts started trickling out of Mexico City, and rumors ran wild that leftist Cuauhtémoc Cárdenas had won the presidency.

It was about this time that the lights went out in federal election headquarters. As Salinas's numbers lagged, the vote-counting computers experienced a mysterious failure. For twenty-four hours, we heard nothing but silence from the government, which had total control of an occult vote-counting process that took place somewhere backstage, beyond public scrutiny. Protesters took to the streets. Miraculously, when the computers came back on, Carlos Salinas de Gortari had won the election with 50.3 percent of the vote.

MEXICO WOULDN'T freely elect a president from outside the PRI for another twelve years. But July 6, 1988, "the night that the lights went out in

Mexico City," became the stuff of legend, a watershed moment in our history. The ruling party, alarmed by the opposition's strong showing and unable to win an outright majority against Cárdenas on the left and Clouthier on the center right, was widely believed to have simply shut down the computers and stolen the election. Incidentally—and pretty well unnoticed at the time—dozens of newcomers like me won seats in Congress in this opposition surge, representing various antigovernment parties on the left, center, and right.

Over the next decade, this band of newly elected opposition leaders in Congress would join with a growing number of reform-minded young leaders within the PRI itself to clean up Mexico's election system. As the Mexican people recoiled against the electoral fraud of 1988, visionary leaders inside the ruling party began to recognize that the country had to change. Consider that in Poland that same year of 1988, Lech Walesa stood on the Solidarity picket line in the Gdansk shipyard. Within a year the Berlin Wall would come down. By 1990, Nelson Mandela would be released after twenty-seven years in prison. With democracy sweeping the earth, a new breed of globally minded technocrats and young-Turk reformers within the PRI began to argue that Mexico must become a democracy in order to take its place among the nations of the world.

Soon PRI reformers like the late Luis Donaldo Colosio (a future PRI presidential candidate who would be assassinated in 1994), enlightened pro-democracy PRI reformers in Congress and the governorships, and eventually the government succumbed to the demand for democratic changes by the new opposition leaders in Congress. In the 1990s these reformers would open up Mexico's electoral system to free and fair competition, paving the way for our victory in 2000.

So in many respects it was not so much our 2000 presidential campaign but these brave souls who brought democracy to Mexico: the voters who cast votes of conscience on that July 6; early opposition leaders like Cárdenas and Clouthier and those who backed them; outspoken reformers within the PRI, some of whom paid with their lives. Twelve years later we rode to victory on the shoulders of these giants.

I CAME to national attention in 1988 in a most inelegant manner, by taping paper ballots to either side of my head to mock the new president's big ears. It wasn't the usual way to take one's seat in the Mexican House of

Deputies, but then the inauguration of the Class of '88 at the congressional Palacio of San Lázaro wasn't exactly business as usual. This was no Washington-style swearing-in, with proud elderly mothers taking pictures and congressmen's children in their laps, doodling at the desks. This was war—or civil disobedience at least. We came in spoiling for a fight, 240 newly elected democratic revolutionary deputies from left and right, united in our determination to reject the results of the PRI's election fraud.

We had spent the previous weeks in Protest School. Here I was, a farmer, former Coca-Cola executive and onetime Catholic-school boy, taking notes alongside Trotskyites, listening to lectures on Walesa's Solidarity movement and Students for a Democratic Society sit-ins against the Vietnam War, learning about Mao's Long March, Rosa Parks's refusal to sit in the back of the bus. We gathered in hotel business centers, university classrooms, and private homes, bringing in longhaired professors to teach us on blackboards borrowed from our children. "If you did your reading of Gandhi last night, you know all about salt and spinning wheels," one of our guest lecturers began. We stared at each other, perplexed. We were amateurs, not political scientists, but we were desperately eager to learn. "Fox!" our teacher shouted (one of the downsides of being tall is that teachers always pick on you in class when you haven't done your homework). "Please explain to the group how Mahatma Gandhi led his people to the sea to make their own salt and taught them to weave their own fabric, and the role this played in overcoming the economic domination of the British Empire."

I read Gandhi and Thoreau, the Russian dissidents, the opponents of apartheid. Our guru in the PAN was a white-bearded democracy activist from Baja in huarache sandals named Norberto Corella, who gave me my first copy of Martin Luther King's "Letter from Birmingham Jail." I took note of the way Corella's every word and deed, even his hippie attire, were visible expressions of solidarity with the poor. For a man like me, who had never believed in fighting violence with violence, the gospel of peaceful resistance as taught by this *panista* street fighter for human freedom was a revelation of biblical proportions.

By the time Congress convened late that summer as an electoral college to certify the July election results, we were trained democracy activists, and our blood was up. The PRI had rigged the results to produce the narrowest of majorities in the 500-member House of Deputies, with the government claiming that they had elected 260 members from the PRI to 240 seats for the opposition parties: 139 members from the four leftist parties of Cárdenas's National Democratic Front and 101 of us from the PAN.

The day before the swearing-in, we met in secret at the Palacio de Hierro shopping center to plot strategy and learn the rules of parliamentary procedure. None of us had ever been in Congress before. We were farmers, teachers, ranchers, doctors, shopkeepers, writers, restaurateurs, boot makers. We didn't know Robert's Rules of Order, how to write a law, the proper way a congressman must approach the tribunal. What we had was our fury: We may have been new at this, but we knew we had been robbed. We all shook hands and swore to keep the peace under the watchful eyes of our protest tutors. But deep inside we were still angry sodbusters ready to stride down Main Street at high noon and face the robber barons who had ridden roughshod over our towns.

Together we walked into the Palacio San Lázaro, into the belly of the beast. I can't tell you how overawed I was to set foot in the halls of Congress for the first time. No place I would enter later—not Los Pinos or the White House, the Kremlin or Beijing's Forbidden City—would so intimidate me. There was this huge five hundred-seat hall of the congressional palace with its green, white, and red Mexican flags. Above it all soared the great golden eagle with the serpent in its claw, the names of Mexico's heroes inscribed on the walls. For the first time in my life, I felt like a patriot, felt that I really could do something noble and good for my country.

Then the speaker called the roll and the government's machine kicked into gear, and I learned firsthand how the PRI really ran Mexico.

Even in democracies like the United States and Britain, newly elected lawmakers are expected to have two ears and one mouth, so they can listen twice as much as they talk; like children, they are to speak only when spoken to. In Mexico this was a permanent state of affairs. Our constitutional policy of "no reelection" covers governors, senators, and congressmen, so the entire legislative branch is composed of perennial freshmen—and perennial lame ducks. Before democracy, PRI loyalists were "placed" into seats with which they often had no connection. The lucky few got governorships, assigned to distant provinces where they could earn fat bribes for their loyal service to the System; others were given lucrative posts in the federal bureaucracy or, if they were very good boys, perhaps a plum cabinet ministry or the ambassadorship to a pleasant country.

Until 2000 the Mexican Congress was not so much a legislative body as it was a lifestyle. Congressmen had no power; they just rubber-stamped the decisions of the executive, approving with no debate laws handed down from Los Pinos. To discuss a bill's flaws would have been heresy, and anyway it would have made them late for their three-tequila lunches. If Los Pinos needed something special from a congressman, the executive branch gave him a "grant." This was not a pork-barrel project for a congressman's district, mind you—the grants were outright cash payments, or maybe a trip to Europe with the family. This was quite a treat for a lowly pol from small-town Michoacán, but if he didn't really want to go to Paris—or had already been while in his sinecure at the commerce department—then the equivalent in cash would do nicely.

These were my seatmates, these veteran politicians of the great hall. When they took to the tribune to pound down the gavel, you could hear the gears of the System grind into action. In late 1988 the House came to order and began the laborious process of certifying the election results in each of three hundred congressional districts.

Normally it was an afternoon's work, this August 15 certification of the July general election results. District 1—we won! District 2—we won! District 3, my, what a surprise—the PRI won again, with 100 percent of the vote! Why, Carlos Salinas has earned just enough votes to be elected president by a majority!

But this time it was tougher for the ruling party. Clearly, the PRI had *not* really won an outright majority. So they carefully calculated exactly how many votes they needed in each district to get 50 percent–plus for Salinas and the PRI, and thus control the Congress and the presidency without looking too ridiculous to a world that was starting to pay attention. It would have been more credible to claim 42 percent for Salinas. (As in the United States, in a three-way race Mexican presidents can be elected with less than an outright majority, as Bill Clinton was in 1992 or I was in 2000.) But then the PRI would have to acknowledge that the two opposition parties had enough votes between us to control Congress. So the PRI went district by district with a secret vote quota that the government's miraculous computers had assigned to each district. At the end they would reach the designated outcome the PRI had determined during that mysterious twenty-four hours that the lights were out: Salinas 50 percent, Cárdenas 30 percent, Clouthier 17 percent.

Cuauhtémoc Cárdenas and Manuel Clouthier joined forces in a mobilization to protest the election fraud. Cuauhtémoc's National Democratic Front, the forerunner of today's leftist PRD, held mass rallies in the square, while my hero Manuel Clouthier went on a hunger strike in a little shack underneath the golden Angel of Independence in the traffic circle on the Paseo de la Reforma.

I grew a fierce black beard in solidarity. Now I was bigger and rougher-looking at 110 kilos—220 pounds—no longer a skinny youth with his big brother to do his fighting for him but a full-blown revolutionary in the best traditions of Latin American guerrillas and U.S. hippies. As usual, we got things late in Mexico—we didn't get the sixties until the eighties. The real democrats had been out on the front lines since the Olympic protests and the shootings at Tlatelolco, but the rest of us were waking up in a hurry.

Outside the congressional palace, we locked arms and marched in the street. Schooled in peaceful resistance, we walked the protest line just slowly enough to impede traffic, careful not to rest on the ground in a true sit-in, so that we never gave the authorities justification to haul us off to jail.

Inside the San Lázaro Palace, we did all we could to frustrate the vote-certification process. Our platform was nullification: The left believed that Cárdenas had won; the PAN knew we had been cheated. Together we united to push the government to throw out these bad election results and hold a new election for president and congress.

The effrontery of those in power knew no bounds. In some districts, needing a maximum score to meet their quota, the speaker would pound his gavel and announce that the PRI had won 100 percent of the vote in the entire congressional district. They would rack up a hundred thousand PRI votes in a district we knew had only a total of twenty or thirty thousand voters on the election rolls. They kept the ballots in the basement of the congressional palace under lock and key, guarded by soldiers with rifles and bayonets, so that no one could determine whether the PRI had voted the dead or double- and triple-voted their supporters (occasionally one single *ejidatario* or union voter could get eleven boxes of food or five pigs for casting as many ballots).

We had reports of other schemes, like the "crazy mice" system, where the PRI changed polling locations at the last minute in opposition-dominated areas, so that Clouthier and Cárdenas voters ran around the city like frenzied rodents while loyal PRI hamsters were taken by government-licensed taxi drivers to polling places to get their little pieces of cheese. The voting was generally held at schools under the tutelage of PRI-union teachers, who often were ready to help the sometimes-illiterate poor to mark the ballots. Three letters of the alphabet were all you needed to get by in Mexico: P-R-I.

I got a firsthand look at the government's election fraud later that year, when I was out campaigning for the PAN in a local municipal by-election in León, where my friend Carlos Medina was running for mayor. Wary of the state party's habit of stuffing ballot boxes, we arrived at midnight on election eve at the schoolhouse in the little rural precinct of La Sandía, on the outskirts of León. As I had learned to do in my congressional race, we stood in line all night, waiting for the polls to open. Sure enough, when they opened the doors, we found the ballot boxes already full, just as they had been in the July national elections. The government had arranged for the printing of ballots, of course; they arrived ready-marked for the ruling party, already in the box before the first voter arrived. We weighed the boxes in our arms: I'd spent my childhood lifting hay bales and knew what a hundred kilos felt like. These boxes weren't made of the transparent plastic we use in Mexico today, but you didn't have to see inside to know they were already full.

We decided to try to wrestle the boxes out of the hands of the municipal election officials to prove that they had filled them with forged ballots. Later that night I came back to La Sandía to find the sun hiding on the hills above the village, as PRI loyalists arrived to stuff their final quota of premarked ballots into the boxes under cover of darkness. "I will just take these," I announced in my deepest voice, standing as tall as I could before the PRI men in their white straw *tejano* cowboy hats.

The meanest-looking of them stuck a pistol in my belly. "No, you won't," he said, digging the snout of the Colt .45 deeper into my shirt.

I would like to tell you that I faced them down and declared, "Do your worst. I am prepared to die for my country." But we surrendered the box.

A month before, in the July 1988 presidential election, we had gone from one polling station to the next, seizing forged ballots and burning them in the streets to protest all across the nation. That year the smoke of burning ballots was the smoldering anger of the Mexican people, the first embers of the peaceful democratic revolution twelve years later.

MANY HAVE CITED the irony of the 2006 election protests at the end of my presidency, when Andrés Manuel López Obrador of the PRD slept in a tent in Mexico City's *zócalo* and called on leftist supporters to block traffic in Mexico City, calling for a recount in the razor-thin 2006 election. The PRD lawmakers even seized control of the congressional palace to disrupt my final Informe, or State of the Union Address, and camped out for days on the congressional dais to try to thwart the swearing-in of Felipe Calderón as my successor. Why, my critics asked, was it right for me to disrupt Congress in 1988 with paper ballots on my ears, to block traffic and burn ballots in order to protest electoral fraud in 1988, yet wrong for the PRD to do the same in 2006?

But there was all the difference in the world between the rigged elections of 1988 and the free and competitive Mexican democracy of 2006. Today elections in Mexico are fair and accurate, run by the new Federal Electoral Institute, the IFE. A multiparty, citizen-run body with no government participation at all, the IFE is a potent symbol of how the PRI began reforming itself under more democratically inclined leaders who began to remake the system during the 1990s. Mexico's Federal Electoral Institute has been hailed as a model of democracy by world bodies like the United Nations. In recent years the IFE has helped run elections from Haiti and Indonesia to Afghanistan and Iraq, monitoring the vote in sixty elections in more than twenty foreign countries. In Mexico's 2006 presidential election, each vote was counted by a committee of all five political parties, the results certified by computers that published a continuous count on the Internet.

The biggest difference of all was that in my presidency, we allowed—and encouraged—the opposition leftists to protest. No one stuck a gun in Andrés Manuel López Obrador's belly under my government. Instead we listened to his wild denunciations and let the courts decide, and the police protected his protesters along the Paseo de la Reforma—because in a democracy every vote is counted and every voice is heard.

There were no foreign election observers allowed in Mexico in 1988: Jimmy Carter came later, during our 2000 presidential campaign. When the PRI was forced by world opinion to allow observers from the opposition parties to watch the voting process, the regime ruled that election monitors would have to stay in place for twelve hours straight—or more—without food or even using the bathroom. Local elections officials would feed the observers poisoned tacos to make them sick. When they fled to the toilets, the elections judges barred the observers from reentering. This was the PRI's machine at work, as it crumbled into a not-so-perfect dictatorship.

All this we protested during late 1988, Mexico's own long hot summer, come twenty years late. When my turn came at the House tribunal that August, I demanded that Congress annul the very election results that had elected me, because they also had rigged outsize majorities from my district for the PRI's Salinas in the presidential race. Having seen my rebel allies gaveled down, I resolved to try a more flamboyant approach.

Not every forged ballot box in my district had been burned or buried in the House basement. We'd been careful to preserve cartons of forged PRI ballots as evidence, though possessing them in private hands was against the law. When the presiding officer called out the results for Guanajuato's District 3, I asked to be recognized. I came tromping up the aisle, this bearded farmer lugging two heavy bales of fraudulent votes. I stepped up to the podium with the PRI's forged ballots stuffed into my pockets, ballots under my shirt, ballots sifting from my hands to the House floor. As the TV cameras rolled to record the PRI's victory, I had two folded paper ballots sticking out of my ears, fashioned to mock the big jug ears of Mexico's fraudulently elected president Carlos Salinas.

The chamber erupted in laughter and raucous applause. Our backbenchers yipped the indigenous *yi-yi-yi* of the opposition amid the booing and catcalls of PRI loyalists. It was political street theater at its best: Mexicans are a fun-loving people; we enjoy a good carnival. My fellow congressmen brought more boxes of forged ballots to the podium, and I waved them about, scrubbed them under my arms, and threw the illegal ballots in the air, daring the authorities to violate the sanctuary of Congress and arrest me for possessing them.

It was a national sensation, and it put Vicente Fox on the map. Even the *priista* media couldn't hush up the spectacle of a young farmer from

Guanajuato, the traditional home of Mexican rebellion, tossing ballots in the air and wearing them as ears to reject the imperial presidency of Carlos Salinas de Gortari. My course was clear now: I set out to become public enemy number one for the new administration. In my head rang the advice of my forefathers: *Keep moving, keep striving.* There was the wise counsel of Clouthier: *Be more aggressive, Fox,* the hollow-cheeked crusader had told me from his little Gandhi hunger shack on the Reforma. *If the wolves can't catch you, they can't eat you.*

Finally we could delay the process no longer. We stormed the tribune, fought with our fists to take the podium, shoved and scrabbled like children playing king of the mountain. For twenty-four hours before the deadline, we lived on the House floor, not eating or sleeping, protesting with all our might. There were two camps in the PAN: the old-line *panistas* who believed democracy was *la brega de la eternidad,* "the work of eternity." They were good Catholics, doctrinaires who wanted to ban public nudity and hewed rigidly to the conservative ideology of the party's northern base. Generally the old-school *panistas* believed we should labor on through the parliamentary procedures and stay faithful to the party's principles, which had gotten us a record 17 percent of the national vote.

Then there were us Clouthier newcomers—farmers and businessmen, amateurs with no experience and less ideology, angry men and women of the humanist center. We wanted change *now,* today. Too impatient to await our rewards in heaven, men like the dark-skinned, mustachioed Rodolfo Elizondo, known as "El Negro" (later one of my top cabinet members), urged conservative party veterans like our House floor leader, Abel Vicencio, to lead us down to the basement of Congress and demand the ballots from the army. On the other side of the debate were men like Bernardo Bátiz, who became the PRD attorney general of Mexico City, doctrinaire veterans who believed that our crusade was missionary work and disliked our violent disruption of their saintly crusade.

But we weren't looking to be canonized. We wanted democracy now, in this life. I respected the conservatives for their principles—they had been in the struggle long before I had—while I was enjoying the good life at Coca-Cola, men like Abel Vicencio had been speaking out for change. But I never respected the old man so much as the moment when he looked us angry young men in the eyes and said, "Let's go get them!"

Which is how, on the day the PRI declared Carlos Salinas president,

I came to have the government's guns in my belly again in yet another Mexican standoff. This time it was army rifles, their bayonets fixed, ready to defend the locked door that hid all the secrets of the PRI's seventy-one years of electoral fraud. We linked arms behind Vicencio, with El Negro at his left, spoiling for a fight, Bátiz nowhere to be found—no doubt upstairs rolling his eyes at us amateurs and our uncouth ways. I stood to Abel's right, staring at the rifle barrels and wondering once again, *What the hell have I gotten myself into?*

"In the name of the nation, in the names of all Mexicans, we come to take these ballots upstairs and open them to eyes of the people!" shouted Abel in a steady, firm voice. "We demand that you let us pass!"

"Stand back!" replied the captain of the guard. "We have orders to protect the ballots. Stand clear!" Behind him in the crowded passageway, 150 soldiers stood at attention between the rebel congressmen and the storeroom, rifles on their shoulders.

"We demand that you let us pass!" Abel repeated.

"¡Listo!" shouted the captain of the guard, and the soldiers presented arms. Ready! The Army cocked their rifles. *"¡Apunten!"* Aim!

It was our moment of truth, a split-second decision that defined the course of Mexico's struggle for democracy. We did what any self-respecting advocates of civil disobedience would do when facing the loaded, cocked rifles of the army. We went back up the stairs and out into the cool air of Mexico City at midnight, found the nearest bar, got stinking drunk on tequila at the Hotel Bristol. And lived to fight another day.

BUT FINALLY Mexico was waking up from its long *somnífero*, the narcotic slumber of the PRI's perfect dictatorship. This is the great lesson of democratic revolution, relevant for those who would bring democracy to Iraq or Nigeria through a rifle barrel today: You can't hand democracy to a people on the point of a bayonet. You can't export it like American tractors on a USAID program. It must come from within. That is the great wisdom of King and Gandhi, Lech Walesa, Václav Havel, Nelson Mandela: Before you can change governments, you must change hearts.

This has been the democratic experience throughout the developing world of the late twentieth century. From Indonesia and the Philippines to Chile and Argentina, democracy came when people were fed up with the failures of their dictatorships—many of them, like that of Marcos in

Manila and Pinochet in Santiago, supported by the United States and the leaders of the so-called Free World. Democracy came not when foreign soldiers brought it in with their M16s but when homemakers and miners, rubber-plantation workers and store clerks faced the rifles of the dictatorship's army to march and speak and vote for change—people who dared to hope, in the face of fear.

Even had we held rifles and bayonets of our own in the basement of Congress that midnight—even if all the soldiers of the U.S. Army or the United Nations had been arrayed behind us, ready to shoot it out with the Mexican army in the basement, Mexico would not yet have been a democracy. We had tried our hands at revolution before: More than a million died from 1910 to 1917. The United States invaded, occupied Veracruz, sent Pershing's army to chase Villa across the desert. After all this blood and sacrifice, the revolutionaries just fought among themselves for power, bandits of the *villistas* and *carrancistas* squabbling over spoils like vultures picking at carrion.

This is what you see in Iraq today, as the dictatorship of one man is replaced by the tyranny of many violent factions. Rifles beget more rifles; bombs over Baghdad give birth to C-4 explosive in Fallujah. More women cry over the corpses of their babies; the only democracy is the equal opportunity of every innocent child to die in the crossfire.

There are ways the Free World can help, other than sending troops. Democracies can apply pressure from the outside: boycott an unjust economy, as the world did with South Africa; quarantine evil, as we should have done with a stricter global boycott of Iraq; demand united action by the UN Security Council, following the original concept of multilateral work for peace and democracy envisioned at Bretton Woods by the founders of the United Nations. But the experience of Latin America, Asia, Eastern Europe, and Africa over the last thirty years teaches us that nations like Mexico won't throw off the yoke of dictatorship until leaders within the society can move souls. The only lasting democracy is the one that comes from within.

The dirty secret of the world's authoritarian regimes is this: They exist because we *let* them exist. It is not that people inside the society are evil, but that an oppressed nation's people are forced by the government's power to *belong* to the System—and thus are party to its crimes, in hundreds of millions of little complicities. Like Iraq under Hussein's Baathist

Party, Germany under Nazism, or the Soviet Union under the Communists, people in Mexico didn't exactly hate the PRI—they *belonged* to the PRI. No matter how badly it failed them, no matter how it abused them, every citizen had a place in the national party. It was the state, the nation, the provider, the stern father figure. Sure, the PRI might have given you (as did my own father, from time to time) *un cuartazo en las petacas,* "a horsewhip to the seat of your pants." But our paternalist system also gave you everything you had.

"Don't take the taco!" we would cry, struggling to alert citizens that the PRI's green-and-red-wrapped treats contained this dangerous narcotic that had hypnotized the Mexican people for over seven decades. "Look at what they're doing to your lives!" But when you are hungry, you eat what is given, until the tacos grow smaller and there is no meat inside.

THIS IS where I came in, *el hijo desobediente,* the uncouth cowboy with muddy boots, the truck driver and Coca-Cola salesman who knew how to speak the language of everyday people. Remember, a key lesson for democratic revolutionaries is that you can't eat a principle. Dogma won't feed the pig. If we wanted to *mover las almas*—"move the souls"—of the people, first we would have to reach their stomachs.

This was my particular gift, my reward for all the mornings I'd spent milking cows, the long days selling soft drinks door-to-door in a khaki jumpsuit, the late nights drinking tequila with the Pepsi drivers before we spiked one another's tires at dawn. Within three days on the floor of Congress, I could see that there was nothing for me there, just more coffee drinking, more smoke-filled rooms occupied by men in suits who talked and talked and talked.

I left the dogma to my brethren in their political Vatican and went to do missionary work in the fields. Like the best revolution theologians, the shipyard electrician Walesa and the farmer Mandela, I aimed for the gut, not the head, the heart, not the brain.

"Why can't you afford milk for your babies?" I would rail as I campaigned to build the PAN, up and down the highways of Yucatán and Chihuahua. "Ladies, what are you willing to do to feed your children? Where is your anger, men?" I challenged. "Why don't we stand up, be real men? Let's fight what they are doing to your wives and children!"

With the ruling party calling the shots from the podium, there was little for me to do in Congress, so I hit the road to start building a grassroots base for our party in the next midterm elections in 1991 for Congress and the governorships of some key states. (In Mexico these are held at the halfway point of the six-year presidential election, although various states hold their gubernatorial elections in off-years, like Virginia or New Jersey—the result being that today in Mexico, as in the United States, there always seems to be an election going on.)

By locking opposition congressmen like me out of the legislative process, the ruling party once again inadvertently sowed the seeds of its own destruction: They left this bunch of angry amateurs with radically different ideologies outside the power structure, grumbling, with lots of free time on our hands to campaign in the countryside. We were like a disparate group of "uncool" kids in high school who'd been excluded by the ruling clique—the computer geeks, the hick farm kids, the parking-lot druggies, and the kids in the marching band. Like teenage outsiders, we united in our exclusion. Rejected by the insiders who ran the school, we became friends, left and right, united in the common cause of radical democratic change.

This is a syndrome one reads about in the works of the political scientist Samuel Huntington, the anti-immigrant scholar and outspoken defender of state parties in Latin America. Opposition parties, Huntington says, are just little boxes of ideology, left and right. But beneath these small boxes of their ideology is the underlying foundation of democratic anger that unites them, the substance of which is greater than the narrow confines of ideology, which divides them into the party boxes above the surface.

We all had been hurt by the System, suffered losses at the polls, in business, and in our personal lives. We had watched from the outside as the System drained and cheated and stole, its gigantic fraud masked by the Big Lie of the government-run election process. In the tradition of Mexican *conspiradores* like Father Hidalgo, we began meeting in secret to plot rebellion with a single goal: to get the PRI out of Los Pinos.

A historic step toward democracy in Mexico was the formation of the Grupo San Ángel, a band of democratic intellectuals, party leaders, congressmen, businessmen, farmers, and artists from widely divergent opposition factions—including young reform-minded upstarts within the PRI itself. In the former village of San Ángel, a quaint little colonial suburb of Mexico City that had been subsumed by the city's urban sprawl, the left's Cuauhtémoc Cárdenas and the right's Manuel Clouthier could meet behind closed doors to plot strategy for hunger strikes and protest rallies, even as they faced each other as presidential contenders of two parties that couldn't be further apart. It was at the Grupo San Ángel that I met leaders who would shape my presidency: Jorge Casteñeda, the former Communist and anti-NAFTA academic who would become my foreign minister; Santiago Creel, the Georgetown-educated law-school dean from a prominent family who would be my interior minister; women's-rights pioneers like Leticia Calzada Gómez, who became a diplomat in our administration; left-wing firebrands like Aldolfo Aguilar Zinser and Porfirio Muñoz Ledo, who became my ambassadors to the United Nations and the European Union, respectively. In the San Ángel meetings, too, was Andrés Manuel López Obrador, AMLO, the reckless agitator who set oil wells on fire to protest the PRI. In those days Andrés Manuel and I were on the same side; later, in 2000, AMLO won the mayor's race in Mexico City over San Ángel member Santiago Creel. Sadly, Andrés Manuel and my government were at cross-purposes from the day I was sworn in as president. But in the early 1990s, we were all friends at San Ángel, united by our intense, seething commitment to democracy.

Though I was new to politics, people in the opposition movement were already talking about the ranchero from Guanajuato who wore the paper ballots on his ears. Even the new president took note. I met Salinas once, on a half-hour bus ride from Irapuato to Celaya in my home state. It was a polite overture from the president, reaching out to try to calm down the opposition by granting me the honor of thirty minutes in the Presidential Presence. I never even spoke with him, just sat in the back of the bus and glowered, nourishing my anger. He was the enemy, the System. Our only focus was to get guys like him out of the presidential palace forever.

On October 1, 1989, I was out campaigning for the PAN in the neighboring state of Aguascalientes when an urgent phone call came: Manuel Clouthier was dead.

I scrambled to borrow a friend's small plane and rushed to the scene of the accident outside of Culiacán. There on the flat plains, on a straight ribbon of highway, a truck had inexplicably crossed the center line and run head-on into the car carrying my idol, killing Manuel and his cold-sober driver instantly on impact.

I walked the accident scene, knelt amid the shattered glass and the tire marks. I saw the car seats, spattered with the blood of a presidential candidate I worshipped. The truck driver survived the crash to face intensive interrogation. The police ransacked every detail of his past. Many believed that Manuel had been assassinated for his political beliefs: Was the trucker a hired killer, paid by the government to silence Clouthier? If so, it seemed a dangerous way to make a living. The technicians found no evidence to support the assassination theory; analysis of the crime scene indicated that the trucker had simply drifted across into the oncoming traffic. There was no evidence to support the rumors that the PRI had somehow tampered with the brakes in Manuel's car.

In the absence of evidence to the contrary, I am inclined to give people the benefit of the doubt. We held a candlelight vigil that night in Culiacán and buried my friend the next day. I poured my grief into action, determined to realize Clouthier's dream. Manuel was a devout Catholic. He would have wanted us to seek not revenge but hope.

CHAPTER 8

MY SCHWARZENEGGER PROBLEM

As EARLY AS my short stint in Congress in 1988–90, there were a few scattered leaders of the democracy movement who thought that an earthy, regular guy like me might be the type who could rally antigovernment forces of left and right to kick the PRI out of Los Pinos. But for my friends to dream of a Fox presidential campaign, there was at least one huge barrier: The Constitution said that I wasn't Mexican enough.

Shaped by our history of invasion by the Spanish, the French, and the Americans, the Mexican Constitution was written in 1917 by nationalists who feared foreign influence—above all they worried about domination by tall, light-skinned, European-blooded descendants of suspect ancestry. So they went one step further than the United States Constitution, which bars immigrants like Arnold Schwarzenegger or Madeleine Albright from the presidency. The Mexican Constitution required that your bloodlines must be pure: Both of a presidential candidate's parents had to be born in Mexico.

My mother had been born in Spain, during one of my grandparents' trips home to import groceries. In fact, all four of my grandparents contrived to be born under politically incorrect circumstances: The Foxes, Quesadas, and Ponts hailed from the very nations most hated by the revolutionary culture of the PRI. The United States had invaded all the way to Mexico City and seized a third of our national territory. Spain, land of the conquistadores, subjugated our ancient Mayans and Aztecs. There was even a French soldier in the family woodpile, who had come with Maximilian's army to marry my one indigenous ancestor.

One lonely Indian great-grandmother would not qualify. If I wanted to run for president, we would have to change Article 82 of the Mexican Constitution.

SO, EARLY IN my political career, I came face-to-face with the core question of the immigration debate: What does it mean to be an American, and what does it mean to be a Mexican? Is it to be blond, tall, and Saxon of blood—or short, swarthy, and Mayan? Are you British if you speak the English language, pray in the Anglican Church, and were born in Surrey—but somehow less than British if your parents were dark-skinned Muslims from Pakistan? Is nationhood a matter of the accident of where you are born, or is what you *are,* what you believe, the values of your culture?

I was Mexican to the core, born and raised on a ranch in the traditional Bajío, the most Mexican place in Mexico. I spoke only Spanish until I was banished to Wisconsin for a year. I then came back to Mexico and spent the rest of my life here. But in the eyes of the law, Vicente Fox was somehow not Mexican enough to be president.

This is still a question for our democracies in the twenty-first century. The Americas, of course, are a hemisphere built by immigration: Both the United States and Mexico were built by pioneers, slaves, Indians, and indentured workers; so were Peru, Brazil, and Argentina. So what does it mean when we say newcomers must "assimilate" and become Americans, Mexicans, or Brazilians? It is strange, this xenophobic demand that all must "assimilate to the mainstream" of a culture, when the mainstream is not one homogeneous, uniracial whole but a diverse tapestry of multihued threads. How does one become "truly Brazilian" when 200,000 of the nation's population are of Japanese and Asian descent, when more than 62 million Brazilians descend from African slaves? Is it Brazilian to trace your ancestors to Lisbon and speak Portugese, or is it that you live in Salvador or Rio de Janeiro, drink *cachaça* rum and dance the samba? Is an American one whose parents and grandparents happened to be born on U.S. soil? Or is an American any immigrant who lives and works to build the society, follows its laws and pays its taxes, and yearns to breathe the free air of the American dream?

For me it was Mexican enough to be born in Mexico City, from whence my mother rushed me home to "cut the umbilical cord at the farm" at Rancho San Cristóbal, to obey the nation's laws and customs, to eat tacos and sing *corridos,* to pay the nation's taxes, raise my children as Mexicans, work the land of my fathers, study at our country's schools, work to export our country's products, and create jobs for my neighbors. Wasn't this enough to be Mexican? Or did both of my parents have to be born here, too?

This is an issue that faces even the most homogeneous nations of Europe or Asia today. The Netherlands and France watch uneasily as nearly a third of their citizens are now Muslims and Africans, born of origins in their former colonies. As the great economies of the planet demand more and more labor from poorer neighbors, among today's rich democracies only Japan even approaches the ethnic homogeneity we once associated with countries like Germany or Britain. This creates huge economic and social unease, as France rejects the European Constitution for fear of Polish plumbers who will work more than thirty-two hours a week for competitive wages and rails against Muslim parents who wrap a traditional head scarf to cover the hair of their daughters in a Paris schoolroom.

In this great explosion of globalism, the Americas have the advantage. We are used to integrating the distinct colors and accents of different cultures into our fabulous mosaics; immigration is not just a fact for us, it is *the* central fact of American history, the driving force of the United States, Canada, Mexico, and the hemisphere. The day America loses its ability to tolerate this diversity, the day our hemisphere fails to foster this immigrant hunger for success, this is the day we say good-bye to the American dream.

For much of the twentieth century, Carlos Fuentes and Octavio Paz were the leading lights of the Latin American intelligentsia. These two brilliant men are artists and thinkers of the first order, outspoken writers and true advocates of freedom whose fearless voices of dissent were tolerated by the regime, given the luster of the Nobel Prize that Paz had won for literature and the global praise for Fuentes as a novelist. Part of the genius of the PRI was to cultivate Mexican academia; it was this patina of democracy that made the dictatorship truly "perfect." But men like Paz and Fuentes could see through the flimsy intellectual drapery of the PRI, and so it was to men like Octavio Paz and Carlos Fuentes that I went to ask for help on Article 82.

If I led the drive in Congress to repeal the restriction on presidential bloodlines, we would fail. There was no way a PRI-dominated Congress would make it easier for the PAN's mad bearded farmer of Guanajuato to kick them out of Los Pinos. But if we could position the constitutional amendment on higher ground and sell it to the government as a democratic reform—as a sop to world opinion and the growing power of the opposition parties—perhaps Salinas could be persuaded to give in.

Like a Coca-Cola salesman looking for new grocery stores, I made a list of prospects—congressmen, artists, intellectuals, business leaders, the men and women I was coming to know through the Grupo San Ángel. I went first to the poet Paz.

"Of course I will help you," the aging Nobel laureate agreed. "It is a matter of democratic principle, of equality and social justice. Where your parents were born cannot govern your right to participate in the political process, or the people's right to choose."

Carlos Fuentes's wife, Silvia Lemus, took my case as a personal crusade. Soon we had backers from left and right as I worked my way down the routes of dissent, selling the brand of democracy. We enlisted Diego Fernández de Cevallos, another bearded revolutionary from the PAN who had his eye on the presidency himself. A conservative lawyer who would debate brilliantly as our party's candidate in 1994, Diego put aside his personal ambitions to come up with a smart strategy on Article 82: We should recruit the supporters of ambitious would-be PRI presidents who were in the same boat. Some key leaders of the System had foreign-born parents; wouldn't they lean on their friends in the Congress and Los Pinos to help?

It worked. Carlos Hank González was one of the nation's wealthiest businessmen, a powerful *priista* cabinet member and governor who lusted for the presidency—but his father had been born in Germany. Another rising young PRI technocrat, Andres de Oteiza, held the high-profile post of comptroller and might be in line for a future *dedazo*—but he was of Spanish ancestry. As Samuel Huntington writes, in politics opposites often attract, drawn together by the magnet of exclusion. Together this unlikely band of poets and farmers, insiders and outsiders, joined to overturn Article 82. Ironically, my old nemesis President Salinas, his arm having been twisted by dinosaurs and technocrats within the PRI, signed the amendment into law—unwittingly paving the way for me to wrest the presidency away from the official party in 2000.

If wearing Salinas's ears brought me to national attention, our success in repealing Article 82 really started tongues wagging. Bored in the PRI's rubber-stamp Congress, I accepted every invitation to speak; where

I wasn't invited, I went anyway, anyplace two or more of the disgruntled were gathered. With my earthy insults that so delighted the increasingly anti-Salinas crowds, I was a popular speaker on the opposition-party circuit. But no one took me too seriously: How could this amateur be a threat to the mighty PRI? The official party still controlled everything said or heard on TV or radio. Even as our rallies grew angrier and bigger, the government made sure that no one heard the tree falling in the forest.

So we went around the media, building our own door-to-door marketing campaign based on my experience at Coca-Cola. Our movement didn't have the money or the media access for the "push-pull" marketing formula of Fortune 500 giants like Coke and Procter & Gamble, which combine the "pull" of ad-driven consumer demand with the "push" of sales at the route-truck level. So we concentrated on the "push," recruiting our own sales network of grassroots citizens who were fed up with the PRI's failures. I also aimed straight at the source of power in the media: El Tigre, Emilio Azcárraga, the *priista* billionaire who controlled Mexican broadcasting with his powerful Televisa network. We staged mass protests against Televisa's refusal to air the opposition parties. Marching gagged along the boulevards of the big cities, we called on citizens to boycott their favorite *telenovela* soap operas and soccer games. Our banners urged consumers to cease buying the brand-name products advertised on Azcárraga's state-controlled networks—P&G soaps, Mexico's major banks and department stores, even Coca-Cola (to the dismay of my former employers). Then I went to see El Tigre.

By now I was a well-known troublemaker who had cultivated my own brand image as a tough guy who shot from the lip. Together we came to a meeting of the minds, Azcárraga the soldier of the PRI and Fox the PAN rebel: I would stop bashing his network with his best audience if he would cover opposition protests on his network. El Tigre may not have seen the light, but at least he felt the heat.

Soon all eyes turned to the 1991 midterm congressional elections and a series of staggered by-elections for the governorships of key states to be held in 1991 and 1992, midway through President Salinas's six-year term. On August 18, 1991, Mexico elected our nation's first opposition governor, the PAN's Ernesto Ruffo in Baja California. In 1992 the focus was on Guanajuato, cradle of Mexican liberty, where the PAN gubernatorial candidate would be the angry rancher and former Coca-Cola CEO Vicente Fox, selling the brand of democracy like cold *aguas frescas* on a hot summer day.

IT WAS about this time that Lilián left me for another man.

Unless it has happened to you, you cannot imagine how it feels to come home to an empty house, where the person you love has left you forever. You think first of your children, still happily ignorant as they play in the yard. But soon they will come inside to ask a question rarely heard in a Mexican home: Where is my mother?

In times of trouble, the human personality rises to its highest capacity. Consider that darkest figure of my youth, Richard Nixon, who wrote about this syndrome after his defeat by one of my heroes, John F. Kennedy. We didn't think much of this Nixon in our part of the world; he had been attacked by mobs when he toured Latin America as Eisenhower's vice president. But I read and prayed and studied widely in those dark days, from the Bible to self-help authors to the tales of the mighty and the fallen. I had been fascinated since childhood with the healing power of faith and the wisdom of those who had overcome great challenges. Certainly no case was stranger than that of Richard Milhous Nixon.

The son of an angry, abusive father and a strict Quaker mother, he grew up dirt poor and obscure on a lemon ranch in California, lost two brothers to tuberculosis, then endured one humiliating defeat after another to become the world's most powerful leader. In 1962's *Six Crises,* Nixon shows that we go through life operating at less than half of full capacity. We never learn that you have another 50 percent to give until you are seriously challenged by crisis. This alerts our systems: Suddenly you are stronger, smarter, more disciplined, like the mother whose child is trapped beneath the wreckage of a truck, as adrenaline gives her the burst of power to lift the tire free. Only when we are fully immersed in challenge can we forget our weaknesses and our fears and summon the courage, stamina, and strength to overcome all obstacles. The opposite also is true, as Nixon's own downfall later proved: The moment of our greatest success, when times are good and we are flying high, is often the moment of greatest danger. It is then that we relax, overreach, and make terrible mistakes.

It is an oddly prophetic book, considering how Nixon was forced to resign by the Watergate scandal after winning a landslide reelection in

1972. But his book made a curious sense to me when I stumbled across it in the late 1980s. It was then that I learned, in the face of great adversity, the key to solving problems is to tackle even more of these challenges. You must challenge yourself to new heights, make yourself so busy climbing the next peak that today's hill does not loom as high. In this way you can rise above great troubles, crisis to crisis, challenge to challenge, to the mountaintop.

It was the toughest time I have ever known. Suddenly I was a single father with four children, two girls eleven and nine years old, two boys of eight and three. My wife had fallen in love with somebody else and left us to fend without her. Our family business was still in trouble. The country was in economic crisis. I had chosen this moment to launch an opposition candidacy for governor in a state where the PRI had controlled the government for the better part of a century. And my name was moving up to the head of the government's blacklist.

So I plunged myself into a custody battle in the courts, a business battle to save the farm, and a democracy battle on the streets. I had seen the American film *Kramer vs. Kramer,* in which Meryl Streep plays a wife who leaves Dustin Hoffman's character, so that he must raise his little boy alone. Watching Hoffman's young father evolve from a typical Madison Avenue executive to master the intricacies of fixing French toast as he finds a new job and rebuilds a life for the two of them—that film showed me that a father could be a mother, too.

Not trusting Hollywood alone, I went to my wise school friend, the banker Roberto Hernández. Now one of Mexico's wealthiest men, Roberto had undergone a painful divorce three years before. He told me that the most important thing for children is a stable home, where they will feel warm and comfortable, not shuttling back and forth in a tug of war between father and mother. I resolved to fight for the right to keep the children. Even though Lilián had abandoned us, Mexican law explicitly favors the mother in custody cases: It is almost impossible for a divorced father to keep the kids. But wisdom prevailed. We worked it out so the children remained with me at San Cristóbal.

I had learned some hard lessons in the failure of my marriage. Most of all I learned that of many wrong things you could do in marriage, the worst by far is staying silent. So instead of pouring energy into a nasty custody fight—as so often happens in these cases, where couples vie to hurt each other in the eyes of their children, looking for villains where generally are found only former loved ones, angry and in pain—I poured myself into love. Every waking hour I could find, I spent loving Ana Cristina, Paulina, Vicente, and little Rodrigo. I made sure I was there to take them to school and pick them up, have dinner and help with their homework. My mother was a pillar as always, a force of unity keeping the family together. My brothers were lions in the battle to defend our business. My sister Mercedes stood by me on the protest lines, fighting for democracy. Through it all, my four kids and I spent hours fishing and playing games together, driving to the beach and going on camping trips and once to Disneyland, even as this historic election campaign for the Guanajuato governorship raged about us.

The ruling party mounted a nasty whisper campaign to attack my marital separation. "Fox can't even handle his own wife," they mocked. "How can he handle the government?"

In response we had only our passion. In place of advertising budgets, we had the "brand separation" that the Harvard marketing professors preach: a unique image that differentiated our product from the opposition. I branded myself with cowboy boots from our factory and a big silver FOX belt buckle, the language of the barnyard and the neighborhood tavern, the Cristero faith of a true believer.

Like our campaign of three years before, our gubernatorial drive took on a religious fervor as I waved the banner of the Virgin, calling on Mexicans to rise up for freedom with tears in my eyes and anger in my voice. By then I had been through a great deal—armed threats and business reversals, adoptions and divorce. I had learned that at every time of struggle, love will show you the way, that even in Mexico a man doesn't have to be afraid to show his emotions, that if you can open your heart to those you love, they will open their arms to you. So together we shouted and cried and laughed and swore at the authorities, me and my little team of amateurs, as we moved souls by talking to the stomach, the spirit, and the heart. My children came with me now on the campaign trail; some of the best times we had were on long bus rides up twisty mountain roads to some ancient town square. Crowds cheered when little Paulina came up to hand me the banner of the Virgin of Guadalupe at one rally. I was surprised: It was just a spontaneous impulse from behind the stage. (I strongly suspect my sister Mercedes, as she usually is the one who starts trouble in our family.) There was an audible hush; the government didn't allow displays of religion at rallies of the PRI. Then the cheering began, people broke into a hymn. I cried tears of pride on the outside and tears of joy within, knowing that with this passion, we would surely win.

And we did. A vast sea of men in muddy boots coursed into the polling stations that July morning—and women in peasant blouses of *panista* blue, for women always seemed to be the first to wake up to what the PRI had been doing to their families. Our polls showed us well ahead going into Election Day. All we needed was to win by a cushion of 5 or 10 percent, so the PRI couldn't steal it.

The official party pulled every trick in the playbook: the vote tortilla, one ballot wrapped around ten forged ones; polling stations that never opened in our urban strongholds; polling stations that we didn't even know existed in the rural areas; government checks written out to buy votes. When the last forged PRI ballot was counted by the regime's extraordinary computers and the last PAN ballot was swept into the trash by their corrupt election judges, the PRI claimed they had won with more than 70 percent.

As with the Salinas fraud in 1988, the official party had overreached. Everyone in Mexico knew that Vicente Fox had been elected governor of Guanajuato. Had the PRI claimed a 51 percent squeaker, perhaps people might have shrugged and said, "Well, that's the way things work in Mexico." Instead the brazenness of the regime angered voters, and they erupted in protest. I kept the focus on me and Salinas, personally: mano a mano, another cowboy standoff on Main Street. Now the media was watching, too, a few courageous eyes peeping from the windows above. Most of television and radio still was roped off to us, but perhaps a third of the news programs would cover our protests. We seized the international airport outside León and occupied the government buildings, my troublemaking sister Mercedes beside me with her battalion of middle-class housewives and rural campesinos, walking slowly, ever so slowly. Soon, all across Mexico, the traffic ground to a halt and the nation dug in its heels in silent rebellion.

Salinas blinked.

Feeling the eyes of the country and the world on him, self-conscious about his own fraudulent election back in 1988, Salinas was by then an aspiring world statesman. He was in the midst of negotiating the NAFTA accords with President George H. W. Bush and Canadian prime minister Brian Mulroney. They would initial the treaty in San Antonio on October 7, 1992, then sign the NAFTA accord on December 17 in highly publicized ceremonies in Mexico City, Washington, and Ottawa. Amid sensitive treaty talks and a hard-fought U.S. presidential election—in which Ross Perot predicted that NAFTA would create a "giant sucking sound" of jobs leaving for Mexico—the last thing Salinas needed was a fight with some cowboy over the governorship of a small state in central Mexico, raising questions about whether his government was corrupt and undemocratic. Under pressure in the face of massive evidence of fraud in Guanajuato, Salinas folded. The president reluctantly agreed to annul the results of the election and sacrificed his pawn, the new PRI governor Ramón Aguirre, to the greater game. (Governor Aguirre, of course, caught the next plane to Europe and didn't surface again until 2003, when he lost a race for Congress as a candidate of the PRI.) The compromise: The government would throw out the results of my election and name a new interim governor from the PAN for the next three years—not me but my friend Carlos Medina, the mayor of León. I called Carlos in Miami, where he was on a business trip.

"You have to come home," I said. "You're going to be named governor."

"You're kidding," he said. "Have you been drinking, Vicente?"

"Salinas caved," I explained. "Get on the next plane to Mexico. You're going to be the first opposition governor of our state in history, and I'm going back to my farm."

THREE YEARS LATER Mercedes stormed into the vegetable-freezing plant. I was back at work getting the broccoli packed to ship to McAllen. Behind her stood more than a hundred campesinos and lots of women, angry women wearing PAN blue.

Like most men, I live in fear of angry women. I looked for the fire exit.

"You're not going anywhere," Mercedes said. "We are staying until you agree to run for the governorship again."

"I've done my thing," I explained firmly. "The kids are getting older, and our business is still struggling. I can't possibly go back into politics."

"Whine, whine, whine," she said, crossing her arms in defiance.

Our newfound converts of the PAN elbowed in between the vegetable bins. "You got us into this!" they accused. "How can you desert us now?"

It was 1994, the year that Mexico teetered at the brink of collapse. The PRI's presidential candidate, reformer Luis Donaldo Colosio, was assassinated on March 23. On September 28, the party's general secretary, José Francisco Ruiz Massieu, was gunned down on the streets of Mexico City. The president's own brother, Raúl Salinas, eventually was arrested and tried for engineering the Massieu murder. Though Raúl was acquitted in the murder case, his wife was arrested in Switzerland withdrawing funds from secret accounts, widely reported to hold well more than $100 million, which may have been bilked from the national treasury or taken in bribes from the cartels. Salinas denies the charges, but they remain the subject of widespread suspicion and intense investigation.

Meanwhile the nation's debts continued to mount. Salinas's bold move to throw the nation's markets wide open with NAFTA riled the nation's protectionist business elite into panic. The peso was on shiftier soil than ever. And by year's end, *zapatista* rebels under the ski-masked Subcomandante Marcos would start shooting soldiers in the jungles of Chiapas, crying, "*¡Tierra y libertad!*" in a bid to spark a new Mexican Revolution.

It was a bad time for a single dad to leave the family business.

"Get comfortable," Mercedes assured me. Her supporters clamored to be heard among the stainless steel and the cauliflower. "We're going to be here all night."

We argued for hours until I bowed to the inevitable. "I'll help with the kids, and so will Mom," Mercedes said. Her fist pounded the table, a sergeant marshaling her troops. "The brothers will run the business, and you will run for governor."

Shit, I thought. *I'm back in politics.*

SIX MONTHS LATER I was governor of Guanajuato, in a landslide this time, a victory even Carlos Salinas couldn't steal. Ernesto Zedillo took office as the nation's new president. The mild-mannered, bespectacled economist was an unknown quantity, the PRI's last-minute replacement after Colosio was killed. Our Constitution requires that presidential candidates must resign any previous office six months before nomination. When the PRI's reform-minded presidential nominee was murdered, Mexico's top cabinet members, governors, and senators were forbidden by law from taking his place. So it fell to Zedillo, because he was available—he had left the government to manage Colosio's campaign. In his first address to the nation as president that December, Ernesto Zedillo seemed blindsided, the proverbial deer blinking in the headlines, as Mexico's economy wavered on the edge of collapse.

Four weeks later, on New Year's Eve, a panic broke out on Wall Street and in the financial markets of London and Geneva, Mexico City and Tokyo: Mexico couldn't pay its debts and was about to default on its loans. The government devalued the peso, and Mexican families watched more than half their life savings wiped out overnight. Within forty-eight hours, shots rang out in the jungle, and the government sent tanks to Chiapas. Mexico was suddenly in economic free fall, its leaders assassinated, its once-perfect dictatorship facing a violent *zapatista* uprising.

And thanks to my hotheaded sister, I had just been sworn in as governor.

CHAPTER 9

THE WINDSHIELD COWBOY

I FIRST MET George W. Bush in Austin in 1996. We were both newly minted governors. He was the son of the U.S. president and elder statesman who had negotiated the NAFTA accords with Salinas, opening our economy to the world market. I was the son of a Mexican farmer and the grandson of an American pioneer. Much has been made of the friendship we shared later, trading boots and cowboys hats in Dallas, attending church in Quebec and rallies in Ohio, sharing stories of our outspoken mothers on our family ranches in San Cristóbal and Crawford. But George Bush didn't have a ranch in those days. Even now George will be the first to admit that he's a "windshield cowboy," more comfortable driving his pickup truck around Crawford than he is on the back of a horse. (I learned this later at San Cristóbal, when I offered to let George ride my beloved horse Dos de Julio. He demurred, backing away from the big palomino. A horse lover can always tell when others don't share our passion for climbing aboard an animal that weighs five hundred pounds and doesn't necessarily stop when you put on the brakes.)

On March 19, 1996, we sat in the governor's office beneath the pink and brown stone of the Texas capitol, surrounded by bookshelves notably bereft of the usual politician's brag wall of photos of himself with world leaders, celebrities, and other politicians. Instead there was baseball memorabilia: bats, balls, caps, helmets from George's past as a baseball player at Yale and managing partner of the Texas Rangers. We talked about American sports: I think he was surprised to find a Mexican governor who understood the infield-fly rule and had caught touchdowns in Wisconsin.

I was certainly surprised by George W. Bush. My expectations were different. He didn't fit the cold, uncaring picture we foreigners often have of

Republicans. When it comes to free markets and fiscal discipline, I suppose I would side with Republicans, but, like most people in Mexico, I'm somewhere well to the left of the Democratic Party when it comes to social justice. On issues like universal health care, antipoverty programs, education funding, and narrowing the gap between rich and poor, I was really more of an admirer of Bill Clinton, who had defeated Bush's father, then helped Mexico out of the devaluation crisis after Salinas's sudden departure for exile in Europe.

In Latin America and so much of the world, we've always felt a special kinship with warm, charismatic Democrats like Kennedy, Carter, and Clinton. They seem to us what we call *sencillo,* which is one of those uniquely Latin words you can't quite translate into English. It is to be compassionate, humble, loving, caring, sensitive, able to shoulder the burdens of another's soul.

Because I knew Bush only as a Republican oilman from conservative Texas, I didn't expect that kind of warmth. I certainly didn't think he'd care much about the concerns of a Mexican politician for the immigrant workers of Texas.

"¡Hola, amigo!" He jumped up to greet me as an old friend, anxious to show off the Spanish he was speed-learning as governor. Bush has a strangely erect way of holding his shoulders, like an athlete poised for action; he holds his arms away from his frame, biceps clenched, as though he has just stepped out of the weight room. His critics on late-night television mock this stance, but in person the effect is of a man taller than Bush really is—full of energy, self-assurance, and a tremendous eagerness to get on with the business at hand. For me, a guy with Grandfather Fox's "bug up my ass," Bush evokes the go-getter qualities I've always admired in Americans. He reminded me of the brash Coca-Cola execs from Atlanta or the friendly, boisterous Texans who used to buy our carrots and onions on the streets of McAllen. Famously, Bush defended his physical confidence in an address to the 2004 Republican Convention when he said, "Some folks look at me and see a certain swagger, which in Texas is called 'walking.'"

In any case, my first impression of George W. Bush was one of total self-confidence. He is, quite simply the cockiest guy I have ever met in my life. *"¿Cómo estás, amigo?"* he said, a bit sheepish as he tried out his grade-school-level Spanish.

"Muy bien, gracias," I said. We switched easily into English, from time to time sprinkling a few words of Tex-Mex Spanglish into the conversation to keep things cordial. It's not as superficial as it sounds, this occasional nod from a U.S. politician to the Latino roots of his border-state population or the use of a Spanish pleasantry by an American business associate or a gringo tourist in Puerto Vallarta. To us it means that you care, that you respect our culture, that you don't automatically expect the rest of the world to speak English whenever we are in your presence.

This is *sencillo*.

So my first surprise was to find in George W. Bush this cultural sensitivity, together with a depth of knowledge about Mexican immigrants and a real compassion for the Latino citizens who lived, worked, prayed, and voted in his state. With Bush this goes well beyond political practicality, but in any case Latino voters respond to him: Hispanics gave him a record majority of their votes in the 1998 race for governor; some 40 percent would back him in the 2000 presidential election, unusual for a Republican.

That day in his office, and on several other visits to Austin, Bush spoke earnestly about growing up among our people in Texas. He had worked with Mexicans and U.S. Latinos in the oil fields of Midland, in baseball, and in the business world of Dallas, and his family had close ties to Mexico, given his father's leadership on NAFTA.

Unlike many Americans, Bush knows the fine-grained legal and cultural differences between Mexican Americans and Mexican citizens. In contrast to many on his party's right wing, he considers both to be human beings of equal worth in the eyes of God. "All this English-only stuff, that Proposition 187 they're doing out in California." He shook his head dismissively at fellow Republican governor Pete Wilson's immigrant-bashing initiative to deny benefits of education and health care to the children of immigrants—who, after all, had done much of the manual labor to build the schools and hospitals of California. "We're not having any of that here in Texas."

This was refreshing. Guanajuato was a poor rural state that had lost an outsize proportion of its population to Texas. Documented or undocumented, virtually all of them were employed, devoutly religious, law-abiding, family-oriented, peaceful, and producing huge value to the U.S. economy. I had grown up with these people. Since my election as governor,

I'd made it a point to visit our emigrants when I came to the United States, whether it was in the hotel kitchens of Austin or the lettuce fields of Fresno.

These workers were as surprised to see me as I was to find a friend of Mexico in the Texas governor's office. Perhaps because I'd been both a farmhand and a busboy myself, I'd always felt close to our migrant workers in the States. As president I would appall many in Mexico by referring to departed emigrants as *mis queridos paisanos,* "my dear countrymen." Mexican society looked down on those who left, considering them exiles of the lowest class who had irrevocably "lost caste" by turning their backs on the land of their birth. If the government had acknowledged the existence of these economic refugees, it would have been acknowledging its failures. When Latinos dared to come home to see their families for Christmas, they faced the corruption of our border guards, who rifled through their luggage and stole the clock radios they had bought with ten dollars scraped from their minimum-wage jobs in meatpacking plants in Chicago. Returning emigrants also faced the hostility of our citizens, who sneered at their broken Spanish grammar, their fancy colored T-shirts with the logos of NBA teams, their nouveau riche American airs. When they returned to the United States, even if they had U.S. passports or green cards, they had to face another shakedown by our own border police, then the hostility of the U.S. border guards, and sometimes brutal local sheriffs: They might be beaten, jailed, or, if they were lucky, merely humiliated in front of their children—all for the crime of paying their mother a visit in Guanajuato.

I wanted to change this, or at least as much of it as I could as a mere governor. Part of my affinity stemmed from the knowledge that my own forefathers were migrant workers, too. When my grandfather rode south through Texas to find his fortune—half a century before George W. Bush's father came there from New England in search of oil—Joseph Fox crossed the Rio Grande into Mexico and met the first great wave of *guanajuatenses* coming the other way, north to the Texas oil fields, the grape harvest in California, the factory floors of Chicago and Detroit. I had seen their poverty and abuse firsthand as a high-school student in the upper Midwest: I would never forget my first trip to visit the Mexican slums along Twenty-sixth Street on Chicago's West Side, where I witnessed some of the bleakest poverty and human-rights abuse I had ever seen. There, just a few hours' drive from the picturesque snowy affluence of small-town Wisconsin, a world apart from the warm sun of Rancho San Cristóbal, I saw the reality of where my childhood playmates had really gone—more Hades than limbo, cardboard shacks whose inhabitants shivered amid the gray slush. These men and women got by on a dollar or two an hour—no pioneers making their fortunes, as George H. W. Bush and Joseph Louis Fox had done, no welfare seekers like those the California talk-show hosts decry, only desperately poor working people spending 100 percent of everything they can earn just to live among the trash on the streets and the raw sewage in the gutters. Chicago was nothing like the sunny, friendly streets of McAllen, where a Mexican boy selling onions and buying pigs traded on equal terms with his Texas neighbors. In the upper Midwest, the immigrants who had come before us, the Polish and the Irish and the Italians and the Germans, looked down on the "filthy Mexicans" and kept my *paisanos* from Guanajuato in the slums, where they worked three jobs night and day to save the extra five- or ten-dollar bill they put in the envelopes to their mothers in Mexico. Often the money found its way into the pocket of the local *priista* postman. If the immigrant decided to play it safe and wire the money home, then he had to cash his check at the corner liquor store, where they didn't ask for ID but charged you 20 percent. Then they went to Western Union, who took another 19 percent. Soon you had paid up to 40 percent for your hard-earned money, worse than the vig charged by the mob.

Even as a callow teenager, I felt for these people, as my Wisconsin Jesuit teachers preached the creed of "men for others," but the wealthy American boys looked down on the "spic" washing dishes in the school cafeteria. I knew how it felt to be ignored and maltreated. But I was just a homesick schoolboy, busing tables and feeling sorry for myself. How must it feel for immigrants in Bakersfield and Charlotte, when they come home from the vegetable fields and textile plants of the world's most productive economy to a sick child they cannot afford to take to the doctor? They know that even if they can afford to pay, someone will ask for their names and may turn them over to the authorities for deportation. How must if feel for the Mexican American father, a Marine Corps veteran of the Vietnam War, who is spread-eagled across the hood of his car by the Border Patrol while his children watch from the backseat, wide-eyed with fear?

Unlike my predecessors, I came to office determined to bring the immigrant out of the shadows of public policy, both in the United States and in Mexico. So was Governor Bush. Traditionally, U.S. politicians didn't care much about Mexican immigrants, because the undocumented could not vote and their descendants often did not turn out on Election Day—but this was changing, rapidly. Today Latinos are 15 percent of the U.S. population and a key swing vote in U.S. elections. They accounted for fully half the population growth of the United States of America between 2000 and 2004. Mexican Americans are valued consumers of major corporations, important viewers of TV networks, powerful influences on music and culture, people who elect American presidents and fight America's wars. But since none of them could vote in Mexico (not even the undocumented, who remain Mexican citizens), their plight mattered little to most Mexican politicians. Good-bye and good riddance, they thought. For the PRI, immigration was the escape valve on the pressure cooker, venting off the steam of economic frustration by sending the poorest, angriest, and most disenfranchised of our people to the other side of the river.

That was how the families of Guanajuato talked about immigration: *Mi hijo se fue al otro lado,* "My son has gone to the other side"—as though your child were dead. For many mothers of emigrants, their sons and daughters might as well be in the grave, for they will never see them again. Kids leave their homes with the clothes on their back, crawl through the muddy river, and slither beneath the barbed wire under the guns of the Border Patrol, never to return. The human-smuggling ferryman of this Styx might be a *coyote* who will leave them in the desert to die of thirst or exposure in the unexpected cold of an Arizona night. At least four hundred immigrants die every year crossing the border, just for the sin of wanting to work for better lives.

Once in the United States, the average immigrant will pay about $80,000 more in taxes than he or she ever collects in government services, a $50 billion surplus to the U.S. government. In George W. Bush's home state alone, the Texas comptroller's office certifies that Mexican immigrants pay $500 million more in state taxes than they take out.

But immigrants are not people in the eyes of the law. When they cross to the other side, they enter a strange limbo of nonhumanity. They live like ghosts. This is 12 *million* people in America, sons and daughters, fathers and mothers, husbands and wives. But no one even really sees them—

working in the fields, building houses for the affluent families of El Norte, picking the fresh strawberries to place atop their breakfast cereal, cleaning the plates of wealthy diners in restaurants and the human waste of retired senior citizens in nursing homes. They are almost never acknowledged, rarely spoken to, their foreign language reviled, their dark faces held solemnly downcast. They are phantoms in the shadows of prosperity.

I came to George Bush's office determined to do something for them in Texas, where more *guanjuatenses* live than in any other state. Nearly a million of my constituents lived in Dallas–Fort Worth and Houston alone; by the time I came to office, more than a third of the population of Guanajuato, nearly 2 million of our citizens, worked in the United States and Canada. I was their governor, too.

This concept is controversial: I would later raise hackles by claiming to be the president not only of more than 100 million citizens of Mexico, but also the 12 million Mexicans who work in the United States, Canada, and elsewhere. They still cherished their tacos and chiles, prayed to the Virgin of Guadalupe, sent money home to Guanajuato to build houses for mothers who wept for them at night. America is lucky to have them, because they still cherish the core human values that built our continent: hard work, faith in God, a hunger to better their families, real hope for the American dream. My job was to try to build a better economy for them in Guanajuato—I believe that, like Ireland, Mexico must bring our people back, give our youth a future, and keep our families home.

I found an unlikely ally in the Capitol of the beautiful Texas hill country on that spring day in 1996. Expecting a coldhearted, all-business Republican, I was surprised to find a man who agreed with me on this basic principle of human concern. As George said then and many times since, "Values are not subject to borders."

Beyond this core spiritual agreement, George Bush and I shared practical concerns about immigration: that it must be made safe, legal, and orderly, as it is within Europe or along the border between the United States and Canada—with full respect to the economic needs of both the sending nation and the receiving nation. But we also agreed to give full respect to human rights, both the civil rights and labor rights of the immigrant who crosses the border to work and the right to security of the U.S. citizens who will be the immigrant's neighbors, employers, customers, and, once in a while, friends.

This was the model that George Bush and I worked to achieve later, as presidents of our respective countries. But in 1996 all this was in the future for George and me, as we moved from Spanish-sprinkled small talk into the meat and potatoes of policy. Meetings with Bush are crisp and "let's get straight to it," a style that many Mexicans find abrupt in me, too. Again I sensed that we were kindred spirits, always in a hurry.

"Look here, George," I said. "You know our people, your father knows us, you've seen the people from my home state here in Texas. They are hardworking, law-abiding citizens who go to church on Sunday."

"Absolutely," he agreed. "They're good people, and we're glad to have them."

"They are just like your pioneers," I said, telling him a bit about my American grandfather. "There will always be some who come with the dream of making it big. But most of these people come because we have failed them, because they just can't find a job in Mexico, and they can't make a living on what our jobs pay."

"What can we do to create opportunities in Guanajuato?" Bush asked.

"Given the choice, they would stay home for a job that pays less," I explained. "But with the current economic crisis, our economy won't provide even that." We talked about how our dysfunctional government had beggared Mexico into poverty, with its walls of protectionism and state control.

"The goal is to get the economy going in your state, so these folks can find good jobs at home," Bush said. "And I understand that with the way things are in Mexico right now, your country can't do this alone. What can we do here in Texas to help?"

The moment had come to spring my big idea.

"Why don't we do a miniature version of the Marshall Plan right here between us, your state and mine?" I asked, an urgent suitor popping the question on a first date. "Like the cohesiveness fund in the European Union, both Texas and Guanajuato could invest in a revolving fund to build up the infrastructure in the poor areas that send the most immigrants," I explained enthusiastically. "For a fraction of what Texas spends patrolling the border, we could create thousands of jobs that would keep my people home. Then we could use the increase in value of our economy in those areas to repay the fund and reinvest in new areas."

He looked at me as though a crazy man had wandered into his office.

In the silence we could hear the traffic on Congress Avenue outside the capitol lawns, the distant ring of a telephone in the outer office.

"Cohesiveness fund," he said, looking at me with those sharp blue eyes. "What's that?"

SINCE MY YEARS at Coca-Cola International and my brief fling at global trade in an attic boot warehouse in Paris, I had been impressed by the Common Market and the European Union. That day in Bush's office, I talked about how the Marshall Plan had rebuilt war-torn Europe and Asia, constructing the highways, airports, and water systems, the electrical and transportation grids of Germany and Japan. I applauded the wisdom of the United States: After the experience of the Versailles Treaty and the rise of Nazism in the defeated, broken Germany after World War I, the United States had the vision to see that rich neighbors made better trading partners than impoverished, bitter, broken enemies.

During the 1980s and '90s, the wealthy nations of Germany, Britain, and France had in turn helped their poorer neighbors in Italy, Spain, Greece, and Portugal, first through immigration, as I have described, then by forming a trading bloc with common tariffs to allow a free flow of goods and labor in the Common Market, and finally by investing a small portion of each nation's annual revenues in a "cohesiveness fund," a continent-wide initiative to build up the roads, schools, trains, power plants, sewage systems, and hospitals of the poorer nations.

As late as the 1970s, citizens in Ireland, Spain, Portugal, and Greece lived in conditions not so very different from those in Mexico, with low standards of living and some of the poorest roads, schools, hospitals, and water systems in the world. Human capital was equally weak: In the early 1970s, more than 90 percent of Spain's population had finished only primary school. Few got job training. Portugal had infant mortality rates approaching those of Mexico under the PRI.

But over the next generation, the European Union invested 2 percent of the annual gross domestic products of all member nations, rich and poor, into a revolving general fund to improve the economies of the poorest areas of Europe—focusing mostly on areas in the poorer nations that produced the most immigrants. What happened next should have surprised no one. By building up the poorest areas of Southern and Eastern Europe, the rich nations hoisted their neighbors out of the muck and made them into good customers. Spanish and Irish farmhands were no longer exiled to Germany and Britain in search of jobs, but stayed home to work on EU building projects, then went to the new schools to learn technical skills, then got jobs in the new factories of Barcelona and Madrid—making products that Spain could now sell tariff-free to its richer EU neighbors.

So they stayed home, this new generation of Spaniards and Portugese whose fathers had been migrant farmers in German fields. Soon countries like Spain, Ireland, and Portugal became affluent consumers of the products and services of Germany, Britain, and France. Now former "welfare" nations are rich taxpayers: Spain and Ireland are paying millions of euros from their ever-growing gross domestic products into the EU cohesiveness fund, which in turn is lifting up the economies of new EU members like Poland, Romania, Bulgaria, Malta, and Cyprus. Someday they will be rich countries, too—and contribute to the fund to boost their neighbors as well.

Certainly, the European Union isn't perfect, and it did not come into being without controversy. Today citizens in France, for example, bitterly oppose the admission of Turkey into the EU. Just as many Americans worry about Mexican "invasion," some in Germany, Britain, and France worry about losing their culture and fret that the EU might weaken their home economies down to the level of their poorer neighbors. In smaller economies, others worry about economic domination and exploitation from richer ones.

Certainly, the richer countries gave up a portion of their growth rate in the short term to help their neighbors. But Germany, the UK, and France still grew in the 1990s, albeit not as fast as the United States. In return for their generosity, Northern Europe got stronger trading partners and more secure allies in the south and east: partners against drugs, terrorism, civil unrest, and crime. Together the nations of the new Europe created what is now the biggest economy in the world—and our chief rival here in the Americas. The old world of Europe has emerged as a new role model of solidarity and social justice, applying the principles of Saint Ignatius Loyola to an entire continent of "nations for others"—proving that countries, too, have souls.

Immigrants still move across Europe. Spaniards and Brits, Germans and Italians circulate freely across a continent. The rich nations draw a growing number of poor and unskilled workers from former colonies in

Africa, the Middle East, and Asia, along with many from Eastern Europe, to meet their labor demands. But where once millions were forced to emigrate out of economic necessity, today the vast majority of citizens have the option of staying home.

The self-appointed "culture warriors" attack the idea of an EU-style integration of the Americas as a "one-world plot" designed to destroy the individual distinctions between nations. But far from "mongrelizing" the cultures of Europe into one homogeneous continental state, smart business ideas like the cohesiveness fund have had the opposite effect. Enriching poor neighbors has actually helped preserve the cultures of both the "old rich" nations like Germany *and* the "new rich" nations like Spain. The reason is simple: Once the cohesiveness fund developed the poor countries, Spaniards could prosper in Spain. So instead of emigrating abroad, they rotated back home in what immigration scholars call "circularity." They brought home German and English language skills, computer literacy, and First World standards of efficiency—but kept their Spanish roots. The people of Spain are still Spaniards, heart and soul (except for the stubborn Basques, like my mother). But now they can afford to vacation in Cancún.

By working more closely with North America, Mexico is finally making some progress. From 2000 to 2006, average earnings in Mexico rose 60 percent, and today we have the highest per capita income in Latin America. But Spain and Ireland have done much better—and the EU cohesiveness fund made all the difference.

"Why can't we do this together with Texas and Guanajuato, George?" I asked. "For every million dollars Texas invests in Guanajuato, we would guarantee the creation of a thousand jobs. That would mean a thousand fewer immigrants here in Texas, a thousand more good customers for Texas products in Guanajuato."

"No way." He shook his head. "The citizens of Texas would never stand for our tax dollars going to build highways and schools in Mexico."

"But we'd pay you back. It would be a revolving investment fund, not a taxpayer giveaway, and we would invest in the fund, too, from Guanajuato," I persisted. "For a fraction of what Texas spends policing the border, you could help us create thousands of jobs that would help me keep our people home."

"It just won't fly, Vicente," he said emphatically. "I could never get something like that through the legislature."

"For Texas today, immigration is a problem," I said, feeling like I was selling onions door-to-door in McAllen again. "But you know our people. They don't come here to rob and steal or to get welfare from the Texas taxpayers. They come here to work. If we could invest just a fraction of the billions that the United States spends on keeping immigrants out and use it to create jobs to keep my people home in Mexico, we could convert that problem into an opportunity for both of our states."

"It's a great idea, but that's not going to happen," he said firmly. "Down deep in their hearts, people here in Texas just wouldn't support a deal like that."

Even a Coca-Cola salesman knows "no" when he hears it. But I didn't take it as a defeat. This is a long-term vision. Politicians have to think about the next election, but statesmen think about the next generation.

From Austin, I moved on to other cities, new leaders, more ideas. Now more than ever before, Fox was in a hurry. With the dire circumstances of Mexico's peso-devaluation crisis—the people of Guanajuato had been hit terribly hard by the post-Salinas economic collapse—I was anxious to get results for my state *now*. Even though I was brimming with exciting ideas of my own, I had an unquenchable thirst for new approaches from the outside world and a bottomless hunger for jobs, foreign investment, and economic-development programs to help the troubled people of Guanajuato.

I went first to our best customer: the United States. We set up Guanajuato trade centers in New York City, Los Angeles, Dallas, Chicago, and other major commercial centers across the United States and Canada. Warehouses for leather goods; distribution networks for agricultural products; marketing centers for our fine furniture, handicrafts, clothing, ironwork, and housewares. It was all based on the model my father and grandfather had used when they opened a little office in McAllen to sell our vegetables. My suitcases were always packed; once again I was on the move, working the routes, selling the product. I would go anywhere to pitch a customer: Detroit to get Ford to build a plant or General Motors to expand; New York to sell the financial community on investing in central Mexico; L.A. to get a movie shot in San Miguel de Allende; Dallas to figure out how to get León shoes into Neiman Marcus. I was in a hurry.

My father always taught me, "Hard work beats anything except death."

Sadly, he passed away just six months after the happy day of my inauguration as governor. But the driving spirit he handed down from his father was always with me. I understood Americans; they responded well to a businessman who started meetings on time, got right to the point, and spoke the language of U.S. business. George Bush and I disagreed about many things, from the cohesiveness fund to the death penalty, but it didn't stop us from making a string of good business deals for our states. I've never needed a speech to talk to businessmen. Just give me a product, whether democracy or the state of Guanajuato, a bottle of Coke or a crate of broccoli, and I'm ready to sell.

The automotive expansion we won from GM brought thirty-four hundred high-paying jobs to the state. Soon we had a string of such success stories, and my state's economy was booming, a sharp contrast to a nation in crisis. NAFTA's sudden opening of the Mexican economy to the United States and Canada upset the applecarts of many in the protectionist business establishment. It was good for the great northern cities of Monterrey and Guadalajara, for hungry pro-business states like Guanajuato and Aguascalientes, and for the border economy, which had always been more oriented to the United States. NAFTA was kind to Texas, Arizona, New Mexico, and California, too, and the midwestern industrial cities at the other end of the NAFTA Corridor along U.S. I-35 from Laredo through Dallas to Kansas City, St. Louis, Chicago, and Detroit.

But NAFTA was not so kind to Mexican farmers. Hit hard by the peso devaluation, now they faced competition from the highly efficient and richly subsidized agribusiness of the United States, where the economic insanity of farm-price supports for millionaire growers and billionaire-run corporations persists even today. Suddenly Mexico was showered with cheap U.S. corn, a boon to hard-pressed consumers in the big cities. But this was a threat to the Mexican farmer, who could not compete with U.S. farmers' superior methods, equipment, capital, productivity, and quality—all funded by the $16 billion in farm subsidies that Washington doles out every year. North America was an impossible Goliath for the 3.5 million Mexican Davids who farmed the little *ejido* plots of ten to twelve acres allotted them by the PRI. Again, free markets work best in the long run, but they are brutally hard on the ill-prepared.

This was even truer in fields like manufacturing, energy, and high technology, big industries that boomed in the United States in the 1990s but did less for the average Mexican in the early years of NAFTA. The core problem was that we simply weren't educated enough yet to fill the jobs of the Information Age. Before I was elected president in 2000, more than 90 percent of Mexicans did not even make it to high school—in the United States, eight out of ten young people earn their diplomas. Over the next decade, we would strive to train our workforce, so that NAFTA became a rising tide that lifted all boats. But in the 1990s our people were drowning—they needed help now.

This is a great challenge of newly freed societies: Leaders must deliver results right away, before people in the formerly protectionist nations grow impatient with all this talk of free markets and go back to the security blanket of what is traditional and familiar. Even if the corrupt, walled-off Mexico had failed our people, at least it was predictable, safe, orderly. In the politics of emerging democracies, this is known as the "nostalgia effect." As memories of the old order's failures fade, people think back fondly on the days when the state made all their decisions for them. Even if life was hard, their lives were in some way protected from the uncertainties of a rapidly changing and terrifyingly competitive world. This has happened in Russia and in other former Communist nations; it threatens democracies from Eastern Europe to Indonesia. It is an old story in Latin America, where nations tend to meander back and forth between state-controlled protectionism and free-market social democracy like drunks weaving between the lanes of public policy. People elect new leaders to drive the car forward, and just about the time you think you're getting somewhere, the guy in the passenger seat reaches over and grabs the wheel and sends the car spinning in a U-turn to head back the other way.

Meanwhile the Free World zooms steadily down the highway, passing us by.

A mere governor, I couldn't change the world, or even Mexico. But I was determined that we would not fall victim to the nostalgia syndrome in Guanajuato. As the first opposition leader elected to run the state, I wanted to deliver the results of democracy *fast*, so that people could feel it in their stomachs *today*. My family and my aides still joke about how I start and end every meeting with the word "*Vamos!*"—"Let's go!"—a most un-Mexican way to operate. But we needed to *move*, fast, before people grew impatient and put the PRI back in charge.

So I went everywhere in search of ideas on how to bring the fruits of

NAFTA past the big corporations, down to the little guy: I wanted free trade that a mother could use to buy milk for her baby, foreign investment in bite-size pieces we could feed to every hungry fourteen-year-old facing the trauma of leaving all he loved to go work "on the other side." I searched and searched. But even as we succeeded on the macroeconomic front, bringing in the big corporations and the factories, I couldn't seem to find the answer.

Until God took a hand one night in San Francisco in the form of Mikhail Gorbachev and a little man from Bangladesh.

CHAPTER 10

THE BREAD WOMAN OF BANGLADESH

In 1996, I attended the State of the World Forum in San Francisco, organized by the former Soviet leader who had overseen his country's transition to democracy. As a rebel seeking to overthrow one-party control in Mexico—the only such regime that had ruled longer than Soviet Communism in the twentieth century—I was anxious to meet Gorbachev. The architect of *perestroika* is a brilliant and charming man whose famous birthmark is actually very striking in person. It's a little like your first view of the Golden Gate Bridge from the top floor of a San Francisco hotel. You think, *Wow, it really looks like that.*

There we stood gazing down upon the bay, in a glittering ballroom full of dignitaries. Jane Goodall talked about her life among the chimpanzees with an intensity that moved me. Love, Goodall says, is the number-one ingredient in leadership, because love moves you to action. From this passionate woman who lived out her dreams in Africa, I heard that love has the power to conquer any obstacle: disease, ignorance, tyranny. It gave me hope for Mexico.

Bill Gates introduced us to the future of a world in the Information Age. It was the billionaire in the wire-rimmed glasses who taught me the concept of "convergence," a global coming-together that means not only the blending of television sets, computer screens, music players and cellular phones with e-mail but a convergence of all the globe's resources to solve critical problems like poverty, AIDS, and genocide. Gates later put his money where his mouth was, donating $30 million to introduce technology to the public libraries of Mexico, connecting the indigenous campesinos of Chiapas and Oaxaca to the brave new world of the Internet. This is philanthropy at its very best, the way Gates and Warren Buffett use their business skills to multiply the effect of their compassion many times over—not only by teaching people "how to fish" but also by giving them the boats, rods, nets, and bait.

The friends I made that day in San Francisco, and at subsequent State of the World Forum gatherings and events like the Clinton Global Initiative, became close allies. First they aided me in the fight for democracy in Mexico; then they contributed to our drive for social justice during my presidency. Some are still helping us in private philanthropy today. Bill Gates, for example, became a partner with my first lady and me in our Vamos Mexico Foundation, helping to fight poverty, promote education, and cure chronic disease for children from Mexico to Haiti and Africa. But even with all this brainpower of the billionaires, statesmen, scientists, and diplomats, the biggest impact came from a little man from Bangladesh who stood at Gorbachev's side.

"Have you met Dr. Muhammad Yunus?" said Gorbachev. A tall man himself, the former czar of the Soviet Communist Party leaned his balding head forward to address the small, dark-skinned, prematurely gray professor wearing the simple white tunic of Islam. "Dr. Yunus, please share your concept with my friend Vicente Fox, governor of Guanajuato in Mexico."

The man who would ten years later win the 2006 Nobel Peace Prize reached forward to grasp my hand, then touched his hand toward his heart in the Muslim fashion. Then Muhammad Yunus shared an idea that would reshape the economy of my state and my country, bringing the economic miracle of the microcredit revolution to women and poor people from Guanajuato to Chiapas, and all around the world.

ONE SWELTERING afternoon thirty years ago, on the crowded streets of the newly created nation of Bangladesh, a young university student in the world's poorest country felt a tap at his elbow.

"Please, sir," implored an elderly woman with a basket in the crook of her arm. Her face was dirty, her cheeks hollow with hunger. "Won't you buy a piece of bread?"

In the basket were small, broken pieces of naan, the flat, crunchy bread of the region. Though the student wasn't hungry, the woman obviously was. So the young scholar took pity on the poor woman and bought a bit of bread for a fraction of a penny. Then, out of curiosity, he asked the question that changed 500 million lives.

"What would you require to do more business?" the college student inquired.

"Money," she replied instantly, "to buy more bread to sell tomorrow."

The young man, a student of economics, believed instinctively that the poor were not the cause of poverty but its victims—that it is the System that creates poverty by denying opportunity to women like this one. The poor lady had all the attributes of a successful entrepreneur. She obviously worked hard and operated in the spirit of free enterprise. She was willing to take risks and sacrifice today to get ahead tomorrow. She sold a necessary product at an attractive price, which she provided at a profit with the value-add of purchasing the bread in bulk, breaking into pieces, transporting it to the college gates, and selling it to targeted customers as they walked out of their classes, hungry for a convenient, bite-size quantity of bread.

So why was the old woman poor, begging students to buy bits of bread, while he and his friends studied high finance inside? Perhaps, thought the young doctoral candidate, there is more to learn from the bread woman than from the professors. "Why don't you take the profits from the bread you sell today and use that to buy more bread tomorrow?" Muhammad Yunus asked the woman.

"Because I am very poor, and I could only afford this one loaf this morning," she explained slowly, as if the student were particularly dense. "This is only enough for three hours of selling, and if I sell it all, I will have only a few pennies, which is barely enough to feed my children and buy one more loaf for tomorrow's selling."

"But what if I gave you a dollar?" asked the young Bangladeshi student. "Then you could buy two loaves and remain here the whole day tomorrow. Could you not then make enough to pay me back my dollar from the first loaf and still have enough profit from the second loaf to buy more bread the next day?"

"Of course, this would be a miracle," she agreed, eyes glowing with hope. "But no one in his right mind lends a dollar to a poor woman."

He lent her the dollar and was pleasantly surprised to receive it back the next day. Experimenting, he lent tiny amounts of working capital to other poor women and was amazed at how quickly they repaid him. Even more astounding was the proportional impact these microcredits had on their miniature businesses.

After turning several beggar women into successful entrepreneurs, the student went to the branch bank on campus to ask whether they would consider lending money to the poor women who sold bread from baskets outside the college gates.

"Of course not!" said the branch manager. "Everyone knows you cannot lend money to the poor. They have no collateral."

"What matters the collateral if they pay back the dollar the next day?" he asked.

"Who can make money on the loan of one dollar?" the banker protested. "Besides, a poor woman will not pay back the dollar. She will use it to buy bread to feed her children, and then the money will be gone. She will have nothing and the bank will get no return."

"What if you lent many dollars to many bread women, but just one dollar each?" Yunus persisted. "And how do you know the women will not pay it back, if you have never tried?"

"We have never tried because any fool knows you cannot lend money to people who have nothing," the banker said firmly.

In other words, the student thought, money can be loaned only to those who already have it. But Yunus refused to accept the idea that those who needed loans the most would not repay them; his experience with the bread woman taught him that her hunger to succeed made her the best of credit risks.

So he went to the big banks in the bustling office towers of downtown Dhaka, the capital of Bangladesh. It was the same story.

"They fell out of the sky laughing at me," he explained that night in San Francisco. "This crazy college student wants us to loan money to poor people!"

So with twenty-seven dollars of his own capital, Dr. Muhammad Yunus became the world's "banker to the poor," lending tiny amounts of money to poor people—largely self-employed women who used their dollar loans to start microbusinesses. Today Dr. Yunus's Grameen Bank has reached more than 90 million families throughout the world, from the 5 million families who now own Grameen microbusinesses in his native Bangladesh to fisherwomen in Haiti, egg sellers in Africa, and basket weavers who export Mayan textiles through the Chiapas project.

By the time Mikhail Gorbachev introduced me to Muhammad Yunus in San Francisco, his "poor people's bank" was helping 200,000 Bangladeshi families a year to escape extreme poverty, adding twenty years to the average life expectancy in Bangladesh.

Here is the miraculous part of Dr. Yunus's concept: 98 percent of all Grameen loans are repaid in full. Committees of five local women meet to review the loans proposed by prospective microbusiness owners, offering credit only to those they can trust to repay them. The committee members follow up with each borrower to make sure the business prospers, so that the microcredit cycle continues.

The result is a vast pool of credit available in bite-size amounts to self-employed poor people in developing economies. Most are women with children or grandchildren in the home, who depend on the female microbusiness owner both for their economic sustenance and their health and education. Self-employment gives mothers the personal freedom to run their businesses from the home, where they can meet the daily needs of caring for children and nurturing families. For the married poor woman whose husband is out doing backbreaking labor day and night to keep the household going, the second income of her microbusiness is a blessing; to the single mother who is the sole source of support for her children, the Grameen Bank is a miracle.

I believe that the work of the gentle Muslim from Bangladesh is truly the hand of God on this earth. At Gorbachev's San Francisco summit, I imagined putting this idea to work in Guanajuato, where the tradition of the mom-and-pop *changarro* was strong. Our culture's relentless focus on maternal child care, as ancient as the Mayans and Aztecs, reinforced by our worship of the Virgin, is often thought quaint and old-fashioned by a postindustrial world where women worked outside the home in banks, laboratories, law firms, corporations, and advertising agencies. But the plain fact was that poor women in the land of machismo were even more poorly educated than the men in the fields: Girls had to leave school at age eight or ten out of economic necessity, to care for baby brothers and sisters. Soon these girls had babies themselves and were locked into the cycle of poverty. Few of the poor mothers I knew in Guanajuato were likely to leave their children, bootstrap their way through law school, and join a blue-chip firm in Mexico City. But could we use microcredit loans to help them start businesses making tortillas on the lava stones of their kitchens? How about a boot-making *changarro* in the toolshed to export leather goods to Dallas?

The more I heard from Dr. Yunus, the more excited I became. "Three things we have learned," he summarized. "One is that small amounts of capital loaned to very poor people produce much more business growth on a proportional, dollar-for-dollar basis than the big loans made by the banks to large corporations. Two, the poor repay their loans much faster, allowing the bank to achieve quicker turnover even though we are investing only tiny amounts of money in a vast number of projects. And three, we have an absolute assurance of getting the money back, because while a corporation might extend the terms of a loan and a businessman may default, the poor woman is desperate to succeed and hungry for more credit. Besides, no poor woman wants to break the cycle and invite the shame of her neighbors."

"We should do this in Guanajuato," I said enthusiastically that night in San Francisco, the lights of the harbor twinkling below. "I will meet with my cabinet the moment I get back."

"Good God, don't do that!" Yunus said quickly. "You will never satisfy the bureaucracy of government. They will strangle you in red tape. Do it privately, and you can change the world overnight. And why would you wait until you return? Make it happen now, immediately. The poor cannot wait."

Now. The poor cannot wait. I had found a soul mate, a man in a hurry, with an idea that could translate the benefits of NAFTA to the poor women of Mexico. The Grameen Bank combined the entrepreneurial spirit of my immigrant grandfathers with the compassionate Catholicism of the Jesuits. I knew it would work in Guanajuato.

As dawn broke over the Golden Gate Bridge, I called my friend Alejandro Arenas and asked him to go down to open an account off the town square of Guanajuato for what became the Santa Fe, a bank for poor people named for the holy faith. Within weeks we had dozens of women operating microbusinesses—home-kitchen tortilla factories and backyard leather shops from my state to neighboring Aguascalientes and Querétaro. Soon Father Hidalgo's route to independence was lined by small family *changarros* where poor people celebrated their freedom from poverty. It was the beginning of our revolution of hope in Mexico.

In a nation where 70 percent of the citizens were "unbankable" on the day I took office as president in 2000, we used this same microcredit formula from Dr. Yunus to help people create 10 million tiny new businesses during my presidency, generating a record 1.4 million new jobs and helping us raise standards of living from an average $6,000 a year to $10,600 today, the highest in Latin America. Dr. Yunus's idea helped us reduce poverty in Mexico to 18 percent—still too high, but much better than the 45 percent of people throughout Latin America who live on less than two dollars a day, the World Bank's definition of poverty. Remember that throughout the world a billion people live even worse than that—the World Bank defines "extreme poverty" as a family living on less than *one* dollar per day, per person. In Mexico the Grameen Bank formula helped us lift nearly a third of such families out of their extreme deprivation.

By the time I left office, 90 percent of Mexicans were banked and bankable, with a social banking system modeled after the Grameen Bank to allow every seller of school supplies to set up her little *changarro* on the bench outside the church, every taco lady to earn an extra 50 percent to supplement the family income—microbusinesses that helped lift some 4 million people out of extreme poverty in six short years. We should do this everywhere—in Haiti and Africa, Chiapas and Cambodia. *Now.* In a hurry. Because the poor cannot wait.

Years later I told Dr. Yunus how his idea had touched millions upon millions of lives in Mexico—that I believed then, as I do now, that in his inspiration I truly see the hand of God on this earth. "Well then, you got your money's worth from the trip to San Francisco!" he cried.

I LATER PERSUADED Gorbachev to bring his State of the World Forum to the old hacienda of San Gabriel de Barrera in Guanajuato. Among the flowering vines of the villa's ancient walls, I was anxious to show the world outside that Mexico could do better in the twenty-first century. I went back to the States again and again to lobby border governors and buttonhole U.S. congressmen and senators in Washington, hammering away at my favorite theme. "The answer to the immigration issue is to create jobs in Guanajuato to keep our people at home," I persisted. "Why can't the United States and Mexico join together in a new Marshall Plan, a cohesiveness fund like the European Union? For a fraction of what you spend policing the border . . ."

I figured that they would show me the door. But a surprising number listened to what I had to say. Like Bush, they seemed genuinely concerned about immigrants and worried about the effects of Mexico's recent economic crisis and the *zapatista* rebellion. At a high level in the United States, I found a core of "Friends of Mexico," farsighted leaders who understand that while a prosperous Mexico is a good business partner under NAFTA, a poor, chaotic Mexico would be a menace to the hemisphere. I solicited advice from every smart man and woman I could find: Henry Kissinger and David Rockefeller in the hushed boardrooms of Manhattan; Mac McLarty, the former Clinton White House chief of staff who was later the president's special ambassador to Latin America, one of the biggest promoters of the Marshall Plan concept for Mexico; Delal Baer, a Latin America scholar in Washington who fell in love with Guanajuato and introduced me to Ted Kennedy and the big leaders in Congress. Though she recently died tragically of cancer, Delal has a special place in my heart: She adopted a child at our orphanage in Guanajuato. Before her untimely death, she raised to adulthood a Mexican child who would otherwise have gone motherless—no mean feat for a single American woman of middle age, given the strong bias in Mexico against adopting our children outside the country (particularly to an unmarried woman who was not Mexican).

Throughout my travels I learned that there are literally thousands of loving, passionate people all around the world who will help you if your cause is just. Some work in think tanks and universities, others in Fortune 500 corporations and elected office. There are Harvard doctors like Paul Farmer, who set up his famous health clinics in Haiti and Peru; UPS employees who build houses for the homeless in Guanajuato; Texas oilmen who dig water wells for the health of the poor. We began to get things done, not just new factories to create jobs in Guanajuato but policy changes from sympathetic American politicians for the 2 million *guanajuatenses* who currently live in the United States.

Texas lawmakers passed a bill giving in-state tuition to the children of undocumented workers. Utah gave them driver's licenses. American banks began accepting the *matrícula,* the consular ID card issued by the Mexican government to our citizens abroad. While the undocumented immigrant cannot prove that he is a citizen or legal resident of the United States, the *matrícula* is vital, because it at least enables immigrants to prove that they are who they say they are. This card certifies that an immigrant is a law-abiding, job-holding, taxpaying worker with a name and this spouse or that child, capable of renting an apartment, opening a bank account, driving a car, getting insurance, repaying a loan, even buying a home. The

Mexican haters in the United States despise the *matrícula,* considering it a backdoor trick of our government to help "illegal aliens" beat the law. In fact it is the opposite: The consular ID merely provides the immigrant with the means of declaring that he or she exists as a human being, ready to comply with the laws and rules of the United States and Canada.

California had been a hotbed of anti-immigrant activism since 1994, when Pete Wilson passed his Proposition 187 banning the extension of government services to the immigrants who worked, lived, and contributed to the growth of America's largest state economy. But the courts overturned the proposition as unconstitutional. I went to California frequently, the first Mexican governor that the migrant workers of Fresno and Bakersfield had ever seen loading cases of vegetables in the San Joaquin Valley. But I knew these campesinos—I had neighbors in Guanajuato who had been lured to the produce fields of California after World War II and into the 1950s, when the shortage of labor in the United States created the bracero program. These migrant farm workers had been the strong backs and arms (literally, the braceros) of U.S. agriculture for decades, and they had been horribly abused. They lived in California shantytown housing little better than the shacks they had left in Mexico, with no electricity or running water, no health care or schooling for their children. I had worked side by side with returning braceros in the fields of Guanajuato; if my back today still hurts from that work hefting fifty-kilo *costales* of hay, imagine how twisted is the spine of the elderly man who lived down the lane from me at Rancho San Cristóbal. For him there was no back surgery, nor even a chiropractor, not one aspirin from the wealthy landowners who talked the U.S. government into bringing guest workers to the United States in the 1950s. They worked the braceros like mules and then deported them back to Mexico, their hands gnarled and backs deformed with twenty years of stoop labor picking American strawberries.

Many of the braceros weren't even paid the money they were promised. During my presidency we sued the huge agricultural interests in the United States for the millions of dollars in back pay they owed the braceros. (They never paid, so we compensated the workers from the funds of the Mexican government; today the repatriated bracero gets at least part of the pension he deserves for his years of slave labor, and a doctor for his back.)

The saddest legacy of this bracero program is the terrible precedent it set for the new, more enlightened program of temporary employment that George W. Bush and I would pursue in our presidencies, based on the modern European model, where an immigrant's human rights are respected and social needs met. South of the border, we encountered great skepticism from a society that still remembers the tragedy of the braceros. North of the border, Mexicans are seen only as migrant crop pickers who have too many babies in the hospitals of California and Texas, expecting border-state taxpayers to pick up the tab.

It is this bleak pattern of mutual misunderstanding that dominates the debate on immigration. On one side of the Rio Grande, the poorer nation, fearful of domination and exploitation; on the other side the wealthy country, fearful of losing its economic advantages, personal security and cultural integrity to a flood of unskilled farmhands who live six to a room and work cheap.

Immigration, say the xenophobes to the south, will destroy our Mexican way of life. Immigration, say the xenophobes to the north, will destroy our American way of life.

But what was this Mexican way of life? Poverty? Authoritarianism? Devaluations? If so, I was ready for change, sure that we could raise standards of living without giving up the things we held dear: family, faith, music, food, history.

And what was this American way of life? Who built the United States, if not immigrants? What does it mean to be an American, if not to be free to move up, as far and as fast as your hard work, education, and sacrifice will take you?

As I traveled the United States and Canada selling the state of Guanajuato in the late 1990s, I began to sense a change. People in Mexico were hungry for democracy. We wanted the benefits of free markets and the social improvements we saw north of the border, where freely elected governments were forced to respond to public demand for education, health care, and good jobs at decent wages. And in the United States, a growing number of progressive leaders, Republicans and Democrats, seemed willing to embrace more thoughtful policies that respected the contributions of our migrants, even as we worked together to generate more opportunities south of the border.

One such visionary was Bill Clinton. The first international crisis of his presidency was the 1994–95 peso devaluation. He successfully led a bipartisan effort of Democrats and Republicans to bail out Mexico with a substantial loan guarantee, averting a global economic recession that could have devastated not only the markets of Mexico (which were already in chaos) but those of the United States, Canada, Europe, and Asia as well.

Another was George W. Bush. While he still hadn't bought my sales pitch for a revolving Marshall Plan–style fund for the Americas (and never would), Bush was part of a group of progressive Republican governors who preached "compassionate conservatism." From Washington to Detroit and Phoenix to Sacramento, I found an astonishing number of U.S. leaders with new ideas about Mexico, free trade, guest workers, and the treatment of immigrants in North America—willing to help a newly elected opposition governor from an obscure state in central Mexico. One future leader I met was an immigrant himself, a bodybuilder from Austria who had made it big in California: Arnold Schwarzenegger.

I LIKE ARNOLD. It is impossible not to like Arnold. At first you are merely struck by his enormous physical presence: I'm a big guy, much taller than Schwarzenegger, but this ex-bodybuilder simply fills the room with his jovial, wine-drinking, cigar-smoking charisma. Behind the muscles and the clever one-liners, what you don't expect is this logical, intense business mind, with a probing interest in what other leaders are doing in the world outside Hollywood and California.

We met at a dinner party in Beverly Hills in the early 1990s, well before the actor got into politics but far enough into my career that people in Hollywood were starting to introduce me as "the next president of Mexico." At the table was Edward James Olmos, who had starred in the film *Stand and Deliver.* The movie tells the story of East L.A. mathematics teacher Jaime Escalante, a hero of mine who was an inspiration to our people in the United States and in states like Guanajuato, where we were struggling to reform a corrupt and uncaring educational system that had failed generations of Mexican kids. Later, Mexican American artists like Eddie Olmos and Mexican stars like ranchero singer Vicente Fernández, NBA basketball sensation Eduardo Nájera, and the popular Los Tigres del Norte became great supporters of our efforts to bring democracy to Mexico. But even back then, Eddie was introducing me around in Los Angeles.

"So I hear you might run for president?" Schwarzenegger said, swirling the red wine in his glass. I certainly had no idea the actor would someday run for governor, but he was obviously interested in politics. He had married a Kennedy, after all—Maria Shriver's father had founded the Peace Corps under JFK, and Maria has a passionate interest in Mexico, as does Arnold.

This was a surprise: I had assumed that the only Mexicans the famous actor would knew were his lawn guys, that his only Spanish was *"Hasta la vista,* baby." But whether you like Arnold's politics or not, he is a shrewd businessman with keen insights into the issues he cares about—like education, health care, poverty reduction, immigration, and the environment.

"I love Mexico," he explained. "I lived there for many months at a time, shooting films, and we edited and produced them there as well. Many people don't appreciate the culture of your country, the great artists and craftsmen, the work ethic and dedication to quality you find in Mexico. But I do."

This of course was music to the ears of a Mexican governor looking for economic opportunity; we hit it off from the start. I explained the progress we were making in Guanajuato, and we talked about immigrants. He shared his experience coming to America, and I mentioned the constitutional barrier I had overcome regarding Article 82.

"So you *are* going to run for president?" he persisted. "That would be something, the son of an immigrant bringing democracy to Mexico and improving the lives of the people there."

"Maybe someday," I responded. "Now, tell me, what is your next film project, and is there any way you can shoot it in Guanajuato?"

By the mid-1990s, things in my state were on the move. I had pitched every customer who would see me, from oilmen in Houston to bankers in New York. But our poor still suffered, patients lacked medical care, young people emigrated, and too many of my constituents still didn't know how to read. So I did what any former Coca-Cola CEO from the conservative PAN would do.

I went to Havana, to see Fidel Castro.

The United States has a curious policy of isolating Cuba from the attractions of free-market capitalism—even as the rest of the world does business with Cuba, even though the United States trades freely with Moscow, Beijing, Tripoli, and Ho Chi Minh City. But the people of Mexico and the people of Cuba have always maintained close and friendly relations. Just as exposure to the benefits of the Free World brought down the Berlin Wall, someday in the not-so-distant future the United States will see the wisdom of opening lines to post-Castro Cuba, so that we can bring this vibrant nation into the global economy.

I always saw Cuba as a neighbor and trading partner, a Communist state with excellent health care, fabulous sports programs, solid basic literacy education. Of course, Castro also has an atrocious record of human-rights abuses and meddling in the domestic politics of other nations. All of Cuba's evils were ignored by the PRI. Throughout the Cold War, Mexico stayed close to Cuba to prove its independence in Latin America, like a teenage daughter who hangs out with a hoodlum boyfriend just to defy her parents.

Later, as president, I would protest Castro's human-rights abuses in the United Nations, casting Mexico's vote with the United States to condemn Cuba on that issue—political heresy in our country. The PRI rarely pointed out the antidemocratic tendencies of other nations, lest they be accused of "calling the kettle black." But I believe that before you judge another society, you ought to see things firsthand. So in 1999 my twelve-year-old son, Rodrigo, and I packed our bags and flew from Mexico City to Havana to meet the region's most infamous revolutionary.

We took home some interesting observations. Cuba did indeed train the best volleyball and baseball players, track and field athletes, and gymnasts we had ever seen. With Castro's help we imported dozens of gymnastics, swimming, and diving instructors to Guanajuato and began what (as a loyal *guanajuatense*) I will say are the best sports teams of any state in Mexico. This helped make my state safer and more educated; sports are a powerful incentive to keep kids in school, a potent deterrent to immigration, and a positive means to redirect young lives away from crime, drugs, alcohol, or violence.

Castro also showed me the benefits of providing universal health coverage in a developing society. He has established huge medical schools; trained doctors are now the Cuban Revolution's hottest exports to Haiti, Venezuela, and Africa. All over the Americas, you will find Cuban doctors, and we welcome them in Mexico. Recently Cuba has even begun recruiting medical students from underprivileged areas of the United States—a clever and effective propaganda move.

Castro also has built one of the better educational systems in Latin America, giving Cuba among the highest literacy rates in the developing world, nearly equal to that of the United States—even if those schools and the media give each new generation only the government's revisionist history of Cuba, replete with the evils of the United States and the glories of Castroism.

But the lasting impressions Rodrigo and I took away from our all-night dinner with Castro recall the bearded revolutionary's inexhaustible energy and brilliant, diverse intelligence. He conversed freely and expertly about a hundred different topics, from the relative qualities of Spanish rioja wines to the best agricultural methods to harvest avocados, from baseball's greatest pitchers to Hollywood movies. He also drank buffalo milk all through the evening and into the wee hours of dawn, interspersing it carefully between sips of finest Galician wine, as though this mix were sustaining his longevity. He had the longest fingernails Rodrigo and I had ever seen, strangely curved talons that Fidel used as pincers to seize little pieces picked out of a long baguette of Spanish bolillo bread stuffed with cheese. This he dipped in sauce and nibbled as the night wore on to three and four and five in the morning—a very late hour for a twelve-year-boy and his farm-raised father, who had risen before dawn on Central Time. But I was riveted. And Rodrigo still does the best impression of Fidel that I have ever seen, right down to Castro's strange habit of pulling his ears between every bite of food.

BY THE LATE 1990S, democracy was working wonders in Guanajuato. We had Castro's gymnasts, Detroit's automotive investments, Hollywood's films and Dr. Yunus's microcredit businesses. At home we did the big things—doubled the state education budget, created record numbers of jobs, brought clean water to cities and farmers, built homes for the poor with an innovative program that coupled private donations with public funds to buy the materials for a house, then enabled the family to build it for themselves, so they would have true pride of ownership. Most of all we rooted out the bribes, kickbacks, and "commissions" paid to state officials by friendly contractors, so that our precious tax money went to buy books and pay teachers, not to buy beach houses for contractors.

I was helped in all this, oddly enough, by the PRI, which still dominated the state legislature of Guanajuato. Among the heroes were young PRI reformers like José Luis Romero Hicks, who became my finance minister and later served in my presidential cabinet; his brother, Juan Carlos, the president of Guanajuato University, succeeded me as PAN governor of the state. As in the United States, partisanship is often less of a driving force at the state level in Mexico. Just as George W. Bush was able to get things done with a Democratic legislature in Texas, we worked across party lines in a state where personal ties of family and love of our neighbors seemed to weigh more heavily on politicians than did the next election. Together, PAN governor and PRI lawmakers, we worked to reform seven decades of corruption and clean up the state. We did little things that made a big difference, like putting state expenditures on the Internet so every citizen could see how the government handled people's money. (The only challenge was teaching me how to use a computer, so that I could set an example by putting my own personal finances on the Web site for everyone to see. Now I'm quite adept at reading the news on my notebook computer every morning and e-mailing my wife and children on my BlackBerry, but this was long before high-speed DSL and Wi-Fi. I've always been fascinated with technology but never quite understood why hitting the mouse pad repeatedly doesn't get you online any faster. To me the Internet should be like a horse—you kick it and it goes.) We also installed streetlamps to highlight the gorgeous architecture of historic cities like San Miguel de Allende, Guanajuato, and Dolores Hidalgo, so that our state could tap its best tourism assets to draw visitors away from the beaches and up to our mountain cultural treasures.

All this added up to more jobs in Guanajuato, with higher incomes and reduced pressure on our young people to leave. But even as our state improved, Mexico nationally was still reeling from the posttraumatic stress of the Colosio and Massieu assassinations, the *zapatista* uprising, and especially the peso devaluation. Instead of ghost stories of La Llorona, now Mexican children were told that if they didn't behave, they would be eaten by a new version of the mythical the *chupacabra*—a half-wolf, half-man monster, with the body of a wild dog and the head of Carlos Salinas.

Ernesto Zedillo was viewed as an accidental president, a cold, bureaucratic technocrat with little stage presence and less compassion. If you met Ernesto today at Yale, you would find him a warm and likable guy in person. But that didn't come across on television. The cartoonists lampooned this grim face of economic crisis and fiscal austerity as a vampire, the dark circles under his eyes no doubt caused by worry.

In 1996, bowing to the pressure of public opinion in Mexico and abroad, Zedillo gave more independence to the Federal Electoral Institute. Freed of presidential control and supervised by citizen committees, the reformed IFE began to clean up the elections process. Public outrage over the 1994 economic crisis led to huge anti-PRI majorities in the 1997 by-elections, when our opposition PAN and PRD won enough seats to create an anti-PRI majority in Congress. With these big reforms, this left-right democracy coalition voted to spend billions to educate voters on a new IFE secret-ballot system, with a thumbprint system of voter identification, international monitors, and scrutiny by the opposition parties. Experts began to debate whether the PRI might finally lose in 2000 to the most popular man in Mexico: Cuauhtémoc Cárdenas, who many still believed had won in 1988.

Now Cárdenas was the dean of the Mexican Left and mayor of Mexico City, where one in five Mexican voters lives. The son of revered former president Lázaro Cárdenas, a Mexican FDR of sorts who had nationalized the oil industry, Cuauhtémoc Cárdenas had universal name identification, a big urban base, and real affection from the 3.5 million *ejidatario* farmers whose land rights had come to them from his father's 1938 edict. By the summer of 1997, a thousand days before the 2000 election, Cárdenas was the frontrunner in the national polls.

But down deep, Mexicans knew that the PRI would win in the end. They could divert up to a billion dollars in government funds to buy votes. (Later, when the Pemexgate scandal came out, officials were investigated for allegedly siphoning off at least $100 million from Pemex for the ruling party's 2000 campaign.) The big *priistas* began jockeying for position to get the finger in the presidential *dedazo*. As usual, the ruling party was split between traditionalist "old PRI" dinosaurs and reform-minded technocrats; to paraphrase the old joke about U.S. senators, every time a cabinet secretary or a PRI governor shaved, he saw a future president in the mirror. But there was an enduring wisdom within the PRI about the ambitions of these would-be presidents: "He who moves while the camera snaps won't come out in the picture." Patient men like Francisco Labastida, who eventually won the carefully orchestrated primary to become the

2000 PRI nominee, watched and waited in obscurity, jogging behind Cárdenas in the horse-race polls like a rider who knows that only one horse has the legs to finish strong.

Few people gave a maverick rancher from the hills a chance at the presidential race; most didn't think I would make it to the track. Guanajuato is a small, rural state, more like Bill Clinton's Arkansas than Hillary's New York or George Bush's Texas. But by 1997 a tiny circle of close friends, family, and business associates—along with a growing network of friends I'd made in the democracy movement of Grupo San Ángel and in the PAN nationwide—began to think Vicente Fox might have what it took.

During the Mexican Revolution, my grandfather Joseph Fox (center, on white horse) and his campesinos braved the bandits of Pancho Villa from the turrets of Rancho San Cristóbal.

Our family farm was literally a part of Mexico's history.

The yanqui pioneer Joseph Fox came from Ohio to become a night watchman at the Irapuato Horse Carriage Factory, saving enough to buy the factory and begin making horseless carriages in the early 1900s.

My grandparents Elena Pont, the daughter of a French soldier and an indígena peasant, and Joseph Louis Fox.

My father, Don José Fox, defied the demands of President Cárdenas in 1938 when the *federales* came to take away the family farm.

The young *ranchero*, my father Don José, and his bride. A merchant's daughter, Doña Mercedes left the brightly lit cafés of Mexico City for a ranch with no running water, no electricity, and snakes in the pond: It must have been love.

The Fox brothers (I'm in the center). I never set out to be in politics; I wanted to be a cowboy.

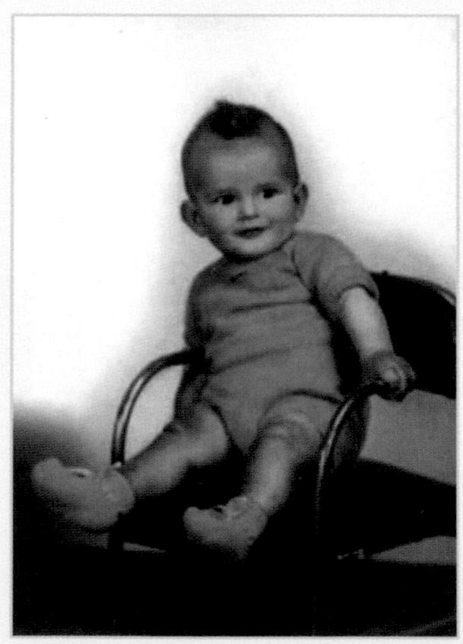

Me, all of nine months old.

The awkward age, thirteen.

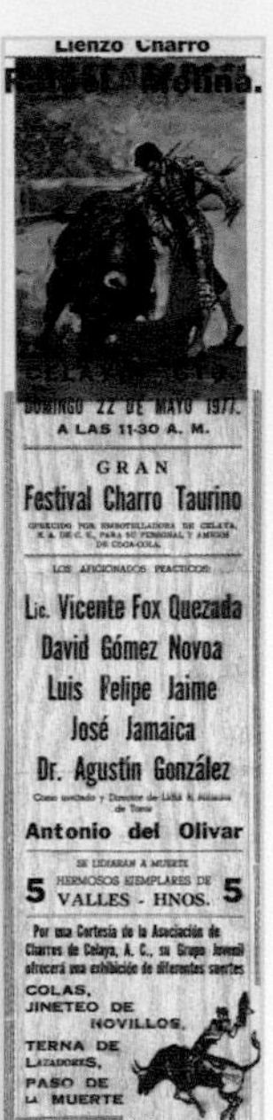

Six years in Los Pinos taught me that in a democracy a president must be the matador and use the cape to wave the bull aside. (Guanajuato, May 1977)

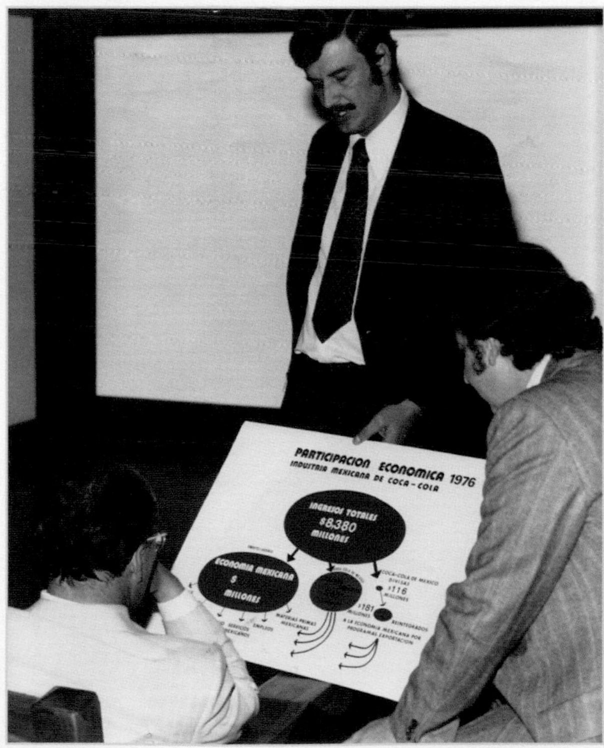

I became president of Coca-Cola Mexico at age thirty-two.

A bearded bull of a man, my mentor, 1988 PAN presidential candidate Manuel Clothier, later went on a hunger strike to protest the alleged electoral fraud.

In politics, whether it was PAN's female candidates or my sister on the picket line, women were in the vanguard of the struggle for democracy. (Guanajuato, 1988).

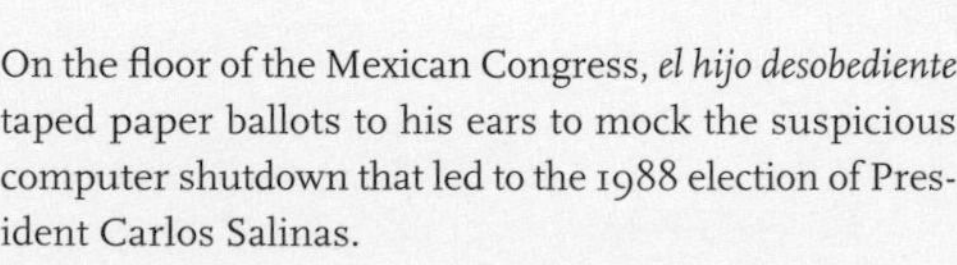

On the floor of the Mexican Congress, *el hijo desobediente* taped paper ballots to his ears to mock the suspicious computer shutdown that led to the 1988 election of President Carlos Salinas.

The congressional class of 1988 produced 240 democratic revolutionaries, amateurs armed only with rage.

In 1990, lacking the ruling party's money and power, we built a door-to-door campaign for governor, pushing our ideas on the back roads of Guanajuato like a route truck driver selling soft drinks.

Together we shouted and cried and laughed and swore at the authorities, me and my little team of amateurs, as we moved souls by talking to the stomach, the spirit, and the heart.

Campaigning for president in 2000.

A congratulatory kiss from my mother on Election Night.

On December 1, 2000, I was sworn in to the presidency as the Mexican people ended seventy-one years of one-party rule that Peruvian novelist Mario Vargas Llosa called "the perfect dictatorship."

On July 2, 2001, a year to the day after the presidential election, Marta Sahagún became the first lady of Mexico.

Doña Mercedes welcomed President Bush to Rancho San Cristóbal in 2001 like a classmate I might have brought home from school: "Oh, you're Vicente's friend!"

The San Cristóbal summit on February 16, 2001 made history as the new U.S. president chose Mexico as his first foreign destination, evoking a new era of harmony in the hemisphere.

At the first summit after the 9/11 attacks, twenty-one world leaders convened in October 2001 in Shanghai for the APEC meeting, eager to see how Bush would rally the world against terrorism.

In August 2002, I became the first Mexican president to welcome the pontiff by kissing the papal ring of Saint Peter: Mexican presidents weren't supposed to enter a church, not even if their daughter was getting married.

Bondadoso and *cariñoso,* Mandela compared notes on building a new democracy: "It is not for you to deliver things to people—it is for the people to do it for themselves." (Houghton, near Johannesburg, South Africa, September 2002)

In February 2002, Marta and I visited Fidel Castro in Cuba. I reached out Mexico's hand in friendship with the goal of increasing trade and financial ties with Havana, but voted against Castro on human rights at the UN.

In 2002, with "Just Call Me Tony" Blair. You may disagree with the British prime minister, as I later did on Iraq, but it's impossible not to like him.

Though President Clinton was headed out of office as I was headed in, we pledged to work closely together to combat poverty. Bill Clinton is a role model for ex-presidents who want to make a difference.

With Hugo Chávez at the Summit of the Americas in January 2004. When he gets long-winded, it's time for the other presidents to go for a bottle of water and some cookies, and try to do some real business in the hallway.

Occasionally I find it necessary to break out of the confining suit-and-tie unctuousness of the presidency. This is usually when I take heat from the press and make people laugh.

At the twenty-sixth Mercosur Summit, July 2004, with Brazilian President Luiz Inácio Lula da Silva, a leader of Latin America's sensible left.

Toasting Putin at the June 2005 state visit at the Kremlin. The Russians are combat drinkers. When I went to bed that night, I had to put one foot on the floor to stop the room from spinning.

At Crawford in March 2004 with Condi Rice—an iron lady, attractive and charming, with a steel-trap mind.

At Crawford with the first ladies in March 2004. Even George will admit that he's a "windshield cowboy" whose ranch grows more brush than cattle.

The proud father of four beautiful children—Vicente, Rodrigo, Paulina, and Ana Cristina.

My grandson Vicente Fox III—never too young to learn the art of bullfighting.

Marta and I plan an active retirement, working for the dreams we share.

On the grounds of Rancho San Cristóbal, we are building Mexico's first presidential librar, a think tank for global democracy and the antipoverty foundation headed by my first lady.

CHAPTER 11

THE BURN BAG

WE MET IN SECRET, at the home of a trusted friend or around the dinner table by the kitchen of my ranch house at San Cristóbal. It was always on Saturday afternoons, for I was "on the clock" as governor from Monday to Friday, and Saturdays are a half workday in Mexico. We were fighting for honesty in government, so we couldn't conduct campaign business on government time, or even use our government cell phones. Besides, they were bugged.

From those early conspiracies of the late 1990s until election day of 2000, an aide went around the room at the end of each meeting and gathered all the paperwork, burning the agendas, shredding the memoranda, locking crucial documents away in coded hard drives and padlocked filing cabinets. It may seem overly dramatic in today's Mexican democracy, but we were living in a one-party dictatorship. As poet Delmore Schwartz put it, "Even paranoids have real enemies." Agents of the Interior Ministry's feared *gobernación* monitored our home and office phones, e-mail, and cellulars. (Note to revolutionaries: Use digital phones, because they're harder to bug, and be careful what you say, because it may end up on the front page of the newspaper anyway.) When we took office and enacted Mexico's first Freedom of Information Act, we found all those tapes in the Interior Ministry's files, right down to private cell-phone conversations between me and my future first lady.

For it was about this time that I did the one thing that has no place on the agenda of an opposition governor and single father with four kids in the midst of a national economic crisis, who was embarking on a budding presidential campaign that aimed to overthrow seventy-one years of dictatorship.

I fell in love.

MARTA SAHAGÚN JIMÉNEZ was a bright, attractive woman of my own generation (though I have a decade on her and she looks younger still, but a gentleman should not tell a lady's age; in any case, Marta will be the first to remind me that I am not much of a gentleman, and she is proud to be fifty-four). The wife and business partner of a respected veterinarian from my home state, Marta ran the family veterinary pharmaceutical business in a country where ranchers did much of their own doctoring. I knew the Sahagúns from my 1994 campaign for governor, when Marta had campaigned vigorously for mayor of Celaya.

The PAN was unusual in that we reserved a third of our candidacies for women. This was a controversial policy, given the conservative roots of our party and the culture of machismo in Mexico. But I was strongly in favor of it: Women were among the strongest advocates for change in our society. Even if the one-third quota system ruffled feathers among male party veterans, over the long run Mexican women would respond.

The year I won the governorship, we lost *priista* strongholds like Celaya, but I had been impressed by Marta's campaign for mayor. She had charisma, intelligence, and communications skills, and she was an early and strong supporter of my presidential candidacy, telling all who would listen, "I'm not just a *panista,* I'm a *foxista*!"

When I asked Marta to join my gubernatorial administration, I first thought of making her secretary of the treasury or secretary of agriculture, as a healthy dose of medicine for the rural PRI good-old-boy network. But she was a wizard with media. A marketing guy myself, I knew the power of communications: He (or she) who controls the information controls the power. So Marta became communications director. With a cultured voice and TV looks, schooled in Ireland and skilled in business, she represented a fresh new voice of change for our administration. For years our relationship was strictly business, not love at all, just professional respect. She was a married woman with children in a conservative Catholic society where marriage was for life; I was still saddened by my divorce and knew for certain that I would never marry again. I poured all my time, love, and energy into four growing kids, the governorship, and the crusade for democracy. Marta did her job ably and enthusiastically. That was all there was to it.

Then one day in 1998, Marta came to me in tears, on the patio outside the Auditorio in downtown Guanajuato. "My husband and I have decided to get divorced," she said, sobbing. Like any friend, I gave her my best advice: Marriage was for life, patch it up, get counseling. "Divorce is the most painful thing you can imagine," I said. "Take it slow. Do everything you can to fix whatever is wrong—and *get back together.*"

She spent days, weeks, months analyzing her decision, but finally she decided—she was leaving the marriage, and getting a divorce. Over time we began to see each other in a different light: as something more than just coworkers and comrades in a political crusade, still professional in public but growing closer and closer in private. Finally I dared to ask her on a trip to Buenos Aires. I don't know if it was the heady music, the splendid architecture, or the Malbec wine, but since that magic week in one of the world's great romantic cities, we have been a couple—drawn together by mutual respect and our careers in public service, but really just a man and woman in love. But even back then, during the long road to the presidency, Marta was my first lady. We shared a secret, partners in our dreams. Love can move mountains, and now we were two on the move, together with our little band of friends, to bring democracy to Mexico.

ALL THIS was in the future, love and democracy and the presidency, as daybreak dawned on a Sunday morning in 1997 on the gorgeous ranch outside Veracruz, where my old friend José Luis González had retired from Coca-Cola. One of the first to encourage me to run for president in the late 1990s, José later died in a tragic accident on an all-terrain vehicle at his ranch. Tlacotalpan is perhaps the most beautiful town in Mexico on a feast day, with the children all dressed in their colorful native *veracruzana* dresses running along the old cobbestone streets, and the marimba trios playing the rosewood keyboards and metal chimes of xylophone instruments that came over with the slaves from Africa. We gathered like Hidalgo's *complot* against the Spaniards in Puebla. Hiding behind the crumbling walls of José Luis's beautiful old villa, we swore an oath to each other, that little cadre of men and women who would work day and night for the next three years to get the PRI out of Los Pinos. That group grew to include José Luis, who would organize our first TV ads; Ramón Muñoz, the organizational genius who would become my de facto chief of staff in Los Pinos and a future PAN senator; Marta, our campaign press secretary; Dr. Juan Hernández, a Mexican American poet and college professor at the University of Texas at Dallas, who would become our chief of scheduling and advance; old friends from my home state and Coca-Cola. They would be at my side from that day to Los Pinos. They moved their families to new cities, then barely saw their spouses and children for three years. Most didn't get paid. All risked their careers, life savings, and reputations to the genteel brutality of PRI retaliation, not to mention the savagery of the PRI-controlled media. They were heedless of personal danger in a country where two of the best-known national politicians had been assassinated in the previous presidential election year—just for trying to *reform* the System. What might they do to democratic revolutionaries who wanted to throw them out of Los Pinos?

Looking back on it now, I see that the PRI was more bluster than bludgeon, more bark than bite. The ruling party was a weakling bully who governed by intimidation, by the appearance of strength rather than its reality; the PRI's carrot of reward always mattered more than its stick of discipline. Once the people could see that the cupboard was bare and the government was running out of carrots, they weren't quite so afraid of the stick.

That day in Tlacotalpan was the beginning of our *pre-campaña,* the two-year-long "pre-campaign" we designed to get my name known and build a nationwide network as we campaigned without campaigning. Every weekend we prowled around Mexico by plane, bus, and car "under the roof" of secrecy. It's not so easy, getting in front of a hundred million people when you're not supposed to tell anyone about it. So we broke all the rules—without breaking any of the laws.

First, like the apostle Paul, we focused our work not on the party faithful but out among what we called "the gentiles." Instead of the traditional political campaign, which is built like military strategy, from the strength of the base outward, we went first to our traditional weakness in the the mass audience. This was controlled in blocs by the PRI, its voters bought, steamrolled, and manipulated by the official party: the union members, the *ejidatario* farmers, teachers, and owners of the mom-and-pop *changarros.*

We also reached out to the leftists I knew from the Grupo San Ángel. This was heresy to some hard-core members of the PAN. Many of them rallied around our party's 1994 standard-bearer, the firebrand orator Diego Fernández de Cevallos, a man all of us admired greatly. Fewer than 350,000 card-carrying party members would decide the nomination; if party loyalty were the only criteria, a maverick like me would surely lose. From the beginning we consciously went "outside the box" of the party's conservative base, many of whom focused on issues like banning public nudity, pornography, even birth control. Even with Diego's strong performance in 1994, the PAN had scored just 28 percent as a right-of-center party in a generally left-of-center Mexico. Courting the mainstream in the political center, our goal was to get so far ahead in the national opinion polls that the PAN could not deny us the nomination. If we could build national name identification, craft a winning campaign message of change, and sell the sizzle of a Fox "brand image" that would show the PAN we could beat the PRI, the nascent "stop Vicente" movement would melt away.

It worked: Diego and his key PAN followers became my strongest supporters. "Let's treat this like the Fox campaign is a product, separate and distinct from Vicente Fox as a person or the PAN as a political party," I would tell the clandestine gatherings of our inner circle. "Now we have to figure out how to sell our campaign. What is our product differentiation? What are the chief weaknesses of the competition's brand?" We teamed up PAN leaders and Fortune 500 types like marketing whiz Paco Ortiz and Aeroméxico CEO Pedro Cerisola; prominent economists like Dr. Eduardo Sojo and the World Bank's Luis Ernesto Derbez; leftists like Che Guevara's biographer, Dr. Jorge Castañeda. Together we laid out a plan that focused on our signature issues—cleaning up corruption; honesty in government; replacing crony capitalism with socially conscious free-market competition; making government respond to basic social needs like housing, health care, poverty, and education—the idea that only a democracy could bring Mexico into the twenty-first century with a sound economy that worked for all its people.

We were amateurs in the political process; no one outside the PRI really knew how to work the levers of the Mexican political machine. But we knew how to sell a brand, how to organize a business and distribute a product. Our brand was democracy, and the creative brief to our account team could be summed up in a single word: "change."

Everything we did needed to be *different,* from the way I dressed and spoke to the issues we raised. It wasn't enough just to articulate the public's anger or play to the far extremes of right and left; the opposition parties had tried that, and it had gotten us less than a third of the vote. As the

PRI scrambled to restore the economy after the post-Salinas devaluation crisis, people knew that the System was broken. Our job was give Mexico *hope* that democracy would change their lives for the better.

In this I was impressed with campaigns in the United States and Britain, where warm, personal, charismatic "Third Way" leaders like Bill Clinton and Tony Blair had articulated themes of hope, compassion, and change. We schooled ourselves on Ronald Reagan's sunny cowboy optimism and his use of humor to transform negatives into positives, as when Reagan turned the tables on Walter Mondale in their 1984 debate: "I will not make age an issue in this campaign. I am not going to exploit for political purposes my opponent's youth and inexperience."

Fascinated as always by the biographies of leaders, I studied how Lincoln had shaped his log-cabin image, how JFK had prepared for televised debates against Nixon. When our team went to Dallas or New York, we would stop at Barnes & Noble or Border's to buy copies of books like Theodore White's Making of the President series; when we went to Madrid or Santiago, we snapped up campaign memoirs of the leaders who brought democracy to Franco's Spain or Pinochet's Chile. We watched political TV ads from the German chancellorship elections, the Chilean referendum; from the Eisenhower campaign to LBJ's famous anti-Goldwater "daisy ad" evoking the danger of nuclear war to the commercial for late Russian president Boris Yeltsin, which raised the specter of a return to the Soviet gulag if voters restored the Communists to power.

People later made much of our campaign's innovative use of state-of-the-art media tactics, but the techniques of democracy weren't really new—they were just new to Mexico. The PRI had never had to campaign on a level playing field in the modern media age, so they never learned how to do it. We had no choice: If we wanted to win, we had to be better than any campaign Mexico had ever seen. So our question to everyone we met around the world, from the day I was elected governor to the 2000 presidential election, whether it was to Mikhail Gorbachev or Henry Kissinger; the advisers of Clinton, Bush, or winning party leaders in Spain or Chile, was not so much "What should we be doing?" but "What should we be reading?"

THERE IS an old political adage that says, "You can't beat somebody with nobody." History had shown that even if a total unknown got the *dedazo*, by Election Day the PRI nominee would be "somebody." The official party won by making sure the opposition candidates remained "nobodies." PAN and PRD candidates were denied media attention by a censored, bribed press, giving our nominees little name identification outside the party faithful and a chronic inability to raise money for advertising or grassroots work. What businessman in his right mind would be caught dead donating to the revolution?

So we set out with a three-pronged strategy. We went first to Ricardo Salinas Pliego. No relation to former president Carlos Salinas, Ricardo was the brash young founder of TV Azteca, a new rival to the Televisa colossus that had been owned by late PRI loyalist Emilio Azcárraga (El Tigre died in 1997) and now was in the hands of his son. To Azcárraga's rival Ricardo, I made the case that covering our opposition campaign could help his new Azteca network challenge Televisa's dominance; to El Tigre's more open-minded son and heir, Emilio Fernando Azcárraga Jean, who totally reorganized the network, we argued that if Televisa didn't open the door at least a crack, an increasingly curious Mexican public might switch the dials to Azteca.

It worked. In response to new reform laws and popular demand, the two main TV and radio networks began to pay attention to the opposition. Now we needed to give them a story.

STARTING A "PRE-CAMPAIGN" two years before the actual election was an unheard-of presumption in Mexican politics. "This just isn't done in Mexico!" insisted my advisers. Heads nodded in agreement around my breakfast table at our ranch. People would say Fox was arrogant, ambitious, opportunistic, disrespectful: too much "in a hurry" for the land of mañana. It was downright un-Mexican.

For me, arguing against a new idea was the kiss of death.

"You know what else has never been done before?" I asked, my fist crashing down on the table, shaking the forks and knives. "We've never *won* before!"

The team laughed and got to work, coming up with the message that would take Mexico by storm. It was that one word again: "change." Even my boots and jeans said it, the belt buckle and cowboy hat, my rough way of speaking to get under the skin of the rural and working people of Mexico and tell them that I was *different*. People said, "Here's a guy who has milked a cow and plowed a field. He worked his way up from truck driver to president of a big company, but he puts on his boots one at a time just like me. He is pissed off just like I am, and he's going to get in there and really *change* things."

But to get our message of change out to people, we needed money—lots of it, because the PRI would get all the cash they wanted from the oligarchy and from the illegal transfer of government funds to buy votes. Experts later determined that the PRI spent hundreds of millions of dollars trying to hang on to power in 2000. We would never be able to match them dollar for dollar, but we at least needed an ante to get into the game.

My friends could afford to chip in ten thousand dollars here and there; some even quit their jobs to join our revolution. But none of us had that kind of money. To raise our first million, I went to the source of the nickel deposits I had collected as a boy, the guys who gave me my first big job: Coca-Cola.

Soft-drink bottlers were wealthy figures, many multimillionaires with close ties to the PRI. We figured none of them would even be seen publicly with us, much less give money to try to overthrow the System. But as so often happens, when you are in trouble and need help, an angel taps on your shoulder. This is the way every church gets built—first you dig a hole, then God finds a way for you to raise the rafters. At our first clandestine meeting at Lagos de Moreno in Jalisco, the bottlers pledged the early resources to start the campaign.

"Mexico has to change," they said, one by one. "I'm with you, Vicente. Just don't mention my name."

We kept our mouths shut and our contributor list a highly guarded secret, which was legal at the time. Oddly enough, in a totalitarian society, full disclosure of campaign contributions makes the peaceful overthrow of a regime by election almost impossible, because no one wants to be seen crossing swords with the established authority. This is an irony of campaign finance reform: Spending limits serve to restrict those who want things to change and thus can aid an incumbent party in power.

Soon we had enough to go on television and fund Amigos de Fox, the independent citizens' organization we assembled to match the PRI's vaunted grassroots machine. This allowed us to expand past the PAN's narrow conservative base in the north of Mexico and take our gospel of change to the urban masses, the rural poor, the churches and the leftists, the owners of the little stores where I had sold soft drinks as a young route-truck driver. Again I spoke wherever two or more were gathered, at evangelical tent meetings in Oaxaca or the corporate conference rooms of Monterrey. The constant hustle and bustle of the campaign trail is always a tonic to me. I took the kids along and made family outings of the trips, singing on the bus like a Mexican Partridge Family.

But this was deadly serious. Once we'd won the PAN nomination and gotten what the Americans call a "bounce" in the polls, suddenly we were in striking distance, and the System got nervous. The music stopped, and the PRI went to war.

By the fall of 1999, I wasn't just Don Quijote anymore. The media began drawing comparisons between our steady gains in the polls and the strong 1988 showing of Cuauhtémoc Cárdenas, the leftist son of former President Lázaro Cárdenas and mayor of Mexico City. As Cuauhtémoc resigned to launch his national campign and I stepped down from the governorship to run for president, we were neck and neck with each other and the PRI in a tight three-way contest for the first time in Mexican history.

Before it had been fun, music and rallies in the *zócalo*. We like a celebratory atmosphere in campaigns in Latin America: People paint the streets and even the boulders along the highway in PRI green, white, and red; PAN blue and orange; PRD yellow. Our events are more like fiestas than the dreary, dull, rubber-chicken dinners of U.S. politics. But now we weren't singing on the bus, striding in blue jeans through the *zócalos*, going horseback riding on Sundays. Now we were in suits and ties with our growing coalition in Mexico City, trying to overthrow the government. Even though we were using the peaceful and legal means of the ballot box, many had been killed in Mexico for less.

Even with my children on the campaign trail, I can't explain why I never worried about assassination. I'm always at my most comfortable out among people, with the campesinos of my state or the *indígenas* of Ttaxcala. I knew these people intimately, we were working to help them—why would they try to hurt me? I've never spoken about this to Václav Havel or Nelson Mandela or any of the much braver revolutionaries I've met. Powerful, far more brutal regimes did much more to try to hurt them: put them in jail, beat them, set dogs on them. In the case of Ellen

Johnson-Sirleaf of Liberia, soldiers took her to a dark field one night at rifle point and told her she was about to die. But I suspect that these democratic presidents would tell you the same: You simply can't worry about this. When you look into the eyes of your neighbors, the children who run along the side of your car making the victory sign with their fingers and singing our slogan of "*¡Ya ganamos!*" (We've already won!), somehow you think only of the great cause you are advancing—and whether you will have time for a bathroom stop for your daughter before the next event.

Advice to aspiring politicians: Never, ever pass up a restroom on the campaign trail. You drink too much coffee along the way. And learn to eat very fast, the minute they put your plate down, because they will immediately introduce you to speak, and then you will stand at the podium looking out longingly at the delicious cake the audience is enjoying. Then they will hand you another cup of coffee and whisk you out the door, hungry and light-headed and a bit cranky. This is about the moment when the press asks you what you think of your presidential opponent, and you reply that he is a sawed-off little shrimp, with little ideas to match.

Francisco Labastida was a man of little stature, though it was no doubt impolitic of me to say so. He was the governor of Sinaloa, a desert northern state with the worst drug-cartel violence in the country. In the PRI's no-reelection tradition of "recycling" politicians, Labastida went on to be secretary of agriculture and secretary of the interior under Zedillo. Like the incumbent president, Labastida was a colorless fellow who offended few, but he lacked Zedillo's depth of intellect and economic savvy. As with Zedillo, the PRI chose Labastida almost by default: Unlike his rival, the ambitious Tabasco governor Roberto Madrazo, Labastida didn't push his way to the top. Afraid to be the moving man who comes out blurry in the photograph, Labastida waited with the chief quality that earned the *dedazo:* patience.

I was high on the government's blacklist, so my state of Guanajuato ranked dead last in federal government largesse. This was critical in a nation where 95 percent of all fiscal income is doled out by the presidency to the states. Normally a governor would go begging for federal aid. But I've never put myself on my knees to any man, only to God. As president I would abolish this system of political patronage, eliminating the discretionary allocation of tax dollars to states with friendly governors. For now

I could only lambaste the PRI's policy of favoring states like Labastida's Sinaloa or Madrazo's Tabasco, making headlines by saying that Zedillo wasn't welcome in Guanajuato.

In Mexico we love this combat of the *burlándose,* the verbal cockfight where a candidate proves his machismo with the spurs of insults. *"¡Chaparrito!"* screamed the newspapers on the eve of the first debate, as I called Labastida the slang for "little shrimp," sort of like calling someone "shorty."

"The little man needs a *banquito* to stand toe to toe with me," I said, ridiculing the two-foot platform that the PRI's strategists had insisted be placed behind Labastida's podium, so that we would seem the same height on television.

¡CHAPARRITO! The bold black letters of Mexico City's tabloids would be sitting on Francisco Labastida's doorstep the morning of the first debate. I was like a boxer before the match, punching the air, like Ali giving lip to Frazier. This is the psych war that goes on behind the scenes before a presidential debate. You've seen it with Bill Clinton or Tony Blair, George W. Bush versus Al Gore or John Kerry, and you will see it again in elections around the planet, as the democracies export America's hottest new product: spin control.

It begins with the candidate's trainers lowering the expectations of the media—"Vicente's never debated a presidential candidate before, Cárdenas has run for president, so he's a pro, Labastida is a professional politician who will have all the answers, and of course the PRI has it all rigged so that Labastida will win, no matter what."

Meanwhile we scrambled to come up with a winning strategy, rehearsing for the big debate behind closed doors in borrowed houses, with the security guys in black flak jackets sleeping shifts in the bunk beds. We squatted on cement floors with all the furniture cleared away and laptops on the knees of our aides, a mock studio set up for the day in the living room. The sliding glass doors were taped up with the wires of antibugging electronics. When something was really sensitive, we walked outside by an overgrown garden or a half-empty swimming pool, where *gobernación* couldn't listen.

We changed location every day that Easter week. Semana Santa is a big holiday in Mexico, a two-week family vacation for many—like Christmas, Hanukkah, and New Year's in the United States and Europe. The capital was eerily quiet, the skies impossibly blue in the April sunshine. Mexico City's notorious pollution had left with the cars to the beach and the countryside. It was the surreal life of peaceful democratic revolution in the perfect dictatorship: Labastida was at the beach, prepping with James Carville and platoons of PRI strategists at a resort, where they taught him to stand tall and attack me for my rudeness in ridiculing his stature in a country where the average male is five foot five. We were in Mexico City in empty houses with For Sale signs in the yard, rotating from place to place like a floating crap game. In the circle, sitting on the floor, were Mexico's foremost intellectuals—leftists and Wharton-schooled World Bank economists, poets and PR men, corporate CEOs—and Marta, who reminded us to speak to the heart. All the time the birds were singing outside, and at the end of each day the fellow with the burn bag came around to gather up the draft speeches for the incinerator, as we practiced the game of political judo against the man who'd "gotten the finger" from the PRI.

It was halfway between a college bull session and a state-of-the-art presidential campaign. We staged mock debates on camera with stand-ins for our opponent. I sparred with my friend Fausto Alzati, a rebel *priista* who had been education secretary in Zedillo's government. Fausto played Labastida; formerly Marxist scholars like Jorge Castañeda and Adolfo Aguilar Zinser took turns playing the PRD's Cuauhtémoc Cárdenas. Advisers stood by with stopwatch in hand, arguing over the fine points of language, rifts in ideology, the correct width of the knot in my tie. We sat in a semicircle before a TV monitor and evaluated each performance. Tirelessly I pressed the members of the group to speak their minds: *"¿Comentarios? ¿Comentarios?"*

Particularly in Mexico, with our tradition of the authoritarian caudillo, it can be difficult to get people to speak their minds. But revolutionaries don't have that problem. With the country's preeminent intellectuals in the room, I had plenty of advice; it was like drinking from a fire hose. Presidential candidates often feel like kids playing baseball in Wisconsin. As you step up to the plate, everyone is shouting advice from behind the fence: coaches, teammates, your brothers, the guy selling ice cream in the stands. Bend your knees! Choke up! Loosen up! Stick your butt out! Quick bat, now! Wait for it, now! But in the end it's just you and the pitcher. In the studio it is you, the presidential candidate, and your opponents, mano a mano.

The trouble with a democracy, of course, is that there are an awful lot of people involved. Every one of them had an opinion for me that Holy Week. I listened and learned. I wish I had a dollar for every time someone told me, "Just be yourself. But you might want to say . . ." The first day we had five people in the room, the next day ten; by D-Day we had sixty, until someone was smart enough to announce, "Fifty of us need to leave this room and give Vicente some peace, and I'll be the first one to go!"

We were still well behind in the polls, and most of the pundits felt that the country bumpkin from Guanajuato could never go toe to toe with the two veterans, Labastida and Cárdenas. But I felt oddly calm on debate night as our campaign caravan, gaily bedecked in the bright blue and Day-Glo orange of the PAN, eased through the crowd outside Mexico City's World Trade Center. Some waved placards with our Fox logo with its big X marked through a ballot box. Others were angry rebels of the PRD and paid union henchmen of the PRI, who shouted insults and pelted our car with tomatoes and heads of lettuce. (The son of austere farmers, I've often wondered how the advocates of the poor could waste good food that way.) I just smiled and thought, *What the hell, at least people are starting to feel free enough to speak their minds!*

When it came my turn, I spoke straight to people's hearts in a way every Mexican could understand, summing up the campaign as a crusade for democracy. "In fewer than seventy days, we will have the historic, unique opportunity to end more than seventy years of bad government, to change more than seventy years of a corrupt system that has stolen from Mexicans the fruit of their labor," I said.

"If you don't believe change is possible, look what has happened around the world," I added. "No one could imagine that a farmer like Mandela, or a miner like Walesa, could break the chains of oppression and authority. Nobody could imagine that students, teachers, and housewives with their bare hands were going to bring the Berlin Wall down. Now the world's gaze is on Mexico, and our country's future is in your hands," I said. "Let's tear down the walls of corruption, poverty, and unemployment that have held Mexico back. . . . The eyes of the world are on Mexico. And only you can decide what country you want and the kind of future you want for you and your family."

Labastida, prepped by Carville & Company, shattered the high tone with a clumsy attack on my *chaparrito* comment before the debate: "He's called me 'shorty,' he's made obscene gestures on television when he's referring to me. But now he's changed his skin. He's come in all polished. He wants us to forget all these gross statements."

Even under the hot lights of the podium after the long, weary days of debate prep, I felt fresh, clearheaded, energized. Somewhere in the back of my mind, I recalled Winston Churchill's brilliant comeback when Bessie Braddock accused him, "Sir, you are drunk." Churchill replied, "Yes, madam, and you are ugly. But in the morning I shall be sober."

"My esteemed friend Señor Labastida, I can lose my vulgar language," I replied. "But you politicians who are cheaters, who are corrupt, who have governed badly, those characteristics you will never lose." It was the sound bite that played over and over again that night, essentially saying, "I can stop being rude, but you can't stop being corrupt."

I knew I had just scored.

And so it went, back and forth, achieving our goal of making this a two-man race with the PRI's Labastida. In the green room, my inner circle gathered around the monitors with their primitive versions of the BlackBerry, the pagers beeping in reports from the live focus groups we had secreted behind two-way mirrors across the city to gauge voter perceptions. On the floor of the studio, Paco Ortiz, the former ad-agency exec we had recruited through corporate headhunters like Horacio McCoy of Korn-Ferry to serve as our communications director, kept me updated through a series of elaborate prearranged hand signals. Like a baseball manager, Paco tapped his shoulder and held up three fingers, then one: We were winning in our flash polls, three to one.

You could feel it as we emerged from the fifty-story tower. The crowds chanted "¡Ya! ¡Ya! ¡Ya!" and flashed the victory signal with their fingers in the slogan Paco had dreamed up. "*¡Ya ganamos!*" I shouted. "We've already won!" We piled into our Suburban like a soccer team who had just triumphed in the World Cup.

This, too, is part of the gamesmanship of the modern presidential campaign: Not only must you win the debate, you also have to "win the spin." Inside the World Trade Center, our team kicked off a carefully choreographed ballet of advisers, senators, and friendly commentators. Our spin doctors prepped them with talking points to emphasize key sound bites that had scored best with the live focus groups. As debate night wore on, PAN senators and Grupo San Ángel allies appeared on talk shows to claim victory, cite weaknesses in Labastida's performance, and call him out on mistakes of fact detected by our quick-response research team.

The mood was exuberant. I had won the first round, but would the referees lift my gloves in victory? The PRI still controlled the media and polling apparatus; they would say that Labastida had won, even if he'd left the ring in a stretcher. But the new capital newspaper, *Reforma,* and some of the TV and radio stations were doing their own polls. In the backseat of the Suburban, my advisers nervously checked their shiny new electronic pagers, cutting-edge stuff back in 2000. Then the car radio blared the results of a flash poll: "*Vicente Fox won tonight's debate, according to our instant survey—*"

That evening Mexico got its first unfiltered look at the presidential candidates, both in the live debate and in the news clips that ran over and over again. There I was, talking about Mandela and freedom and mothers who needed money to buy milk, versus Labastida in his high-pitched, nasal tone, meandering through vague points of public policy. Most of all there was the *chaparrito* exchange. Presidential debates often turn on key moments: Ronald Reagan turning the tables on George H. W. Bush in New Hampshire with the line "I am paying for this microphone, Mr. Green!"—and Lloyd Bentsen's famous riposte to Dan Quayle—"I knew Jack Kennedy. Jack Kennedy was a friend of mine. Senator, you are no Jack Kennedy." The trivial exchange about the height of Labastida's debate platform knocked the props out from under the PRI. Somehow this passing remark summed up the contrast between an uncouth rebel and the smooth, polished gangster veneer of the ruling party: *I can stop being rude, but you can't stop governing badly, and you won't stop being corrupt.*

By week's end we were ahead of Labastida in the presidential head-to-head by three points in our internal polling. We poured on the ads, raising every peso we could squeeze from the "bandwagon effect" of the debate victory. Big businessmen began to worry that we might actually beat the System, so we encouraged them to cover their bets. We couldn't keep up with the PRI's billion-dollar budget. But even if we could match one ad to every three of the official party, we could win: Our product was better; we had successfully differentiated our brand of democracy from the PRI's liabilities.

Our slogan of "*¡Ya ganamos!*" came true: We *were* winning. I could see the differences in my closest aides and friends, who stopped calling me "Vicente" and started calling me "Governor," much to my annoyance. (While I differ with George Bush and Tony Blair on Iraq, we share a common distaste for the pomp and ceremony of high office, for the same reason: It wastes time.)

I could sense a difference in the alert eyes of the unusually tall *guanajuatenses* who served as my security guards. As we moved ahead in the polls, they worked harder to shield me from the growing crowds. Suddenly I wasn't merely some cowboy loudmouth, but the front-running candidate for president of Mexico. This is when I should have remembered Richard Nixon's admonition that just when you are on top and everything is going brilliantly, this is when you make your biggest mistakes.

By the middle of May, we headed into the warm-up for the second debate confident of victory. We had beaten them once, and while expectations were higher now, we all felt that I could deliver in the second round. Then came Black Tuesday and the infamous "debate over the debates," when I lost my temper and nearly blew the presidency.

THE PRI DIDN'T WANT another debate. The ruling party had tried all the Carville-inspired trappings of pseudodemocracy: a simulated primary election within the party to nominate Labastida; slick TV ads with a new slogan promising "a new PRI, closer to the people." But we climbed in the polls. So they decided to "go negative" with those hatchet-job commercials that are surely the worst export of the United States. In the dark, scary voices so beloved of Washington spin doctors, the ads warned that Vicente Fox was a dangerous radical whose election would lead to revolutionary overthrow of the established order.

What Carville & Company missed was that the Mexican people *wanted* to overthrow the system. Mexicans were fed up with corruption, economic crises, poverty, illiteracy, and disease. Having worked for Bill Clinton, the "Man From Hope," Labastida's American advisers should have understood: Our people needed *la esperanza*—hope.

Our campaign ads focused on the single theme of change and this single benefit of hope. Facing that sudden onslaught from a PRI with its back to the wall, we made a conscious decision to move up above the fray. Mexicans had never before elected a maverick. Our research showed that they might be angry enough at the System to risk it—we didn't need to spend our time and precious advertising dollars on articulating PRI negatives. But Mexico is a culturally conservative country, and voters were still apprehensive about the uncertainty of their future under democracy. The PRI's Mexico, for all its ills, was a paternalistic caretaker society, though the caretakers had failed to take care of us very well. Even if the regime sometimes beat us and behaved like drunken criminals, they were still the only parents we had ever known.

In any presidential campaign, the big hill the challenger must climb in the final debate is to "look presidential"—to project the father-figure gravitas that is the voters' ideal of a head of state. In a nation where our imperial presidents wore elegant gray suits and a presidential sash, a rancher in blue jeans and a FOX belt buckle faced a mountain of doubt. The heading on one strategy memo that survived our burn bag shows that we debated this weighty issue: *¿Corbata o no corbata?*—"Tie or no tie?" I worked harder to act presidential: If Henry IV was said to have thought Paris was worth a mass, surely democracy in Mexico was worth a gray tie.

NEGOTIATIONS FOR the second debate dragged on that May, as the PRI threw up roadblocks to avert another weak showing by Labastida. The regime was no longer concerned about the height of the *banquito*. No doubt, their focus groups came up with the same results that ours did: Voters told pollsters that Fox seemed more in command, more presidential, and more intelligent than Labastida—three key assets the PRI expected to have on their side. With our full-court advertising press stressing hope and change, the PRI went into a stall, hoping they could wear us down over the final two months with their three-to-one advantage in media spending—if they could just keep anyone from seeing Labastida and me together again, live and unfiltered.

Every day our debate negotiator, the chain-smoking former Aeroméxico CEO Pedro Cerisola, came into our headquarters looking drawn and pale from hours of wrangling. The PRI wanted to restrict us to preformatted topics, a single interviewer, no rebuttals or interchange between the candidates—essentially, they wanted side-by-side campaign commercials, not a debate. Most devastating to us was their demand to limit the second debate to a highbrow Mexico City public-affairs channel watched primarily by the intelligentsia, where it wouldn't be seen by the majority of voters.

"I've negotiated with the unions, banks, regulators, and politicians," Pedro said. "But never before with someone who just didn't want to make a deal." Not eager to be seen as cowardly for ducking the debate, the PRI's tactic was delay, delay, delay. This is the classic Mexican game of mañana: Don't say no, just say "tomorrow."

Finally negotiations broke off altogether. There would be no second debate. This was cataclysmic for us. We were neck and neck with Labastida for first place, but if it was that close, we were sure the PRI would steal the election through fraud, as they had in 1988. We gathered at midnight in the Presidential Suite of the JW Marriott, which in our heady ascent in the polls we had commandeered—an act of political hubris for which, in my Catholic guilt, I am quite sure we paid dearly. Paco Ortiz and his crew whipped together a short national TV broadcast that I delivered at midnight, attacking the PRI for denying Mexicans the opportunity to hear the candidates.

Cuauhtémoc Cárdenas, the leftist PRD candidate who had been cheated in that contest, was not yet ready to throw in the towel. The early front-runner now lagged well behind the two of us, so Cuauhtémoc sought to boost his third-place status by mediating the "debate over the debate." Around noon on Tuesday, May 23, Cárdenas called to invite me to an impromptu meeting with Labastida at Cuauhtémoc's headquarters to break the impasse. I accepted on the spot, jumped into the Suburban, and rushed over to his office.

And walked straight into an ambush.

Temper is not a presidential emotion. Voters expect presidents to be calm, cool, collected. Once in a great while, a resolute, controlled anger might be in order, like George W. Bush's resolve to go after the 9/11 terrorists and "smoke the rattlesnakes out of their holes." But a tantrum with my hair askew, clothes rumpled, face sweaty in the spring heat—this was not part of the strategy memo.

As I climbed out of the Suburban for our "private" meeting, I knew we were in trouble. Forty or fifty cameras crowded the lawn of the little garden in front of Cuauhtémoc's *casa de campaña*. A hundred reporters milled on the grass. The sky was blue, the birds chirped peacefully above the media's murmurs, and we were in trouble.

Cárdenas—a man I admire greatly, even though our politics differ—

had made a little deal with the devil. He and Labastida had cooked up a plan to invite me to a private *debate sobre los debates*—a "debate over the debates." Then the two of them submarined us, by inviting the media. Looking back, I have to hand it to Cuauhtémoc: He looked like the leader, and I'd just been had.

There were three microphones on the table. I nodded grimly and took my seat. My two opponents smiled smugly. They were in full makeup, with carefully typed talking points in front of them. I had one thought, which best translates to impeccable English as follows: *I am in deep shit.* I wish I could tell you that I deftly recovered my composure, uttered some polished bon mot, coupled perhaps with a literary quotation from Octavio Paz. Instead I pounded the table with my fist and demanded an open debate, "Today, today, today!"

"¡Hoy!" I barked hoarsely, thumping my hand with each word. *"¡Hoy, hoy, hoy!"*

IT WAS A DISASTER. In three seconds of discomposure, I had confirmed the worst fears that the PRI had spent millions of TV ad dollars pushing in their scare campaign: This angry cowboy from Guanajuato would be a wild man, a dangerous populist—unpredictable, ungovernable, unfit for the presidency.

Here was the genius of the trap my opponents had laid: After I fell apart on national television, they smiled and agreed genially to a prearranged deal for a second debate that Friday. This should have been good news. But there wasn't a necktie in the world gray enough to make me look presidential after the debacle on Cuauhtémoc Cárdenas's front lawn.

BLACK TUESDAY! shouted the headlines. Within twenty-four hours, the Carville-trained machine of the PRI churned out one of those gringo negative ads with grainy footage of my Black Tuesday debacle, asking voters whether they could trust this revolutionary who pounded his fist on the table and shouted at his opponents.

We were in free fall, dropping like a stone. On Monday we had been ahead of Labastida in the polls. By Friday we were seven points behind, a landslide margin in a five-way race. We holed up in one of our "safe houses" in Las Lomas to prepare. In the backyard I walked with my team, and we thought, *How the hell do we get out of this?*

Apologize, most of them advised. Stop the bleeding, say you're sorry, move on. Then one of my strategists recalled a conversation he'd had with my mother years before, when he had gone to Doña Mercedes to learn what kind of man I was.

"*¡Terco!*" she replied, which means "stubborn." But it is slang, like the English term "bullheaded."

"She told me, 'Vicente is too *terco* to be president,'" the adviser recounted. "'He is what he is, and you'll never change him. He uses bad language that embarrasses the family, and he wears boots and jeans, like he never had a mother who taught him to wear a nice coat and tie, like a president should. But you will never change him,'" the young man recalled. "And here's the thing, Vicente—she said that with pride!"

He was right. *Terco*—firm, stubborn, bullheaded—in Mexico these can be terms of affection. Doña Mercedes was really saying that her son was a man of principle, that he was who he was, that politics would never change him. So when the cameras rolled at the debate in the Museo Tecnológico that night, I acknowledged that as I was pushing for an open debate that previous week, "Some think I was a little stubborn, *terco*. Even my mother used to tell me that." Then I took a deep breath and plunged in. "But you need firm character and true leadership to end seventy years of corruption, poverty, and desperation. Do you think a weak and gray person could stand up to the PRI and its allies?" I was pounding my fist verbally on the table, just as in Cuauhtémoc's garden: *Hoy, hoy, hoy*. In that moment I had no idea whether I had achieved a feat of political judo and turned our biggest negative into a strength—or just sealed the lid on my political coffin.

As THE DEBATE wore on, Paco waved frantic signals. Thumbs-up, did that mean we were doing well or that I needed to pump up the energy? I just concentrated on the message: Mexico needed change, *hoy, hoy, hoy*.

Afterward, crowded into the Suburban with all the beepers and pagers, I really wasn't sure how well I had done until after we arrived at an improvised midnight rally at the golden Angel of Independence, the national symbol of Mexico which stands amid a great traffic circle on the Paseo de la Reforma. As I mounted the steps of the hastily erected platform, I heard the boom of ten thousand voices shouting in unison, a continuous rhythmic rolling rumble, nothing our partisans had started, just the spontaneous roar of the massing crowd:

"¡HOY! ¡HOY! ¡HOY! ¡HOY! ¡HOY! ¡HOY!"

We had won. A poll of viewers by Mexico City's *Reforma* newpaper said I had won the second debate by 49 percent to Labastida's 17 percent. As we arrived back at campaign headquarters in the wee hours, exhausted and victorious, I hugged my daughters and told my aides that we would win the vote on July 2. "Now," I said, "we just have to keep the bad guys from stealing it."

IT WASN'T EVEN CLOSE. Children ran along the side of our caravans, still flashing the victory sign but shouting now their new slogan demanding change, *"¡Hoy! ¡Hoy, hoy, hoy!"* The Mexican people wanted democracy *today*. On July 2, 2000, they got it.

As it happens, the second of July is my birthday and the name of my favorite horse, the big white stallion Dos de Julio that George W. Bush would later decide was not on his printed agenda for our summit meeting. I slept like a baby on election eve and rose that July 2 feeling fresh, eager, alive. Despite all the doom and gloom in the media—all but one of the major media polls forecast victory for the PRI—I *knew* we would win. You could feel it on the streets. People might be telling pollsters that they would vote PRI, for fear they might lose their government benefits, but our polls said that while they might still smile and "take the taco," they would vote for Fox and the Alliance for Change, the coalition we had built with dissident leftists and the Green Party.

I went to ten o'clock morning mass with my mother and children at the little chapel outside the former hacienda gates. Then we walked to the nearby school to vote. The kids and I walked Doña Mercedes home, gave her a kiss and a big Mexican *abrazo,* then went to our favorite taco stand, Chuy's Tacos. Chuy took my picture for his wall, exulting, "Now they will see that a president of Mexico ate my tacos!"

By the time we arrived in Mexico City, the capital was in a mood of suppressed excitement. Everywhere people flashed the victory sign at each other, hanging bodily out of their car windows and shouting, *"¡Hoy! ¡Hoy! ¡Hoy!"* But by one or two in the afternoon, we began to worry. Exit polls showed that we were winning the big urban *casillas,* the polling stations in the major cities. But what kind of chicanery was going on in the *priista* rural strongholds? The mystery was how far the PRI dinosaurs might go. Would Zedillo let them steal the election?

Our campaign had scoured the world, lobbying all my contacts to beseech world leaders to serve as election monitors. Jimmy Carter came. So did former U.S. Secretary of State James A. Baker III, who would later that year head George W. Bush's team in the Florida recount.

In the final days before an election, Mexico bans polls, speechmaking, and alcohol, three vices to which politicians are notoriously addicted. But we were allowed to conduct exit polls on Election Day.

"The Cowboys are ahead of the Redskins by a touchdown!" the exit pollster said over the cell phone to my aides, who strained to hear over the growing crowd at campaign headquarters, talking in a hastily improvised sports code to confuse the agents of *gobernación*. Our campaign advance chief, UT Dallas professor Dr. Juan Hernández, looked puzzled—he was no fan of American sports. "A touchdown, is that six points or seven?" Juan whispered into his cell phone. "There's a kick involved, right? Or is that where you get three points?"

"That's a field goal," said the exasperated pollster. "Jesus, just tell Fox he's won by seven points!"

We had won. But would the PRI give us the sash? We felt better that afternoon, when President Zedillo's private secretary, Liebano Saenz, made a polite courtesy call to Marta to say we were ahead in the government's internal polling. Then, as I emerged from mass that July evening with my children—you can't pray too much on Election Day, even if your teenagers are bored stiff—the radio reports of our victory began trickling out, despite the government's ban on election results until after the polls had closed in Baja California, an hour later than the rest of Mexico.

Then President Zedillo shocked the nation with a bold move. He went on television to announce that Vicente Fox had been elected president of Mexico.

THERE ARE STILL those old-guard *priistas* who consider Ernesto Zedillo a traitor to his class for his actions on the night of July 2, 2000, as the party boss who betrayed the machine. But in that moment President Zedillo became a true democrat. He spoke about eight hundred words that night, directed not so much to the nation as a whole but to the PRI itself, urging his followers in Mexico's official party to accept the outcome of a free election. It was Zedillo's "Gorbachev moment." In minutes he preempted any possibility of violent resistance from hard-line *priistas*. It was an act of electoral integrity that will forever mark the mild-mannered economist as a historic figure of Mexico's peaceful transition to democracy. His approval rating shot up to 66 percent.

Five thousand people, gathered in the giant toy-block contemporary architecture of the PAN's headquarters in Mexico City, gave an audible gasp when Zedillo's image popped up on the big screens above our heads. What was the president doing? Would he claim victory for Labastida? Was he massing the tanks on the lawns of Los Pinos? When Zedillo publicly acceded to our victory, the crowd simply went wild. One of my sharpest memories of that evening is the impromptu news conference we held downstairs in a glass-walled conference center. There the notoriously cynical, PRI-controlled media joined me in singing the Mexican national anthem, many of the reporters with tears streaming down their cheeks: *"Mexicanos al grito de guerra . . ."*

A hundred thousand or more of our supporters gathered again at the Angel of Independence, holding up their babies for a first glimpse of democracy, singing and crying and laughing and shouting for democracy: *"¡Hoy! ¡Hoy! ¡Hoy!"* Foreign correspondents reported that the ground literally shook beneath the stomping feet of the crowd. Was Mexico City's famously unstable subsoil experiencing another earthquake? No, one of my aides assured me as I stepped to the podium, "That's the sound of a hundred million people who just got their freedom."

VÁCLAV HAVEL, the playwright-poet, president, and hero of Czech democracy, called me to congratulate me. Lech Walesa called. Bill Clinton, president of the United States, called. George W. Bush, not yet president of the United States, called. So did Al Gore, almost-but-not-quite-president of the United States. Henry Kissinger called, and Tony Blair, and Vladimir Putin. About the time the king of Spain called, we ran out of cell-phone minutes.

We were broke. My ex-Coca-Cola friends, Fortune 500 executives, and fellow maverick *panista* businessmen like my old friend Carlos Rojas had outdone themselves trying to raise enough money from private sources in Mexico to match the hundreds of millions of dollars the PRI was milking from government funds. But we had spent it all trying to compete with Labastida's advertising buy, and we couldn't afford to keep the phones on. My aides were running up their personal credit cards, charging campaign events to hotel bills they had no idea how to pay, digging into their pockets to hand fistfuls of pesos to student volunteers who ran down the street to the Telmex store and traded in one mobile-phone plan for another, hoping that the telecommunications giant Carlos Slim—now the world's richest man—wouldn't notice. One of my friends has a photo of my future first lady, Marta, sitting at a table in the Fiesta Americana Hotel the day after the election tearing the plastic from a pile of shrink-wrapped phone cards so I could talk to Nelson Mandela.

For the first time in the campaign, I was scared. A hundred million people sat on my shoulders, expecting me to deliver the fruits of democracy. Later, during the transition, when I groused that people expected me to walk on water, one of my advisers said, "What do you expect, Mr. President? At the end of every rally, you told the crowd, 'Suffer the little children to come unto me!' " We had needed to give people hope. The close of every campaign speech in those final days was an invitation to the children, who were the future of Mexico, to come forward and join me as we crusaded for a country where they would be free to rise as high as their talents would take them. In my campaigns there was a religious zeal for which I will never apologize and never recant. This was God's work, and if we failed Him, it was our fault, not His.

Jesus Christ, I thought, *what a burden.* But then, as the first day dawned and I realized that Mexico was finally a real democracy, it hit me: *Jesus Christ, we did it!* From that day forward, I was at peace, even if the world around me was not.

CHAPTER 12

THE SPIRIT OF SAN CRISTÓBAL

YOU CANNOT IMAGINE what a sensation it caused in Mexico when the president of the United States chose our family ranch in Guanajuato for his first foreign state visit. Never before in the long and troubled history between our nations had Mexico been extended such dignity. The unswerving tradition of U.S. presidents for nearly a century, back to Warren G. Harding in 1923, has been to honor Canada with the first state visit, then perhaps London or Paris, even Moscow or Beijing. But not Mexico.

On February 16, 2001, George W. Bush bounded off Air Force One at the little León International Airport, which my sister and I had once held hostage—"international" because we have flights to Dallas and Houston, but the terminal is still just six gates and one Dunkin' Donuts stand. Behind the new U.S. president came Secretary of State Colin Powell and Condoleezza Rice, then Bush's national security adviser; Andrew Card, the White House chief of staff; Jeff Davidow, the U.S. ambassador to Mexico, a Clinton holdover whom Bush regarded highly and had retained. Colin Powell is a big bear of a man, warm and affable and hearty; Condi Rice is an iron lady, attractive and charming but with a steel-trap mind; Andrew Card is like a corporate executive, affable but all business, with a watchful eye on the clock; Davidow is a bearded Latin American specialist at State, prone to open-necked guayabera shirts and good cigars. Within minutes the whole entourage of a visiting U.S. president—which can number up to a thousand people—headed in a single line of Suburbans down the rural road to Rancho San Cristóbal.

The Secret Service had spent the first month of George Bush's presidency combing over the ranch with the Mexican army officers of Estado Mayor, getting their feet muddy in the rows of broccoli and generally disturbing my mother—"They are *everywhere,* Vicente, and they are very polite, but how am I going to *feed* them all?" Doña Mercedes later greeted George Bush with casually gracious Mexican hospitality. "Oh, you're Vicente's friend!" she said, as though I had brought a schoolmate home for the weekend. "Please make yourself at home, you are always welcome here." President Bush took it in stride. He has a mother, too.

Doña Mercedes's nonchalance belied the fever with which she had supervised six weeks of landscaping, housecleaning, and makeshift construction at San Cristóbal since early January, after I casually mentioned at Sunday dinner that the first summit of the Bush administration would be held at her house. San Cristóbal is a beautiful place, but it is a working farm, not the Ritz-Carlton. I suppose it looked familiar to a fellow who had grown up in Midland, Texas, and spent the previous year traveling the back roads of Missouri, Iowa, and Ohio. The presidential motorcade went by the tollbooth, the electric power lines and the Pemex station that mark the final boundaries of town. We passed the silo and the fertilizer warehouse, the drivers watching for the marker for their left turn at the feed store with the Cruz Azul logo, famous to Mexican soccer fans.

Inside the new fence that Estado Mayor had built around the ranch, we had scrambled to erect barracks for the security guards and cut a road for the security vehicles. We built a little addition to my house, closing in the sunroom to create the big, comfortable glassed-in dining room where I tell you this story today, surrounded by Mexican leather sofas and a collection of the saddles from foreign heads of state. The room would come in handy later when King Juan Carlos and Queen Sofia came to the ranch. (My mother would have been horrified if we'd served Spain's monarchs in my breakfast nook.)

That day in February 2001, every farmhand at San Cristóbal had on his Sunday best to welcome the first U.S. president who had made this gesture of coming to Mexico on equal terms. This was the great honor George Bush paid to Mexico, the reason I will always be his friend, no matter how sharply we may disagree on Iraq. Whether we stand fiercely together in the face of Hugo Chávez or find ourselves divided by the Berlin Wall that his Congress wants to build along the Rio Grande, down deep I believe that George Bush brought Mexico and the United States closer than ever in our troubled history. What the media later dubbed the "Spirit of San Cristóbal" was first and foremost a friendship between two former governors, both of us ranchers and newly elected presidents, each taking tremendous heat for our willingness to stand up for each other: Bush attacked as too pro-Mexico for the anti-immigrant right wing of his party, Fox attacked as too pro–United States by the anti-American intelligentsia of the Mexican left.

But the left had a leader at my side that day, Dr. Jorge Castañeda, the anti-NAFTA crusader, eminent historian and part-time NYU professor who had left the Mexican Communist Party to join our broad-based "Alliance for Change," which was our name for the united front of the PAN and the environmentalist Green Party in 2000. I had rankled my own party's right wing by naming Castañeda as foreign minister, but he was a good counterweight to the Wharton-educated economists and corporate CEOs in my inner circle, the free-market advocates that the Left derided as the "Guanawashingtons."

Getting too close to Bush was politically dangerous for us in Mexico, where we needed to build coalitions with the nationalist PRI and the leftist PRD in order to get our reforms through Congress. Shortly after the presidential election, back in August of 2000, I visited both Washington and Dallas in my first trip to the United States as president-elect, carefully staying neutral in the 2000 Bush-Gore race. Jorge took me to the vice presidential residence at the National Observatory to meet Al Gore, the impressively intelligent Democratic vice president, whose views on the environment I greatly admired—I had been the Green Party's presidential candidate in 2000, too. Back in August 2000, most of us abroad expected that Gore and the Democrats would win in November. President Clinton seemed to have weathered the impeachment scandal; the U.S. economy was strong; Gore was handsome, articulate, clean-cut and above reproach; and the Clinton-Gore approval numbers remained high. On my transition team, only Dr. Juan Hernández, a dual citizen whose mother came from Fort Worth, was in the minority—we often chided him for being George W. Bush's number-one fan. "Watch this guy," Juan persisted. "I saw what he did as governor in Texas. Bush is going to win."

Since our meetings in Austin, I had considered George a friend and admired his strong stance against California's anti-immigrant Proposition 187, as Bush declared, "We are going to educate the children of immigrants, period." But I can't honestly say that I had ever seen George W. Bush getting to the White House. I suppose I underestimated his resolve—

as have so many, from domestic opponents like his predecessor as governor, Ann Richards, to Al Gore, John Kerry, the international community, the media, even the Taliban and Saddam Hussein. Those who see only the George W. Bush of the surface—the cocky, simplistic baseball-loving son of an ex-president who went in six years from never having won a political race to the presidency of the most powerful nation on the planet—miss the core of inner resolve behind those sharp blue eyes. Even before 9/11, Bush always struck me as a man in a hurry, tight-lipped and determined and straight to the point. Bush may be the single most *focused* individual I have ever met.

On my transition trip to the United States as president-elect that previous August of 2000, I had gone from the Gore meeting to see Bush at the University of Texas at Dallas, where my adviser Juan Hernández headed UTD's Institute for U.S.-Mexico Studies. We had deliberately avoided any perception of favoritism between Republicans and Democrats, but the Bush team did a much better job of taking political advantage from this meeting with Mexico's first freely elected president. Condoleezza Rice, Karen Hughes, Karl Rove, and Josh Bolten planned the UTD event with meticulous care, anxious to burnish Governor Bush's foreign-policy credentials—at that point limited primarily to Mexico. By then critics were already ripping Bush for his occasional verbal gaffes, mispronunciations, and mangled syntax. (I can sympathize, having recently mentioned the "Colombian Nobelist Mario Vargas Llosa"—though he is actually from Peru, and his only Nobel Prize was the one I gave him that day in Los Angeles. But Vargas Llosa deserves the Nobel for his apt description of the "perfect dictatorship," and if you want to read a really good Colombian Nobelist, there is always Gabriel García Márquez.) During the New Hampshire primary, Bush had been ambushed by a media "pop quiz" at a Boston television station, drawing a blank when asked to name the presidents of India, Taiwan, Chechnya, and Pakistan (Bush got one of them, from Taiwan). The Bush team wasn't about to be caught out twice. Karl Rove called one of my advisers to triple-check the exact pronunciation of my first name, which Americans often mispronounce "Vincente," by inserting an extra *n*.

"It's *Vee*-cente, not *Vin*-cente, right?" said Rove, who is famous for his mastery of detailed minutiae of politics. Later we heard that Rice, Rove, and Hughes prowled the halls of campaign headquarters in Austin, Rove calling out, "Pop quiz, gang—who's the new president of Mexico? *Vee*-cente FOX! *Vee*-cente FOX!"

Bush carried off the event with the aplomb of a practiced statesman. From the stage in the university auditorium, we exchanged cowboy boots and hats, the subject of a frantic call to our team from Gordon Johndroe, the press aide of Karen Hughes and now Laura Bush's press secretary: "Is this really his correct size? Gee, Fox must be a really big guy!"

Behind the scenes Bush and I met in a classroom, then brought in our aides, my future foreign minister Jorge Castañeda and Bush's future Secretary of State Condi Rice; my press secretary and future first lady Marta Sahagún and his future senior counselor and undersecretary of state Karen Hughes; my chief economic adviser Dr. Eduardo Sojo and future White House chief of staff Josh Bolten. Campaign strategists like Mark McKinnon, Bush's ad guru, hovered outside to make sure they got it on film. Later Bush would cite our close relationship in the campaign against Gore, where he made the point that if Texas were its own country, Bush would have been chief executive of the world's eighth-largest economy.

We watched the impossibly close Bush-Gore election from afar that fall. It was ironic: At our request the United States had sent election monitors to protect the balloting process in Mexico, but where they might have been more useful that year was in Florida. To its eternal credit, the Mexican government had reformed the Federal Electoral Institute, which became a model of election accuracy; our IFE would later work to advise electoral authorities and advance democracy in Colombia, Algeria, Zambia, and Iraq, while even Palm Beach couldn't get the butterfly ballots to work. As we watched the thirty-six days of suspense in Florida on CNN, with judges holding up ballots to look for hanging chads, we never dreamed that my own presidency would end with a similar cliffhanger in 2006, when hundreds of thousands marched in protest, lawmakers seized the congressional palace, and my successor's victory was contested for two months in court.

BY THE TIME George W. Bush was set to arrive at our ranch, I had been president of Mexico for three months. My friend the windshield cowboy was no longer the governor of a state the size of France, but president of the world's reigning superpower, hanging chads and all. As my mother scrambled around San Cristóbal doing what any host does when company is coming—dusting the furniture, repainting the hall—we began the staggering task of setting Mexico's house in order after seventy-one years of corruption and decay.

We started cleaning house at the top. But like any new democracy, we faced a dilemma: Should we focus on punishing the past or building the future? Whether it is South Africa or the nations of Eastern Europe, whether Iraq, Liberia, or Afghanistan, every newly freed society faces this core issue of retribution. Is it more important to mete out justice to those who did wrong in the regime that preceded you or do you try to learn from the mistakes of the past and concentrate on delivering the fruits of democracy, before people run out of patience?

My team and I were greatly impressed with the models of Mandela's Truth Commission in South Africa, the experiences of former Communist nations, and the Moncloa Pact that governed the approach of Spain's constitutional monarchy after Franco, each of which had investigated some of the worst abuses of the past but focused primarily on the future. In a country like Mexico, where virtually *everyone* was complicit in the System—from the tiny corruptions of the *mordida* that an urban worker paid to beat a traffic ticket or get a phone hooked up, to the party dues that a poor *ejidatario* paid to the agrarian union to keep his ten acres of land, to the thousand-dollar bribe a local businessman paid to operate his tourist boat in Acapulco, to the million-dollar bribes the big family *grupos* of the One Hundred wired to the Swiss accounts of cabinet members and presidents. It was nearly impossible to go back and punish all that was wrong with the old ways. Our government set up commissions to investigate and prosecute the worst abuses—the human-rights abuses of Echeverría, for example, or the $100 million the old PRI had stolen from the state-run Pemex oil company. But our focus was on cracking down on corruption from December 1, 2000, forward. Jailing everyone who had ever been corrupt would simply have shut down the country and sent it back into crisis, which would have been the end of Mexico's democratic experiment forever.

In 2000 our PAN-Green Alliance for Change had won with just 42 percent of the vote in a five-way race, so the PAN was a minority in Congress. But in our first hundred days, we joined with the leftist PRD and reform-minded members of the PRI to promote a series of tough new laws imposing unprecedented transparency in government. Five months after I took office, Congress passed Mexico's first Freedom of Information Act, requiring that everything be made public, from the president's schedule to the vegetables we ate at Los Pinos, from the Russian military boots Vladimir Putin gave me as a welcome gift to every government contract and public official's salary. We moved to enforce our own version of the Bill of Rights, guaranteeing freedom of the press, freedom of religion, and freedom of assembly. By executive order I immediately dismantled all the police-state apparatus of the PRI, opening *gobernación*'s secret files to reveal a treasure trove that would have made J. Edgar Hoover proud—even my private cell-phone conversations with my press secretary and future first lady were on those tapes. And we cut off all of the corruption that had given the Mexican presidency so much power—the "grant" payments to keep members of Congress sweet on administration proposals, the president's discretionary authority to direct 95 percent of Mexico's fiscal income to governors and mayors who toed the party line, the multimillion-dollar government advertising budgets that were awarded to newspapers and TV/radio networks who censored their broadcasts to make the president and ruling party look good. It was in the first few months that Marta, whom I had named presidential press secretary, earned the undying enmity of the Mexican media by ending the time-honored government practice of paying under-the-table bribes to reporters to write favorable stories. (A U.S. media consultant once gave a four-hour workshop to campaign press secretaries across Mexico explaining how to deal with the media in a free society—the art of message discipline, how to bridge from negative questions to positive objectives, the best techniques for answering reporters' questions but getting your point across. At the end, every hand went up as the Mexican press operatives asked, "That's all fine and good, but you haven't told us the most important thing—how much do you usually pay a reporter in the U.S. for a good story?")

This sudden transition to freedom brought us to the second major challenge facing a new democracy: If you give everyone the right to speak out—the media, Congress, the churches, business, the unions, the opposition parties, the former regime—they will probably speak out against *you*. One of the things you don't think about as you give the entire society free rein to lash out at the established authority is that their first target will be the new democratic president. Congress was angry with us because their System no longer ran the country—so they wouldn't be taking their wives and kids to Paris that summer. The unions were mad because their gangster bosses weren't getting kickbacks for concluding wage agreements that screwed the workers to the benefit of the big *priistas,* and the businessmen were mad because they could no longer get a fat government contract that wasted the taxpayers' money on graft. The media was angry with us because their bosses were laying off reporters due to the cutbacks in government advertising—Mexico City then had more daily newspapers that no one reads than any capital city on earth, and here comes this new female press secretary who won't even buy them lunch, much less pass them an envelope containing a thousand pesos under the table. (After Marta got in hot water with the press over cutting off their subsidies, I joked that the only answer was to fire her as my press secretary and marry her as my first lady.)

When all these mighty forces in a dictatorship suddenly lose their power, they strike back, *hard*. In the dramatic changes we made during my first few months in office, our government had made sure they had the freedom to do so. This presented huge challenges for the third and most important challenge of an infant democracy: to produce quick results.

Our campaign of hope had raised the *expectativas* of the Mexican people impossibly high, promising a liberalization of the economy to free up market forces, so Mexico could deliver a 7 percent annual growth rate. When we got to Los Pinos, veteran governmental experts we recruited to join our team at the Mexican White House would often grouse at those who had served in our campaign: The criticism we were now facing was all their fault for raising hopes so impossibly high. This was an argument I cut short. "If we hadn't given the people hope, we wouldn't be here," I reminded our team. "It's a good problem to have."

In early 2001 we moved swiftly in the honeymoon glow of victory to present an aggressive package of economic reforms to Congress. We began work on a labor-reform bill to overhaul Mexico's archaic laws, which make it almost impossible to hire and fire employees—a huge disincentive for global business to invest and create the new higher-paying jobs we needed so desperately. We got our experts cracking on an innovative energy-reform package to open up the state-controlled oil, natural-gas, and electricity industries to investment—not privatize them, which would be political heresy in Mexico; we just wanted to recruit private money for investment in drilling and power plants. Mexico needed capital to improve the horribly outdated equipment and technological systems of Pemex—then one of the world's largest and worst-run oil companies, larger than Exxon or Shell—a state-run company whose technology is so grossly inefficient that it costs Pemex about $8 to extract the same barrel of oil that Shell produces for $6.49.

Finally, to make a hundred-year leap and lead Mexico into the twenty-first century (after having missed the twentieth century altogether), we needed a sweeping fiscal-reform package to help government pay for itself. The goal was to balance the budget and get Mexico out of the deep hole of debt the old regime had handed over with the keys to Los Pinos—yet still fund the ambitious education, housing, health care and antipoverty programs we envisioned as the fruits of our new democracy. We also proposed a new pension-reform law to help Mexico avoid crippling debt in the future.

Under the crooked rule of the old PRI, Mexico's scofflaw businessmen could avoid paying taxes by paying a bribe to someone in Hacienda, the Mexican IRS. Virtually the entire public did business in cash to avoid income taxes: Mexico had one of the lowest tax-collection rates in the hemisphere. We needed a fair and practical tax system to capture the government's share of the economy, so we could pay for a world-class education system, universal health care, aid to the poor, and a massive program of homeownership to give Mexicans a stake in society.

All of these—labor reform, energy reform, pension reform, tax reform—were of course terribly controversial. In politics, every time you make a change, you gore the ox of someone who likes things the way they are. Congress, controlled by the dethroned PRI and the leftist PRD, was determined to oppose us at every step. By enacting a series of new laws to empower Mexico's democracy, we had just given them the power to do it.

ON DECEMBER 1, 2000, the day I was sworn in as president, there was a collective gasp from the crowd in the Auditorio Nacional as I accepted a crucifix from my daughter Paulina. After the gasp you could have heard a pin drop—until a wave of cheers erupted from the hard-core *panistas* in the hall.

We had begun the day of our *toma de posesión* (literally, taking possession) with a similar expression of religious freedom. Feeling the need to get on my knees and ask for God's help in the great task before us, I shocked the sensibilities of Mexico City's anticlerical establishment by attending morning mass at the Basilica of the Virgin of Guadalupe, the site of the miracle where San Juan Diego, an indigenous peasant, implored his bishop time and time again to build a church, because the Virgin had appeared to him and told him that it must be so. "But how will the bishop believe me?" asked Juan Diego. "You must bring him some roses," instructed the Virgin. When Juan Diego arrived at the current site of the Basilica in Mexico City and reached inside his robes to pull out the flowers for the bishop, the Virgin revealed herself in the indigenous garb of Juan Diego. These ancient robes have been preserved in the basilica's reliquary, the holiest of symbols of Mexico's revered Madrecita, the "Little Mother," our Virgin of Guadalupe.

Leading a religious procession down the hill, I stopped at a taco stand to eat lunch with the drug addicts at Tepito—hardly the usual fare of Mexico's imperial presidency, but Rodrigo was hungry. The mood was bright and celebratory in the December sunshine—Mexico City is at seventy-two hundred feet, higher than Denver but with the weather of Los Angeles, generally in the seventies Fahrenheit year-round. Riding in an open car down the Paseo de la Reforma in a red, green, and white snowstorm of confetti, I watched as thousands upon thousands of Mexicans flashed the victory sign: "*¡Ya ganamos!*"

Eleven days later, on December 12, 2000, the volcano of Popocatepetl erupted outside Mexico City, spewing fire and smoke and ashes all the way to the capital's suburbs. I went instantly to the scene of the devastation with the Mexican army's crack disaster-relief unit. As the United States would learn after Hurricane Katrina, when Mexican army soldiers delivered relief to New Orleans, despite Mexico's dysfunction in many areas of government, our nation has surprisingly strong resources for helping people recover from natural disasters. This is perhaps because Mexico straddles the narrowing base of the North American continent, sitting astride volcanoes and hurricanes; we also suffer terrible floods and droughts exacerbated by more than a century of thoughtless environmental exploitation. In any case, I responded immediately and personally to the volcanic eruption. Given our history, I believed it was vital that the president take personal charge of making sure all the victims got the help they needed.

I also had appointed my friend Dr. Juan Hernández as our country's first director for Mexicans living abroad, the first dual citizen of the United States and Mexico to serve in a presidential administration. This was a controversial move in a country that had too often looked down on immigrants who left in search of a better life. That December of 2000, Juan and I went to the border and literally lined up the guards who had spent decades systematically ripping off the families of immigrant workers coming home for Christmas. "This stops today!" I said with the authoritarian presence that law-enforcement officers respect. I let them know that regardless of how things had been in the past, I was president now. We would tolerate no harassment, theft, or abuse of our *paisanos;* I called our immigrants heroes in the face of a bureaucracy that despised them as economic refugees and traitors.

My government's quick response to the volcano, the swift passage of the new democracy and transparency laws, our outreach to indigenous citizens and immigrants, and a series of executive actions to clean up corruption sent our administration's job-approval numbers through the roof. By the time George W. Bush stepped off the plane in the León airport, my popularity had peaked at close to 80 percent in the polls. Mexico's new house was in order. The "democracy bonus" experienced by newly freed nations from Eastern Europe to South Africa could not be far behind, now that the eyes of the world were on Mexico.

Little did we know that even on that very day in San Cristóbal, they would turn instead to Iraq.

As I WOULD LEARN over the six years of presidential globetrotting from the UN to Number 10 Downing Street, from the Vatican to Shanghai, from Caracas to Havana and Moscow to Johannesburg, summitry is a highly ritualized business, where very little happens on the altar of public view. At long, liquid dinners, First World politicians give wearisome toasts to their own generosity, and Third World demagogues harangue the summit with endless rhetoric. All the real business takes place in what they call the "green room," usually some windowless conference room down the back hallway of a nameless hotel, where world leaders are given coffee and cookies while aides tighten the knots in our ties and push our hair into place for the photo ops.

The San Cristóbal summit was completely different, perhaps because

George W. Bush and I were both so new to our jobs that we assumed it was okay to just meet and talk straight, one-on-one. Surely two friends whose nations shared one of the world's longest and most active land borders could speak frankly to each other and get something done.

We had a lot in common. The media made much of the fact that we were both ranchers, but this was the least important bond between us. Even George will admit that Crawford is a hobby ranch where he grows more brush than cattle. And San Cristóbal is really a vegetable farm with a few horses and milk cows; a thousand acres wouldn't rate as much of a cattle ranch in Texas, where I am told everything is bigger. (Before I met with Bush, a friend from Dallas gave me this piece of advice: "Never ask a Texan where he's from. If he's from Texas, he will tell you. And if he's not, you don't want to embarrass him.")

More salient was the fact that we were both beginning our terms. New presidents of the United States and Mexico take office together only once every twelve years. The last two were presidents Carlos Salinas and George H. W. Bush—and that led to NAFTA.

George and I had helped each other as governors. We each came from the right side of the political spectrum, but this can be misleading. Though I was considered an economic conservative in Mexico because I wanted to balance the federal budget, open markets to competition, and build a strong peso, I was a liberal by U.S. standards on most social issues. I stood for universal health coverage, direct payments to the poor, and a ban on the death penalty, so Bush is much further to the right than I am. But we both had business backgrounds, the first presidents of either country who had studied business rather than law, politics, or the military. Neither of us had set out in life to become president: Bush wanted to be a baseball player; I wanted to be a cowboy.

Finally we managed to separate ourselves from the watchful eyes of Colin Powell, Condi Rice, Jorge Castañeda, the White House staff, the Los Pinos staff, my cabinet, my friend Juan Carlos Romero Hicks, the new governor of Guanajuato, the U.S. Secret Service, the Mexican army's Estado Mayor, my mother, my brother, and more than a few curious farmhands. A one-on-one chat between presidents at a summit is like the courting ritual of the *zócalo*: You have to take advantage of any moment the two of you can steal away from the piercing gazes of your chaperones.

"We can do great things together, Vicente," Bush began as we walked down the path to feed the horses, cameras whirring at a safe distance. The protocol portion of the event was over. We had shaken hands on the red carpet at the airport, saluted the soldiers, paid respect to all the dignitaries. Now it was classic Bush and Fox, straight down to business, two men in a hurry. "You've got six years, Vicente," Bush said, "I will have eight." Already, less than a month into his first term, Bush was open about his plans to run for a second term. "Now that Mexico is a democracy, there is no limit to what we can do to bring our countries closer together," Bush added, obviously well briefed on our hopes for a "democracy bonus" in dealing with the United States.

"What can we do for the immigrants?" I said, plunging in before the aides could find us and keep us from actually accomplishing anything. "You know our people don't come to rob and steal, and they don't have their hands out for welfare. We don't expect to send our unemployed to you. From now on, we just want human dignity and fair treatment for those with jobs waiting for them in the United States."

"I respect the people who come to our country," Bush said. "That's what America is all about, and we're going to make immigration safe and orderly and treat people humanely. But we can't open the border, Vicente."

I waved him off. "Of course not," I said. I had stirred up a fuss during the Bush-Gore campaign when, as president-elect, I airily outlined my dream of a North American trade union like the EU in thirty or forty years, with free movement of goods and labor across the borders of the United States, Canada, and Mexico. My aides had warned me not to push this idea at the summit. As they say in Texas, that dog would not hunt with George Bush.

"We can help you secure the border." I nodded. "But the only way to slow down the flow of immigrants is to raise the standard of living in Mexico."

"Mexico can't do that without partnering with the United States," Bush said. "We have to work more closely together to build out the opportunities of NAFTA."

"Your economy needs our workers, George," I said. "As long as Mexico has a magnet next door with an economy sixteen times bigger than ours and wage rates ten times higher, the United States is going to draw some of our people to a better life. But if we can build up our economy here at home, we can give people a reason to stay. There will always be a few with the talent and the drive to go north, just like your pioneers. But really, these are good people who work hard, go to church, and love their families. Given a chance, they would rather make it here at home."

"I've said it over and over in my campaigns," he agreed. "Family values don't stop at the border. We need to find a way to bring these folks out of the shadows and into the legal system, so we know who they are, educate their children, collect the taxes, and keep people safe on both sides of the border."

Summits are all about the photo op; sensitive matters are rarely discussed president to president. As in an old-fashioned gentlemen's duel, the details are worked out in advance by the principals' seconds. Once the cameras are rolling, world leaders are expected to smile and go through the motions on the grassy field with the horses in the background. George and I wanted to do better, so we signed an agreement on the spot. This Guanajuato Accord pledged both nations to work for comprehensive reform to make immigration safe, legal, orderly, meeting economic needs and respecting human rights—and to establish an aggressive program to build prosperity in Mexico and the United States.

Neither of us had the power to do this by decree. Bush would struggle to get support for the idea in his Congress, while I would take tremendous heat from my country's anti-gringo political establishment for moving Mexico closer to the United States. But for the first time, the presidents of the United States and Mexico agreed on a plan to improve the standards of living on both sides of our border and a guest-worker program to document the undocumented. We had different perspectives: Bush was more focused on securing the border; I was more focused on humane treatment of our people. But George and I shared each other's aims: I believe that it is Mexico's responsibility to help control immigration and provide jobs to keep our people home; George believes that the United States needs guest workers from Mexico and that all immigrants should be treated with dignity.

Like the abolition of slavery in the nineteenth century, immigration reform is a three-legged stool: a moral question, an economic issue, and a legal matter. At its core the debate is about the equal treatment of all people regardless of color, ethnicity, or origin: quite simply, a matter of human dignity. It is wrong to criminalize the essentially moral behavior of workers who hurt no one, people who sacrifice all to help their families.

Making immigration a felony also hurts the economies of both countries, because the United States needs the labor and Mexico needs the capital that immigrants wire home—and the job skills these guest workers bring home when they return.

Finally, keeping immigrants in the shadows is a danger to the rule of law and public security. Undocumented workers are forced to hide from police, so they can't aid law enforcement or report crimes even when they are the victims. Their illegal status makes it nearly impossible for them to follow the law and arrange for basics like auto insurance, health coverage, and education for their children.

So as George and I took pens in hand to sign the 2001 Guanajuato Accord in the bright February sunshine, we also agreed to the basic prinicíples of what became our "Security and Prosperity Partnership."

"Mexico can't advance to its full potential without moving closer to the U.S. in economic policy," Bush told me that day. "You can make changes here that will change the hemisphere forever, Vicente. You need energy reform to open up your markets to private investment. We've got some issues between us on water rights, immigration, drugs, and security at the border. But the main thing I want to say is, we're going to focus on Mexico in a way that Washington has never done before."

Then his aides signaled the meeting to an abrupt close: There was a crisis in Iraq.

OUT OF OUR VIEW on the other side of the pond, Colin Powell and Condi Rice had broken off their discussions with our foreign minister, Jorge Castañeda. Powell and Rice rushed off to the makeshift White House communications center that the Secret Service had erected at the ranch. In an eerie foreshadowing of the events that would soon extinguish the Spirit of San Cristóbal, Saddam Hussein's antiaircraft missiles had violated the no-fly zone. Suddenly the summit was over. President Bush hustled back to Air Force One, to launch an airstrike against Iraq.

The newly freed media in Mexico had a field day, lashing out with all the pent-up frustration of reporters who had endured many decades of government censorship. BUSH SNUBS FOX TO BOMB IRAQ! read the headlines. On CNN the camera cut from film of George Bush and me shaking hands to Saddam Hussein in his general's uniform, daring the United States to take action, then to stock footage of a U.S. Navy plane dropping bombs on Baghdad during Operation Desert Storm.

My team was downcast. "Like they couldn't wait two hours until they were back on Air Force One to launch the airstrike?" fumed Jorge Castañeda, never a fan of Republicans. "Shit, they could bomb Iraq anytime—they do that once a week. This was a moment in history for Latin America, and they blew it."

But I was upbeat. The ranch summit *had* made history, a new chapter in U.S.-Mexico relations. A noted scholar of the PRI, Reyes Heroles, once wrote that in politics *la forma es fondo*—"form is fundamental." George Bush's form at San Cristóbal was the fundamental accomplishment. In some ways the fact that the U.S. president could order an airstrike halfway around the world from our family's ranch underscored the gesture Bush had made: Here was the commander in chief of the world's reigning superpower, summoning the humility to come to the family ranch of Mexico's first democratically elected president. For the first time in history, this put Mexico on equal footing with the mighty United States, and the world.

A great deal of what the United States may read as anti-Americanism in countries like mine is really just fear and envy—fear of U.S. dominance, envy of U.S. prosperity. The rest of us too often stand ready to take offense at every perceived slight by the American colossus, which frequently acts in a manner that seems arrogant and dismissive. In one short visit to my house, George W. Bush had changed that in Mexico, at least for the moment. In any case we had the form—two amigos pledging to bring our countries together, signing an accord pledging sweeping reforms for a "NAFTA-Plus" approach to immigration, security, and free trade. Now it was time to deliver the fundamentals.

THERE IS a basic principle of physics called *vasos comunicantes*—the communicating vessels. Fill two jars of water, one nearly full and one nearly empty, then connect them with a tube at the base of each jar. The water will of course flow from the full jar to the empty jar, until both have reached what physicists call equilibrium.

This is the mythic view of immigration and free trade: economic junk science that says if you open the tube of globalism from the rich country's full jar to the poor country's empty jar, the level of per capita income in the rich country will drop to the lower level of cheap labor from the poor country. This model is of course absurd, because it treats the global economy as a zero-sum game. *Vasos comunicantes* fails to account for what happens when you add water to both jars and make the total volume of economic growth much greater on both sides of the tube.

What really happens is that immigration and free trade dramatically increase the per capita incomes of countries like Mexico, Ireland, or Spain—pouring gallons and gallons of water into the empty jar. In Mexico, income from our workers abroad was $23 billion in 2006; today this is Mexico's second-largest source of foreign direct investment, after the tourism industry.

Free trade and immigration also raise wage rates in the wealthy countries, as newly enriched consumers in Mexico start buying more products from our richer neighbors. Immigrant labor also gives a competitive advantage to the host country's industries and adds value to boost the richer country's standard of living. For example, a recent study shows that the influx of immigrant labor since 1990 actually has *increased* the per capita incomes of California—good news for Arnold Schwarzenegger.

In other words, when you dump gallons and gallons of economic growth into *both* vessels, incomes rise on *both* sides of the border—and you have to go get bigger jars. Free trade and immigration add up to more jobs at better wages for all countries smart enough to get into the game, because globalism is the ultimate win-win proposition.

Consider the alternative: Spain was the sick man of Europe through forty years of Franco's walled-off dictatorship, from the 1930s to the 1970s. Miracles don't happen overnight—it took thirty years under King Juan Carlos's constitutional monarchy, including a decade of wise leadership by democratic socialists like Felipe González. But eventually the EU helped lift per capita income in Spain from about $4,500 in 1975—not far from Mexico's—to more than $25,000 today, a fivefold increase that has made the average Spaniard much richer than the average Mexican.

What about Spain's wealthier northern neighbors in Germany, the vessel at the other end of the tube? Real incomes in Germany rose over that same generation—not as fast as those in Spain, but then Spain had much further to go. The point is that *both* vessels gained water. The rich country of course grows at a slower rate, but, as any owner of a mature business understands, it is much harder to grow on a percentage basis the container that is already pretty full. For Mexico, a container that starts out much emptier, every inch or two of water poured in from the top will raise our income levels very quickly.

Imagine how much better a neighbor a rich, prosperous Mexico would be, what integration of our economies could mean for the Americas and the world. Remember, according to Goldman Sachs, Mexico is already on its way to becoming the fifth-largest economy on the planet. If the U.S. economy continues to grow at its mature, full-jar rate of 2 to 3 percent a year, and the Mexican economy keeps growing at 5 percent, within our lifetimes Mexican incomes will average 60 percent to 70 percent of wage rates in the United States and Canada—still not quite what they are north of the Rio Grande but respectably in the ballpark. Certainly, the income gap would no longer drive immigration and outsourcing the way it does now, when today's Mexican workers earn only a tenth of what they can make in El Norte.

NAFTA boosted income levels within the United States, especially in formerly poor regions like the Rio Grande Valley of Texas. NAFTA has created 190,000 jobs in the Lone Star State since its passage, versus 21,019 jobs that have been negatively affected—a net gain of more than 9 jobs gained for every 1 job lost.

The exciting part of globalism comes when you stop worrying about what you might lose alone and start thinking about what we might win together. This was the vision that George Bush and I discussed as we signed our agreement and fed the horses at San Cristóbal. I offered to let George ride Dos de Julio. "Secret Service doesn't have it on the program"—he grinned—"and I'm not much of a horseman anyway." (A cowboy can always tell when a guy doesn't want to ride a horse; a friend won't push it. But a guy who will confess that he doesn't *want* to ride your horse—that's an *honest* friend).

Even if George W. Bush wasn't yet buying the idea of a North American trade union, I didn't go away disappointed. As the aides scurried toward the new U.S. president, I was walking on air. If we could work together to free 12 million people from second-class citizenship with a guest-worker program that Bush could sell to the right wing of his party, the new Republican president could become the Great Emancipator of Mexican immigrants in the United States, and we could declare another "democracy bonus" for our new government in Mexico.

It is a great tragedy that the moment didn't last. The Spirit of San Cristóbal would not survive the tragedy of September 11.

CHAPTER 13

SEPTEMBER 7

FOR THREE DAYS from September 4 to 7, 2001, my first lady, Marta, and I went to the United States, where I was to address a historic joint session of the U.S. Congress, speak with President Bush at a rally in Ohio, and have dinner with Laura and George Bush at the White House, the first state dinner of his presidency. Again, it was a signal honor that recognized how democracy was working in Mexico: We were two free nations with linked economies, open societies, honest elections, a free press, and the rule of law.

Laura Bush is a most delightful dinner companion, warm and funny, deeply devoted to family and many causes we shared in common: education, literacy, children. Though she was relatively new to the job of first lady, she shared tips with Marta, who had just become the first woman ever to get married in Los Pinos.

That previous summer I had waked up at dawn, bent down on one knee, and asked Marta to marry me that very morning—on my birthday, July 2, 2001, one year to the day after I'd been elected to the presidency. It had been a surprise, to Marta and to the country. People knew I was a bachelor, but divorce is still sort of unmentionable in our largely Catholic society. We still use the term *separado*—"separated"—to describe a divorced couple. Still, I'd been single for a decade, my children were pretty well grown up, and I was in love. Fortunately, so was Marta.

We had come together as a political couple, in love with the dream of a better Mexico—of bringing democracy to our people, equal rights to women, help for the downtrodden. But we also had the little dreams every couple shares, of bringing our lives together with our families, children, and grandchildren. Somehow we put all that together, so we could give love to each other and to those in need—the sick, poor, indigenous, and immigrant. At eight o'clock on that July morning in 2001, our Catholic country woke up to find that the president had married his first lady at a small, private ceremony with Marta, her children, and my brother and sister-in-law. Then we went straight to receive President Aznar on a state visit from Spain—not terribly romantic. But ever since we fell in love during my presidential campaign, Marta and I have lived in a permanent honeymoon, connected physically, mentally, and spiritually, day and night—a hopelessly old-fashioned romance in a thoroughly modern marriage, whether cuddling affectionately in public (to the great disapproval of our critics) or connecting by telephone, cable, Internet, instant messaging, mobile text and wireless (this is true love, these days—BlackBerry love).

But to marry the presidential press secretary, a party leader who was a prominent political figure in her own right—this had been a jolt to the political establishment, to say the least. Almost immediately the press labeled Marta the "Mexican Hillary" or, worse yet, the "Mexican Evita," speculating that she would seek the presidency to succeed me in 2006. My first lady was politically popular in those early years of the administration, before the long knives of my opponents came out. But the idea of a *dedazo* from me to hand her the presidency was preposterous—Marta's only ambition was to build a charitable foundation to help women, children, and the victims of domestic violence, breast and cervical cancer, and abject poverty.

Still, you can understand what it was for the land of machismo to suddenly wake up one morning to a new first lady with a mind of her own and the professional expertise to make things happen. I can't say I liked all the nasty things the media would write about my wife in the years to come, but I couldn't deny that it was big news. In Mexico's democracy, newspapers were now free to print whatever they wanted to say—even when they were wrong.

Los Pinos is very different from the stately alabaster White House, where on September 5, 2001, George Bush greeted us in black tie. He and Laura led us to the Blue Room, where the assembled VIPs of Washington mingled with film stars, athletes, and musicians: Clint Eastwood and Alan Greenspan, Plácido Domingo and the NBA's Eduardo Nájera, John McCain and Dick Gephardt, William Rehnquist and Emilio Estefan. Bush's friends from Texas and the 2000 campaign were there, along with key

Latinos and leaders of business. The Bushes had invited everyone from Joe Biden to Trent Lott, even the heads of Coca-Cola and Pepsi—truly a bipartisan affair.

The residence of the U.S. president actually is a house—a big house and a very grand one, with a very exclusive address—but still, when you step inside the White House, you really have the feeling of entering someone's private home. Though today the elegant Palladian features the offices of powerful aides and government officials, it is really just a big, rambling old house with rather nice furniture. The floors creak in a genteel, historic way as you walk down the narrow corridors. The windows are the old-fashioned kind that would open if the Secret Service allowed it, with shutters and deep casements like the ones you see on a plantation tour in the Old South.

I had been to the White House before, to pay my respects to my friend Bill Clinton just after my election as president. I liked both the White House and its previous occupant. Clinton is a big, hearty guy. He has powerful listening skills, a wide-ranging, inquisitive mind, and a loose, easygoing style that is nearly Mexican in its disregard for the clock. President Clinton had a sincere enthusiasm for our microcredit revolution in Guanajuato; he had been to Bangladesh himself to see Dr. Yunus's little miracles in action. Though Bill was headed out of office as I was headed in, we pledged to work closely together to combat poverty, a promise he has certainly kept—like Jimmy Carter, Clinton is a human dynamo and a role model for ex-presidents around the world. Between us, Marta and I have since modeled our own Fox Center at San Cristóbal, for poverty reduction, microcredits, and global democracy, on what he has done with the Clinton Foundation, and we've toured the Carter Center in Atlanta, the Clinton Presidential Library in Little Rock, and the centers built around the legacies of former presidents Bush and Reagan. It does not surprise me that Bill Clinton has been so active in the world. Foreign leaders who came to the Clinton White House prepared for a perfunctory photo opportunity and a polite brush-off instead got the full measure of Clinton's intellectual curiosity, and to this day, like Fidel Castro, he conveys that sense of wanting to stay up all night to shoot the bull.

Sometimes I think some foreign heads of state come to the White House looking for a slight, and invariably they find it. Others come with the expectation of a warm welcome; they, too, will find it. This was my experience with Clinton and Bush, two very different presidents, both sincerely interested in Mexico. It is like the old story of the man walking north along a country road, toward a strange town. He encounters another man riding south on horseback out of the town.

"How are the people up north?" asks the walker.

"Terrible," growls the rider. "Rudest, meanest people I have ever met. How are they down south, where you have been?"

"About the same," says the walking man.

Then comes another rider out of the town. "How are the people up north in that town?" asks the walker.

"Wonderful!" cries the second rider. "The nicest, friendliest people I have ever met. How will I find the people down south?"

The walker says, "About the same."

If my own experience as president is any guide, meeting another head of state is first and foremost a matter of personal curiosity. It's like seeing yourself through the other side of the glass. What is this president like, and how does he differ from others? How did he win this job? What can I learn from him in half an hour that will help me do mine? Then there are practical concerns. What does he want? How can I help him achieve it and get something for my country in return?

In any case, hosting foreign dignitaries is nearly always a relief from the day-to-day hassles of dealing with your own Congress and the entrenched bureaucracy: Presidents and prime ministers have much about which we can commiserate. Long ago I learned one of the ironies of being at the top of an organization: Instead of having one boss, now you answer to *everyone*—your own employees, customers, shareholders, government, franchisees. The presidency is like that, a constant catering to a thousand different constituencies on a hundred different topics every week. You go from one half-hour meeting to the next: a predawn meeting with your antidrug task force, then indigenous village leaders from Chiapas, the miners' union of Chihuahua, a reporter from *Reforma*. Now, finally, it's time for breakfast (with the prime minister of Austria, or is it Australia?). Then into the helicopter to put computers in a school in Puebla; back to the presidential jet *Benito Juárez* for an hourlong flight to the border to put the fear of God into notoriously corrupt border guards, during which staff briefs you on the success of the raid that captured a cartel leader; then a meeting with your attorney general to figure out how you can extradite the drug dealer to the United States. Now you fly onward to inaugurate a new prenatal health-care unit in Sinaloa, have lunch with business leaders in Monterrey, hear the concerns of reform-minded *priistas* in Congress that your economic reforms are too radical. All of this is tightly scheduled to the precise stopwatch of the army officers of Estado Mayor so that you can get back to Los Pinos in time to meet Mel Gibson, who was in the Yucatán peninsula during Hurricane Stan, shooting his film *Apocalypto*, about the Mayans, and wants to give you a million dollars for disaster relief. You are very grateful for this, because your next meeting is with the governors of the states hardest hit by flooding, as you begin the "second workday" of a Mexican president and try to finish in time to put on a fresh suit for dinner with the president of Poland, or the prime minister of Singapore, or the governor of Tamaulipas.

The interaction between presidents is planned out over briefing books and PowerPoint presentations in high-tech basement "war rooms" like the one Ramón Muñoz had constructed at Los Pinos. The book on George W. Bush was that he was the opposite of Clinton, who was known for rambling policy discussions and a casual attitude to the daily agenda—appealing to foreign visitors but occasionally vexing to his aides, who called it "Clinton Standard Time." Bush was more of the typical American, perpetually checking his watch. I respect this. I hate to waste time and dislike keeping others waiting. Bush-Fox meetings were crisp and to the point, starting and ending on the dot.

That evening at the White House was more relaxed and social; the president and Mrs. Bush could not have been more gracious. A man who dislikes pomp and ceremony (he rarely even allows the band to play "Hail to the Chief"), Bush had been in office eight months before hosting his first state dinner, heresy in a Washington that loves the who's-who game of which VIPs get invited to what formal dinner.

After dinner the president and Laura led us out on the balcony for the most magnificent fireworks show I have ever seen. Later I read that Condi Rice leaned over to Karen Hughes and quipped, "We're testing the missile-defense system." It's strange to think of it now, after all the tragedy that came later. But at the time it was as though we had gone for a barbecue in a neighbor's backyard, and the United States government just happened to light up the sky.

Los Pinos is not nearly so cozy. Unlike the White House, where you can nearly see in through the windows of the president's front parlor from Pennsylvania Avenue—callers in the more innocent times of Jackson and Lincoln could simply stroll in the front door to see the president—the Mexican presidential residence is not a house at all. Los Pinos is a vast, secluded military compound, well protected by our version of the Secret Service, the army's loyal and vigilant Estado Mayor. The palace sits hidden a quarter mile back from the road amid a huge expanse of green lawns, forests, and gardens. All this is surrounded by army soldiers and a high green wrought-iron fence, a quiet oasis in the heart of the biggest, busiest, noisiest metropolis in the Americas. You would never know you were in the midst of the world's second-largest city. Inside, the Federal District's 20-million-plus people seem far away as you stroll the peaceful paths of Los Pinos, birds chirping under what feels like the only patch of clear blue sky for miles as the late-afternoon pollution begins to whiten the rest of Mexico City.

Like Los Angeles, Mexico's Federal District sits in a bowl of mountains that create an atmospheric inversion to trap the exhaust of millions of cars snarled in its notorious traffic. (As I was also the presidential nominee of the Green Party, partners in our Alliance for Change in 2000, I am pleased that air quality is improving markedly in our nation's capital.) I often disagreed with Andres Manuel López Obrador while he was mayor of Mexico City and I was president, but cleaning up the environment is a passion we share. AMLO made good progress on air quality. Now we are using technology to clean up pollution across the country. Mexico introduced low-sulfur gasoline in 2006; by 2009 every gas station in the country will sell only this cleaner-burning fuel.

We made big changes at Los Pinos. With the austerity of my dad and his forebears, I was determined to throw open the remote, imperial isolation of this fool's paradise, where our former presidents had lived in splendid serenity while the economy crashed around them. Most Mexicans had never seen the inside; our people had a better idea of what the White House looks like, from CNN or programs like *The West Wing*. Before I took office, Los Pinos sat behind its locked gates like Willy Wonka's Chocolate Factory, a secret place where the wizards of government did their magic. We threw the doors open and invited the public inside, for the first time in Mexican history.

I didn't think much of the place we had worked so hard to wrestle out of the hands of the ruling party. Though Los Pinos had always been shrouded in the mystique of authority, there was none of the sense of patriotic awe that I felt when I first walked into the great congressional hall of San Lázaro. I had been in Los Pinos before, of course, waiting in Echeverría's lobby with gifts of shrimp and cookware from the Coca-Cola Company. Perhaps because so many of our former presidents had looted the palace at the ends of their *sexenios,* by the time I got there Los Pinos looked shabby, run-down at the edges. It was like walking into an aging hotel where you'd once stayed long ago: The paneling in the lobby was still impressive, but upstairs the rooms are seedy, windows crusted over with peeling paint, fans clacking in the corners of offices, soiled ceiling tiles sagging with exposed electrical wires—our authoritarian presidents didn't need to worry much about building codes.

I had no interest in living in a museum and wanted to set an example of fiscal discipline by cutting costs. With so many Mexican families in poverty, we would no longer waste precious tax dollars so that a dozen butlers could spend their days polishing brass railings. We slashed the budget of the office of the presidency, which had rented buildings all over Mexico City—a metropolis with some of the higher office-rental prices in the Americas. My "reinventing government" guru, Ramón Muñoz, the Al Gore of our administration who was one of my top advisers, brought all these offices to a new, more businesslike Los Pinos—he reengineered the whole compound as a campus of office buildings rather than an imperial court surrounded by the palace guard. Dining rooms became conference rooms, receiving lobbies became administrative offices; Ramón equipped the basement with a White House–style "war room" communications center, where staff and cabinet members could link to the Internet and keep us in constant communication during volcanoes and hurricanes.

We also set an example of discipline, running Los Pinos on time—no more keeping people waiting ten hours in the lobby, then sending them home until they brought a platter of seafood. If we wanted to bring Mexico into the twenty-first century, first we had to get Los Pinos out of the autocratic habits of the past.

I kept my campaign promise never to live in that palace—it is a cold and formal place anyway; the best part of it is outside. For occasions when

I needed to impress a union boss with my authority or put on Mexico's best face for a foreign leader, I would meet a dignitary downtown at the Palacio Nacional, where the great Diego Rivera murals along the staircases tell the history of Mexico from the point of view of our most distinguished artist. Committed Communists, Rivera and Frida Kahlo once hid Leon Trotsky in the couple's famous Blue House in the Mexico City suburb of Coyoacán, a site not to be missed the next time you are in Mexico City—nor is the fortresslike Trotsky home where the Russian revolutionary was killed by a Stalinist agent wielding an ice pick on August 21, 1940, despite a ring of armed guards and the steel-door bank vault in which the revolutionary slept. There is so much more to Mexican history and culture than people know—as president I used every opportunity to show off our product's unique selling points to the world.

For my first month in office, I lived at the Fiesta Americana Hotel while we renovated an old gardening shack on the grounds, a few minutes' walk from the old presidential palace. Now the shack is a little two-room *cabaña,* a cottage that looks more like a pleasant Mexican-contemporary casita of middle-class newlyweds than a presidential residence. But houses are for love and family, not to impress the neighbors. There was room in the *cabaña* for my books and the woman I intended to marry, with a spare bedroom for the kids when they visited from school.

All this sent the message that our administration would be down to earth and down to business; no longer would the government waste money on the trappings of power. Of course, the best-laid plans of presidents nearly always go wrong: When Bill Clinton was president, he balanced the budget for the first time in decades, but the media focused on a two hundred-dollar haircut he got in Los Angeles. Our team learned our first lesson when a staffer paid four hundred dollars for a monogrammed set of bathroom towels that I never even saw. Faced with taxing tortillas in order to keep the government solvent, the last thing you want is a flap over the price of linens in Los Pinos—a scandal that was made public only because we were the first administration in history to disclose every centavo our government spent. But I looked at the bright side. "We're going to make mistakes," I reminded the crestfallen staff. "They're going to be public, they're going to be painful, and the press is going to be free to criticize. That's why we fought to get this job."

I WAS RAISED to believe that you must do the difficult things early in the day or you never get them done at all. This is true whether you are milking cows, or jogging, or reforming your nation's chronically dysfunctional finances. If we wanted to make big changes in the second half of my presidency on education, health care, and poverty—and we weren't willing to plunge the nation back into debt—we needed money, lots of it.

Very little of a president's time is spent handing out paper cups of vaccine to schoolchildren or painting the three-millionth new home for your housing program. This is what voters see on television, but the bulk of your day is spent figuring out how to pay for it all. Ask world leaders from Washington to Moscow, and they will tell you. It is budget, budget, budget, all day long—the greatest dreams and most visionary programs will change your country only if you can pay for them without bankrupting the economy.

By September 2001, I was a newlywed and the toast of Washington, but my political honeymoon was about to end. We'd had a good first year. In late August 2000, just after the presidential election but before I took office, our opposition movement had even ousted the PRI from its stronghold in Chiapas, forming a joint PAN-PRD coalition to elect as governor indigenous-rights activist Pablo Salazar, who brought peace to the jungles of the *zapatista* rebellion. But by February 25, 2001, just short of my first hundred days in office, Subcomandante Marcos announced that he, too, would take advantage of the new era of freedom. Marcos unveiled plans to march the rebel *zapatista* army to the nation's capital and seize the streets to protest the previous government's policy of ignoring the people of Chiapas. The rebels were coming, Marcos said, to back Vicente Fox's bill for indigenous rights. With friends like this, who needed enemies?

In my inaugural address, I announced our intent to pass one of the most comprehensive indigenous-rights laws in the world, honoring the tribal rights of villages and granting partial autonomy, social benefits, and economic opportunities to indigenous communities that had been overlooked for seven decades. Well over 13 percent of Mexico's population is indigenous, more than 12 million people who live primarily in the southern region of the country; many of Mexico's people do not speak Spanish, but Mayan and sixty-two other dialects. This of course makes it terribly difficult for them to integrate into the economic mainstream; just as our immigrants in the United States must learn English to prosper, the indigenous of Mexico desperately need Spanish-language skills in order to survive.

These are Mexico's poorest and most downtrodden people, the old ladies and children with bellies swollen by malnutrition, begging on the streets wrapped in Indian shawls. If I did nothing else as president, I was determined to change their lives. On inauguration day we had appointed Mexico's first cabinet-level chief of indigenous affairs, a woman named Xóchitl Gálvez, one of the true stars of my presidential administration. Xóchitl created an award-winning program of indigenous development that the United Nations now holds up as a model for the emerging world. That February of 2001, she had called to alert me to a potential crisis.

"I saw it on television," I said, taking the call on a secure line at Los Pinos.

"Marcos says he's going to lead a march from Chiapas to Mexico City," Xóchitl said, her voice tense. "He's bringing the whole army with him to protest."

"Let him," I said without hesitation. "As long as it's peaceful."

"They'll be unarmed," she assured me. "I think this is a wise decision, but of course there will be a political price. Some people will say you are weak."

"Mexico is a democracy now," I replied. "They have the right. As long as the march is peaceful, all Marcos will do is tie up traffic. That will wear out his welcome in a hurry."

While the international media doted on Marcos as the voice of the indigenous of southern Mexico, the *zapatista* leader was not popular among the great mass of our mestizo population, which remembered the initial violence of his movement and the shooting of innocent Mexican soldiers in the 1994 Chiapas rebellion—which, together with the peso devaluation, had thrown our country into a terrible crisis. Most Mexicans saw the pipe-smoking radical as either a dangerous revolutionary or a vainglorious joke. Few outside the extreme left and the foreign press wanted Marcos to march his *zapatista* army to clog the streets of the nation's capital. But, like everyone else, the media-savvy rebel was looking to take advantage of the new climate of freedom.

In the end, Marcos was true to his word: The march was peaceful. While some thought I was being too soft on the rebels, Mexicans preferred democracy to repression, even at the price of a few traffic jams. Frustrated commuters blamed the disorder on Marcos, and he plummeted in the eyes of the citizens, while polls showed that they approved of our handling of the crisis. Six years later, defeated presidential candidate Andres Manuel López Obrador would use the same protest tactics to challenge the results of his defeat—with the same result.

But the era of peace and harmony and the sky-high approval ratings could not possibly last. We knew we had to invest this popularity in the tough things that we needed to do early in 2001, while we still had political capital. Here we were guided by the example of Bill Clinton, who took heat for raising taxes and balancing the budget early in his first term, then had the benefit of a healthier economy and strong economic growth to help him win a second.

We set out to balance Mexico's federal budget. This meant dealing with Congress, where some of the PRI old guard was hostile and ready for payback, some *priista* reformers were ready to help us, and the leftist PRD was feeling its oats. On big issues like tax reform and economic liberalization, we worked hard to build a coalition with members of the PRI who were pro-business and pro-democracy and knew we needed reforms to open up our economy. But the dinosaur wing still ran the party of the former regime. Their agenda was to block anything that might help our administration succeed. The promises of support that congressmen and senators gave us in private had a way of vanishing on the floor, like a girl who agrees to go out with an unpopular boy, then melts away when her friends see her at the dance.

The PRD was even more obstructionist. The leftists wanted to fold up the PRI's nationalist base and become the leftward half of a two-party, right-left divide that would make our PAN the Tory or Republican party of Mexico and position the PRD like the Labor Party or the Democrats. From the day Andres Manuel López Obrador took office as mayor of Mexico City in 2000, he and the PRD were angling to replace us in the presidency in 2006. They lashed out at anything we proposed—even simple reforms like putting Mexico City on daylight saving time to cut down on electric bills.

Mexican presidents cannot run for reelection, but for us the stakes were even higher: the "democracy bonus." People were expecting miracles. If we didn't produce immediate results that they could see and touch—better schools, medical care, new houses, a strong peso so they could afford basics like food, clothing, and medicine—then they might give up on democracy altogether and run back to the familiar arms of dictatorship. We had seen this "nostalgia effect" in Russia, Eastern Europe, Asia, and all over Latin America; citizens of an emerging democracy often simply don't have patience to stick with a consistent economic policy until it works. When democracy and free-market reforms fail to deliver immediate results, a hard-liner of the old regime or a demagogue of the radical left will jump up on his white horse and promise to solve all the country's problems with the siren song of a government that will "take care of you." This translates into a return to a paternalistic state crippled by cronyism and a state-controlled economy. Then they nationalize industries, set wage and price controls, and spend the country billions into debt, hoping that voters won't think ahead to what happens when the oil runs out and the government goes bankrupt.

The immutable rule of political capital is "use it or lose it"—a president who takes no risks accomplishes nothing. A real leader should be willing to burn the credit card of his political popularity to get things done. Political capital is renewable energy anyway. If you succeed, you get more of it. If you fail, you can always do something else to win back the people's support.

Our cure for the country's fiscal woes gave the opposition all the ammunition they needed to hurt us. We wanted to extend the 15 percent sales tax to the broad mass of consumer spending in Mexico—even to some higher-priced food and medicinal items, though not basic necessities. Still, in politics this translated to the "tortilla tax," anathema in a poor country like Mexico.

For us this was the fastest way to redistribute income to the needy, by applying a more collectible tax on the more affluent consumers, then investing that money into education, nutrition, housing, and health programs for working people and the poor. Politically we had no choice: We had to take our lumps early and raise taxes on the wealthier consumer class, or we would simply run out of money for antipoverty programs.

In a cash economy like ours, people have a thousand ways to beat the income tax. The rich have lawyers and accountants to dodge the tax system or simply move their funds to U.S. dollar accounts in Miami or Houston. Workers are often paid in cash, and they buy everything that way, too—so unless you collect taxes at the point of purchase, you won't raise much income for your social programs.

Based on the success models we had seen in Europe and Canada, we wanted to lower the income taxes—which were hard to collect and discouraged savings and investment—so that Mexicans would save their money and invest it at home in our banks and businesses, instead of avoiding the tax laws altogether. To pay for our ambitious social programs, we could raise revenue more effectively through a value-added tax, or VAT, levied on higher-priced consumer goods. The idea was to rebate these taxes back to the poor, with cash payments and social programs for those in need.

A VAT-style sales tax is much harder to avoid than income taxes and much less expensive for government to collect. Our plan was to have one flat tax of 15 percent on everything, whether the money was earned in salary or via product sales. A 15 percent flat tax rate also would draw more foreign investment to Mexico, the quickest way to create the new jobs we needed to help the poor and keep our emigrants home.

The government of an emerging economy has two main challenges. It must bake a larger pie, but it also must distribute that pie more evenly, so that the poor and working class share equally in that growth. The first challenge is easier; the free market is an enormously powerful tool for achieving growth. Mexico has terrific natural resources, a phenomenal labor pool, and immediate access to the richest economic engine on earth: North America.

By far the tougher challenge is to spread that prosperity fairly across the income ladder in a developing country with lopsided gaps in wealth and educational attainment, so that all share in the benefits of the free market. The Europeans have had tremendous success with broad income distribution. In social democracies like Sweden, Germany, and now even Spain or Portugal, the baker and the lawyer both do very well, as do the machinist and the teacher. A citizen may make a bit more or less, based on experience and education, but most everyone has a home or a nice apartment, even if it is not a lavish penthouse or a country estate. All have access to health care, retirement pensions, even free college education for their children. This flatter distribution of the benefits of society is made possible in part by a broad-based VAT tax, so that everyone shares in the burden of building a society where every citizen will have a true social safety net.

So, taking a cue from Europe, we set out to tax consumption rather than production with a VAT that would have fallen most heavily on the most affluent consumers of Mexico, taxing the richest people of our society fairly for the first time in the nation's history. Regardless of how they dodged and weaved on their income-tax forms, the rich would have to pay 15 percent at the point of sale for Cadillacs or perfume.

The trouble is, while a small sliver of Mexican society is very wealthy, there just aren't that many Cadillac and perfume buyers in the country. To generate the kind of income we needed to fund education, health care, and social welfare for the poor, everyone in Mexico would have to contribute at least a little bit—so we had to tax some of the higher-priced food and medicinal items, because most people in Mexico didn't spend money on anything else.

Our goal was to reduce the flat income-tax rate (then 36 percent in Mexico; now 28 percent). We would cut the tax rate on working-class automobiles while hiking taxes on luxuries and imposing a 15 percent VAT on everything else. Where the prospects for income redistribution got exciting was on the government spending side—we could use that money to make direct payments to those in extreme poverty, give scholarships to enable poor parents to keep their kids in school, offer pregnant women and the elderly the first medical coverage they'd ever had, build highways and airports, and bring clean water and electricity to rural areas and indigenous villages—taking Mexico into the twentieth century, at least before we got too deep into the twenty-first.

Of course, opposition politicians reduced this visionary plan to the more easily vilified "tortilla tax." The Democrats learned this lesson after Clinton hiked taxes to balance the budget early in his term, then got clobbered for it by Republicans in 1994. In politics it doesn't matter how well your program works to lift up the poor or revive the economy. If you propose tax reform, your opponents say you want to tax the poor people's tortillas; if you want to open up energy to private investment, opponents say you have a "secret plan" to privatize Pemex and throw oil-field workers out of their jobs.

This was the greatest disappointment to me in the presidency. Politics is a Tower of Babel where everyone speaks and no one listens, and where few act beyond their own narrow, selfish, partisan interests. The member of Congress, the party leader, the reporter, the businessman, the union boss—all of them communicate outward in the tongues of their own tribal interests, but few make any effort whatever to appreciate the concerns of others. There aren't many Jesuit "men for others" in Congress. I had better luck with female lawmakers, many of whom had entered politics recently and were more open to change. Even the opposition parties were full of reform-minded "women for others," both in Congress and groups like the teachers' unions.

My critics often said that as a business executive I should have been better at the give-and-take of negotiations between competing interests. But in this way politics is the polar opposite of business. Two parties negotiating a contract think always of how to "make the deal"—What do they want? How can I deliver that and make a profit? In business you look for the win-win, not the win-lose: better that both parties gain from a transaction than one profits at another's expense. Only then will they be able to do business with a satisfied customer again.

This is the way family life works. They are the rules of neighborhood and community and church, values that virtually every child learns from his mother, whether in the suburban sandboxes of the United States or on a farm in Guanajuato. Work together for the common good. Play well with the other kids. Don't fight, or you will only end up hurting each other. And always do what you know in your heart is right.

Somewhere along the way, politicians the world over have forgotten the simple rules of our mothers. Our ambitious plans for tax reform went down in flames in the Mexican Congress, a serious setback for my government. My critics said I was too naïve for real political infighting, and perhaps they were right. It is not a skill I aspire to learn.

IN WASHINGTON that autumn, George W. Bush was learning about partisanship, too. The District of Columbia is little more than two hours from Texas by air, but it was light-years from Austin, where Bush had worked with Democrats and Republicans in a much more bipartisan environment to make big changes—better public education in Texas for the children of Mexican immigrants, for example. By the time I stepped up to the Speaker's dais of the U.S. House on September 6, 2001—the first Mexican president ever to address a joint session of Congress—we knew that Bush had his hands full.

Vermont senator James Jeffords had bolted the Republican Party on May 21, 2001, handing control of the Senate to the Democrats. While this was a blow to Bush, it was good for our immigration bill—most Democrats were for the guest-worker reforms that Bush and I had envisioned at San Cristóbal. Over the intervening seven months, our cabinets and staffs had worked together reasonably well—with the exception of U.S. Attorney General John Ashcroft, whom we dubbed "the water man" for his obsessive focus on a side issue over water rights along the Rio Grande and whose right-wing views led him to oppose the guest-worker initiative with every legalistic argument the Justice Department could dredge up. By September we had an agreement on the basic principles—a temporary-worker program that would make immigration safe, legal, and orderly, documenting all those immigrants who had a job, allowing only those guest workers into the United States who had jobs waiting for them. The Bush and Fox administrations had worked out a process for uniting parents and children in our shared belief that "family values don't stop at the border." And we had agreed on a policy of civil rights and worker protections that would respect the human dignity of these "New American Pioneers," that wonderful phrase which titles an excellent book on immigration written by Dr. Juan Hernández.

My speech to Congress, carefully crafted by my foreign minister, Jorge Castañeda, focused on trust—a term I used over and over in that address. "I am aware that for many Americans and for many Mexicans, the idea of trusting their neighbor may seem risky and, perhaps, unwise. I am sure that many on both sides of the border would rather have stuck to the old saying that 'good fences make good neighbors,'" I told the senators and congressmen gathered in the House chamber for the joint session. "These perceptions have deep roots in history. In Mexico they derive from a long-held suspicion and apprehension about a powerful neighbor. And in the U.S. they stem from previous experience with a political regime governing Mexico, which for the most part was regarded as undemocratic and untrustworthy."

I knew that this would cause a firestorm in Mexico, where politicians hated any mention of our country's sordid past of corruption, narcotraffic, and economic crisis. But I told the U.S. Congress that it was time we began to trust each other. "Circumstances have changed, and we are now closely bound together. . . . No two nations are more important to the immediate prosperity and well-being of one another than Mexico and the United States."

The Congress rose as one, Republicans and Democrats, in a thunderous standing ovation. In closed-door meetings with key senators and congressmen from both parties, like John McCain, Ted Kennedy, Fritz Hollings, Phil Gramm, Dick Gephardt, Tom Daschle—even Jesse Helms and Trent Lott—it was clear: Passage of the immigration-reform package was in the bag.

"We're with you on this, Mr. President," said the lawmakers, even anti-NAFTA union Democrats and the same right-wingers who would later oppose Bush on our guest-worker proposals. "We've got the votes, President Fox, and we're going to pass an immigration-reform bill," the lawmakers told me, one after another. The halls of Congress rang with their pledges to "bring immigrants out of the shadows." As their applause and good wishes echoed in my ears under the Capitol dome that September 6, I remember wishing that I could get that kind of reaction from my own Congress in Mexico City.

That afternoon I boarded Air Force One to fly with President Bush to Ohio, where I had the unique experience of speaking for immigration reform and free trade alongside George W. Bush at a pep rally at the University of Toledo. This was highly unusual, for a foreign president to appear beside the president of the United States in a campaign-style setting. Bush is very good on the stump; the president rallied the crowd with great skill and passion. Ironically, Bush said on that day, September 6, 2001, "I want to remind people: Fearful people build walls; confident people tear them down."

While Bush is often criticized for his inarticulate performances in televised press conferences, he is an amazingly effective hall speaker, with a dynamic energy and a punchy, straightforward delivery that conveys a great sense of conviction. Whether or not you agree with everything he says, you know that *he* believes it; in person, Bush seems like a man who operates from principle and governs from the heart.

The White House was eager to feature me in Ohio, a key swing state, to help attract Latino voters. Growing numbers of Mexican immigrants and their Mexican American descendants live in the big "purple" swing states of the Midwest; the traditional Hispanic strength in California, Texas, and the Southwest now extends to millions of people of Mexican origin in states like Illinois, Ohio, Iowa, Missouri, North Carolina, New York, Florida, and Virginia. For me the Toledo appearance was one more chance to assure conservatives in America's heartland that Mexico was an ally, a business partner, and a friend.

On Air Force One on the way back to Washington, it was all hugs and high fives. "We're going to get this done," Bush said enthusiastically as he pumped my hand and we slapped each other's backs in a farewell *abrazo* at Andrews Air Force Base. I was touched by the gesture—Bush not only had improved his Spanish, a language that George will admit he speaks bravely, rather than well—but he had mastered the traditional male hug of Mexican culture. The *abrazo* dates back to our country's lawless past, when men needed to check each other's backs to check for hidden weapons. There were no secrets between us now.

As we returned to Blair House that evening and Marta went back to the White House for a private dinner with Laura Bush, I wished President Bush farewell and realized that we were partners now. By singling out Mexico for his first foreign trip and hosting me at his first state dinner, Bush had bet his political capital on the controversial issue of immigration reform. By associating my administration with the United States instead of Mexico's traditional tilt toward Castro and the Latin American left, I had cast my lot with the often-reviled El Norte. Bush and I were back-to-back against the anti-Mexico crowd to the north and the anti-America crowd to the south. I firmly believe that until that fateful week George W. Bush had the opportunity to become the Latino Lincoln—giving hope to 12 million Mexican immigrants and, not coincidentially, realigning Hispanic voters into the Republican Party for a century.

Instead, four days after I left Washington, the men of hate flew airplanes full of passengers into the World Trade Center, the Pentagon, and a field in Shanksville, Pennsylvania, killing more than three thousand innocent people. Fifteen of them were Mexicans. Overnight the world changed. America's borders clanged shut. Our revolution of hope came face-to-face with the walls of fear.

CHAPTER 14

FORTRESS AMERICA

Around the world we remember where we were on the morning of September 11, 2001. I was in the front seat of a Chevy Suburban in Mexico City, flush with the success of our trip to Washington and the bright prospects for an immigration bill. Over the car radio came reports of a small plane striking the World Trade Center in New York.

"I've been in that building," I said, having visited there on Mexico trade business over the years. "Turn that up." Taking the secure cell phone from the guard, I called Santiago Creel, my interior minister, a Georgetown-educated former law-school dean and comrade from the Grupo San Ángel democracy movement.

"They don't know, it could just be an accident, but it might be terrorists," said Creel, whose ministry oversaw law enforcement and intragovernmental affairs. "We're not sure what's going on. The White House isn't saying anything, but our people in Washington say there are rumors that this is some kind of orchestrated attack."

"Keep me posted," I said uneasily as we drew up to the site of my speech that morning—oddly enough, Mexico City's own World Trade Center, a fifty-story complex with a big convention center, where our final 2000 presidential debate had been held. We walked inside, and for once I didn't protest when the security detail led us in through the kitchen. Presidents get used to the smell of rotting vegetables—my next book should be a guidebook: *Freight Elevators and Loading Docks of the World's Convention Centers and Hotels.* I kept my speech brief. Midway through, the army officer from Estado Mayor came up to the dais and handed me a note: The United States was under attack, according to media reports. I broke off abruptly, and we hustled back to the car, while our team gathered in the underground war room of Los Pinos.

Communications to New York and Washington were impossible;

phone lines were jammed. Our Foreign Ministry and the U.S. ambassador to Mexico, Jeff Davidow, a brilliant career diplomat whom Bush had retained after Clinton's departure, knew no more than we did. The U.S. government hadn't yet said anything. But the news trickling out on CNN en Español was horrifying: The tall towers that had been the twin signatures of the world's financial markets toppling in pillars of smoke; a smoldering hole in the side of the Pentagon, headquarters of the planet's mightiest military. There were rumors of more terrorist attacks headed to the White House and Capitol Hill.

My first thought was, *God, help those poor people.* I said a quick, silent prayer for their deliverance from this evil. My second thought was for the Mexicans trapped inside the burning buildings: the busboys and waiters at Windows on the World restaurant; executives or diplomats who might be having meetings in the Twin Towers; the visiting Mexican army officer or immigrant worker who might be in the Pentagon.

Only then did I think like a president: Was Mexico City next?

The tallest skyscrapers everywhere in the world were evacuated, and government buildings went on alert. I issued the orders for *centinela,* Mexico's version of red alert. We doubled the guards at the border, ports, oil refineries, and government facilities like Congress and Los Pinos. We helped the United States to shut down the borders along the Rio Grande and accommodated inbound flights that were grounded by the shutdown of air traffic inside the United States. We put our armed forces on the highest-level alert and put our law-enforcement agencies to work investigating any possibility that the terrorists had entered via Mexico (they had not, coming in through Europe and U.S. airports, though some early media reports immediately pointed the finger southward). Once we knew what had happened, I went on television and radio to express our sympathies and support for our neighbor in the face of this terrible tragedy, rejecting the "terrible criminal terrorist acts" and expressing our support for all the victims and their families. We held a massive candlelight vigil at our own World Trade Center. Mexicans prayed for the victims, expressed outrage at what terrorists had done to our closest neighbors. Many scrambled to try to contact family in the United States. Our nation was appalled by the handful of far-left radicals in Mexico who suggested that the United States deserved this attack in reprisal for its imperialism and military aggression. But this was the fringe. Mexico was completely united in the days after 9/11 in our compassion for those who died at the hands of the terrorists and in our determination to do all we could to secure the hemisphere so that this would never happen again.

Immigration reform was now the furthest thing from anyone's mind. This was just as well: We had been the talk of Washington the weekend before, but by September 12, Mexico did not exist for the United States. We accepted this new reality, keeping the borders closed and clamping down on our ports. My government beefed up security along Mexico's southern border with Guatemala and Belize and controlled rail and air transit along our frontiers to help the United States lock down the security of the hemisphere, despite the staggering cost to our fragile economy. To paraphrase Franklin D. Roosevelt's famous defense of the Lend-Lease Act to aid Britain during World War II, when your neighbor's house is on fire, you don't argue over the price of the hose.

While of course we mourned first the loss of life and the danger to the United States, the damage of 9/11 to Mexico was incalculable. Not only did 9/11 derail an immigration accord that three days before had seemed imminent. Now, instead of a "democracy bonus," Mexicans faced the potential collapse of our economy.

I'd been in office only nine months when the airplanes struck the World Trade Center and the Pentagon and crashed in Pennsylvania. Mexico was deep in debt from Salinas and his PRI predecessors, despite the Clinton bailout of the peso and Zedillo's approach to fiscal discipline. But the 1994 crisis had utterly destroyed our banks, real estate, aviation, the housing and financial markets; the homes and life savings of Mexicans had vanished overnight. Just as we were beginning to recover, 9/11 closed the borders to all trade with the United States and Canada—and virtually shut down tourism, one of the largest industries in the country. Wall Street and the world's financial markets, still reeling from the previous year's collapse of the high-tech bubble, tumbled, recovered slightly, then dropped again as the anthrax scare swept the United States that winter.

It is impossible to overstate how deeply and inextricably entwined our economies are. The saying here is that when the United States catches a cold, Mexico gets pneumonia. Now the United States had pneumonia; 9/11 could easily have killed Mexico altogether. It still seems callous and calculating, to measure in economic terms the impact of a tragedy, when so many good people died. I am mindful at all times that only the swift actions of the Bush administration and its allies in the Free World have to date averted more such tragedies. Mexico, too, lost sons and daughters in the September 11 attacks, a fact I cite not to curry sympathy for my country but to remind you that we are all in this together—all peace-loving, democratic nations now lie at risk to terror and hate. Though President Bush is frequently mocked on late-night television for speaking about the authors of these attacks in moral terms, as "the evil terrorists"—September 11 *was* evil, and I applauded him aloud the day he promised to "smoke them out of their holes" and "get them running and find them and hunt them down," so we can "bring them to justice." The U.S. president and I later disagreed sharply on the plan to invade Iraq. But my disappointment in the U.S. decision to go to war despite the world's objections at the United Nations does not lessen my admiration for George W. Bush's handling of those dark days of late 2001, when the entire earth was in great danger and our continental economy teetered on the edge of collapse.

Closing the borders hurt us the most, and for the longest duration. Before September 11 the average wait for a cargo truck at the Rio Grande was an hour and a half; after 9/11 they could not cross at all. When the border was reopened, the average wait was nearly six hours. The cost to all North America was huge, but since the vast majority of Mexico's trade is with the United States and Canada, the damage to us was cataclysmic. Even for the mighty U.S. economy, closing the border with its biggest trading partners was painful: Fully 62 percent of all U.S. trade to Latin America is with the Republic of Mexico.

The effect on tourism was staggering. Visits by Americans and Canadians, by far our biggest customers, plunged. The hotels of Cancún and Puerto Vallarta were empty, causing layoffs and unemployment along both the Pacific and Caribbean coasts. The ripple effect to real-estate values, construction, and the housing sector was devastating. Tourism eventually recovered, once Bush's new Transportation Security Administration got North Americans over their fear of flying. Mexico later gained in an odd way from U.S. travelers, who saw us as a comfortable, familiar, and close alternative to more distant travel overseas. But 2001 and 2002 were disasters for tourism and the more than 2 million Mexican workers who depend on this lucrative business for their daily bread.

Shutting down the NAFTA trade across the borders also hit the *maquiladora* assembly plants, the transportation industry, and retail outlets on both sides of the U.S.-Mexico border from Brownsville-Matamoros to San Diego–Tijuana. There were layoffs in agriculture and factory closures in the Mexican interior, as workers who picked crops or manufactured products with freshness dates were no longer needed for goods that couldn't reach their destinations in time. This caused spot unemployment throughout Mexico—and in south Texas, too, where 80 percent of the NAFTA trade passes before moving on to the upper Midwest, the Northeast, the far West, and Canada. The end result, according to the International Monetary Fund, was that while Mexico's economy should have grown at least 4 percent that year, after 9/11 our growth was flat—not nearly enough for our young people entering the workforce, who needed good jobs at higher wages to keep them home.

With our proposed economic reforms already facing stiff resistance from an opposition-controlled Congress, I decided at our first January 2002 cabinet meeting to focus on what we could do by ourselves. The United States had its own problems. In his address to the U.S. Congress, Bush had announced an all-out war on terror, which leaders of both U.S. parties and the world backed wholeheartedly—including Mexico, which had much at risk. If our own Congress was too consumed with selfish political agendas to back our economic reforms—remember, neither the Mexican Congress nor the president faces reelection, so there was no way to pressure the legislature with public opinion—there were only three courses of action available to us to revive the economy.

We could resort to the same tactics of authoritarianism and corruption used by previous Mexican presidents to force through our economic reforms—pay journalists under the table, shell out grants to buy congressmen's votes, threaten opponents by cutting off discretionary spending to their states, blacklist their personal business interests. But I wasn't about to go down that road. We had not fought for the better part of a century to bring Mexico into full democracy just so that we could impose a new dicatorship in order to pass our reforms. As the Bible says in Mark 8:36, "For what shall it profit a man, if he shall gain the whole world, and lose his own soul?"

A second option was to do nothing. This would result in collapse. I suppose that the ensuing unemployment, bankruptcy, and panic might have pressured Congress into passing some reforms to keep government solvent, but that strategy would have been callous and Machiavellian in the extreme. I would not run the risk of returning to the cycle of devaluation, debt, and crisis that had made Mexico the great loser of the twentieth century.

The only course remaining was to make incremental changes in those areas where we could find common ground with reform-minded opponents—and bold changes in areas we controlled directly, through executive action. The most dramatic—and politically costly—of those moves was to raise electricity rates, which we did in January 2002.

Between our so-called tortilla tax and the utility-rate hike, my personal popularity tumbled from a high near 80 percent the year before to 50 percent in a January 2002 poll. This mattered little to a guy who couldn't run for reelection, but it would allow the PRI to regain ground in a series of gubernatorial by-elections and the 2003 congressional elections, making prospects even bleaker for reform. Freed of its traditional control by the executive branch, the Mexican Congress was like a classroom with a substitute teacher. Resolutions, investigations, subpoenas, and silly laws sailed through the air at the Speaker's dais like so many spitballs.

But we found ways around obstructionist lawmakers. On energy reform, our lawyers and industry experts crafted a carefully vetted system to enable the private investment we needed so desperately to upgrade our oil and gas industry. Pemex was Mexico's number-one source of revenue. We made it even more profitable by offering "multiple service contracts" to bring in private money from domestic Mexican and foreign investors, without privatizing Pemex or giving up government ownership of oil and gas.

Together with the electricity rate hikes, these private investments in Pemex yielded huge revenues to government. But unlike the reckless petrocracies of our past, Mexico no longer ran the country into debt when oil prices were high, leaving future generations to figure out what to do when the oil price drops. Instead we saved 25 percent of our windfall profits from higher oil prices in a "rainy-day fund" to offset future drops in oil prices and invested 50 percent into improving Pemex to make the state-owned energy giant more profitable and productive. Only then did we invest the remaining 25 percent of excess profits into education, health care, housing, and the social-welfare needs of the poor.

When the state owns all the nation's oil reserves, mineral rights, gas stations, and airports of a big country, that nation's president is also the de facto chairman of the board of one of the biggest corporations in the world. Pemex is the earth's second-largest oil company, after Saudi Arabia's Aramco; our state oil company has 50 percent more oil production and employees than Exxon. Yet even in today's high-priced oil market, Pemex reaps only $77 billion in annual revenues (about a third of Mexico's federal budget), while ExxonMobil makes $377 billion. Pemex has $24 billion in debt; Exxon earns nearly $40 billion in annual profits. So there is great potential for improvement—but we have to be careful not to drain Pemex of the capital it needs to modernize operations, as had too often been the case in Mexico's past.

For example, even back in 2001, our geologists knew that deep-water drilling in the Gulf of Mexico could more than double our energy reserves. We had more than 40 billion barrels of oil in the ground and under the sea floor, but with Pemex's inefficient and outdated methods of extraction, Mexico had only twenty-five years more before we'd run out of energy altogether. Deep-water drilling could help us find a hundred-year supply of oil and gas. But that took money, billions of dollars to drill deep in the Gulf and develop the vast pools of gas and hydrocarbons in our Cuenca de Burgos reserves. Our new public-private energy partnerships brought in the money we needed. Then we used this tactic on electricity to build thirty-six new power plants and boost our electricity supply by 35 percent.

We took a similar approach to the nation's airports, tollways, and railyards, finding innovative ways to tap the private sector to run air-terminal operations and toll plazas. I found these ideas in Britain, where government has long worked hand in hand with the free market; Tony Blair has found a "Third Way" between raw free-market capitalism and state-controlled socialism.

For us, billions from public-private partnerships and cost savings on state-owned enterprises were nearly as good as tax reform; money, after all, is money. "It's all coming out of the same bag," I told my aides. There was political heat. In Congress the opposition howled that we were selling off Mexico's patrimony by the barrel. One day I saw a mob of protesters marching along Reforma wearing Fox masks, carrying coffins with the corpse of "Mexico" knifed to death, oil leaking from her chest. "We must be making a difference," I said to myself, thinking of how many kids we could educate with the money that private investors were saving us at Pemex.

Still, it hurt, seeing masked, cartoonish figures of myself "raping" a lady called Mexico, alongside men dressed up as Uncle Sam. Change is pain.

In case I was ever tempted to forget this elemental fact of political life, at the village of Atenco there were angry men and women ready to remind me. It all began just after September 11, when our government announced plans to build a new international airport near the nation's capital.

By 2002, the airport of Mexico City, the second-largest metropolis in the world, was more than ninety years old. It had only two runways, just one of which could normally be used. Completely inadequate for Mexico in the new global economy, the airport is hemmed in by residential neighborhoods and was a cripping limitation on our country's ability to grow and create jobs for the poor. We researched the options and decided to build a new $2.3 billion airport in Texcoco, the most environmentally sound, cost-effective site we could find, located in a lake bed of cornfields about about twenty miles outside Mexico City, in an adjoining state, which (confusingly) is called Estado de Mexico.

When our first offer to local farmers was too low, we upped the ante from about three thousand dollars an acre to twenty-one thousand dollars an acre. But a small group of locals, whipped up by antiglobalist organizers linked to the *zapatista* movement and radical leftists, took to the streets armed with machetes to block the highway. Violence spiraled out of control as rioters seized police cars and blew up gasoline trucks, kidnapped police officers and a deputy attorney general, threatened to light them on fire, and paraded them as hostages before the media, demanding that we drop the plans to buy the land for the airport.

"Even if they gave us all the gold in the world, we wouldn't leave our land, because it's all we have," said one protester. This sounds admirable, until you remember that the land in question belonged to the government—it was *ejido* land, so it was held in the public domain with hereditary rights given to farmers, who tilled small plots of corn and beans. I could sympathize with the campesinos—I knew how my family had felt when the government came to take away the land we farmed. I understood them, the emotional bond a family forms with a particular piece of land. But developing countries like mine must have airports, highways, reservoirs, hospitals, and schools in order to grow and make life better for people. Where can we put them, if we cannot use lake-bed farmland?

By 2002 there were four thousand police in and around Atenco. People were getting hurt. Reports of police brutality trickled out of what had become a virtual war zone. Atenco was the right place to build, we were operating within the rule of law, the new airport was important for our economy—but it wasn't worth people's lives. Our interior minister, Santiago Creel, negotiated patiently with the rioters to secure the release of the hostages, but the hard core of the protest movement didn't want a solution—they wanted a cause.

Finally I summoned my cabinet and told them we were dropping plans for the new airport. "Democracy is more important than new runways," I said. "We can't have people getting killed over this."

Pedro Cerisola, the former Aeroméxico CEO who had worked tirelessly on the issue as my secretary of communications and transporation, was crestfallen. "But it's the ideal site!" he said.

"No doubt, no doubt." I shook my head sadly. "But we will just have to make do with what we have." In the end we took half a loaf as better than none: Creative and skillful manager that he is, Pedro engineered a solution to renovate the existing airport. But the new airport we planned at Atenco would have been better.

The media and the critics, who had screamed for a year that the government was being too harsh in expropriating the land of poor farmers, now howled that Fox was being weak. Businessmen and hardline *panistas* complained that the government had folded too quickly; the opposition said I had failed to solve the nation's air-transporation crisis. It would not be the last time I was forced to choose between democracy and the rule of law, between social order and the prospect of violence.

Change is pain.

As WORLD MARKETS adjusted to the post-9/11 reality, Mexico began to recover on its own. We began to earn new revenues from our Third Way partnerships at Pemex and the transportation sector, where Pedro worked miracles. "We can't worry about what we can't control," I told my team again and again that difficult year. "If the laws block us, let's figure out a loophole. If Congress won't reform, let's focus on what we can do within the executive branch. If the U.S. is too busy to work with us, let's pull ourselves up here in Mexico. God helps those who help themselves."

Immigration reform was dead for now, as the United States turned inward and isolationists in Washington began talking about building a Fortress America. It was a stark contrast to where we'd been two years ago, when I had urged Mexico to tear down walls of corruption and Bush had told Ohioans that only fearful people build walls, that confident people tear them down. Now there was talk of a new Berlin Wall along the Rio Grande.

At home our own Congress was still balking at economic reform, but we eked out a modest compromise that put us on the road to a balanced budget and a strong peso. Finally we had some money to invest in education, housing, health care, and poverty. We could wait no longer for a democracy bonus. It was time to earn one on our own.

Seven decades of neglect had left Mexicans utterly unprepared for the global economy. If Mexico was to stand up among the nations of the twenty-first century, the spine of our government had to be a revolution in education.

Today the average child in the United States gets twelve years of education, still the most in the world. More than 80 percent of U.S. kids finish high school; an astonishing 70 percent of them attend college. When I came to office, Mexican children got an average of just *five* years of education. Remember Clinton labor secretary Robert Reich's point about the average of his height and Wilt Chamberlain's? The tragedy behind median statistics is this: Five years on average means that for every Mexican kid who makes it to high school, there is another Mexican kid who never got *any* schooling at *all*. Only 5 percent of our young people went to college, while 10 percent of Mexican adults were still fully illiterate.

This of course leads to underemployment and low wages in a global economy that demands more and more intellectual ability. Our people needed to know mathematics, the sciences, and computer technology; language skills in a world where English is not only the language of our biggest trading partner but also the new lingua franca of world commerce and the Internet; citizenship values, the rule of law, ethics, personal responsibility, on-time performance; cultural advancement in literature, music, and the arts, which opens the right brain to the creative possibilities of ideas undreamed.

For most of the twentieth century, education in Mexico had progressed little from the days when peasants were kept unlettered by Porfirio's *hacendados*. Just as they controlled artists and intellectuals, censoring what we saw in the movies and on television, the government used the schools to keep the children of peasants and urban workers ignorant and in their places. The old PRI had cared more about providing full employment for 1.5 million teachers in the government-controlled unions than in developing the minds of the next generation. Besides, if kids were given access to information about how people lived in the rest of the world, they might foment democratic revolution here at home.

This is another reason that that the authorities turned their backs on immigrants who left Mexico. The brave young men and women who went north were not welcomed home, because they returned with a new worldview, like American soldiers after the world wars. Like the old song lyric, the old PRI worried: How would they keep immigrants down on the farm after they'd seen the sights of gay Paree?

This was the view of the old dinosaurs of the PRI. But by the time I came to Los Pinos, a group of young reformers had risen up within the PRI. There was a new crop of visionary, honest young PRI governors in their thirties and forties who wanted to remodel schools for the twenty-first century. Dedicated *priistas* at the highest levels of the teacher's unions shared the professional pride of classroom educators to help children, even if it meant that the union's teachers had to take tests and work harder to get results. Many reform-oriented PRI lawmakers were willing to work side by side with us to bridge the education gap that was the most tragic legacy of Mexico's authoritarian past.

This inequality of knowledge was widening even faster than our income gap with the industrialized nations. Mexico's problem is not so much unemployment—in 2007 our jobless rate was 3.6 percent, lower than in the United States. Our chronic problem is *under*employment. For nearly a century, Mexico had failed to prepare our citizens to compete in the global economy; it didn't even produce enough high-wage jobs for those we *did* prepare with good educations.

Impressed by "best practice" models we had seen around the world, we built our education reforms on a foundation of human values, with three pillars: equity, quality, and evaluation. We stressed teacher testing, school discipline, an end to social promotion, and the encouragement of parental involvement. In the past, parents had not been welcome in our schools. There were no PTAs, no regular meetings with teachers to assess students' progress. The poor and the indigenous were particularly unwelcome at the schoolhouse doors, which had been closed as surely to parents of one underclass as white schools of Alabama under George Wallace had been to African Americans.

We encouraged parents to get involved in their child's education, to attend meetings, to complain when a teacher acted improperly or failed to show up on Fridays—a sadly common occurrence in Mexico even as late as 2000. This was especially true in rural schools that served the poor, far from the eyes of the more sophisticated and demanding parents of the middle and upper classes. Even in the big cities, Mexican culture, downtrodden under centuries of dominance by Spanish conquistadores, wealthy *hacendados* and military caudillos, strongman presidents and even the indigenous village caciques, tells us to bow to authority, never to complain, to take what little one is given and survive without making any trouble. As parents, consumers, students, or voters, historically we were not demanding people like the Anglo-Saxons of the north. Our culture was a Latin lifestyle: get along, live and let live, take it easy, don't make any waves.

We wanted parents to stand up for their rights to see their children educated, to demand more from our schools. I was struck by the example of the heroic Latina mother who came up and grabbed my sleeve one afternoon in Los Angeles and told me how she had fought all through the 1960s just to be allowed to join her children's PTA, after her cookies were turned away from the grade-school bake sale because they were "too Mexican."

Working in partnership with Mexico's largest teachers' union, Marta's Vamos Mexico nonprofit foundation launched an innovative program of parent education, publishing a three-volume guidebook for parents. Vamos Mexico put the three-volume set into 11.5 million homes, more than half of Mexico's 22 million families. This *Guía de Padres,* or *Parents' Guide,* became as common a staple in Mexican living rooms as Dr. Spock's books were in the United States during the 1960s. Vamos Mexico and the national teachers' union joined together to help create a Sunday-morning TV show to encourage parental responsibility for education and promote healthy social values.

Perhaps in other countries a mother storming down to the school to complain is the bane of the educational establishment. In Mexico it was simply not done. But, oddly enough, the 1.5 million teachers of Mexico became our biggest allies. Female teachers in particular—who had only recently entered the teaching profession in large numbers and were anxious to have a positive impact on their students' lives—were very receptive to our efforts to promote parental involvement. A good teacher knows that parents can make all the difference, just by helping the child with homework. If they were unable to do so, as were so many poor and uneducated adults, parents could help just by making school a priority and by supporting the child's decision to stay in school.

We coupled those aspects of reform that we thought the teachers' unions might resist—like encouraging parents to report absent or abusive teachers, and the stringent teacher testing we implemented for the first time in the country's history—with strong financial support for schools. We wanted teachers to do a better job, but we knew we needed to pay for it—by boosting salaries of this notoriously underpaid profession and by giving teachers the books, computers, and training they needed to do their job well.

Finally we had our education-reform package ready. It was time for me to confront the two things I dreaded most in the world—angry women and demanding teachers.

"Why do you want to meet with the teachers' unions?" my advisers chimed down the long conference table in the basement war room of Los Pinos, looking at me like I was a madman. "They're all PRI. Those women won't help us."

"We at least have to face the music," I said. "If not, they will say we imposed these changes undemocratically and didn't even consult with them."

So I went into the lion's den and laid out our plans to the impassive faces of the women who lead the nation's million and a half teachers, like a student taking an oral exam. Inwardly I flinched, expecting a rap across the knuckles. Teacher testing, parental involvement, standard evaluation of students—all this would be anathema to the union rank and file. "Well, what do you think?" I said. There was a small pause as I waited for the lecture.

"Thank you, Mr. President," one lady said, breaking the uncomfortable silence. "When do we begin?" The educators plunged into the conversation enthusiastically, embracing our radical ideas and adding their own.

Afterward I took the woman aside. "I am pleasantly surprised, and so grateful for your support," I said. "But I have to say, I was expecting resistance. What do you teachers really think about this?"

"No one's ever asked us what we think, Mr. President," she said. "We're only teachers. What do we know about educating children?"

"But you're from the PRI, I just thought—"

"We're *teachers,* sir." She smiled. "Our party is the children. We take pride in educating them, and we'll work to make our schools better, no matter what the politics. Do you understand?"

"Yes, señora," I said dutifully.

"You respect our profession, I can tell. You can't fool a teacher."

"I know, señora," I said.

"So don't try."

"Yes, señora."

"And don't give up on this. I know you can do it."

"Yes, señora."

IN A DEVELOPING SOCIETY, it is not only the students who need to learn to use computers or to speak English—we had to "educate the educators" as well. Few of our 1.5 million teachers were even slightly bilingual, for example. This led us to the electronic blackboard, an innovative technology that allows teachers and students to self-teach English and other subjects with interactive learning, using computers and the Internet. Here again, as promised, I had the enthusiastic support of the teachers, even though it used to be the most *priista* of PRI unions. With their help we launched Enciclomedia, a nationwide program of electronic blackboards to connect every school in Mexico to the Internet, from the bustling big-city high schools to the poorest elementary school in Chiapas. Imagine this: A Mayan child in the Yucatán Peninsula walks barefoot to the rural school, which still lacks walls and windows, its roof thatched indigenous style. The child walks up the wooden planks at the door and sits down at the computer and reads Cervantes, puts on headphones to listen to the Berlin Symphony Orchestra, learns the story of Nelson Mandela's struggle against apartheid.

This is globalism. This is the revolution of hope.

I HAVE DESCRIBED the syndrome we face in the developing world: Even if public education is free, parents are often forced by economic necessity to take their kids out of school, or never even let them out of the home, so they can tend other children and work for the family's survival. This practice had to stop. But if you are scraping to buy milk for a baby and the only way you can do it is to keep your ten-year-old home to tend the baby while you go to work, this is what a loving parent will do, no matter the long-term social cost—anything else is rather abstract when your baby is crying, your purse is empty, and your cupboard is bare.

With Oportunidades, our direct scholarship payments to the poor, we were able to increase school attendance and reach an average of eight years of education. We reduced illiteracy, boosted college attendance, and gave out 6.2 million scholarships to poor, rural, and working-class families to enable them to keep their kids in school longer. This is not enough, but it gets us closer. Our new president, Felipe Calderón, has pledged to carry on and strengthen these education reforms, so that soon Mexican children will stand in educational parity with our wealthier neighbors.

This is critical, because even as I write today, a hundred thousand high-paying jobs sit unfilled in the *maquiladora* factories of northern Mexico. Those jobs alone would keep home in Mexico many of those who emigrate north every year. Think of the impact of good jobs for the heads of households of a hundred thousand families—Mexican parents and children who could immediately reach financial security, without being forced to cross deserts or crawl under barbed wire. But these jobs require a high-school diploma, and Mexico doesn't yet have enough young people educated to fill them.

We also deliberately addressed controversial social topics that had been largely taboo in Mexico. With help from the teachers' unions, the new parenting textbooks, funded privately by Marta's Vamos Mexico foundation, were distributed free in bus and subway stations. Along with a companion weekly Sunday-morning show, the curriculum taught sex education, gender equity, values, and ethics. Education reform also opened students' minds to diverse views of history, teaching young people to think for themselves as free citizens—not brainwashed by a government whose revisionist historians would have done well in the Soviet Union or Franco's Spain.

Here again is another great lesson that may serve those striving to bring democracy to the Middle East, Africa, Asia, and the Americas: Dictatorships always work first to capture the minds of the children. Control them, make sure they do not learn how others live in freedom, and you will control the country forever—at least until young people discover that life can be better. If the world's policy makers really want global democracy, they should focus on hooking up the classrooms of Afghanistan, Haiti, Iraq, and Africa to the Internet.

Because education is freedom. Education is revolution. Education is *hope.*

WOMEN LED the fight to reform education in Mexico. There is no doubt in my mind: Had men remained in charge of the teachers' unions and the schools, Mexico would still languish light-years behind the big industrialized nations. From Doña Mercedes to my outspoken first lady to the forceful women who now run the educational unions, women have always been a powerful influence for change in my life and for change in Mexico. In politics, whether it was the PAN's quota requiring female candidates or whether it was my sister on the picket line, women were in the vanguard of the struggle for democracy.

This was remarkable in a macho nation that in the past had its version of the view that women should be kept "barefoot and pregnant." Too many Mexicans believed that *las mujeres fueron como las escopetas; hay que mantenerlas cargadas y en la esquina*—"women were like shotguns; they should be kept loaded and in the corner." This sexism dated back to the Mayans and Aztecs, who gave women no rights whatsoever, traded them like cattle, and beat them into submission. The Spanish conquerors were no better, nor the strongman caudillo presidents of our past. Perhaps nowhere on earth did the gender gap yawn so wide as in the Mexico we inherited in 2000.

I was determined that our revolution of hope would also be a revolution for women. All over the world, women were the leading agents of change. This is true of the pioneer rancher's wife who ministers to sick farmhands as well as of the bread seller in Bangladesh who uses microcredits to build a small business. My heroes were Mother Teresa tending the untouchables of Calcutta; the remarkable Aung San Suu Kyi fighting for human rights in Myanmar; Cory Aquino leading a peaceful revolution of democracy in the Philippines; Rosa Parks, keeping her rightful seat on the bus in Montgomery, Alabama; our own Xóchitl Gálvez, Mexico's first cabinet minister for indigenous rights, honored by the United Nations for the advancement of disadvantaged minorities.

Along with rights for tribal peoples, immigrants, the disabled, and others who lived outside the economic mainstream, gender equity became a hallmark of our government. At times I deliberately administered shock therapy to our male-dominated society. As if marrying a political leader weren't enough, I insisted on beginning every speech by addressing the audience, "Ladies and gentlemen." This may seem pretty tame by global standards, but it was unprecedented in Mexico, where presidents and leaders had always begun their speeches with the male universal "Señores." Imagine if George W. Bush, Bill Clinton, or Tony Blair began their speeches saying, "Gentlemen, here are my goals," or started a cabinet meeting, "Well, men, let's get to work." This was Mexico before democracy.

"*Chiquillas y chiquillos*"—this became the signature of late-night comics and radio deejays in Mexico when they did impressions of me—and some of them do it remarkably well. My favorites were the comedians Alfonso Villapando and Andrés Bustamante, who ridiculed me worse than Dana Carvey ever did former president Bush. One of the happier aspects of our new democratic climate is the freedom of TV stations to create hilarious parodies. They savaged me, Marta, and the political figures of the country, from the Muppet-like characters of *Hechos de Peluche,* which spoof the antics of "Chente Fox" and "Marta Según," to the cast of *La Parodia*, where a whole family of zany Fox family look-likes mocked the foibles and missteps of my presidency. Sometimes telling, occasionally cruel, these programs are nonetheless fruits of democracy. However much they may pain me at times, my advice to future presidents is grin and bear it. We fought long and hard to give the comedians the power to make fun of us: it's rough on your poll numbers but good for your humility.

To advance the cause of the long-suffering women of Mexico, we tackled the most sensitive issues head-on. We cracked down on domestic violence, for example, historically treated in Mexico not as a crime against women and children, but as a right of husbands and fathers. We also worked to break the glass ceiling that had kept women out of key positions. Mexican women had finally made it into the workforce, especially in education. But you rarely saw a woman CEO or even a vice president or business partner. They certainly had not featured as visibly in presidential cabinets as they did in mine or the cabinet appointed in 2006 by President Calderón.

I made a conscious decision to lead on difficult issues like the morning-after pill, despite the outcry we faced from our best allies in the Catholic Church and the evangelic movement. I considered this issue very carefully, consulting with the top professional medical minds, scientists, doctors, and my world-renowned health minister. Science is clear on this:

The morning-after pill is birth control, not abortion. The morning-after pill only avoids conception; as a Catholic, I strongly oppose abortion and support the protection of any human life that occurs after conception. The decision to use a morning-after pill is in no way the ending of a life, but a choice to prevent the conception of unwanted pregnancies—much like condoms or birth-control pills, two other "untouchable" subjects we were criticized for including in our educational outreach. But AIDS, accidental pregnancy, lack of prenatal care, and "children having children" all stem from a shortage of knowledge, good values, and social responsibility. I was determined to provide young people with the right information to make intelligent decisons.

We created a women's institute to make our laws and policies gender-neutral and advance women in the government. We established our authority to punish those who discriminated or committed acts of violence against women and those powerless to defend themselves. This Institute for Women acted horizontally through all ranks of government—Pemex, the state energy giant; the electric monopoly Comisión Federal de Electricidad; labor, where we could insist that private employers give equal opportunity to promote women and disadvantaged minorities; education, where two thirds of teachers were now female.

Perhaps most controversial was our decision to make welfare payments directly to women instead of to male "heads of household." Sadly, in Mexico the stereotype was too often true: Payments made to men frequently went for beer. The studies show that mothers are more likely to put the money to good use—to feed, clothe, educate, and house their children. When we were fighting for every peso we could find for social programs, I wasn't about to see the fruits of democracy wasted on liquor and cigarettes.

DETERMINED TO RAISE private funds to help the poor, rather than relying solely on tax revenues, Marta had set up the Vamos Mexico foundation to help women and children, the indigenous, rural families, and those in the urban slums. Even this nonprofit foundation was controversial from the start: Critics lambasted my new first lady as a scheming Evita, charging that she was using the foundation to advance her alleged presidential ambitions. The irony is that Marta stayed completely out of government from the morning we got married, resigning her post as communications director and handing it over to Paco Ortiz, our advertising director from the campaign; later the job would go to Rodolfo Elizondo, that same El Negro who stood arm in arm with me in the basement of Congress to face the bayonets of the army.

Marta poured her time, energy, and considerable fund-raising prowess into twisting the arms of generous billionaires, corporations, and philanthropists. With their help she set up mobile breast-cancer and cervical-cancer screening units, drug-education and rehab centers to get Mexico's young people out of substance abuse, and shelters to help mothers and children escape abusive husbands and fathers. She used innovative ideas, distributing aid kits to midwives to help dramatically reduce the infant-mortality rate and setting up "bus classrooms" to educate the poor about childbirth, drugs, and violence.

These were touchy matters you just didn't talk about in Mexico, much less allow the first lady to put them "in your face." Marta was popular with women and the poor, who finally had someone to speak for them. This, too, alarmed the political establishment. Worried that Marta would be a force in the 2006 elections, either as a presidential candidate or as a PAN draw for women and the poor, our enemies in the old regime and the fast-rising PRD of López Obrador went after Marta with guns blazing.

In Mexico we have a culture of social cannibalism common to oppressed peoples. It is sometimes called the "crab bucket syndrome": When one climbs up out of the pail, the others have this bizarre natural desire to pull that one back down where they are. In Mexico this cultural envy is an enormously powerful force in the political establishment against any visible agent of change—particularly the press, which resented Marta bitterly for carrying out my orders to end the *mordida*, the "bite" that PRI press secretaries traditionally handed out to reporters like so many chocolates to keep them sweet.

As the U.S. press had done with Nancy Reagan and Hillary Clinton, as Fleet Street did with Cherie Blair, the Mexican media sought to hurt a popular chief executive by going after his spouse. Headlines questioned the prices of the gowns Marta wore to meet foreign heads of state. Talk shows gossiped about her "pillowcase influence" on the presidency. So-called investigative reporters sought to tarnish the first lady with absurd charges of financial chicanery. There were false allegations about her fund-raising tactics and an ugly smear campaign against her children. An Argentine writer falsely accused the first lady's family of influence peddling. (Marta later won a $178,000 libel judgment against the writer in court; she plans to distribute the money to help the poor.) The critics never came out and questioned my integrity or the honesty of our administration. But the intent was clear: We can't touch Vicente Fox, so let's go after Marta and her family to bring down the Fox presidency, before the 2006 election.

They could throw an atom bomb at me and I didn't care. This was a democracy, and they had a right to print what they wanted, even when it wasn't true. This is how it is: You run for president of the United States, the next thing they want to know is what kind of shorts you wear. If you can't stand the heat, you get out of the kitchen.

But I wasn't just a president, I am also a man and a husband—and it hurts to see your wife torn apart in the media for the good work she does, just so your opponents can gain political advantage. Your friends read those newspapers, too, and your mother and your neighbors, and your wife's youngest son, who is away at college. So do the businessmen she asks to help provide prenatal education for poor indigenous women.

I am convinced that behind these scurrilous attacks there lay a darker truth, rooted in Mexico's deeply ingrained tradition of machismo. The PRI and the PRD resented the changes that Marta and I were making in Mexican society. So they raised the not-so-subliminal question "Who's wearing the pants in Los Pinos?"

Our public-opinion research showed that their mudslinging got that message across. Citizens began to think, *Donde hay humo, seguro hay fuego*—Where there's smoke, there must be fire. People still cited the scandals, even after every single charge was proved in court to be false. But my first lady's foundation helped save thousands of newborn babies who would otherwise have died. She helped build a hundred hospitals, clinics, and shelters to get Mexican kids off drugs, treat cancer patients, protect the indigenous, and aid women and children as they escaped domestic violence to take shelter in totally equipped havens where they can get back on their feet and keep their kids in school. A few bad headlines seemed to us a pretty small price to pay.

CHAPTER 15

THE FARMERS IN THE ROAD

I ARRIVED in Shanghai for the first big summit after 9/11, the APEC meeting of twenty-one heads of state from the Pacific Rim, the Americas, and Europe, representing well over half the planet's economic output. Our host for the October 2001 summit was Chinese president Jiang Zemin. As the new kid on the block, I watched carefully as President Jiang greeted Vladimir Putin and the other heads of state; they were to be my guests at the next APEC summit at Los Cabos. Canada's Prime Minister Jean Chrétien and the Latin Americans I already knew well, along with George W. Bush. All eyes were on Bush as he worked the room, eager to see how he would rally the world against terrorism.

Shanghai is staggering. Whatever you have read or imagined about the explosive growth of China, multiply it by a hundred and you begin to approach the reality of your first glimpse of Shanghai's skyline—like a dozen shiny new Manhattans, all built within the last decade. Marta and I stepped to the window of our high-rise hotel room and gaped in wonder. My first glimpse of New York as a teenager paled in comparison: Shanghai was a glittering, endless panoply of stars, like the night sky over San Cristóbal. When I go back to New York now, it seems cramped, old, and dowdy in contrast to that endless galaxy. The first thought any president has on arriving in China is, *These people are going to be tough competition.* Mexico had a lot of catching up to do.

This is as true for the United States and Europe, too. Big industrialized nations grow at 2 or 3 percent in a good year; countries like mine are lucky to grow in the 5 to 7 percent range. (Remember that it is statistically much harder to grow that which is already large—a child's growth in height from three feet to four feet tall is a 33 percent increase, but a basketball player's increase of that same single foot of height, from six to seven feet tall, is a growth rate of only 12.5 percent.) But even though China is the most populous nation on earth and its second-largest economy, it grows as much as 10 percent annually, year after year; some of the other Asian tigers are growing even faster, at rates up to 20 percent.

This is an inspiration to countries like mine—and a competitive threat to wealthy nations like the United States and Canada, which are steadily losing global market share to the Asians. Meanwhile China is using its newfound prosperity to exert influence around the planet—making deals with Hugo Chávez, for example. The Chávez government has nineteen trade agreements with China, five of them to feed China's demand for petroleum. Venezuela has even signed a deal with China to launch a satellite. By 2010, China will have ninety times more cars on the road than it did in 1990. We often hear the statistic about how the United States has only 5 percent of the world's population but uses 40 percent of its fossil fuels. A dozen years from now, the Chinese will need 150 percent more energy than they use today, and, like the United States—which buys 60 percent of Hugo's oil—the leaders of China will get this energy wherever they can find it.

In fact, it is the rapacious demand of Chinese industry—not the war in Iraq—that was the primary cause of the dramatic rise in global energy prices during my presidency. As the de facto CEO of one of the world's largest oil companies, Pemex, I was glad to have the revenue. But I was more worried about the struggles of our wealthy neighbors to the north to cope with the economic challenges of rising oil prices, the increasing competition from Asia, and the painful economic realities of the post-9/11 era.

I cannot stress enough how much the future of our three nations are linked within North America. Without U.S. and Canadian trade, Mexico would never be able to compete with faster-growing developing countries like China. And without Mexican labor, the United States will lose the competitive race with the Asian juggernaut and surrender its role as global economic superpower to China.

Where does all the investment capital come from to build these thousands of skyscrapers, those thousands of miles of roads where all those cars will burn all that gasoline in China? From us—the rest of the world. China offers huge incentives to foreign investors to operate, sell products, manufacture, and build in China. But the Chinese push foreigners to reinvest their profits in the People's Republic. Since multinationals pay little or no taxes if they use their profits to build out China, the companies pour money into Chinese factories and retail complexes until they need no more capacity. Then they plow billions upon billions of dollars into Chinese real estate: office buildings, hotels, and skyscraper complexes—many of which sit empty behind the glittering lights of the skylines of Shanghai and Beijing.

PUDONG IS the biggest city you have never heard of. It is a suburb of more than 1.5 million Chinese next to Shanghai, a satellite city larger than most big urban centers—bigger than Amsterdam, Munich, Dallas, Brussels, Dubai, or Kuala Lampur. It is a completely new city, which did not even exist in 1990, a futuristic showplace out of a science-fiction movie, with great towers of twenty, fifty, eighty stories of dazzling architecture in glass, aluminum, and granite, including the second-tallest building in the world, the Jin Mao Tower. All this grandeur lines broad avenues and perfect gardens, where only a decade ago there were a few ramshackle fishing huts and a muddy harbor with some wooden Chinese junks floating in it.

The car picked me up from the hotel in downtown Shanghai on time—I am an early riser and appreciate punctuality, but Chinese efficiency is something else altogether. The motorcade pulled up at precisely three minutes past the hour, the allotted time for Mexico's president. We proceeded at a prerehearsed speed to reach exact GPS waypoints along the route at various stopwatch intervals: eight minutes and twenty seconds past the hour, thirteen minutes and fifty seconds past the hour. The line of armored limousines and SUVs carrying the leaders of the world's great powers moved in synchronized rhythm out of the city center. From the backseat I watched the dots on the driver's navigational screen as we massed on the bridge to the suburb.

We crossed over into Pudong, where the APEC meeting was to be held. Suddenly there was no one—*no one*—on the streets. The boulevards and park benches were empty. There were no pedestrians, no cars, no buses, no motion behind the shop windows. No one ate in the restaurants or worked in the office towers. There was only this line of vehicles bearing dignitaries who stared at this brave new world through bulletproof glass.

The Chinese, concerned about security at the first global summit a month after 9/11, were anxious to impress the world that nothing could go wrong in the perfect city they had built on the banks of the Huangpu River. Our hosts had evacuated the entire city of a million and a half people the week before our arrival in China.

It was eerie beyond belief. As heir to the Teutonic punctuality of my father and grandfather (I still struggle with my wife, Marta, over this; she is rather more Latin in her approach to time), I appreciated the clockwork accuracy of it all—especially in view of the very real threat of terrorism we all felt after the September 11 attacks. This new world felt secure but strange: this brutally efficient China that sends bulldozers through ancient neighborhoods to erect new high-rise apartment blocks, exiles the less educated to distant zones in the countryside, and builds new metropolises overnight for the booming middle class—then evacuates them overnight, lest the government lose face with foreign leaders. This would never happen in Mexico, I thought; we were lucky to get a foreign visitor through the heavy traffic along the Reforma, which can make a twenty-minute trip last an hour and a half. Our culture is far too attached to home and family to tolerate the staggering social cost of Chinese prosperity—try moving an *ejidatario* off his ten acres or telling a Mexican mother she can have only one child and see how long your government would last. I was impressed by the Chinese, but I do not envy them.

INSIDE THE ELEGANT conference room of the Hyatt at Jin Mao Tower, security was on the mind of every head of state. Normally the subject of such summits is trade, trade, and more trade. But after 9/11, leaders of the world's democracies had only terrorism on the agenda. We were all completely united behind President Bush back then—it is amazing to think how different things were in the world just a few short years ago. Determined and focused, Bush's speech was met with thunderous applause. President after prime minister, from Russia's Vladimir Putin to Japan's Junichiro Koizumi and the other heads of state from Latin America to Singapore outlined the actions our nations would take to combat the clear and present danger to our people and our economies.

George W. Bush had us in the palm of his hand at Pudong. A united front of twenty-one leaders of the world's great powers arrayed ourselves in solidarity, standing with the United States for peace against the violent killing of innocents. It is a measure of just how wrong things went that two years later the nations of the world would be bitterly divided into opposing camps.

I WASN'T ALWAYS able to attend such summits. There is an odd loophole in our Mexican Constitution that requires the president to ask Congress for permission to leave the country. A mere formality in the rubber-stamp era of the past, this law now gave my critics the opportunity to put rocks in my road. Congress literally held Mexico's president hostage for months at a time. They forced me to cancel a trip to the western United States and Vancouver early in my presidency and ended it by forbidding me to attend the 2006 APEC Summit in Vietnam.

These summits and state visits to foreign leaders were enormously valuable to Mexico. We made trade deals, brought home massive investments, and gave Mexico the strongest peso it had ever known. The most important parts of a summit are the private business meetings. The big plenary sessions are mostly blather, with lengthy harangues from Hugo Chávez or some tinpot dictator in Africa raving on for hours about how badly they are being exploited by those who are buying their oil and giving them foreign aid. But in between these eight-hour marathons, veteran world leaders learn to schedule five or six bilateral meetings, where you meet one-on-one with George Bush, Vladimir Putin, Jean Chrétien, or Peter MacKay of Canada. There, or in the green room before you go out onstage, you can hash out a deal that means billions for your country's agriculture or a complex legal agreement to extradite drug dealers you'd like to banish from Mexico.

When I boarded Mexican Air Force One, the *Benito Juárez*—a 737 reequipped with a sleeping cabin and conference-room seats emblazoned with Mexico's eagle and serpent, where I was briefed by cabinet members and diplomats and security officers—I felt like I was back at Coca-Cola, out on the route truck. Our product was democracy, a new Mexico, ready to take its place among the free-market economies of the world.

Mexico's population doubled in the twentieth century. That will never happen again: Experts predict that by 2040 our population will level out at about 130 million. By then Mexico will have the world's fifth-richest economy for the planet's ninth-largest population. You do the math—within our lifetimes Mexico will be more prosperous than all but a handful of the world's nations. Where today our average worker makes only 10 percent of what people earn in the United States and Canada, by 2040 Mexicans will make salaries much closer to those of our northern neighbors.

Like China, Mexico is enthusiastic about this prospect of material prosperity, but in its pursuit we must not lose our soul. I once angered U.S. audiences by saying that our people were "a step ahead" to be born in Mexico. I stand by this. All good things in life cannot be bought. To us, Americans seem fearsome competitors: People who live to work. But Mexican culture is Latin; like Europeans, we work to live. As president I wanted to bring my country closer to the prosperity of the First World. But we love the lifestyle values of our culture, which cherish peace, serenity, and family as much as material success. Shanghai was a powerful reminder: As Mexico opened itself to the world, our soul was not for sale.

TODAY SOME 35 MILLION Chinese tourists go abroad every year; soon it will be 100 million. Now they go to Hong Kong to shop and to the beaches of Southeast Asia, but we of course want them to come to Mexico. This is a testament to China—this nation of 1.3 billion people who were starving a generation ago today represents a target market for Los Cabos and Puerto Vallarta.

As of now only 20 percent of China's population—about 260 million Chinese—have reached the consumer class. Still, this is nearly as large a consumer market as the United States, with 280 million people. Consider how big China's market will be when the *other* 80 percent of its mammoth population become consumers. (And believe me, if China can move a million and a half people out of a city for a summit and completely rebuild one of the world's great capitals of Beijing in five years for the Olympics—to paraphrase an old motivational dictum, what the mind of China can conceive, it can achieve.)

All over the world, presidents and prime ministers are scratching their heads and asking, "How do we beat China?" In Mexico we looked at China and said, "We can't." We learned this lesson from living next door to a behemoth: The answer is not to compete *against* the giant but to partner *with* our neighbors toward mutual success. This is why the Americas must join hands to create our own hemispheric economic union, or China will displace the United States as the world's principal superpower.

China is very ambitious in Latin America. You see businessmen from Shanghai in every hotel of Mexico City and Monterrey, São Paulo and

Santiago. Mexico's partnerships with China have been phenomenally successful, led by an innovative group of young entrepreneurs who came as part of our program to send two hundred Mexican university students to China to learn the Chinese language, study the country's dynamic business culture, and foster Mexico-China business as entrepreneurs. Now Interceramic of Mexico makes tiles in China for homes in San Diego and Guadalajara, and our bakers at Maseca have one of the biggest tortilla factories in the world in Shanghai, a $100 million Mexican investment in the Chinese economy. China is an export market for delicious Mexican avocados from Tinguindin, where my wife Marta's family comes from, a lovely town whose name itself is poetry, a place of melodic indigenous music and heartbreakingly gorgeous scenery whose peacefully named village of Cotija de la Paz has produced more artists, bishops, doctors, and politicians for its size than perhaps any town in the world. Think about this, and imagine how the indigenous farmers of Tinguindin or my beloved Marquitos at San Cristóbal would feel to know that our tortillas and guacamole now feed the hungry urban consumers of the new China.

The People's Republic of China has built a massive textile plant in Ciudad Obregón that employs thirteen hundred Mexican workers, but with a Chinese state-capitalism twist—they ship in all the building materials and import more than a thousand employees from China, because their government mandates that more than half of an overseas Chinese plant's workers must be Chinese citizens. The spirit of our own laws in Mexico allows foreign investors to bring in technicians and managers, but the Chinese are smart: They classify more than half of a plant's jobs as "technical."

The United States should respect China as a trade adversary. U.S. markets are being flooded with Chinese products, to the great benefit of the American consumer. And the number-one investor in China's explosive growth is U.S. business. So North America has a great deal to gain—but we also could lose. Already the United States and Mexico are losing jobs to China as investment capital that might have built plants in our countries goes to erect skyscrapers that sit vacant in Pudong and Beijing. We could lose again, when U.S. and foreign investors figure out that all the gilt edging in those elegant hotel ballrooms and all those sparkling lights on the Shanghai skyline distract one's attention from the fact that most of those buildings are *vacant*—that all that glitters is not gold. The fancy incentives

China hands out may decorate your corporate balance sheet, but in fact they represent frozen capital in a vacant office building in a state-controlled economy half a world away—an authoritarian government that can take your fine building from you just as quickly as it sprung up. On that day we may be glad that we explored China's brave new world but found common ground here in the Americas—where Mexico still provides a real return on real-estate investment and our three NAFTA countries comprise what remains the biggest marketplace in the world.

IN ONE GENERATION China has transformed itself from a country of walls to the world's most aggressively globalist economy. Once China's closed market was so shrouded in secrecy that port cities like Shanghai and Canton were literally walled off to foreigners. Europeans were kept in permanent quarantine in ghettos, forbidden to bring their families to China, to study the language, or to go so far from the Western cantonment that traders could not return by nightfall. As recently as the Maoist late twentieth century, few foreign companies did business in China: Pepsi entered the Soviet market well before U.S. soft drinks came to Communist China.

Now the People's Republic is one of the most open markets in the world. Their pitch is smart and seductive: If you want into our market, soon to be the largest on the planet, then we want into yours. With its post-9/11 lurch toward walled-off nationalism, the United States is making things easy for China. As the Asian juggernaut streaks upward, the United States is retreating into a bomb shelter.

The best example of this was the recent Dubai Ports fiasco. Mexico's and America's trading partners around the world looked on aghast as President Bush took a beating from the Congress and U.S. public opinion for allowing an international company—owned by private interests in a staunch U.S. ally in the Middle East—to continue operating cargo ports in the United States, after a merger of the Dubai Ports World company and the British Peninsular and Steam Navigation company, which had the contract. In the face of such hostility, Dubai Ports World bowed out. As with immigration reform, Bush's globalist instincts occasionally put him at odds with the surge of nationalism in the United States after 9/11, as the America First crowd seized on September 11 to legitimize their xenophobia.

The Dubai Ports deal never would have collapsed if the company had been Canadian or Dutch. No one had qualms about foreign companies operating U.S. ports when the company was British. But Dubai is a country of dark-skinned Arabs, no matter that they are allied with the United States against terrorism. The dirty secret of xenophobia, immigrant bashing, and antiglobalism is that all three frequently are driven by race, whether in the anti-Japanese riots in California during the "Yellow Peril" of Theodore Roosevelt's time or the massacre of 250 Chinese workers in Torreón during the Mexican Revolution, when those who came to help build our railways were looted, beheaded, and dragged at the horse's tail to their deaths by a pogrom against the "Jews of Mexico."

The U.S. rejection of the Dubai Ports deal sent a terrible signal to a world that had already begun to question U.S. commitment to global democracy after the invasion of Iraq. For the authors of the American dream to retreat behind cantonment walls into some isolationist Forbidden City—while China sends out trade emissaries around the world, opening its markets to countries like mine in trade for our willingness to allow China into our countries—leaves the United States in an awkward position. Having sold the developing world on opening our markets to free trade, now the United States appears to be turning 180 degrees and retreating back into a new Fortress America. Consider how poorly a walled-off China fared in the mercantile explosion of the nineteenth century—or how walled-off Mexico lost out in the the twentieth century—and you begin to see where isolationism will lead the United States in the future.

The United States still has the best technology, the most creative people, the most productive economy, the competitive spirit, the greatest freedom of ideas, the most sophisticated laws to protect intellectual property, the most abundant agriculture, the most advanced industrial plants and equipment, and the stablest democratic system and rule of law on the planet. Americans should trust in themselves, just as they have asked us to trust their system. This is why I worked to bring Mexico closer to the United States—because if we can unite our economies, America will win.

It grates on me every time some scholar or media pundit trots out that tired old quote attributed to Porfirio Díaz: "Poor Mexico, so far from God, so near to the United States." Many historians don't even believe that the dictator actually said it. After all, Porfirio doled out more than half of Mexico's wealth to U.S. and British interests; it is unlikely that he found God as he escaped on Lord Cowdray's yacht. In any case the statement is the opposite of truth: *Mexico's greatest business advantage is our closeness to the*

United States. And in the future, the U.S.A.'s biggest advantage globally will be American access to a vast hemispheric market of more than a billion people from Canada to Argentina. Faced with competition from the cheap labor and open markets of China, the United States desperately needs to unite with us to survive.

President Hu, China's dynamic new leader, is, like his predecessor Jiang Zemin, a stark contrast to the impassive, elderly Maoists who sent tanks into Tiananmen Square. Hu is young, humble, incredibly smart, energetic, strategic, and visionary. China has five-year plans for everything: agriculture, housing, airports, highways, technology, military, pure science. In just twenty years, they will move a billion and a half people who were starving peasants just a few years ago to become the most brutally efficient economic force on earth.

I saw how far China has come during a state visit in April 2001, on the road to Xian.

"Stop the car," I said suddenly. The guard swerved to a halt on the winding road through Shaanxi province. I had unnerved his Chinese security partner, who eyed the dash clock uneasily—this would throw us at least sixty seconds off schedule.

My farmer's eye had caught an oddly familiar sight: a hundred Chinese peasants, bowed to the waist under broad-rimmed bamboo hats with straps under their chins, spreading out hay in the oncoming lane of the highway. Another phalanx of Chinese farmers led a cavalry troop of horses plodding up the endless miles of hay to grind the grain beneath their hooves. Women in smocks and bamboo hats trailed behind with wooden rakes to toss the straw in the air to dry it and separate the wheat from the chaff. I had done this work under my grandfather's regime, and my back still aches from it. Here were peasants seventy and eighty years old doing stoop labor in an ancient practice that dated back before the fifteenth century, when the Ming dynasty had built the Great Wall in a vain attempt to keep out the Mongols. (Neither the Great Wall nor the walled ghettos of Shanghai and Canton succeeded in keeping foreigners out. The Manchus crossed the Great Wall in 1644—and today Shanghai is full of Kentucky Fried Chicken stands, McDonald's hamburgers, and a Maseca tortilla factory.)

The world had come to China. In Beijing we had just concluded successful trade negotiations to bring Mexican avocados and tortillas to feed China's consumer class. But President Jiang did not yet have good jobs for these peasants on the highway, nor can his successor President Hu yet employ more than a billion Chinese who have been banned from the narrow cantonments of the "Economic Zones," China's Emerald Cities of globalist consumerism. So they had been exiled here, to do stoop labor in the countryside. These peasants, young and old, were not left to starve; they were put to work in these labor battalions that advanced one horseshoe at a time over the hay. There they will work, plodding and stooping and raking the hay into the air, until President Hu calls their number. There is not much individual initiative in China; all progress is planned and cooperative, a nation of highly efficient workers who do as they are told—until one man trudging over the hay in Hunan learns that his countrymen in Pudong have television sets and Mexican guacamole. *We can compete with these people and win,* I thought. In the Americas we just need to keep our doors open to change.

OCCASIONALLY I FIND IT necessary to break out of the confining suit-and-tie unctuousness of the presidency: the tiresome political correctness, the oily politeness of summitry, the wearisome diplomatic protocol, the endless ceremony and ritual, the relentless need of politicians to conform to the binding straitjacket of public opinion. This is usually when I screw up, badly and publicly; this is when I take some heat from the Mexican press for embarrassing the nation and make people laugh. What the capital intelligentsia never understood was that people *like* this in a leader, this comfort in yourself that allows you to clown around once in a while, this reminder that you are a regular guy with *tus botas en la tierra,* "your boots on the ground." Reagan had this quality, and it made him the "Teflon President"; so did Bill Clinton, in a different way. At times a president's foibles are what make him seem human, as long as he leads for what is right.

That day in Xian, my first lady and I went to view the famous terra-cotta soldiers, the life-size rows and rows of clay warriors unearthed by archaeologists in 1974, standing as straight as the six-foot-plus guards that the Communist Chinese government handpicks to patrol Tiananmen Square today.

Marta and I are affectionate together in public. Mexicans aren't shy about this. We do not have that discomfort at seeing a couple smooching on a park bench. North Americans call these PDAs—public displays of affection—but we consider it everyday life, now that lovers can kiss in the *zócalo* without escorts. But what happened at the terra-cotta soldiers shocked the folks back home—in a playful moment someone in our party allegedly reached out and rubbed one of the clay soldiers from behind.

Advice to aspiring world leaders: Next time you get an urge to kid around with your wife, keep your hands off the terra-cotta soldier's ass.

I WENT from Shanghai to Europe to pay court to the king of Spain, whose transition to constitutional monarchy, democracy, and prosperity had been an inspiration to us in Mexico. Despite our long and troubled history with Spain, back to the Conquest and our war of independence, we share so much culture that our nations are forever inextricably entwined, much like the United States and Britain. Of course I had a special love and admiration for Spain, both because my mother was born there and because Spain is a case study of how Mexico could move forward.

With its great leap upward in this past generation, Spain's financial investments in Latin America have increased dramatically. Spain is Mexico's lead trading partner in Europe, responsible for a healthy bit of foreign investment in Mexico, around $18 billion at last count—Spaniards own some of our biggest banks, power plants, and hotel chains, increasing their trade with Mexico by more than 150 percent just in the last decade.

And of course both of our nations speak Spanish, of a sort—Spaniards may disdain the way we fail to lisp our *s*'s, but we in Mexico stand by our pronunciation. (Legend holds that the Castilian pronunciation of *S* with a *th* sound began with Spanish courtiers who aped the speech defect of a lisping king, but scholars say this is just a myth.) In any case, as George Bernard Shaw once said of England and America, we are "two nations divided by a common language." Spain's fabulous literature, religion, art, architecture, clothing, ethnicity, and folkways all came to us in the fusion of European and indigenous cultures. So it was with enthusiasm and a proper sense of respect that I planned for my first trip to a palace to dine with a king. Presidents, governors, senators, and archbishops I had met, but I had never broken bread with a king.

It was a formal state dinner in our honor. For the occasion I ordered the finest black patent-leather footwear from the Fox Boot Company in León. The media had a fit. The other dignitaries all wore traditional shiny patent-leather tuxedo shoes, of course, and here comes Vicente Fox to disgrace us by wearing cowboy boots, like Jimmy Carter carrying his own garment bag to signal a shift away from the imperial presidency. In my inaugural speech I had promised to keep *mis botas en la tierra*. I guess people just didn't expect me to wear them to the palace.

I also went to the Vatican on that round-the-world trip in October 2001, to invite the pope to visit Mexico City. That following August, I became the first president of our country to welcome the pontiff by bending down to kiss the papal ring of St. Peter. Though Mexico has more Catholics than any other nation on earth except Brazil, our Constitution and tradition—dating back to the freemasons like Benito Juárez and the early military dictators after the revolution, carrying through officially secular PRI presidents right up to Zedillo—held that presidents and first ladies did not even enter a church. It shocked our political establishment when President López Portillo's aging mother was allowed to go to mass. For me to bow my head down to welcome the pope to the Basilica of the Virgin of Guadalupe was constitutional heresy.

But if there was a law against the president's praying to the God of his choice, I broke it every day. I suppose that Congress could have removed the immunity and gone after me for violating constitutional provisions against presidential expression of faith. But that was a fight I would have relished. It was important that our new democracy established not only the right of the press to criticize me for such actions but also that we enshrined forever in the Mexican consciousness the right of our leaders to act from religious principles. If not, then the only thing left to guide us is earthly material gain. Power, money, corruption, partisanship—we had seen where secular goals had led Mexico. I preferred an imperfect democracy, where flawed and human leaders were free to ask for spiritual guidance from a perfect God and His representative on earth, His Holiness John Paul II or the Prophet Muhammad, the Talmud, the Koran or the Buddha—surely any moral impulse of the world's great religions will serve as better guideposts than party platforms and material greed.

You cannot imagine the raw spiritual energy emanating from this elderly, white-haired man. By then the Holy Father was shaky and infirm of body, but he was ever so powerful of spirit. His touch was electric as he laid his hands on my head. I kissed his ring, and he blessed the work we were doing for God's children in Mexico. Here was a man who had survived the

Nazis and the Communists, helped free Poland and the entire Soviet Bloc, brought the light of divine inspiration to illuminate dark corners throughout the world. I was speechless: a rare occurrence for a guy in politics.

Churches of all denominations—Catholic, Jewish, evangelicals, Protestants—were among our best allies in the new Mexico. Catholic schools and hospitals tend to the needs of indigenous children who would otherwise go hungry and sick. Cardinal Mahony of Los Angeles and Underground Railroad–style operations in evangelical and Catholic churches from Chicago to Texas lead on immigration reform, sheltering innocent, God-fearing families from discrimination, deportation, and abuse.

As for the pope, even as his voice grew old and wavery, thinned with the Parkinson's disease that ground his once-powerful instrument to a whisper, John Paul II was the mightiest voice on the planet for healing the global divide between rich and poor. He was the ideal "man for others": a religious leader who did not hesitate to transcend the bounds of faith into the good fights—for democracy, human rights, social justice, and peace.

I went to the Vatican again in April 2005 to attend the pope's funeral. I do not mind admitting that I wept the day he died, when a bright light went out in the world.

CHAPTER 16

COMPARING NOTES

In September 2002, I called on former president Mandela in his modest office building on Thirteenth Avenue in Houghton, just outside Johannesburg. Nelson Mandela is an elderly and wise man we would call *bondadoso* and *cariñoso*—"bonding" and "kind," I guess; these are distinctly Mexican terms of affection that don't quite translate. This idol of my days as a rebel for democracy is a generous and peaceful soul. He broke rocks for decades in prison, remained locked out for years on Robben Island, yet seems to have no anger in him; he would not hurt a fly.

"You grew up in these very poor conditions, survived prison, and won this great struggle," I said, in awe of this distinguished man who had freed his people and made the new South Africa one of the great success stories of democracy. "How did you do it? There are so many problems in countries like ours—the budget, crime, drugs, corruption, health care, education, housing. Where do you focus? How do we build a democracy among people who have never had that power?"

"They need food," he began simply. "A roof over their heads, medicine for their babies, schools for the young people—"

"So we need to feed them, give them homes," I jumped in excitedly. "Our government has a program to give them—"

"You must give them nothing," Mandela said firmly. "Mexico is a democracy now. It is not for you to deliver things to people. It is for the people to do it for themselves."

"But if we don't give people the fruits of democracy, they will give up."

"They already have the fruits of democracy," Mandela said, patiently explaining his now-famous philosophy that with freedom comes responsibility. In a democracy the people of Mexico were free to succeed or free to fail, he said. Our government could not build the house of a new Mexico for them. Our job was only to give them the tools and let the people do the job. "It is for people to build a new society, not the leaders."

I nodded. "The next time someone asks me when we are going to deliver on our promises for democracy . . ."

"You must ask them what they are doing with their freedom, to help build a better country for their children and grandchildren."

Mandela sat in a rocking chair on his porch among all that was beloved and familiar. Just to sit at his feet and listen to his story was a privilege I will tell my grandchildren about (as soon as my daughter Paulina, now joyously pregnant with her first child, and my other children all do their Catholic duty to give me many, many, many more grandchildren).

Like Gandhi and King, Mandela used the power of peace to advance the end of apartheid in South Africa; he has that rare inner harmony that moves multitudes. But as the son of poor farmers and a man who has experienced the pain of hunger, beatings, and decades of hard labor, he has never lost his sense of the simple. This trait I revere in the great reformers: Gandhi reducing the British Empire to the need of the Indian people for salt and cloth; Dr. King, Rosa Parks, and the civil-rights leaders translating the struggle for equality into a seat at a lunch counter, or the front of a bus. In this, Mandela is much like another hero of democracy, Lech Walesa, who came to my inauguration to celebrate democracy in Mexico; he danced the polka with the women on my campaign team in the lobby of the Camino Real Hotel. Their stories are a model of inspiration for changing nations by moving souls. I resolved to do my best to walk in their big footsteps. There will not be many more like them.

From South Africa, Marta and I traveled to Nigeria to protest the imposition of the death penalty by stoning against Amina Lawal, who had been sentenced without trial by an Islamic court for having borne a child out of wedlock. In Africa, amid cultures where female genitalia are mutilated to curtail a girl's sexual appetites, this punishment of stoning is even more horrible than the biblical term implies: Amina Lawal's body would literally be severed into pieces by the mob. In the year since she became my first lady, Marta had become a global leader on women's issues; at her initiative we went to Nigeria to help Amina.

I thought I had seen extreme poverty in the indigenous villages of Chiapas and the urban slums of Tijuana or Mexico City, but African poverty is another thing altogether. A million or more beggars lined our route into the city. They walk miles each day for the privilege of begging from any urban worker who might have a few pennies for bread, supplicating on their knees, crying out aloud in misery. Nigeria is the human face of the great evil of this vast global divide we allow between rich and poor, while so many remain indifferent.

President Olusegun Obasanjo greeted us at the head of a red carpet. The leader of Nigeria proceeded to grasp me firmly by my buttocks and walk me down the twin lines of photographers and TV cameras, assuring me in voluble English that all would be well. Apparently this is Nigerian custom. Where Mexican men hug and slap each other's backs in an *abrazo,* and Italian men walk arm in arm, in Nigeria a man grabs a friend's hand, then reaches around to grasp his . . . ah, lower back and walks him down the red carpet, flashbulbs glaring. I remembered the terra-cotta soldiers in Hunan and thought, *If a guy tried this in Mexico, he'd get the shit kicked out of him.*

Exposure to the world's culture is a wonderful thing. Sometimes we judge the Muslim culture too harshly just because we see a girl attending school with her head covered or a man dropping to his knees in Amsterdam or Jakarta to pray. The rituals of each culture and faith seem strange to others, just as a man in a black cassock shaking a censer of burning incense in my cathedral seems strange to strict Baptists, who plunge each other into vats of cold water to find the Lord. But my tolerance of other cultures draws its limit at the Islamic law requiring the stoning of Amina Lawal to death for having a baby outside marriage. The fight for gender equity is more than breaking the glass ceiling at Pemex or using the word "woman" instead of "girl"—it is a global crusade to protect women and girls from mutilation, subjugation, and malnutrition in a world where every woman's life is precious and all too many are at risk.

After we left, thanks to pressure by world leaders and the great work of organizations like Amnesty International, Amina Lawal got a lawyer and a reprieve. President Obansajo bade me good-bye, but I did not ask him to walk me back up the red carpet to the *Benito Juárez.*

When you are the president of a developing country that needs *everything*—schools, health care, jobs for the poor, housing for the homeless—you come back from every foreign trip brimming with the ideas you have gleaned from China, the example of Spain, the inspiration of the pope, the philosophy of Mandela. You get up in your little cabaña at Los Pinos and kiss your wife good-bye as she helicopters off to give out parenting guidebooks in Oaxaca and literally run across the grass with your long legs striding so fast that the much younger army officers who guard you are puffing to keep up, the jet lag and the dull pain in your back from the long ride nothing compared to the urgency you feel to *hurry*. Though now you're past sixty years old and the lawn sprinklers get you wet when you cut across the lawn—sending the gardener scrambling to turn them off before he soaks the president of Mexico—you simply *run* to the office to fix your country, before you lose another minute. As you whisk through the metal detector and ignore the beeping sound, you envision yourself bursting into the office and gathering your cabinet to put all the great wisdom you've picked up abroad into action. All right, ladies and gentlemen, what are we doing for the poor? How many families have we put into new homes? What have we done this week to reduce infant mortality?

Then you walk through the door and run smack into a congressman from a district you can't recall and a senator who is chairman of some committee that you will gratefully forget, who have arrived at this very un-Mexican early hour to discuss—at length—the need to help save a good company in their home state. Then your press secretary bustles in to correct you on the latest grammatical error you made the day before (now page one in Mexico, because the poet you misnamed or the statistic you misquoted is somehow more newsworthy than the millions of Mexicans still living below the poverty line). The foreign minister calls on the red phone: Castro is on the line, and, by the way, the UN wants to know what you think about the weapons of mass destruction in Iraq. Soon, before the lawn crew has finished watering the grass beyond your window, you have lost control of the nation's agenda—unless you slap your hand on the table and say, "Enough. Let's talk about poverty."

ONE SUCH MORNING in September 2002, fresh back from a state visit to see Fidel Castro in Havana and my trip to Africa to attend a Sustainable Development Summit on poverty and the environment, hold my life-changing one-on-one meeting to compare notes with Nelson Mandela, and do my best to help avert the tragedy of Amina Lawal in the country of Nigeria, I could hardly focus on what the two lawmakers were saying. We went through the weary process of sorting out whether the congressman and the senator were after a legitimate interest of a vital industry or whether this was just some subtle shakedown for a contract: Los Pinos had been out of that business for a long time. I would hope that my predecessor, Ernesto Zedillo, didn't stoop to that sort of thing; in any case, we had passed strict transparency laws in my first year in office to weed out corruption in every level of the federal government. But maybe these guys hadn't gotten the memo.

As it turned out, the lawmakers in my office were good guys, reform-minded members of the opposition who were trying to help workers in their state. I asked what the company was doing to provide health care. "Are they teaching people the English and computer skills to retrain them for the new economy?" I queried. "What are they doing to hire poor and indigenous citizens? How do they house the people they move in from other states?"

They surprised me by having the answers. "This is a good company, Mr. President," said one lawmaker, one of the PRI's bright young stars who had been active in cleaning up his party from within. "But, with respect, the free market can't do it all. People in my state just aren't ready to compete with Microsoft. Government has to help." The young congressman, a reformer within the PRI, added, "Frankly, Mr. President, our party may have made mistakes in the past, but at least we took care of people. We are still waiting for you to deliver on your promises."

Sometimes, just when you think you've been knocked off track, you get a kick in the right direction from where you least expect it. "Will you work with us on Oportunidades, even though we have our differences on taxes?" I asked, anxious to push my pet antipoverty program to reward poor parents for keeping their kids in school. Thinking about Mandela, I said, "We can't just give things to people out of thin air. If we can work together, your party and our government, strengthen the fiscal discipline of the Mexican government and balance the budget, we can have sound market policies that pay for social welfare and help people get the tools they need to succeed—housing, health care, education. Will you help me, even though we come from different parties?"

"Absolutely," said the young congressman without hesitation.

The older senator, a veteran in the ways of politics, cleared his throat uncomfortably. He looked behind me, where yet someone else had entered the room. "Mr. President, I'll help you, too. But . . . er, there is one thing I'd like to ask from you."

Uh-oh, I thought. *Here it comes.* "Yes?" I asked, bracing myself.

The senator eyed the steward at my elbow. "Could I just get a cup of coffee?"

POVERTY REDUCTION IS perhaps the most stubborn challenge for my country. The free market is the greatest engine of economic growth known to man (or woman). But it leaves a lot of people behind (especially women, who are the poorest members of nearly every society on earth).

In recent years millions of Mexican men and women have worked their way up out of the worst levels of poverty. As measured by the World Bank, nearly a third of those living below the dollar-a-day level in Mexico escaped this extreme poverty just in the last six years. *But there are still millions of Mexicans trapped below that line.* My country has made progress, but not enough.

What is staggering to leaders of the "have-not" developing nations is how little effort it would take from the "have" nations to help fix this problem. Mexico is not so far from prosperity. We may seem poor on a relative basis to people in the United States, juxtaposed next door to the richest nation on earth. But thanks to that proximity and the fiscal discipline of this last decade, both in Zedillo's government and in mine, Mexico today is the wealthiest country in Latin America. During the last ten years, we advanced from seventh place in the hemisphere to attain the highest per capita income south of the United States. Indeed, by world standards we are not the poorest of countries: Mexico is rather middle-class among the nations, ranking behind New Zealand, Spain, and Greece but ahead of Poland, Chile, Turkey, Brazil, and Argentina. If the United States was to take even a fraction of the $6.5 billion it plans to spend building a wall that will not work—or a tiny sliver of the $500 billion it has spent on the Iraq war—and invested it in a revolving investment fund to create jobs within Mexico and keep our people at home . . . Well, by now you have heard my pitch for a new Marshall Plan of the Americas.

But the United States had problems of its own during my administration, as it does today. We couldn't wait for help from our neighbors; as Mandela taught me, Mexico has to take responsibility for itself. We have everything we need within Mexico's borders to succeed as a nation—

natural resources, a vast pool of hardworking people, a sound culture of family and religion. But now, for the first time in history, we have a democratic system, with the rule of law and leadership to clean up corruption.

So we started by expanding the Oportunidades program to provide scholarship payments to the poor—a socialist concept straight from the playbook of a Nelson Mandela or a socialist like President Luiz Inácio Lula da Silva of Brazil. But as long as we could balance the budget and pay for it with real revenues and not debt, we had a moral responsibility to do as Mandela advised: "Give them the tools—and let them build a new Mexico."

Then we went one step better—showing people how they could put their own roofs over their heads. If you want democracy to become something people can see, feel, taste, and touch—and jump-start an economy so that you meet human needs and create jobs in the bargain—housing is a good place to begin. Under the old regime, interest rates in Mexico were as much as five times higher than in the United States. We had no mortgage system or title industry. It was nearly impossible for middle-class people to buy a home of their own, much less working people. As for the poor—too many were still living in cardboard shacks or in the streets.

By reducing Mexico's debt and bringing economic stability to the country, we went beyond the discipline imposed by Ernesto Zedillo. By compromising with Congress on tax reform and cutting wasteful spending on corrupt deals, we balanced the federal budget, reduced inflation below that of the United States, and brought interest rates even lower than those north of the border. This paved the way for one of our biggest goals: to put 3 million families into their first homes with low-interest loans.

My favorite housing program was the one we had in Guanajuato, where we matched federal, state, and local dollars three to one with private contributions to give families the bricks, mortar, building plans, and land—then let them build their own home. This concept is working now all over Mexico and all over the world.

In just six short years, roughly 15 percent of Mexico's 22 million families went from being renters to proud homeowners. This completely changed us from a nation of itinerant subjects to permanent stakeholders in a democratic society, building a new culture of responsibility. A quote widely attributed to Lawrence Summers observes, "No one has ever washed a rental car"—people take better care of what they own. Now, the system is in place to put more Mexican families into their own homes in six years.

One day I came to help a family move into their first house. As everyone bustled about applying last-minute finishing touches, I stood there, paint dripping from my brush, and handed the keys to the husband as he carried his wife proudly across the threshold. Tears ran down their cheeks, and mine. Then the wife looked at me, her eyes shining with pride.

"Mr. President," she began nervously. "I have something to say, and I . . . well, I don't know how to say it—"

"Yes." I beamed encouragement. "Please, I'd love to hear."

She burst out, "You're getting paint all over my floor, sir!" I handed her the brush. Correctly assessing my capabilities, she handed me a broom.

This is what it is to change a country. This is the reason Jimmy Carter hammers nails for Habitat for Humanity. This is the revolution of hope.

I HAD GOOD health insurance at the Coca-Cola Company. One of the ironies of antiglobalism is that the same demagogues who accuse Fortune 500 corporations of exploiting the workers of Latin America rarely mention that their own governments don't provide nearly as generous benefits to their citizens as do Ford, Cemex, or the Coca-Cola Company. Multinational corporations do this not out of philanthropy but enlightened self-interest; healthy employees are more productive, happier, and they make you a great deal more money. The wonder is that even in the wealthy United States, more leaders of government do not apply this reasoning and provide universal health coverage to the whole of their societies.

In Mexico the day I took office, only 45 percent of our population had health insurance. Only 3 percent of them had health insurance of the same quality I received at Coca-Cola. Most mothers did not receive prenatal care. Only three out of ten births were attended by medical professionals.

This is intolerable, even for a nation as poor as ours; the mystery of why a nation as rich as the United States does not provide universal health-care coverage is one I leave between U.S. citizens and their politicians. But for Mexico, I was determined that every citizen should have the same coverage I had from my Fortune 500 employer.

Consider this: For a brief few years of my boyhood, I hefted heavy bales of hay and dug irrigation trenches in the early mornings and late afternoons, doing farm chores on weekends and working as a ranch hand on school vacations. I was young and spry then, feeling fit and proud of myself after eating copious breakfasts of Marquitos's lovely tortillas and eggs, ham, cheese, and fruit—while the campesinos got by on a cup of coffee, perhaps a handful of beans. Since then I have always done a moderate amount of physical labor—in part because I enjoy it and find it much less taxing than mental work, which is stressful and exhausting in contrast to the sheer joy of roping a calf or building a fence. But all my life I have had complete access to professional medical care, from the personal attention of Dr. Solís to the best specialists any sixty-four-year-old retired president can find.

Yet my legacy from boyhood farmwork is excruciating pain in my back, with vertebrae permanently twisted by lifting those *costales* of hay. Perhaps you, too, have some ache that flares from time to time, or even some chronic ailment that you must have treated with surgery or medicine.

Imagine what life is like for those who cannot see a doctor. Think of men who lift those hay bales all their lives with muscles weak from malnutrition. Many have never seen the inside of a doctor's office; when I came into the presidency, most of their wives had babies without medical care—and lost many of them. Most Mexicans did backbreaking labor all their lives, women and children, too. How must *their* backs feel at sixty-four? How do their wives cope with the loss of their babies?

In many countries of the Americas, things are much, much worse. In Haiti, just a short flight from Miami—a country of almost a million people, which the rest of the world could help transform overnight without a feather's weight of difference in our own prosperity—conditions are horrific. Eighty percent of the population lives in abject poverty. Sixty percent of people do not have access to clean drinking water. The same is true in other nations of Central and South America, where citizens in Nicaragua or Bolivia face far worse conditions than those in Mexico.

As president I could not do much to help the problems of Haiti or Peru (though I intend to do so now, because the doctors say my back is straight enough to get out of this chair and on the road again). In Mexico we expanded Seguro Popular, the "People's Insurance," into a program of universal health-care coverage. In a radical departure from the norm, we worked from the bottom up—versus the top-down approach we had seen in Mexico and the United States, where, traditionally, fully employed middle-class people have good health insurance and the working poor have little or none. Fully 55 percent of our people had no health coverage at all, so we enrolled about 20 million Mexicans in Seguro Popular and increased maternity care to cover eight of ten births.

All this social change sounds easy, like we waved a magic wand and Presto!, suddenly there were more jobs, new homes for low-income workers, health-care coverage for the poor. But every change you make upsets someone's applecart: The doctor who must work harder for less money as we push down health-care costs. The nurse whose easiest tasks are now performed by a clerical assistant. The untrained indigenous midwife who is displaced by a licensed nurse-midwife.

Then there's the politics. In the old days, a governor got a big ribbon-cutting ceremony at the massive downtown hospital, which might have borne his name—now he gets a privately funded van to teach women about breast cancer, which will help reach a lot of poor people in the rural areas but won't get the governor many votes in the big city. When one governor launches a pilot project funded by the state and private interests to provide mobile medical vans, the reform-minded PRI governor of the state next door calls you at Los Pinos: "I'm doing more to help you than he is, Mr. President—why can't we have vans, too?" Then there's the old party hack in Congress who thinks that all this mobile-van stuff is a bunch of bullshit and won't vote to expand health coverage until you build a hospital in his hometown, preferably with his name on the door. (You won't get his vote anyway, because what he really wants is a contract for his cousin's medical-supply company.)

But on social issues, even though the opposition PRI still controlled most of the state governorships, many leaders pitched in to help.

"Mr. President, welcome to my state!" The young *priista* governor greeted me on the red carpet, as I stepped off the *Benito Juárez* to help him open a new neighborhood clinic. The cameras whirred behind us, capturing the reform-PRI governor and the president whose PAN party had thrown the old guard out of Los Pinos. We clasped each other's arms in an *abrazo*. "Here comes the motorcade," the governor said proudly.

There was the usual line of SUVs on the tarmac, where officers of Estado Mayor led me to the Suburban in which the governor and I would ride together. By now I knew the drill: It was vital that the local politicians got appropriate "face time" with the president and even more important they were seen on television getting out of the presidential motorcade with the nation's head of state. But when we arrived at the clinic in a poor *colonia* and shook hands with the doctor and the nurses, there was no media there.

I leaned over to the governor, murmuring, "I'm surprised there's no press here."

Ever alert, the officers of Estado Mayor pricked up their ears. The world over, Secret Service men do not like the word "surprise."

"Press?" The young reformer looked back, puzzled. I'm pretty sure that he was in grade school about the time I got into politics. Now he's reforming the worst excesses of the old PRI, which he read about in his college textbooks. "I thought we'd skip all that today," he said nonchalantly. "These are the people you need to meet." He pointed to a massive line of poor and working-class patients waiting to see the doctor, who obviously was a bigger draw in this town than the governor—or the president.

"Come this way, sir." The governor smiled, helping me across the dirt road with the solicitous concern of a Boy Scout helping an old lady across the street. "Just don't tell the folks down in Michoacán that we got you here first."

Today there are still Mexican neighborhoods where the clinics do not serve and the vans do not come, and too many Mexicans still lack health insurance. But under President Calderón, soon 100 percent of our people will have Seguro Popular. Poor and working-class Mexicans have the first access to medical care they have ever known in their lives—the first their family has known going back for generations, before the Spanish Conquest, to the Mayans and the Aztecs. These are the fruits of democracy, the gospel we need to spread to Bolivia, Haiti, Africa, and all over the world. This gospel and the unlikely apostles who helped us spread it across Mexico are the vanguard of hope.

As Al Gore says, the planet is sick, too; like the poor, the earth cannot wait. We had won the presidency in a coalition with the Green Party in 2000, and, having grown up in nature, amid God's bounty, I was determined to put the environment on Mexico's agenda for the first time in our history.

There are moments when you can see all of your country's problems at once. Not long after I took office, I visited a school in southern Mexico, in a rural indigenous village far from the globalized cities of our more affluent north. There was no computer yet in this school, not even schoolbooks, just a careworn teacher with dark circles under her eyes, who stood before a blackboard drawing letters in chalk to teach Mayan children how to read in Spanish. As usual I had drunk too much coffee on the plane coming down from Mexico City, so I raised my hand.

"Yes, Mr. President?" the instructor said, calling on me with that same patient expression a teacher reserves for children who interrupt the class.

"Uh, where might I find the bathroom?"

The students tittered nervously behind their hands. She paused, embarrassed for me, I thought. She shot a meaningful glance toward the back door.

Extricating myself from the little student desk, I excused myself and walked out of the class—to the sewage ditch behind the school, where students and teachers alike were expected to squat in the muddy river. Upriver to one side was a textile mill that polluted the river to a mere trickle, where a strange greenish foam choked the reeds. Downstream lay the indigenous village where women washed their clothes and hauled the foul water by hand in buckets to the rough kitchens outside their doors.

It was the legacy of three quarters of a century of authoritarian neglect in a nutshell: a tireless teacher with no resources to educate children who grew up in unspeakable conditions; mothers and fathers who had been left on the margins of the new global economy with no way to better themselves; a public-health disaster in the making as rampant development nearby destroyed the only thing these people had left—the natural environment that had fed, housed, clothed, and cleaned the Mayan people for thousands of years.

I thought of this village frequently as I traveled the world looking for ways to move Mexico into the twenty-first century without destroying what we have left from the human and environmental wasteland of the twentieth. In Ireland I saw towns that had leaped in one generation from Third World conditions to become jewels in the crown of one of the world's richest economies—yet Ireland has remained the Emerald Isle, one of the greenest environmentally sustainable economies on earth. I was greatly impressed with the models I saw there and in Canada, Costa Rica, and New Zealand, four countries that have made huge strides forward while protecting their natural assets—green in cash, yet green in nature.

Mexico had NADBank developed in cooperation with the United States in the NAFTA agreement. Paid for by the booming NAFTA trade, this fund was designed to clean up the environment and build social needs like sanitary water systems along the border. This was the closest thing to the Marshall Plan–type, EU-style "cohesiveness fund" I had pitched to George Bush, both as governor and again at our San Cristóbal presidential summit.

But we couldn't foist this problem off on our neighbors. Mexico needed to do more by ourselves. Here again the great exploiters of antiglobalist myth—the big corporations, both foreign and domestic—were our best allies.

"You have to help us clean up this mess," I told one industrialist in Monterrey.

"We already are," he said, leading me to the wastewater-recycling plant outside. Mexico, a nation with pressing human needs, lacked public funds for environmental cleanup, so companies like Ford, General Motors, and Mexico's Cemex cement makers and Vitro glass manufacturers, two of the world's biggest success stories, are stepping up to fill the gap. Global corporations simply don't create new wastewater these days unless they can recycle cleanly—they are heavily regulated in the EU especially, where values matter more than short-term economic interests. If they want to do business in green countries, they must be good environmental stewards everywhere on the planet.

Once the Lerma River came to my home state of Guanajuato from Toluca in all its beauty, fresh with lagoons of lily pads and clean water for millions. Today the Lerma has just 10 percent of its former capacity. The canals and rivers that once ran through Mexico City are dried up and gone. Foul pollution soils our urban skies. Even here on the *cerro* above my home, along the ridgeline where once stood the white cross where I intended to be buried in peace, today there is only the ugly gash of the bulldozer blades driven by rampant commercial development.

During my administration we followed the example of Costa Rica—which has turned most of the nation into national parks for ecotourism—and declared fifteen protected regions of Mexico, shielding 10 percent of our territory from development. This is some 4 million acres of jungle, mountains, deserts, and marshlands, and someday people in indigenous villages like the one with the Mayan school I visited will gain from ecotourists who visit them, bringing jobs, revenue for schools, fresh water, and environmental cleanup. This doesn't happen without a fight—*ejidatarios* resist the government's putting an end to slash-and-burn agriculture or land that reverts back from farm use to protected nature. At times this has even been violent, as men wield machetes to protect their traditional rights to cut trees, burn forests, or foul rivers with banned pesticides. Change is pain.

This is a tough balancing act for developing countries, where most people focus more on the need to create jobs and economic growth to help the poor *now,* in this lifetime; the need to preserve earth's precious natural gifts seems esoteric to those who are starving. As countries like Mexico, Brazil, and Malaysia join our richer neighbors to become "have" nations, we must remember that this earth is neither First World nor Third World but God's world—and we are its stewards. Global democracy—even global affluence—will mean little if the result is global warming.

THE UNITED KINGDOM is a different kind of environmental success story. The world's oldest globalized economy, it has, during the Tony Blair decade, completely reversed the course of British environmental self-destruction. When I visited Number 10 Downing Street in late November 2002, the prime minister was waiting out in front, standing like a proud homeowner eager to show you his new flat. The innocuous black door looks like any other row house in the pleasant, clean streets of London.

Inside, the cramped, busy quarters of the British prime minister are comfortable and hectic, like the campaign headquarters of my ten-year ascent from precinct worker to president, bustling with bright, smiling young people who called my host Tony. He remains the only leader who met me out in the street, a touching gesture of hospitality that makes a state visit to London a success from the start.

"Mexico is the gateway to Latin America for the rest of the world," said the man I, too, would call Tony. His smile is permanent and unfeigned: I think that it must take death or tragedy, or Blair's steely resolve to fight terrorism, to chase the natural good humor from that perennial grin. You can disagree with Tony Blair on policy grounds, as I did on Iraq, but it is absolutely impossible not to like him.

We talked about trade, development of "have-not" nations, fighting crime, and his passion for protecting the environment, but the looming prospect of an invasion to topple Saddam Hussein was the elephant in the room. Blair is a consummate politician. Instead of pressing me on Iraq, he used the visit to build a relationship that he would lean on heavily in the months ahead, as he and George Bush formed a global tag team to lobby the world on the war.

Blair encouraged me to sell Mexico to British business: "You can do great things for your country here in London." I thanked him and praised his support for public-private initiatives and his successful fusion of the free market with a socialist welfare state—advances we had studied carefully in designing our own Third Way in Mexico. "You've got a powerhouse luncheon in the City, I understand," Blair said, referring to my speech to five hundred heavyweight foreign investors in London's one-mile-square financial district, which guides how investment capital will flow around the planet. The British historically had been major players in Latin America during the previous century, but in recent years their interest had waned.

"We want to get closer to Mexico," Tony said as we sat on love seats beside the fireplace. His office was decorated not with the usual seals and flags but with pictures of his children and crayon drawings from an elementary-school class. Tony impresses world leaders not with the trappings of power but with the colossal force of his personality. His political acumen is nearly unparalleled; today only Bill Clinton is such a master. Blair has the enthusiastic gift of salesmanship and the wizardly articulate and witty intellect of that particularly British stripe, honed in debates with parliamentarians on the floor of the House of Commons. With Tony you look at the picture, not the frame.

"Our relationship has been good, but it is too distant," I agreed. We decided that I would send a team of experts headed by the chief of our economic cabinet, my close friend and adviser Dr. Eduardo Sojo, to study the advances that Britain could share with Mexico—how the UK rewarded private business for building airports, roads, and public works; joint security initiatives with Scotland Yard to learn how the United Kingdom had such low crime rates when its policemen still did not carry guns; Third Way social programs balancing capitalism with the public good; the ethics and efficiency of Britain, whose rule of law and punctual performance have long been the envy of the world.

I left elated by the sense of joy in this young leader—he is like a kid,

Tony Blair, literally hopping up and down with the sheer pleasure of making your acquaintance. I've never met anyone who so enjoys the process of getting government to work. One good salesman can always recognize another: Tony Blair is the ultimate PR man, and he could sell ice to Eskimos. The only thing he couldn't sell me was the invasion of Iraq.

CHAPTER 17

BE CAREFUL WHAT YOU WISH FOR

THINGS GREW UNCOMFORTABLE with George W. Bush after my return from London. The Republican campaign in that November's 2002 U.S. congressional elections made it clear that Bush intended to take his country, and the world, to war against Iraq. The world responded with a diplomatically worded UN version of "Hell, no, we won't go."

More than a year had passed since 9/11. In Mexico we had hoped, once the security fever passed and the United States got through the midterm elections, that the White House would give GOP lawmakers the nudge they needed to get immigration back on the agenda. Instead, in late November 2002, Colin Powell told our foreign minister, Jorge Castañeda, that there would be no immigration bill until after Bush's 2004 reelection, at the earliest. In the meantime, Powell said, the United States wanted Mexico's vote in the United Nations for the war in Iraq.

It was Mexico's worst diplomatic nightmare: to have our most important issue with the United States put on the back burner for years to come, then be the swing vote on the Security Council when it came to the biggest foreign-policy flashpoint on the planet. We had only ourselves to blame. Early in my presidency, to celebrate Mexico's arrival among the world's democracies, our foreign ministry had campaigned successfully to win a seat for Mexico on the UN Security Council. When the United States came to the UN for a vote to authorize the invasion of Iraq, Mexico was in the hot seat. It was a classic case of the old adage: Be careful what you wish for—you may get it.

You are probably wondering, who cared what Mexico thought? It's not as though we could send troops—our Constitution forbids the deployment of Mexican armed forces abroad, and it's not as though Mexico was a military superpower. But Mexico and Canada were seen as the closest neighbors of the United States, hemispheric allies and trading partners whose people were most affected by the threat of terrorism. Also, there was my highly visible personal friendship with Bush. If Mexico's Fox wouldn't support George Bush on Iraq, how could Europe, Russia, or China be expected to fall in line?

Worse yet, the dynamics of the Security Council vote made Mexico the one thing we never wanted to be: the decisive vote that might block the United States from gaining UN passage of the war resolution. There are fifteen member nations on the Security Council. Ten are nonpermanent nations like Mexico, elected by the General Assembly to serve on a rotating basis. The other five are permanent members with veto power: the United States, Russia, China, the United Kingdom, and France. Mexico's vote would likely sway the vote of the other Latin American nonpermanent member, Chile. Chilean president Ricardo Lagos was one of my closest allies; we agreed early on to stick together on Iraq. If Mexico and Chile opposed the United States, safely esconced between two oceans within the Americas, it would be impossible for Pakistan and Angola—two other Security Council "undecideds" with much greater exposure to Mideast terrorism—to back the U.S.-sponsored invasion plan. Suddenly all eyes fell on Mexico.

Thus began a steady stream of phone calls from secure "red phones" around the globe, as the world divided quickly into two camps. There was the war party: Bush, Blair, Prime Minister Koizumi of Japan, Silvio Berlusconi of Italy, and another of my closest friends, the conservative President José María Aznar of Spain. Their ralling cry was that Iraq was the front line of "the war on terror"—that Hussein's weapons of mass destruction were an imminent threat to the Free World. On the other side was the "peace party" of Jacques Chirac, Vladimir Putin, Chancellor Gerhard Schroeder of Germany, and the majority of world leaders—their view was "wait for the inspections report."

My response was "what's the rush?" Mexico wanted much more before we could vote for war—more evidence of WMDs, more time to let the UN weapons inspectors do their work, more discussion of the implications of invading a sovereign nation, and more details about how a postwar Iraq might be governed.

"¡Vicente, mi amigo!" came Bush's voice over the line, hearty and amicable.

"¿Cómo estás, Presidente?" Aznar's familiar voice asked from Madrid.

"President Fox, hello." Putin's voice was deep, sober.

"President Fox!" Blair called several times that winter, bubbling over with the most articulate arguments about the long-term threat posed by Hussein. Despite the seriousness of the matter, you could literally hear his smile as he sat by his cozy London fireside. "Here's the case, Vicente," he began brightly, summing up with the one question the United States rarely asks of prospective allies: "What do *you* think, my friend?"

Soon they began showing up in person. I imagine they had planning sessions among themselves. Who knows Fox best? How can we get Chrétien on board? Does anyone have a line on where Lagos stands? Should we get Aznar to go see Fox at the ranch? The peace party plotted, too: Who should call Mexico next, Chirac or Schroeder?

As 2002 became 2003 and then January turned into February, the pressure mounted. The prime minister of Canada and I exchanged phone calls almost daily to compare what it was like to "sleep with the elephant." Canada was not a Security Council member, but Bush needed his two NAFTA neighbors on board, else the world would say, "If Canada and Mexico don't back the United States, why should we?" Chrétien and I compared the offers we were getting, the carrot-and-stick diplomacy the United States was using to woo us at the diplomatic midlevel, where promises and threats are deftly deniable. In the past it had always been more stick than carrot when the United States dealt with Mexico—all the way back to Woodrow Wilson's time, when the United States drew up war plans to invade our northern states if it didn't get its way. Now it was subtler. Bush always treated me with dignity, but we got strong hints from second-tier U.S. diplomats that it would be awfully "difficult for Congress to back an immigration bill if Mexico opposes the U.S. in its time of need." There was the occasional comment from the Bush cabinet member or GOP senator who told our diplomats that a "no" vote from Mexico on Iraq could "imperil the progress" we were making on immigration. "What progress?" groused one of my ministers. "We're not just on the back burner—we're not even in the kitchen!"

The trouble was, the United States didn't really have much carrot with Mexico, and no stick at all. Congress and the Bush administration had already dropped the guest-worker reforms in the 2002 frenzy to "secure the border." The United States wasn't going to pull back on NAFTA—free trade was in both of our interests as the North American economy struggled to recover from September 11. Mexico had paid back all of its debt to the International Monetary Fund and made good on the U.S. loans from the peso bailout after our 1994 economic crisis; in fact, we were well on our way to reducing all our foreign debt by half, nearly doubling our monetary reserves during my presidency—so it wasn't as if the United States could call our loans. Our nations worked together well on crime and drug matters—the Americans would not cut off DEA assistance when it was helping them fight crime. They could slow up the passage of trucks across the Rio Grande to send us a message, but they had tried that before, and it had caused an outcry from Bush's own constituents in South Texas. Even if the Bush administration had wanted to punish us, there was little they could do. While we appreciate our friendship with the United States, Mexico is not one of those nations that depend on massive U.S. foreign aid or military assistance.

In any case Bush is a man of principle. Whether you agree or disagree with his determination to go to war, you must concede that once George W. Bush decides where he stands, it is virtually impossible to move him. On immigration this has been a good thing: The president's support for a guest-worker program was deep, heartfelt, and unflinching. No matter how much U.S. officials blustered about "derailing progress in bilateral relations," neither Bush nor I would have bought into any threats that the White House might submarine immigration reform to pay Mexico back for opposing the war.

But this *terco* stubbornness in George Bush was his undoing in the drive to garner support of world leaders for the invasion of Iraq. From the start, Bush tackled the selling of the Iraq war with the air of a man who already had his mind made up. Perhaps when he discussed Iraq with Tony Blair, there was real consultation. But with the rest of us, it was never, "What do you think we should do about Iraq, Vicente?"—rather it was, "Here's what we intend to do, and we really need to have Mexico with us." This was not a leader of the new global democracy listening to his allies, soliciting our views, and then building a multilateral consensus to take action. This ship was going to sail, and Bush just wanted everyone else on board with him. Bush and his team executed their war plan in line with the old American business saying: "Lead, follow, or get the hell out of the way."

In the year leading up to the March 2003 invasion, our face-to-face meetings and phone conferences were one-way affairs: Bush and the war party selling, the peace party not buying. Bush and his team made it clear that the United States was going to war, with the world or without us. We replied, "If that's the choice, then you must do it without us."

As early as March 2002, a year before the UN debate, I had a firsthand glimpse of how completely George's mind was made up on Iraq. At a joint news conference in Monterrey—oddly enough, the same March 2002 press conference where the two of us were accused of lying about alleged pressure to force Fidel Castro to leave the Summit of the Americas—Bush responded forcefully to a question about Iraq.

Hussein was "a dangerous man who possesses the world's most dangerous weapons," Bush said, framing the issue as a personal confrontation. "And it is incumbent upon freedom-loving nations to hold him accountable, which is precisely what the United States of America will do. I haven't had a chance to explain this to our Mexican friends, but a nightmare scenario, of course, would be if a terrorist organization, such as Al Qaeda, were to link up with a barbaric regime such as Iraq and, thereby, in essence, possess weapons of mass destruction. We cannot allow that to happen."

Bush assured me publicly that the United States had no imminent plans for military action. "We'll be deliberate, we'll consult with our friends and allies," he pledged in Monterrey. But even then, a full year before the invasion, he immediately added an ominous postcript: "But we'll deal with Saddam Hussein."

Does that mean, a reporter asked, that you'll remove him?

Bush replied bluntly, "As I said, yes, we'd like to see a regime change in Iraq."

I stood at my own podium beside him, thinking, *He just said he's going to war.*

Bush went on to once again promise "close consultations with our friends from all around the world" and expressed his hope that Hussein allowed "inspectors to go into his country, like he promised he would do. Not for the sake of letting inspectors in, but to show the world that he has no weapons of mass destruction." Yet when Iraq did allow the UN weapons inspectors in, and the inspectors asked for more time in early 2003 to do their jobs, it was the United States who ordered them out—because the war party was about to invade.

"Where is the evidence?" our team demanded, over and over again from November 2002 to February 2003—of Colin Powell, of Condi Rice, eventually of President Bush and Prime Minister Blair and their allies from Japan and Spain. "Where are the maps, the photographs, the documents?" Here was this global economic superpower with the most vaunted intelligence capacity the world had ever known, with satellites that could read newspapers from miles in the sky, electronic intercepts, spies and informers on the ground in the Middle East. In February 2003 they sent Colin Powell into the United Nations with a few fuzzy photographs and a sophomoric PowerPoint presentation. But where was the clear-cut evidence of nuclear-weapons facilities, like what Kennedy's team had shown the UN when the Russians put missiles into Cuba?

If the war party could prove that the U.S. desire to go to war in Iraq was to cripple Hussein's capacity to deliver nuclear and biological weapons to terrorist cells for use in attacking the world's great democracies, military action was something we could understand, even support. But if this was vengeance for 9/11, some sort of "Sicilian message" the United States wanted to send to the evil regimes of the world that terrorize their own peoples and use state resources to fund terrorists—and Saddam certainly had done both—then there were *many* such nations around the world, from Syria to Iran to North Korea. Would the United States have us invade them all? Thousands had died in the World Trade Center, the Pentagon, and on United Flight 93, and we mourned them in Mexico. But killing thousands of innocent civilians by dropping bombs on Baghdad would not bring them back—or make us safer.

In many, many conversations between President Bush and me on Iraq that winter, our discussions were always cordial and polite: two friends who disagreed, each trying to convince the other that he was on the wrong track. "We need to have Mexico's vote with the United States on this," Bush repeated several times that winter and early spring of 2003. "This is vital to our security, and that's important to both of us." I responded, "We need more time, George—to gather evidence, to discuss the best way to deal with this."

But Bush and his top aides presented the war plan as a unilateral fait accompli, not a subject for multilateral debate; if his tone grew icier with frustration at my unwillingness to commit, he was no less frustrated than we foreign leaders were with the unwillingness of the White House to just slow down and *listen*. Even as the issue went before the United Nations in public, behind the scenes U.S. officials were making it clear that the U.S.-led coalition would invade Iraq with the UN's support or without it. "But it would be so much better if you were with us," Bush told me in one phone call, as the Security Council vote drew near.

It was a worst-case scenario for Mexico. By February 5, the day Colin Powell gave his dramatic speech to the United Nations Security Council with its multicolored slides but a puzzling lack of hard evidence, it was clear that our vote would be pivotal. Bush called yet again, then Blair with his highly persuasive arguments—the difference between presidents and prime ministers is that the latter must face Question Time in Parliament, while presidents generally appear only in highly controlled situations. This has made Tony Blair the best debater on the planet.

But there was no way Mexico was going to vote to authorize an invasion of Iraq without more evidence of WMDs than anyone had shown us yet. As a nation we knew firsthand what it was like to be occupied. We had been invaded by Spain, France, and the United States, and no true son of Mexico could ever back the invasion of a sovereign country unless that nation was a danger to the rest of the world. Our only prayer now was that this would not come down to a vote. We hoped that the United States and the United Kingdom would see that the world was not with them and reconsider their plans to go to war.

On March 12, as I was headed into the hospital for a difficult spinal surgery, President Bush called one last time. "The vote at the United Nations is tomorrow," he said tersely. "It's very important that we have Mexico's support." The president alluded to the September 11 attacks and his certainty that Saddam Hussein had weapons of mass destruction, pressing hard for my support. "We need your vote, President Fox." No more "Vicente," I noticed. Bush laid it out cold and bare: "The security of the United States and the Free World is at stake here, and Mexico is either with us or against us on this. We need Mexico with us."

We needed more evidence, I said, and more time—repeating the argument I had used over and over again with Bush, with no discernible effect. Bush made it clear that his mind was made up, and the time for discussion was over. "The vote is tomorrow," he repeated flatly. "I just need to know whether we can count on Mexico's vote."

I am sure that George was surprised to find himself at the eleventh hour pressing for a "yes" vote from his closest neighbor, the Mexican rancher he had swapped boots and hats with, the foreign leader he was presumed to know best. But the real surprise was that anyone in the Bush administration ever thought that Latin American countries like Mexico and Chile would support the Iraq invasion on such flimsy grounds. Remember that Mexico has suffered one U.S. invasion after another, losing a third of our territory to the U.S. Army, enduring the occupation of our ports and expeditions into our northern states by the American military during World War I. Chile, in the adult lifetimes of President Ricardo Lagos and that country's current Socialist government, suffered horrendous human-rights abuses by the CIA-backed tyrant Augusto Pinochet, after a U.S.-sponsored 1973 coup during the Nixon administration ousted and murdered Chile's democratically elected Marxist president, Salvador Allende. All too often in our region's troubled past, the Monroe Doctrine meant "sending in the marines" to back vicious dictators like Nicaragua's Anastasio Somoza, the Dominican Republic's Trujillo, and ruthless military dictatorships in countries like Brazil, Haiti, and Guatemala. This long history of U.S. gunboat diplomacy made it inconceivable for nations that had suffered under those regimes to rally behind a U.S.-led war plan to oust a similar dictator who also had been backed with U.S. assistance, delivered to Saddam Hussein personally by Donald Rumsfeld. There is a famous photograph of the two of them shaking hands, with Rumsfeld smiling like the college dean handing his prize student a scholarship.

Surely the U.S. State Department knew this history well enough to brief President Bush before these calls. But somehow they missed its relevance. From early 2002, when Bush raised the subject at that summit in Monterrey, I had the sense that he considered the support of countries like Mexico and Chile to be what basketball fans call a "slam dunk"—as though we were still puppet regimes backing the United States against the Communists in the Cold War. But given Mexico's history, there was never any possibility that countries like mine would cast a Security Council vote to invade Iraq on such shaky grounds.

So at this point in that pivotal March 12 call, Bush and I disagreed, politely and courteously, as presidents do. He wanted my support, I refused to commit it, and we hung up the phone. My only hope now was that the United States and Britain would not push it to a vote at the Security Council the next day, so that Mexico wouldn't have to cast the deciding vote against our friends.

Before I underwent anesthesia for the operation on my spine, I gave strict instructions to my new foreign minister, former World Bank economist and Commerce Secretary Dr. Luis Ernesto Derbez (Dr. Castañeda had just resigned, contemplating a 2006 presidential bid as an independent): "Negotiate for more time, and keep pushing for more evidence," I told Derbez. "Do your best to get the U.S. to see the wisdom of having no vote at all, and be sure you stay in touch with Lagos." President Lagos, my Chilean seatmate on the Security Council hot seat, also would face the unpleasant task of turning down George Bush on the telephone that day. "In no case," I ordered Derbez, "is Mexico to vote for war."

The next day, as doctors operated on my vertebrae, the United States and the United Kingdom withdrew their resolution from the United Nations Security Council. A week later, on March 20, my friends George W. Bush and Tony Blair invaded Iraq.

Bob Woodward is a brilliant and thoughtful Washington journalist whose books offer great insight into world affairs. In his book *Plan of Attack,* Woodward gets the gist of my March 12 conversation with President Bush correct but draws the wrong conclusions. (I have often wondered how authors can recount such one-on-one conversations, since I assume that no one was taping the call—but then, Castro taped phone calls between him and me, and Woodward's nemesis Richard Nixon tapped his own phone.) Mr. Woodward's account implies that the White House was frustrated that I wouldn't give them a straight answer, as though my back surgery were some sort of dodge. Woodward also claims that instead of responding to Bush with a yes-or-no answer, I asked him what the UN resolution said, as though I were ignorant of its contents.

That's not really accurate. Bush knew where I stood: Mexico wanted more time and more evidence and would not vote for war without it. I knew where Bush and Blair stood: They were going to war, with the world or without us. Since Woodward was on neither the telephone nor the operating table, let me say first that George Bush expressed no anger at me, in that call or at any other time in the ten years we have known each other. Second, I never questioned President Bush about what was in the resolution—we both knew what it said. And finally, for what it's worth, the surgery on my spine was real, it was excrutiatingly painful, and it didn't do me much good anyway. (If you're ever presented with a choice, skip the operation and do the therapy.)

If the discussions in early 2003 between President Bush and me on Iraq lacked the warmth of our previous one-on-one encounters, it was because president-to-president phone conferences about a war are highly scripted affairs. Both parties have precise written talking points. Aides, cabinet secretaries, diplomats, and intelligence chiefs hover nearby, passing notes to keep each president on message. (Perhaps they keep these notes, so that they can tell their side of things later to Bob Woodward.) There is enormous and palpable focus by both presidents to make sure that every word conveys exactly what he means. If a foreign leader seems vague or noncommittal—as was often the case in my responses to Bush on Iraq—this is intentional. Mexico could not support the invasion on such weak data, and we could not understand this great rush to judgment. But neither did we want to cast the deciding vote against the United States at the United Nations.

This was difficult for me personally, opposing George Bush, because I trusted the president, he trusted me, and I still trust George W. Bush to do what he believes is right—even when I think that he is wrong. As I hung up the phone that March 12 of 2003, I thought back to two years before when, at Summit of the Americas in Quebec, President Bush had taken me to my first non-Catholic church service. The way I was raised, you just didn't worship in Protestant churches, at evangelical services or Jewish temples. There weren't many around in rural Mexico (though there are now; evangelical Protestantism is the fastest-growing faith in Latin America). Anyway, in Catholic Mexico of the 1950s, worshipping with the heretics would have brought you a sharp reprimand from the priest. But George was my friend and the president of the United States, so I attended the early-morning service. Few of the other hemispheric leaders were there—few Latins are early risers, but George and I share this, too, in common.

I remember looking at this deeply compassionate and spiritual man and wondering, how was it that someone so devoted to God's word could support the death penalty? To a Mexican and a Catholic, the death penalty seems more like vengeance than deterrence. And now, how could the president of the world's proudest democracy support the invasion of a sovereign nation, causing the inevitable bloodshed of thousands of innocents? Was all life not precious in the eyes of his Lord?

I face the same perplexity when I think of any conservative Catholic who can at once oppose abortion, arguing passionately for the sancity of life, then support the death penalty, or a military invasion that will kill thousands of innocent children, or a border policy that lets four hundred or more immigrants die in the deserts of Arizona and the American Southwest every year, or a law that denies medical care to some category of human beings. My Christian faith instructs me, as does nearly every denomination, to be peaceful, humane, compassionate, to help my neighbor, and to protect life at all costs.

I know that George W. Bush is a loving Christian. My friend must have wrangled with these issues very seriously before making the difficult decision to send his country to war. I am absolutely certain that George W. Bush did what he believed he had to do, in order to protect his country and the world from evil. Surely those who accuse him of playing politics must be wrong, since the politics of his wartime presidency have turned out rather badly. Wrong, too, are those armchair psychologists who concoct bizarre theories about the son's need to depose Saddam Hussein to vindicate his father. On Iraq, I think that George W. Bush did what he deeply believed was right. The sad thing is that he was so deeply, deeply wrong.

There is a more profound principle at stake here: the future of global democracy. After the United States admitted that its intelligence had been incorrect, that there were no weapons of mass destruction, the war party changed its rationale for the occupation of Iraq as a battle for democracy. But where was this passion for global democracy when the United States went to the United Nations for the vote to authorize the use of force? When the United States and the United Kingdom couldn't get the majority of votes from the institution of world peace that they had created at the Bretton Woods after World War II, the United States simply withdrew from the process of global democracy and invaded Iraq anyway.

So when people ask me, "Why does the world hate America?" I answer that we don't hate America. But at times we do wonder whether America hates the world—or at least does not respect us. In a true global democracy, our vote should count, too, when decisions are made that affect the planet. When the United States does not always value the opinions of others, it should not surprise anyone that this diminishes the world's admiration for American democracy.

By ignoring the process of global democracy and just doing what Bush had planned to do all along, whether the world liked it or not, the United States set itself up as the world's judge, jury, and policeman, the sole arbiter of which regimes should be allowed to survive and which sovereign nations should be invaded to have their governments changed. Can the United States afford the cost, in blood and treasure, of invading every nation with which it does not agree? Will the United States next invade North Korea? Iran? Venezuela? Syria? What world leaders wonder, whether we say it out loud or not, is this: Could a displeased United States, without the sanction of the United Nations, invade my country next?

Even now, four years and $500 billion into the war, if the United States and what is left of its coalition decided today to leave Iraq and hand the country over to the United Nations, I believe that the world would accept the challenge gratefully. Few in the United States would believe this, given the opposition of most foreign leaders to the invasion. But I believe strongly that world leaders would agree to roll up their sleeves and work through the United Nations to restore order, peace, and security to Iraq.

George W. Bush would have to eat humble pie. The case to world leaders would have to be this: The United States has learned that it cannot do this alone. (Spain's Aznar and Italy's Berlusconi would not have to join them in this act of contrition; their governments fell after they backed Bush on Iraq. With Tony Blair's departure, the United Kingdom plans to withdraw its troops this year.) It would be an unprecedented act of humility on the part of George W. Bush to admit the failings of unilateralism and ask for the world's help. But this man whom much of the world sees as a belligerent cowboy is at heart a humble and Christian man, with a core of compassion. I have met world leaders—the Muslims, Buddhists, atheists, Catholics, Protestants, and agnostics who lead the great nations. I know that they would debate and discuss and reflect, and some would pray. But they would meet with joy such a bold act of American contrition. It would be a visible symbol that the United States had returned to the path of Bretton Woods, with the United Nations as the cornerstone of a new global democracy.

There is a clear way forward on Iraq. It lies in four steps.

First, the United States should agree to a phased withdrawal of U.S. and British-led forces from Iraq, handing over the job of security to a UN peacekeeping force, which might include for a time the participation of U.S. and coalition forces under UN command.

Second, the United Nations must help rebuild a democracy in Iraq organized under a federal system with local autonomies in the wake of a U.S. departure, so that nationalist-Islamist anger is no longer focused against the sitting target of the U.S. and British forces.

Third, the United States should agree to trust the process of global democracy and the vote of the United Nations, before launching future invasions designed to achieve regime change. The United States and its allies gave birth to the United Nations, but as parents of global democracy there comes a time when the great powers of the Free World must embrace the young democracies of the planet and let us become adults.

Finally, there must be sweeping reform of the United Nations led by a strong U.S. commitment to help reinvent that institution. We must give the UN the teeth it requires to more forcefully resolve conflicts and lead the world to harmony. There is an urgent need to reform the world body so that it is truly democratic, with both the moral authority and the state-of-the-art efficiency it has lacked in recent years. Still, with all its failings, the UN is the last and greatest hope for peace and freedom on this earth. As Winston Churchill once said, "Democracy is the worst form of government, except for all those other forms that have been tried from time to time."

CHAPTER 18

ONE FOOT ON THE FLOOR

WITH THE IMMIGRATION issue tabled and the White House utterly absorbed with Iraq, 2003 was not the best time to visit the United States. President Bush and I remained on good terms, though I wasn't exactly the man of the hour in Washington any longer. I understood the realpolitik at work and was sincerely touched later that year, when George and Laura invited Marta and me to visit them at Crawford in March 2004—this in the midst of a presidential election year in wartime, when U.S. voters were focused on homeland security and the "crisis at our borders."

Eager to expand Mexico's global trade, I went first to Japan, where I had done business in my Coca-Cola days. I was well prepared for the unique dynamics of a business meeting in Tokyo: the bowing over business cards; the impassive faces whose expressionless taciturnity hide a precise knowledge of English, despite the presence of a Japanese interpreter; the strict ritual of protocol, giving seniority to the most important man in the room; the utter absorption in process in a culture where the form truly is fundamental. In Japan a meeting is not a means to an end—it *is* the end.

What I was not prepared for was the friendly welcome of this prime minister who had been a staunch ally of President Bush and Prime Minister Blair on Iraq. With Samson's hair and a Hollywood smile, Japan's animated, gesticulating Junichiro Koizumi greeted me just as warmly as Bush would that following March at his Crawford ranch. (With Tony Blair, too, it was as though we had never clashed on Iraq. He had visited me that August, when we toured the oil fields and offshore wells of Campeche, visited a British nitrogen plant, and dined with Marta and Cherie in Cancún. All of us—Bush, Blair, Koizumi, me, or other world leaders—were anxious not to let Iraq overshadow our friendships or the progress we were making on trade, security, and other fronts.)

Even the Energizer Bunny hyperactivity of Tony Blair pales in comparison with that of former Prime Minister Koizumi, the first of a new breed of leaders in Japan. I happened to see Koizumi in action the night we arrived in Tokyo in October 2003, on the hotel-room television set flickering high above the futuristic science-fiction movie of neon that is the Tokyo skyline. How fortunate, I thought, to catch the prime minister's act on the floor of the Diet. He waved his arms and slapped the lecturn, pivoting and shouting and laughing and chopping his fingers just like the whirling martial-arts champion on the next channel. Later I discovered that I had not been fortunate at all: Japanese prime ministers take the floor *every day* to tangle with opponents. They fence with backbenchers of the opposition party, joust with the media, fend off questions from rebels within the governing Liberal Democratic Party. Surely such a workout would benefit the George Bushes and Vicente Foxes of the world. Like most good exercise, it would be painful but healthy—for democracy and, no doubt, very good for our verbal skills.

Koizumi was equally animated in person. His great mop of salt-and-pepper hair had been elaborately styled at some point in the day, but it flew askew as he nodded and waved his hands and utterly, utterly charmed anyone lucky enough to meet him. This remarkable man breathed fresh life into a Japanese political system that had ossified into genteel decay. Now his new generation of "Koizumi babies" is bringing Japan into the twenty-first century with energy and spirit.

I've never met a man with better skills of corporal expression than Koizumi-san. Like Blair, this man can *sell*—his dreams, his vision, his ambitions for new trade and economic expansion. The deal he and I signed during my state visit to Tokyo helped Mexico become the most open market on the planet: We now have free-trade agreements with forty-two nations altogether, more than any other country.

Like the old Mexico, Japan had been a notoriously protectionist society, especially when it came to agriculture. Mountainous Japan's lack of arable land makes its agriculture less than 1 percent of the total economy. Historically Japan protected its rice farmers zealously, because rice farming lies at the core of Japanese culture—and because a nation always wants some semblance of the ability to feed itself. But rice costs ten times more to grow in Japan than just about anywhere else in the world. So protectionism is terribly unfair to Japanese consumers—they'd be far better off buying rice, meat, and vegetables from Mexico, even with the shipping cost. If we fully opened our markets to Japanese electronics in return, we would unbalance our trade deficit overnight. Mexico would be flooded with attractively priced televisions and cell phones whose value is much higher than bales of rice. So this must be worked out step by step, in trade agreements. The deal Koizumi and I signed spurred Mexican exports to Japan to grow at a rate of 30 to 40 percent a year, to the benefit of Japanese consumers and ours—they get cheaper rice, we get Japanese electronics at prices that our fast-growing, gadget-thirsty middle class can afford. And in the process my country gains billions of dollars in Japanese investment to create new jobs in Mexico.

At the end of our meeting, Koizumi showed how well briefed he was. "I understand you had back surgery recently," he said solicitously. "How's that going?"

"It aches pretty much every day," I confessed. "I've tried swimming, walking, strengthening the muscles on the weight machines. But the doctors say I damaged my back when I was very young, and just may never recover to a hundred percent."

"I've struggled with the same thing," the prime minister said. "And I found a brilliant doctor for this condition here in Japan. I'm going to send him to you tonight."

Sure enough there was a discreet knock at the door that evening. The doctor bowed and asked permission to enter. "I don't do surgery on people's backs," he explained as he examined me. "When the pain gets too great, we just give you an injection here, between the vertebrae. The injection itself is very painful, and there are side effects, but it will kill the ache in your back."

I was desperate to regain my mobility—I couldn't walk, ride horses, or wear cowboy boots anymore, and the pain can be vicious at times. So I inquired about returning to Japan for the procedure. Then I learned that it only lasts for twenty-four hours: I would have to get a shot like that every day. It hurts less to get gored by a bull.

Most of my foreign travel through six years of the presidency was inside Latin America, where we worked hard to build closer ties. The socialist

Ricardo Lagos in Chile became my particular friend and ally, as Mexico and Chile went beyond a trade agreement to build a virtual economic union between our countries. Chile's blend of social-democrat welfare state and free-market economics are a model for Mexico and the developing world. North America could worry less about demagogic presidents like Hugo Chávez if the United States could build closer ties with socialist democracies like Chile under its new president, the warm and charismatic forward thinker Michelle Bachelet.

Fidel Castro had been kind enough to attend my inauguration, despite our differences. So did Hugo Chávez, though he became my principal opponent on the other side of the Latin American divide. The twenty-first-century dialectic of our region splits Latin America in two.

On one side lie countries like Mexico, Costa Rica, Colombia, and Chile—free-market social democracies of "capitalism with a human face," where human rights are respected, the rule of law and property rights have meaning for citizens and foreign investors alike, economic policies are based on sound fiscal discipline, and presidents actually leave at the ends of their terms.

Then you have Venezuela, where Hugo's bully-populist regime of oil-funded demagoguery pays little respect to democracy, law, or basic economic principles. Sadly, now Bolivia and Ecuador are following the same example, with state-run economies. If you think these *chavismo* regimes are dangerous today, wait until you see what happens when the price of oil and natural gas drops and they cannot repay their debts—the next step is revolution or repression, the sad old Latin American story.

In the middle lie large, pivotal nations that can tilt one way or the other: big socialist democracies like Lula's Brazil, Alan García's Peru, or Néstor Kirchner's Argentina. Washington would do better to work more closely with these sane and reasonable leftist governments, rather than pushing them toward Hugoism.

A trip to the Caracas of Hugo Chávez is an experience unlike any presidential visit on earth. In April 2001, I went to Venezuela to try to resurrect the traditional G-3 alliance between Colombia, Venezuela, and Mexico, which had atrophied in recent years. As Mexico's Air Force One flew south over the Caribbean beaches, crossing into the verdant jungles of Venezuela's interior, the voice of a fighter pilot squawked over the radio. *"You are entering the control of the armed forces of the democratic Bolivarian Republic of*

Venezuela," the disembodied voice said. I looked up from my coffee to a sight I had never witnessed, before or since, not in state visits to Washington or Moscow, Beijing or Johannesburg—two fighter jets shrieking up beside us to escort us down to the landing field.

The entire experience of Hugo's Venezuela is military, from the jackbooted soldiers who greet you on the Tarmac to the truckloads of young men whose AK-47s dangle loosely on the floorboards. You sense that these weapons are loaded and ready at half cock. So is their maximum leader: Chávez is a seething presence at summit meetings, in presidential state visits, at the United Nations, ever about to explode into a two-hour diatribe against George Bush and the exploitation of Latin America by global corporations, shouting and raving about the devil and the smell of sulfur at the podium—Chávez said he could still smell the reek of Hades as he took the dais after President Bush had addressed the opening of the UN in New York in 2006. (Hugo, by the way, is an immensely personable conversationalist, even if he always has his mental walkie-talkie button pressed on "send." I am fairly sure that he drinks more coffee than any human being on the planet, twenty to thirty cups a day, he says—which explains a lot.) At events like the Summit of the Americas in Monterrey in 2004, Bush and I and the other presidents—most of us impatient at the long-winded oratory—just rolled our eyes when Hugo took the podium. You knew that the three-minute time limit was about to be ignored. The next two hours were a good time to go for a bottle of water and some cookies, and try to do some real business in the hallway by the restroom.

The timekeepers of these functions no doubt breathed a sigh of relief when Castro stopped attending most summits after Chile's former dictator Pinochet was arrested on human-rights charges in London to face trial in Chile in 2002. If the West would arrest a dictator of the right on human-rights abuses, Fidel must have reasoned, might I not be next? Between his fear of arrest and worsening health, we saw little of Castro outside Cuba after I visited him there in 2002.

But Hugo has picked up where the Cuban left off, positioning his brand as the new Fidel: Chávez exports his revolution of the proletariat along with barrels of oil, buying influence from Haiti to Harlem, Africa to Argentina. He launched a Pan-American television network as the Al Jazeera of our hemisphere. He has struck oil deals with anti-American leftist governments from Jamaica and Nigeria to Angola and Libya.

Recently Hugo invited Iran's president to Venezuela to make plans for a new axis of hate in our hemisphere. He also ordered Venezuela's largest independent TV network to shut down despite massive protests against the closure, and he has backed copycat demagogues to win the presidencies of one South American nation after another. Only in Peru and Mexico have his allies lost to the advocates of democracy—even then, Andrés Manuel López Obrador was very nearly elected president of the nation that shares a two thousand-mile border with Hugo's Great Satan, the United States of America.

We started out with an olive branch to Hugo Chávez. At my inauguration I met with Hugo and Colombia's President Andrés Pastrana to see whether we could resurrect the Group of Three or G-3. Between the three of our nations, we once had been nearly half of Latin America's economy. (Mexico is a big player, with 36 percent of the gross domestic product of Latin America; Mexico and Brazil alone comprise two thirds of the region's economy.) I was anxious to help mediate the ongoing rebel activity of narcoterrorists against the Colombian government, which many accused Chávez of fostering. Venezuela shares a disputed border with Colombia; Hugo has been suspected of arming the rebels and funding them with oil revenues, although this has never been proved.

Our own *zapatista* uprising in Chiapas was settling down. By the time I visited Caracas in April 2001, the rebellion had evolved into a peaceful civil-disobedience protest march to Mexico City. "What a pity we don't have rebels like yours," President Pastrana said wistfully. But Chávez would have no part of negotiation and had no intention of rebuilding an alliance with free-market countries like Mexico and Colombia. His goal is not to ally with democracies but to destabilize them. The classic Chávez modus operandi is to back leftist-populist radicals who win an election by promising everything to the poor. Then they can become old-style Latin "presidents for life" like Hugo, winning reelection through expropriation, corruption, repression, and state-controlled cronyism, using the country's wealth to reward friends and punish opponents.

I WENT TO SEE Fidel Castro on his home turf in February 2002, as I had done with Hugo in 2001, holding out my hand in friendship with the goal of increasing trade and financial ties with Havana. I believed then, as I do now, that the United States is foolish to redline Cuba with the embargo.

When the Berlin Wall came down, the West's triumph of over Communism showed once and for all that exposure to the values, products, and unquestioned economic success of liberal democracy is the most powerful way to bring down tyranny. Instead of boycotting Cuba and beaming over Radio Martí, the United States should send Coca-Cola and reruns of *Friends*.

But despite the personal friendship between Fidel and me, we soon got crossways.

In April 2002, Fidel accused us of forcing him to leave the Monterrey Summit of the Americas early so that George W. Bush wouldn't have to meet him face-to-face. In a bizarre episode, Fidel even taped conversations between himself and me, then played them for the media, calling George Bush and me "liars" and "hypocrites." At the United Nations, I had reversed Mexico's long-standing policy of not criticizing Castro's deplorable record on human rights, voting with the United States for the UN resolution condemning Cuba's abuse of its people. (Eventually Peru joined us in condemning Castro, a new wave in Latin American politics.) These early feuds were diplomatic statecraft, but I remained committed to bringing Cuba into the world of global trade. I kept the channels of communication open with Fidel—until 2004, when Cuba began meddling in Mexico's domestic politics.

Like Castro or Chávez, Mexico City Mayor Andrés Manuel López Obrador had a public image as one of those messianic characters who project that whatever the leader decrees *is* the law. This is the danger of bully populists, the reason that an election in and of itself does not a democracy make. As the United States is learning today in the Middle East, it is what happens *after* the vote that determines whether a fragile democracy will survive. Remember, Hitler was elected, Hugo Chávez was elected, the president of Iran was elected. The question is, will elected leaders respect the nation's institutions and obey its laws? Will they live within the checks and balances of the executive, legislative, and judicial branches? Will they allow freedom of the press and the primacy of written law over the rule of one man?

Andrés Manuel's answer is, like Hugo's or Fidel's, to offer himself as the voice of the people, the savior of the downtrodden. AMLO's philosophy conveys to the nation, like Sylvester Stallone's character in a bad science-fiction movie: "I am the law." This became evident in 2006, when López Obrador refused to accept the results of a democratic defeat and made a fool of himself by declaring that he would henceforth be known as the "alternative president" of Mexico.

But back in 2004, AMLO was still popular nationwide. Then a top aide to the Mexico City mayor was caught on videotape stuffing huge wads of cash into a briefcase in a major corruption scandal. As reported in many media accounts, one of AMLO's top advisers, finance chief Gustavo Ponce, reportedly made some thirty-seven trips to the Bellagio in Las Vegas and was accused of stealing $3 million from the Mexico City government. The wealthy businessman Carlos Ahumada, whose blurry image was captured on the videotapes handing cash to AMLO's top aide, denied the charges and fled to Cuba. There, Castro's government jailed Ahumada and backed AMLO's side of the story. Andrés Manuel and his Cuban allies made wild accusations of a "conspiracy" against AMLO by our federal government and the United States, saying that the whole thing had been a sting cooked up by the Fox administration to discredit AMLO before the 2006 election, even claiming that my government and the U.S. Treasury Department were at fault, because we should have warned AMLO that aides in his top circle were corrupt.

Our ambassador in Havana filed papers to extradite Ahumada from Cuba; he was deported back to a Mexican prison. Castro lashed out at Mexico in his May Day speech, criticizing Mexico's stand at the UN against his human-rights violations and echoing AMLO's claim that he was the victim of a *complot* by my government. PRD officials later admitted that they had met with Cuban officials in the affair, a gross violation of our sovereignty in matters of domestic politics.

The opposition of Castro and Chávez to Mexico's free-market policies or my friendship with George W. Bush, these I could accept. Fidel and Hugo were presidents of sovereign nations, and they had the right to criticize me, to oppose our views at summits, in speeches and communiqués, at the United Nations. But we could not allow the sitting government of Cuba to interfere in Mexico's affairs. We also wanted to send a strong signal to Fidel and Hugo to stay out of our politics, so that Chávez would not be tempted to funnel his oil money to his favored presidential candidate, as he is widely believed to have done in some countries of the hemisphere. No doubt Fidel and Hugo wanted to see AMLO turn Mexico's democracy back into one-man rule, and they had the right to their opinions—but not to take action within our borders.

Despite Mexico's close relations with the people of Cuba and my past friendship with Fidel, I made the difficult decision to withdraw our ambassador, Roberta Lajous, from Havana, and expel Cuba's ambassador from Mexico City—in part because of Castro's attack on our support for the UN resolution on human rights and also due to the unauthorized activities of Cuban Communist Party officials on our soil. Castro labeled my government a "mafia at the beck and call of Washington." Hugo Chávez stepped up his rhetoric, telling Bush's "lapdog" Fox to "shut up." This would come back to haunt their Mexican ally in 2006, when Andrés Manuel would try to do the same.

SOMETIMES THE TENDENCY to speak on the run or act out of turn is not such a good quality. In May 2005 my own propensity for verbal gaffes brought me into contact with the Reverends Jesse Jackson and Al Sharpton.

As my presidency moved into its maturity, immigration reform in the United States faced the constant banging of the anti-Mexico drum by right-wing talk shows. There also was criticism from the American left against immigration and free trade, especially from labor-union protectionists from Rust Belt states who blamed Mexicans for "taking our jobs away." Some African Americans even complained that immigrants and Latinos were "cashing in" on the hard-won progress they had fought for in the civil-rights movement.

Speaking in Spanish from Mexico City, I said that the United States needed our workers, because "there is no doubt that Mexicans, filled with dignity, willingness, and ability to work, are doing jobs that not even blacks want to do there in the United States."

Bad wording. Bad day at Los Pinos.

First, it was a borderline racist thing to say. Implicit in the way I misspoke was the idea that African Americans were willing to take *some* jobs that Anglos didn't want, but not those jobs that were going to immigrants, or, worse, that Mexicans were harder-working than African Americans. It was the wrong thing to say, and I never meant it to come out that way.

It is true that Mexican workers fill jobs that U.S. citizens don't want. Experts predict that 70 percent of all new jobs in the U.S. economy are unskilled jobs for those without a high-school diploma. But 80 percent of U.S. citizens *do* earn a high school diploma: Americans of course do not want to work in jobs for which they are overqualified, so these jobs attract our immigrants.

It would have been far, far better to put it like that than to express things in racial terms; the French call these second thoughts "stairway wit," the more clever and intellectually sound things you realize you *should* have said—after you leave the room.

In any case it was wrong to say what I said, and I was sorry to have done so. My entire life had been devoted to ending the ruthless discrimination within Mexico against the poorer, darker children of indigenous and mestizo heritage that I grew up with at San Cristóbal. Perhaps what hurt the most was that my own adopted children come in all colors of God's rainbow, and when I look at each of them, I see only those I love.

It pained me, as have few other things in public life, to read in the international press that the Reverend Jesse Jackson had called me a racist. The Reverend Al Sharpton phoned to demand that I apologize. So I did, inviting them to come down to Los Pinos to accept my heartfelt apology in person. This is how the Reverend Al Sharpton of New York City came to the presidential palace of the Republic of Mexico to take me to the woodshed and explain the dynamics of racism to a man who had learned his lesson. I called Jesse Jackson to apologize: Reverend Jackson took me at my word that I had intended no racial offense. I hoped for a rapprochement with African American civil-rights leaders, because Mexicans must engage more closely with those who have suffered discrimination. We have common cause on the moral high ground of human rights and social justice for the dispossessed. When we argue over who has it worst, we all lose.

Weeks later some bureaucrat in the Mexican post office issued a five-part installment in a long-planned series commemorating the history of Mexican comic books, each with cartoon illustrations depicting a character of the nation's folklore. Memín Pinguín is a black 1940s cartoon character. A comic-book hero that Mexican kids have loved since my boyhood, Memín is a kind and generous youth based on stories of the Afro-Mexicans of our Caribbean coast. He stands up against racial injustice, refuses to take communion when he is told that "blacks aren't allowed in heaven," travels to Texas to play soccer with his friends, where they encounter discrimination against people of color and fight racist bullies. But the stamp, like the comic-book character, was drawn with outlandish red lips and bulging white eyes—an exaggerated, cartoonish ethnic stereotype, like the American cartoon character Speedy Gonzalez (who, by the way, never provoked much outrage from civil-rights leaders in the United States). The reaction from U.S. media was savage.

The first I knew of this was in the newspaper. I did my best to explain that the government meant no offense to people of color, among either African Americans or the Afro-Mexican community. The Bush White House attacked the stamp. Jesse Jackson demanded that Mexico withdraw the stamp. Bidders on eBay offered $125 for the five-stamp series. They cost sixty cents in Mexico.

JUST AFTER the postage-stamp flap, I headed to Russia, an important customer and one of the last stops on my global sales route to peddle the wares of the new Mexico. The drive into Moscow from Sheremetyevo International Airport takes you past a giant gray monument in the shape of the antitank traps that halted Hitler's armies just thirty kilometers from the Kremlin, crossed steel beams that look like massive versions of the toys little kids toss on the pavement, in the game of jacks. Moscow is like that, gigantic and grandiose and over the top, carefully designed to awe, impress, and cow you into submission, whether you were a dissident in the Soviet era or a president coming to meet Vladimir Putin to sell the former head of the KGB on building helicopters in Mexico.

The Kremlin is a city within a city, with nine churches and a host of czarist palaces and government buildings hidden behind its massive crenellated walls of red brick. I had hosted Putin at the APEC summit at Los Cabos in 2002; now he was returning the favor. But first his aides took us on an all-day tour of the Kremlin. It was the only state visit where the host insisted on dazzling me first with the power of his mighty empire, before sitting down with the president of little Mexico.

We had more in common than you might think: Russia's economy is not much larger than Mexico's, with big oil and gas reserves like ours. Its empire spans the continent from one ocean to the other, as does Mexico's. Both nations have long histories of obsession with the United States; early in the 1900s, Mexico and Russia both were invaded by U.S. expeditionary troops in the wake of our simultaneous revolutions and counterrevolutions. Mexico and Russia struggled toward democracy after a twentieth century spent largely under one-party control. But Putin's background and mine could not be more different: He was a KGB insider from the old regime; I was a rebel outsider who had been spied on by our own softer version of the Soviet police state.

Like Mexico, Russia is a deeply spiritual place, despite decades of iron rule by antireligious governments. The tiny Kremlin apartment of Czar Nicholas II and Alexandra has a secret door behind the wall to the chapel where the royals spent hours each day. Orthodox churches in Russia have no pews. Passionate adherents prefer the discomfort of praying on their feet during mass, which goes on for hours. Fasting parishioners have been known to swoon and tumble to the stone floors on Easter Sunday.

We toured the great halls, the spectacular golden throne room, the chandeliered conference rooms where Lenin and Stalin and Brezhnev had held sway. But never was there a mention that Russia had ever been Communist. Putin has carefully repositioned his country's brand, as if Russian history had leaped straight from the czar's Winter Palace (in what is now, again, St. Petersburg) and the Orthodox churches (reopened this past decade), with not a stop in the many decades of Soviet tyranny. While it is good that the Communists are gone, historical revisionism always makes me a little uneasy.

It was the same the next day. Apparently we had been insufficiently reeducated, so we spent the morning touring Red Square, evoking memories of the May Day parades of Red Army tanks and rockets, the Soviet leaders standing stiff and grim in overcoats and fur hats. Putin's aides focused instead on the onion domes of the landmark church. I debated whether I could diplomatically ask the fellow from the Russian Foreign Ministry to point out the Lubyanka Prison, headquarters of Putin's former colleagues.

Only then were we suitably indoctrinated for the meeting with Vladimir Putin. Thus began my afternoon playing musical chairs in the Kremlin. I was led from one waiting room to the next, each more elaborate than the last, like a character in a fairy tale who goes to grander and grander palaces as he seeks favor first from his squire, then his duke, then king, emperor, and pope. I assume the point was to put me at some sort of disadvantage. But I rather enjoyed the whole psychological gamesmanship of the thing. First I was brought to a huge hall decorated with fresh flowers and left to sit in an antique chair. Then a well-coiffed lady came to say, "President Putin is ready to see you now," and I was led to a second room, this one all in gold—golden walls, golden ceilings, golden statues, golden chairs and couches. Again I was left to ponder all this magnificence. Then I was led to the end of the long room, where a huge golden door some twelve feet tall and six feet across swung wide open—I imagined the sound of golden trumpets. I entered the inner sanctum and stood at attention.

At the far end of the room, another great golden door burst open, and Putin strode in trailing a line of aides, walking with that aggressive, athletic, world-leader strut that conveys dynamism and strength. Vladimir Putin and George Bush both walk like they're carrying a watermelon under each arm.

It was all perfectly choreographed. He took twelve steps to my three. We sat on a bench so that the photographers could snap the requisite pictures. Putin is a man of immediate and surprising personal charm, the usual attribute of world leaders. He has electric blue eyes, sharp features, a quick wit, and a ready smile. We sat side by side, but still we were not really together, just props for the opening act. Behind us was the stage set: Act 1—czarist Russia. Background—ornate splendor. Finally we got our speaking parts, the thirty minutes for which you travel halfway around the planet.

The details of our business discussions would bore you—unless you have an unnatural interest in Ural disaster-relief trucks for our navy's hurricane-relief units; Russian investment in construction-equipment plants for Mexican road building; or my pitch for a Russian helicopter-maintenance facility in Veracruz. The United States was worried that Mexico was buying military equipment from Russia, but it was all civilian commerce, the humdrum but highly profitable stuff of most head-of-state discussions. Few people realize that diplomats spend little time on high policy; U.S. ambassadors will tell you that they spend 95 percent of their time lobbying for American business.

That evening's state dinner took place in a splendid Kremlin ballroom with painted ceilings and thick, lavishly hued columns looming all around us. You could smell the history in the Kremlin, amid savory hints of beef soup, sturgeon, and potato salad. You must be careful at state dinners, because each time you empty a glass, they will refill it. You are so busy exchanging family chitchat with the President and Mrs. Putin that you will not count the number of glasses of iced vodka you toss down as if it were so much soda—the Russians are combat drinkers, of course, and vodka is thought to be very good for the digestion. But when you walk out into the cold of the Russian night, you realize that the red brick walls have gone fuzzy at the edges. When you go to bed, the mattress is moving around in slow circles, so that you must reach out and put one foot on the floor.

UKRAINE IS NOT nearly so splendid. Even Russia, with all its privatization millionaires in Range Rovers and Mercedes-Benz limousines, is a poorer country than Mexico, with per capita income 15 percent below ours. Ukraine is Russia's even poorer neighbor, with average incomes less than 30 percent what the average Mexican earns. Unlike Mexico or Russia, Ukraine lacks vast energy resources and manufacturing wealth—that somehow ended up on Russia's side of the ledger when the old Soviet Union broke up.

I went there en route to Russia because Viktor Yushchenko's "Orange Revolution" had just made Ukraine the latest addition to the growing club of democratic nations. I admired the dramatic peaceful-resistance movement of this scarred president, whose handsome visage had been mottled by his brush with death when Yushchenko was allegedly poisoned by his opponents from the previous Russian-aligned regime. We had experienced much the same path to power, fighting electoral fraud and tyranny. Yushchenko and I also had the common dilemma of living next door to a colossus.

Ukraine is as linked to Russia's economy as Mexico is to that of the United States but is much more dependent on the favor of its giant neighbor. Even after the fall of the Soviet Union, Russia kept control of its former SSRs—Ukraine relies on Russia for oil and gas; it also is the site of a massive pipeline carrying Russian petroleum to Europe.

In keeping with his people's poverty, Yushchenko's presidential office is the humblest I have seen. A lover of Ukrainian folk hymns, he hummed pleasantly as we waited for the Televisa anchorman Joaquín López-Dóriga, Mexico's Walter Cronkite, to complete the sound check for a TV interview. I also met with Ukraine's stunning vice president, the dynamic Yulia Tymoshenko, who had united her party with Yushchenko's despite the differences between them. She is a remarkably talented and persuasive woman: I left Ukraine carrying a plea from their government to encourage Putin to ease Russia's foot on Ukraine's neck.

When I arrived at the Kremlin, Vladimir did not receive it well.

"It would have been better for Ukraine if Yushchenko's enemies had won," Putin said shortly. The conversation shifted abruptly back to family and Russian helicopter plants in Veracruz. The former KGB czar did not speak of Ukraine again.

CHAPTER 19

DEPARTURES

I BELIEVE that the most important thing the president of a new democracy does is to leave. As Shakespeare writes of the Thane of Cawdor, "nothing in his life so became him like the leaving it." So it is with a new democracy—the true test occurs not with the election of the peaceful revolutionary but when that leader has delivered enough results that he or she is able to pass the torch to another freely elected leader, who in turn will respect the institutions of democracy, open government, and the rule of law.

By early 2005, despite the advances we had made, democracy was still in great peril in Mexico. Andrés Manuel López Obrador, the populist mayor of Mexico City, was sure to be the 2006 nominee of the leftist PRD. He stood well ahead in the polls, with popularity ratings rivaling mine and a solid lead over any presidential candidate from the PRI or the PAN. This, in and of itself, would have been fine: Mexico was a democracy; I would turn over power to anyone elected by the people, regardless of party. As 2005 began, it looked more and more as if this would be López Obrador.

A passionate public speaker and adroit media handler, Andrés Manuel had mastered the political street theater of the populist candidate. He drove his own Tsuru compact to work. A hardworking bachelor who lived in a cramped, spartan apartment, he picked his battles carefully to position himself the champion of the poor and dispossessed. Taking aim at our administration's center-right economic policies, AMLO made himself the anti-Fox. For three years AMLO had been the darling of the Mexico City intelligentsia, the international media, and Mexico's TV and radio stations. His daily dawn news conferences were dubbed *las mañaneras* by the reporters, as they gulped their coffee and got their daily ration of AMLO-isms, which became the fodder of conversations in street markets and factory lines. "Did you hear Andrés Manuel this morning?" people would say, laughing at AMLO's latest attacks on the foibles of my administration.

He started with trivial matters, like our feud over my plan to reset Mexico's clocks to daylight saving time in order to save on energy. Soon it escalated into major battles over anything our administration did in Mexico City, where one fifth of the country's population lives.

This is a mighty base for any national politician. It's like being governor of California or senator from New York in a U.S. presidential election, where coming from a big home state can allow a Ronald Reagan, a Hillary Clinton, a Robert F. Kennedy, or a Rudy Giuliani to start out with a huge chunk of the party's convention delegates, plus forty or fifty votes in the electoral college. AMLO used his bully pulpit to decry our shortcomings, whether it was missing our 7 percent economic-growth target (never mind that 9/11 had a bit of impact) or the inevitable miscues of a government in a new democracy. Most of these, of course, were my fault. I have "the gift of the gaffe"—and besides, I was the CEO. As the sign on Harry Truman's desk said, when you are president, "The buck stops here."

On the international scene, the era of harmony was over for us. We were at odds with the United States over the war in Iraq. In 2004 we had withdrawn our ambassador from Cuba over human-rights issues and Castro's meddling in our presidential election. In 2005 we had done the same to Venezuela, after Hugo Chávez threatened me at the Summit of the Americas in Argentina, saying, "Don't mess with me, sir, because you'll get stung," calling me a "puppy of the empire" of the United States for my support of the Free Trade Area of the Americas. (Bush and I and other free-market nations back FTAA as a huge leap beyond NAFTA for our hemisphere, but Chávez excoriates it as a yanqui plot to allow the Fortune 500 to rape and pillage the poor.)

As our 2006 election drew closer, I was being savaged regularly by the trio of AMLO, Castro, and Chávez. As the surf lapped on the beaches of the November 2005 Mar del Plata summit, Hugo exulted that "President Fox left bleeding from his wounds." Even the Argentine soccer star Diego Maradona got in on the act, appearing at Hugo's side to attack my defense of free-market ideas, as Latin America swung further to the antiglobalist left. A longtime ally of Castro's and Chávez's, Maradona helped draw an anti-Bush, anti-trade crowd of forty thousand to the Argentine seaside resort. Near the summit hotel, antiglobalist demonstrators threw gasoline bombs, shelled police with stones, and set a bank on fire; eight thousand police were summoned to quell the riots with tear gas. I responded that the onetime soccer idol had a "good foot for kicking, but he does not have a good brain for talking."

I had become the leader in the region for market policies with a human face—even as senior Bush-administration officials fumed over our refusal to back the United States on Iraq. By then I was catching it from all sides. The extreme right in the United States was angry because I was protesting the idea of a wall along the Rio Grande, the extreme left in Latin America was angry because I was seen as being too close to George W. Bush, and those around Bush were angry because I'd opposed him on Iraq. In politics you judge a man by the caliber of his enemies. I figured, if I was annoying Hugo Chávez, Donald Rumsfeld, Fidel Castro, Tom DeLay, Diego Maradona, and Tom Tancredo, then I must be doing a pretty good job.

When it comes to Latin America, the United States can be a bit tone deaf, particularly when dealing with governments that lie somewhere to the left of a Republican administration—which is nearly all of us, here in the hemisphere and around the world. In Latin America some governments are centrist free-market democracies led by social-welfare democrats like me or former president Fernando Henrique Cardoso of Brazil. There are truly socialist democracies, like Chile under Ricardo Lagos and Michelle Bachelet. Still further to the left, you have radical socialist-populist countries whose far-left presidents recognize market realities and have made peace with the business community (like Brazil's Lula da Silva, Argentina's Kirchner, or Peru's Alan García).

But there is an ugly new strain of radical populism that lies well outside the pale of ideological difference from right to left, somewhere off the chart altogether. These are the nationalist-socialist regimes of strongmen like Hugo Chávez, the coca farmer Evo Morales of Bolivia, the *sandinista* Daniel Ortega of Nicaragua, or Rafael Correa of Ecuador: all allied with Venezuela and Cuba, taking on the mantle of Castro's extreme anti-American, antiglobal demagoguery. These men are not real leftists; they are not true socialists, Marxists, or social democrats, though each was popularly elected. They are populists who cater to the mob, and they have capitalized brilliantly on the inability of the United States to cultivate potential allies to the social-democrat center and the sensible left. To lead again in the Americas, the United States must learn to transcend its traditionally Cuba-obsessed, Cold War view of the hemisphere—which Washington too often sees as a battleground between leftist socialism and rightward capitalism. To help our half of the world escape from *chavismo,* U.S. leaders must find a Third Way to work with leftist social democracies to heal the divide between haves and have-nots.

When talking to the rest of the world, the United States would do better to stress its best values, rather than its best interests. Around the globe many people see the United States of America as selfish and insular, obsessed with its own material well-being. This is ironic, in a way: As private citizens the people of the United States can be the most generous in the world. U.S. citizens, corporations, charities, and colleges gave away $71 billion in 2004—much more than Europeans give in private philanthropy and far more than the $20 billion the U.S. government gave out in foreign aid. With much justification, Americans see themselves as a kind and compassionate nation of freedom, democracy, hope, and opportunity—values the United States holds up as a model for the rest of the world.

But this is not how the world sees America. Contrary to popular belief, the generosity of private citizens in the United States is not exactly matched by its government. While the U.S. government spends more total dollars on foreign aid than does any other nation, the United States also is the world's richest economy—so Americans have the most to give. In fact, the United States ranks second to *last* among the world's industrialized nations in the percentage of national income devoted to foreign aid. The countries of the European Union devote about three times as much of their economies to foreign aid. As the Bush administration ran up its $500 billion tab for the war in Iraq, U.S. foreign aid dropped 20 percent, while EU assistance to poor nations rose. The world looks at this pattern and sees a United States obsessed with war—while Europe and Japan devote an ever bigger share of their national incomes to address poverty, disease, environmental issues, and disaster relief in the developing world.

When I travel in the United States, three complaints I hear most often from Americans are as follows: First, "Why does everyone in the world hate us, when we give away so much tax money to other countries?" Second, "Why can't they solve their own problems?" And third, "Shouldn't we spend that money to address our own problems here at home?"

Here are the answers of a Mexican president: First of all, the world appreciates American generosity, both public and private. But it has been half a century since the Marshall Plan and the vision of FDR, Truman, and Eisenhower that rebuilt Europe and Japan; now the governments of these countries do more for others than does the United States, the wealthiest country on earth. If America wants to lead again in the world, the best place to start would be with a new Marshall Plan to lift up the poorest countries of our hemisphere.

We *can* solve our own problems in the developing world, and the United States is not to blame for them. But the United States benefited enormously from building up Europe and Asia after World War II, and it gained even more by opening markets like Mexico to free trade. As the world's biggest economy, the United States would gain more than any nation if it can turn poor nations into business partners, as John F. Kennedy sought to do with his unfulfilled dream of an Alliance for Progress in the Americas.

The United States will, of course, do as it likes with its tax dollars. No doubt America will continue to invest in the educational systems, scientific advances, highways, airports, military strength, and infrastructure that make the United States the mightiest and richest nation on earth. But the problems of the developing world are absolutely staggering. Here I am not talking about just Mexico, which is now the most prosperous country in Latin America. But around the world today, *a majority of human beings live on less than two dollars a day*—billions of families in Africa, Haiti, Central and South America, Asia—and, yes, still too many in our Mexico. As you read this, think about the fact that on this day thirty thousand children will die of poverty—*thirty thousand* little girls and boys just like the children of your family or your neighborhood, and mine. It is mind-boggling. Thirty thousand children will die today, another thirty thousand tomorrow, another thirty thousand the next day and every day, until we take action against starvation, malnutrition, and disease to solve the economic problems that produce these ills. To this the richest and most powerful nation on earth cannot be indifferent. Regardless of what problems any of our nations face at home, the United States must join with the world to heal our global divide.

America must lead in this, because America can. The United States is not required to do this—the problems of the world are not America's fault, any more than the man fallen at the side of the road is the fault of the Good Samaritan. The Samaritan stops to help the man not because he is to blame for the poor man's condition but because it is in the power of the Samaritan to aid his fellow man. He was among our faith's first "men for others"; in his spirit America and all of us must build Nations for Others.

Europe is doing this, even as I write these words. My experience with foreign leaders yielded this surprise: EU nations are much more focused on values and social equity, while the United States is more focused on interests. When Mexico negotiates a trade agreement in the EU, European leaders are primarily concerned with how the agreement will affect social conditions. Will the growth from trade protect our environment? Will Mexico invest the gains in education, health care, and aid to the poor? Will trade with Europe help Mexico build a better country and improve its quality of life?

In contrast, trade agreements with the United States are all about the best business deal, driven by that hard-bargaining Yankee business sense: What's the best deal we can make for the United States? How can we get the most products for the lowest cost? How will trade advance the interests of U.S. consumers, exporters, farmers, and citizens?

My faith, my family, and my life have taught me that the best way to be loved is to love. There is a way to get the world to love America: It is for America to love the world.

ON A SUNNY MORNING in May 2004, the same month we withdrew our ambassador from Havana, my attorney general came to see me. "We have a little problem in Mexico City," he said.

The *desafuero* issue began as a simple dispute over a piece of land in the bustling neighborhood of Santa Fe, the richest and most modern corporate suburb of the city, where the city government of Mayor Andrés Manuel López Obrador wanted to build a private hospital. AMLO's administration had seized access to the hospital site from private property, without going through the procedure laid down in the rules of eminent domain. Soon the issue of this access road would bring hundreds of thousands of protesters into the capital's streets, threatening Mexico's fragile young democracy.

As a matter of law, the dispute was clear: The courts had ruled that the mayor had no right to take the private property. So if AMLO would not relent, the federal government was required by law to step in and enforce the rules on behalf of the landowner. López Obrador, by then gearing up for his 2006 presidential campaign, was always looking for any opportunity to embarrass me in public, anxious to provoke the same sort of confrontations that had made me famous for standing up to Salinas. So AMLO refused to negotiate. When threatened with prosecution by federal authorities, the mayor claimed his electoral rights to run as the PRD's presidential candidate and asserted the protection of government immunity—or *fuero*—that automatically protects Mexico's elected officials from being put in jail for such legalities.

In Congress the PAN and PRI—the two largest blocs of congressional votes—were in agreement, for once. Allied against AMLO's illegal actions, this majority coalition moved to pass a congressional *desafuero* to strip López Obrador of his immunity. The PRD leader allegedly was breaking the law after all; the PAN and PRI were both law-and-order parties with no interest in protecting AMLO from his crime, however minor. But deimmunizing López Obrador with a *desafuero* would force the federal government to put the popular Mexico City mayor in jail—and with a criminal record, López Obrador would no longer be able to qualify as a presidential candidate in 2006.

The wily mayor had the other parties on the horns of the bull. On one hand, our administration was 100 percent committed to the rule of law, so we were required to strip him of immunity with the *desafuero* and prosecute AMLO for his crime. If the federal government interfered with the right of the courts to prosecute him, *we* could be in violation of the law, for tampering with the mandate of the judiciary. On the other hand, my government believed in democracy, and López Obrador was the clear favorite in the race to succeed me. How would it look if we allowed the letter of the law to knock him out of contention?

The optics of the specific case were bad, too. López Obrador had chosen his battleground well: The legal violation was at most a fairly minor technicality, pitting a populist mayor working to build a hospital against a well-to-do landowner who, people figured, probably just wanted more money for his lot. Certainly it was not a major crime like the corruption case, where AMLO's top aides had been caught on videotape stuffing dollars into briefcases. Looking to deflect attention from the bribery scandal, López Obrador seized gleefully on the issue, posing as the martyr of democracy—the *desafuero* of Congress, Andrés Manuel said, was yet another *complot*, a political conspiracy by powerful forces in the Fox government that feared the champion of the poor and wanted to bar him from the presidency.

AMLO's supporters agreed with him. By the spring of 2005, mobs of protesters had taken to the streets in the mayor's political base of Mexico City. Our nation's capital was frozen in gridlock. The international media loved the story of the crusading, self-styled Robin Hood. The *desafuero* issue sent the radical leftist even higher in the polls.

Late that spring, I went to Rancho San Cristóbal one weekend to ponder the issue. It was a critical moment for Mexican democracy: If we followed the letter of the law, accepted the *desafuero* of Congress, and let the courts try López Obrador, they might send him to jail. Then AMLO would become even more of a martyr. Many radicals, from Adolf Hitler and Hugo Chávez to good men like Vaclav Havel, Nelson Mandela, and Mexican president Francisco Madero came to power after a stint in jail. My roots were in the civil-disobedience movement, and I knew its dynamics. When Henry David Thoreau went to jail rather than pay war taxes to protest the U.S. invasion of Mexico, Ralph Waldo Emerson visited him in his cell and asked Thoreau, "David, what are you doing in there?" The author of "Civil Disobedience" looked out through the bars and replied calmly, "The question is, Ralph, what are you doing out there?"

In the end you could have argued either side, rule of law or democracy. As I walked the paths of my youth and rode horseback on high on the *cerro,* the choice was very clear. The next day I called my team and told them that we needed to find a loophole to drop the case. Our legal wizards pored through the statutes and found a way to reverse the proceedings, so that the judiciary would have to revise the case and Congress would have to back out of the *desafuero.* I met with Andrés Manuel and told him he was off the hook. AMLO got his immunity—and his victory. His supporters rejoiced in the streets; my advisers worried that I looked weak. My poll numbers suffered for a bit, and López Obrador's jumped even higher.

But in my heart I knew that Mexico had won, even though AMLO had been allowed to thumb his nose at the law. Our democracy was intact, and the 2006 elections would be free and fair. No one could complain of being cheated out of the chance to run. Now it would be up to the PAN's candidate to beat AMLO fair and square on his own, so that our democracy didn't end up in the hands of another Hugo Chávez.

WITH AMLO STILL the favorite to succeed me, running as the anti-Fox, a rebel within my own party, Felipe Calderón, quit my cabinet to challenge my much better-known interior minister in a free-for-all for the PAN presidential nomination. But with my own poll numbers down, common wisdom in Mexico City at the time was that the PAN would lose in 2006. Most thought the choice would be between a leftward lurch to the PRD or a return to the PRI, where a growing number of young, reform-minded leaders had won governorships and swept the midterm congressional elections.

If Andrés Manuel López Obrador had been in my shoes, there would have been no dilemma at all. He had a reputation for recklessness with the law dating back to 1996 protests at Pemex refineries, where rocks were thrown and people injured. This is what defines Hugo-style *populismo*: this utter disrespect for any law but the strongman's own opinion.

As 2005 wore on, things looked good for AMLO. Chávez allies like Evo Morales won the presidency in Bolivia and were running strong in Ecuador, Nicaragua, and Peru; the leftist-populist tide was engulfing Latin America. The United States was too immersed in the Iraq War to worry; besides, any effort by Bush to rein in Chávez would only have backfired, because the U.S. president was by then terribly unpopular in Latin America. "We need to be bolder in confronting *chavismo*," I told my team. It was up to Mexico to promote the only real answer to poverty: sound market policies to create jobs and income for the poor and fund the social programs that build human capital. Just as Andrés Manuel López Obrador picked his fight with me, it was time to draw a clear line between democracy and Hugo's populism, so that the people could see the real issue at stake in the Americas. Would our region have presidents who respect the rule of law, democratic institutions, and sound economics? Or would we revert to authoritarian regimes that might spend us back into debt, devaluation, and economic crisis? More than anyone in our society, the poor would pay the cost if Latin America went back to economies run by strongmen and their cronies.

I couldn't criticize AMLO directly for his *chavismo*, because he was a presidential candidate. As much as I would have loved to roll up my sleeves and wade into the 2006 campaign, I had to stay strictly out of the electoral process. This I did, right up until I handed over power. Unlike in the United States, where a Ronald Reagan or a Bill Clinton can campaign for George H. W. Bush or Al Gore, Mexican presidents cannot legally play a public role in the campaign to succeed themselves—ironic, I know, in a country where the presidency had always been determined by the behind-the-scenes *dedazo*. But then, it was exactly this culture that we were trying to change.

I did, however, have the right to defend the policies I believed in and the values I shared with the PAN and the reformers within the opposition parties: a free and democratic Mexico, the rule of law, clean government, respect for human dignity, and vigorous programs to combat poverty. Ferociously I began to promote the results of our democracy: the sound economy we had achieved through fiscal discipline, social-welfare programs to cure the sick and aid the poor, information technology to teach our young people, housing for first-time homeowners, and scholarships to keep kids in school.

On the international front, I was free to speak out. At summits I took every opportunity to advocate clearly for free-market policies; showing what sound economics could do to fund social justice; arguing for globalism, NAFTA, and the Free Trade Area of the Americas—all of which put me on the side of North America. This was a red cape to Hugo—he has a blind hatred of George W. Bush and the United States. It is easy to get that bull to charge.

The Mexican people watched all this with growing interest. Our vast and fast-growing middle class by then included many of the former poor and working class, with their first-ever homes, cars and refrigerators—and television sets, to watch the whole thing on the evening news. They began to realize that Mexico could soon go the way of Venezuela and the other chaotic, crisis-ridden regimes of South America, where Hugo's *chavismo* was spreading like wildfire. We had already withdrawn Mexico's ambassador from Cuba to protest Castro's meddling in our elective process. When Hugo Chávez began attacking me as George Bush's "puppy"—ironic, because if I was George's puppy, I hardly would have bit him on the arm on Iraq—Hugo dropped his ally AMLO neatly into a trap. We pulled our ambassador out of Caracas, and I went on TV to protest Hugo's offensive remarks. Even in AMLO's base in Mexico City, the crowds cheered their president on in the feud with Chávez, chanting, *"¡México! ¡México! ¡México!"*

After the chapter of the *desafuero,* we had shaken up our own team at

Los Pinos and gotten back to the basics of communicating the key benefits that our democracy had brought to Mexico: housing, education, health care, and poverty reduction, the four areas where citizens gave us the most credit. We couldn't get involved in the 2006 election—our administration would remain strictly nonpartisan to the end. But we could certainly do a much better job of communicating the good things that democracy had done for the country.

I gathered my team around me—stalwarts like Ramón Muñoz, our wizard of government innovation; our scheduling chief, Emilio Goicoechea, now the Mexican ambassador to Canada; new recruits like Rubén Aguilar, the revolution theologian and former Jesuit seminarian who had been with the *sandinistas* in Nicaragua, by then my presidential spokesman; Roberto Mourey, my new communications director, a top marketing executive for my old enemies at Pepsi (this was treason for me, but I solved it by making Roberto switch to drinking Diet Coke). As we prepared for our version of the 2005 State of the Union Address, we created an entirely new strategy to get back to our roots of the 2000 democracy movement, when we had been the brand of hope and change in Mexico.

Once in government, we had fallen into the trap of allowing our opponents to constantly harp on the differences between the high hopes we had raised for democracy in 2000 and what we had achieved so far by 2005. In essence it was Fox versus Fox—President Fox of 2005 was running against Candidate Fox of 2000. We needed to change that dialectic to the real question: Were Mexicans better off under democracy than they were before 2000?

We had made good progress—millions of families in their first homes, 6.2 million kids kept in school by scholarships, a 30 percent reduction in extreme poverty, 25 million new families covered by health insurance. The road of democracy wasn't perfect; it was sometimes slow and messy, the results took time, and once in a while you had protesters in the streets. But surely it was better to keep going down that road than to turn back to the failed, walled-off, debt-ridden, authoritarian Mexico of the past.

We cut a new series of brief television speeches and a short, punchy State of the Union Address. This was a stark contrast to the traditional style of our Congress, which called for a lengthy, tiresome annual Informe from the president to show how much he had accomplished. (In many political cultures outside the media-savvy United States, if you don't speak for at least two hours, people don't take you seriously.) But the reality is, no one really listens to a speech that rambles on that long.

Instead I zeroed in on our key social reforms and talked about the gradually improving economy. The years of fiscal discipline were finally paying off: Mexico was growing faster now. Our balanced budget had produced low inflation, reduced our foreign debt from $75 billion to $40 billion, and brought interest rates down to affordable levels. Our strong peso was giving consumers more buying power for poor people to buy food, and helping working-class families to gain a foothold in prosperity. Now 97 percent of Mexican homes had electricity and 90 percent had telephones. Millions of families had bought their first refrigerators, computers, washing machines, and cars. Democracy was working—we just had to make sure people knew it.

As I walked into the congressional palace of San Lázaro in September 2005 to relaunch our administration with the annual Informe, our job-approval numbers were still lower than they had been in our honeymoon. Part of this was due to AMLO's *desafuero* issue, the slow recovery of the economy after 9/11, and our own shortcomings in Congress, which had blocked many of our plans for economic reform. But I was also paying a political price for the subject where my administration earned its lowest achievement scores: fighting crime.

CHAPTER 20

AT THE FEET OF THE HORSES

Narcotraffic has become a chronic problem for Mexico. It is tragic, the legacy of seventy-one years of corruption, and we have only ourselves, and our leaders, to blame. But to some extent Mexico is also a victim of our geography.

Until the late 1960s, we had little or no history of drugs in our country. But Mexico has the bad luck to lie "at the feet of the horses." From the 1970s to the 1990s, Mexico became the transit route between the drug consumers of the world's biggest and richest importer of illegal narcotics—the United States—and the vast and highly organized drug cartels of the world's biggest drug exporters—the Andean nations, especially Colombia, Peru, and Bolivia, which grew and exported the vast majority of the world's cocaine.

Though there was much less drug use in Mexico than in most other countries, our country became the preferred route of the *narcotraficantes*, first by land, then by air and sea. The more fiercely our authorities fought the drug cartels, the more sophisticated the gangs became in developing new distribution channels, buying new weapons, bribing judges and law-enforcement officials, and founding sophisticated new criminal organizations. Soon Mexico had its own homegrown drug gangs, which began to manufacture, grow, and move their own drug exports inside our country for sale to the United States—and now, sadly, to more and more young drug abusers here in Mexico, a new phenomenon that is deeply troubling to our family-oriented, child-protective society.

Remember, it is the narcotics customer in North America who funds all this criminal activity from South America to Mexico, funneling billions upon billions of dollars into poorer and more corrupt Latin American countries, where the money of U.S. drug consumers purchases the automatic weapons and pays the bribes by the cartels to buy off the police and the prison wardens. The *narcotraficantes* are a tremendous threat to the fragile democracies of countries like Mexico and Colombia, presenting enormous challenges to leaders like Andrés Pastrana and me—or brave new presidents like Colombia's Álvaro Uribe and Mexico's Felipe Calderón—as they work to assert the rule of law in countries where police officers and prison guards, too, work for a tenth of U.S. wages. Then there is the constant threat of assassination of honest judges, elected officials, police chiefs, and drug-enforcement officials who risk their lives daily against the cartels, from the U.S.-Mexico border to the Andes Mountains.

The corrupt climate of Mexico's past made things even worse. During the crack epidemic of the 1980s—and again with the resurgence of demand for marijuana and laboratory drugs like methamphetamines and ecstasy in the United States during the 1990s—the Mexican drug cartels grew stronger and bolder, competing against the Colombian *narcotraficantes* with firepower and influence. For a police officer making eight hundred dollars a month, a bribe of ten thousand dollars was a year's salary. Many high-ranking Mexican officials made less than a street cop in the United States. Some could be bought for a bribe of fifty thousand or hundred thouand dollars. A cartel leader could easily afford to pay a judge or prison warden a million dollars to buy a "get-out-of-jail-free card." Soon powerful Mexican cartels in mountainous states like Sinaloa and Guerrero or border cities like Tijuana and Ciudad Juárez, matched the Colombians for brutality, as the *narcos* fought among themselves for control of the most lucrative corridors to the United States.

When I was elected in 2000, we immediately cracked down hard on the *narcotraficantes,* arresting twenty top cartel leaders, fifty subchiefs, and a total of seventy thousand narcotraffickers over the six years of my presidency. But when you shine the light in the corners, the cockroaches run out. The pressure we applied resulted in a terrible wave of violence among cartel leaders, as they squabbled among themselves for the spoils. Who would take over for the leaders we had arrested? Drug traffickers sought to outdo each other in showy violence against their rivals, dismembering the corpses of their competitors and displaying their cojones by gunning down police chiefs in broad daylight.

It was not so much the number of crimes but the vivid and brutal nature of the cartels that shocked and horrified the nation and drew headlines in the foreign press. Cartel leaders, savvy to the media effects of theatrical violence, knew just what placement they would get in the next day's tabloids when they rolled a beheaded enemy's skull out onto the floor of a crowded nightclub. Like any sophisticated terrorists, the *narcos* wanted the shock value of their violence on television, where gory pictures were designed to intimidate their *narcotraficante* rivals, impress foot soldiers and subchiefs to recruit them for the cartel, and strike fear into the hearts of those police chiefs, journalists, or authorities who were courageous enough to confront them.

To this Molotov cocktail of drugs and cartel violence, Mexico added the surge of street crime that occurs every time our economy fails to keep up with the job creation that a young, developing nation needs to keep its youth gainfully employed. After 9/11 our tourism industry was shattered, world financial markets were reeling, and big corporations in the troubled U.S. economy stopped investing on the margins in overseas markets. Inevitably the slowdown led to an increase in robberies, car thefts, burglaries, and a string of high-profile kidnappings from late 2001 to 2004. When our policies of fiscal discipline and economic stability turned the economy around and began creating more jobs in 2005 and 2006, non-drug-related crimes dropped 15 percent. In fact, according to the United Nations survey of the number of crimes per hundred thousand residents in the world's countries, Mexico today has an overall crime rate less than half that of the United States, with far fewer aggravated assaults, rapes, and crimes with firearms.

But we have a higher murder rate than the United States—even after five years of anticorruption reforms and our crackdown on the drug cartels, there was still far too much crime in Mexico. As we geared up to turn around our public communications with the September 2005 Informe, crime was the talk of every neighborhood, factory floor, and office building in the country, particularly in the big cities. With the headline-grabbing decapitations of the more daring drug cartels front and center, Mexico was painted by the media as though it were Chicago in the 1920s.

Despite the tragedy of September 11, my "trust" speech before the U.S. Congress on September 7, 2001, opened up a new chapter of cooperation with U.S. officials on crime and security matters—a partnership we accelerated rapidly after 9/11, by clamping down on both sides of our border. First I ordered Mexico's armed forces on *centinela* or "red alert"; now we invested heavily in high-tech X-ray equipment, optical scanners, and a new system of electronic visas to control the million people a day who cross our northern frontier. We also tightened control of our southern border. While much is said about the job-hungry Mexican immigrants who cross into the United States and Canada each year, few realize that Mexico receives somewhere between 300,000 and 400,000 immigrants a year from Guatemala, El Salvador, Nicaragua, and the rest of Central America—nearly as many as the half million or so Mexicans who go north to work every year.

Early in my administration, we had a major breakthrough when we convinced the Bush administration and the U.S. Congress to drop the humiliating and useless process of so-called drug certification. During Mexico's corrupt past, the United States had insisted on "certifying" whether Mexico was making valid efforts against narcotraffic. But now that Mexico had a clean government committed to cracking down on corruption and the cartels, the process was a colossal waste of time—the sort of nonsense bureaucracies live for. Drug certification made for bad blood between the two countries, as each blamed the other for a problem we both shared, yet here we were with our top law-enforcement agencies wasting precious resources pointing fingers. We agreed with the White House that from now on, drug enforcement would be neither country's fault and both nations' responsibility—a shared burden. We put our top experts together with the FBI, DEA, Scotland Yard, Interpol, and the excellent local law-enforcement authorities in U.S. border cities like San Diego, where Mexican officials now work closely and well with U.S. police.

Another area where we made progress hand in hand with the United States was the extradition of drug criminals wanted for crimes north of the border. This is a thorny area in Mexican law, primarily because the United States allows the death penalty, while Mexico and most modern democracies do not. It took years of complex legal maneuvers to get around the constitutional barriers erected by previous Mexican governments. They had been afraid to be seen extraditing criminals to the United States by anti-American nationalist elements; Mexican presidents thought it would make them look weak, that extradition in some way undercut our nation's sovereignty.

Early in my presidency, I called the White House to try to find a solution.

"George, I want to talk to you about the death penalty," I said.

"The death penalty is very important to me, Vicente," President Bush replied.

"We both know where we stand," I said, treading cautiously. I had canceled one visit to the United States to protest the planned execution of a Mexican national, and this whole subject had been a touchy one between me and the former governor of Texas, where several Mexicans had been on death row. "But, George, we can agree to disagree on the death penalty and still work something out to extradite these drug dealers."

I cared deeply about the death-penalty issue, because I am committed to protecting human life in all its forms—but I cared not a whit for the nationalist pandering that had led our former leaders to hang on to drug dealers as symbols of Mexican machismo. To me it simply made good sense to rid Mexico of a cartel leader who could offer a million-dollar bribe to our underpaid prison wardens. For this reason we also rotated captured drug lords from one prison to the next, to avoid getting them too comfortable with the guards and wardens.

Bush and I, together with our legal experts and diplomats, worked out a deal in which the United States agreed to forgo the death penalty and give life sentences to cartel leaders who had committed crimes in both countries. We were able to extradite sixty-three drug lords to safer U.S. prisons. Immediately after taking office, President Calderón used these legal tools to extradite fifteen more drug kingpins. Now he is leading the most aggressive war on drugs in Mexico's history—with some big successes. And late in my presidency, after we had solved knotty legal issues around extradition and built trust with U.S. officials, the bilateral partnership between Mexico and the United States produced some big breaks.

THE SUN beat down mercilessly on the sea as it lapped lazily against the *Dock Holiday,* the forty-three-foot sportfishing yacht named playfully for the Old West gunfighter. In the cabin cruiser's lee frolicked a young man in his thirties, fit and tanned, clad only in a weak mustache and a rather hideous pair of beige and green plaid boxer shorts. The boat had gone out deep off the Baja Coast, where the good tuna could be found, fifteen miles or more from the shore. The young man liked to have the best of everything—

the prettiest girls, the fastest cars, the best liquor, the finest yachts. And the best fishing was out deep—in international waters.

Suddenly there was a commotion on deck, a scramble for weapons, binoculars, clothes, the dumping of evidence, the cursing of navigational charts. "This is the United States Coast Guard!" came the tinny voice of a loudspeaker, echoing over the Pacific swell. Out of nowhere, a 169-foot former navy patrol boat loomed on the horizon, manned by coast guard personnel in crisp uniforms. There followed a quick, disciplined casting of lines, a locking and loading of weapons, a monotone reading of rights. It was "El Tigrillo," the "wildcat"—enforcer of the Tijuana drug cartel, who was widely reported to have been linked by the DEA to the slaying of a brave Roman Catholic cardinal. Law-enforcement agencies and newspaper accounts also suspected his cartel of involvement in orchestrating a massacre in a Puerto Vallarta disco and alleged beheadings of enemy cartel leaders. Media reports claimed that he and his family had made a splash by allegedly hanging the decapitated head of a rival from a highway overpass with a sign reading WELCOME TO TIJUANA. El Tigrillo, proud playboy scion of one of Mexico's most ruthless drug clans, one of the world's most wanted men—hastily covered himself with a coral T-shirt and a pair of orange flip-flops. It was in this style that Francisco Javier Arellano Félix was hauled onto the pier at San Diego in DEA handcuffs with law-enforcement officers on either side of him like proud fisherman, weighing in the catch of the day.

EL TIGRILLO WAS one of the most wanted men in the world, but nobody wanted him more than we did. In 1993–94, late in the presidency of Carlos Salinas, the newly empowered Mexican drug gangs had ran amok, with impunity. Francisco Javier was a member of the powerful Arellano Félix clan, who ran Baja California's notorious Tijuana cartel. He was perhaps the most vicious of the lot—no small distinction in that family. Then barely into his twenties, according to newspaper accounts El Tigrillo was linked by U.S. drug-enforcement officials to the planning of the 1993 gangland-style execution of Roman Catholic Cardinal Juan Jesús Posadas Ocampo, whose body was riddled with fourteen gunshots at the Guadalajara International Airport. The former government had the nerve to blame the assassination on "accidental crossfire," claiming that the cardinal had been mistaken for a drug lord. The reality, according to media accounts and some law-enforcement officials, likely was much simpler: The cardinal had talked openly about his suspicions of collusion between the cartels and corrupt authorities; in 1993, someone decided to make sure the cardinal never spoke again.

When I came to the presidency, we opened a commission of inquiry to investigate the cardinal's murder, headed by brave Deputy Attorney General María de la Luz Lima Malvido. Her name means "of the light"; María's reward for shining the light of truth on the cartels was the abduction of her teenage daughter and two incidents where her sons were shot at in their cars. So when my attorney general, Eduardo Medina Mora, called me in May 2006 with a triumphant, "They got him!" it mattered little to me whether El Tigrillo rotted in a jail in San Diego, a U.S. federal prison, or the worst *cárcel* in Mexico. For me, the issues of extradition and antinarcotics cooperation were never about national pride; they were about putting men like that in prison for the rest of their lives, preferably far from their home turf, where they had no connections and could not buy influence.

This cooperation worked both ways. Earlier that same year, in January 2006, we discovered the infamous "drug tunnel" dug by the Arellano Félix gang from Tijuana to San Diego. Ironically, Mexico was vilified for this during the 2006 immigration debate; the hue and cry of the American talk-show hosts was, "The Mexicans are digging tunnels under our border!" But the drug tunnel actually was discovered by *our* officers at the Mexican end, then brought to the attention of law enforcement on the U.S. side, so we could coordinate a joint bust. It was one more big break in the case against men like Arellano Félix, whose arrest came as a result of an anonymous tip to the DEA that May.

Anti-Mexico voices in the United States often seize on these high-profile busts as evidence that ours is a dangerous, drug-infested country whose government is run by corrupt drug lords. In fact the opposite is true: Mexican drug cartels are in the news primarily *because* administrations like Felipe Calderón's and mine worked so closely and publicly with U.S. authorities to crack down, arrest cartel leaders, and extradite these thugs. To suggest otherwise denigrates the courage of the police chiefs who have been slain, the prosecutors whose families have been kidnapped, the crusading journalists whose offices are bombed. Remember, these brave Mexicans are more at risk than anyone in the fight against drugs. Had we swept drug crime under the rug like previous governments, Mexico's image would have been better—but the drugs and corruption would have been worse.

Change is pain.

The international extradition system needs work, not all of it on Mexico's side. The deluxe condominiums of Miami and the South of France are rife with corrupt former presidents of Latin American countries, drug lords, and money launderers. The United States under President Bush has been unwilling to sign the treaty empowering the Court of Rome to deal with human-rights violations, corruption cases, and extraditions for high crimes—perhaps for fear that the international tribunal could exert jurisdiction over the abuses at Abu Ghraib or Guantánamo Bay.

But in 1999 a courageous and brilliant Spanish judge named Baltasar Garzón tried exiled Chilean dictator Augusto Pinochet in absentia and put out an international warrant for his arrest. Living in luxurious exile, the arrogant Pinochet was arrested as he was recovering from minor surgery in a London hospital, on charges of torture, kidnappings, and the reign of terror from his era of *los desaparecidos*—"the disappeared."

The world's dictators and human-rights abusers have taken note: Ever since then Castro has stopped traveling much outside of Cuba. Long before his health began to fail, Castro started skipping summits of Spanish-speaking countries that he normally attended—in Peru in 2001, the Dominican Republic in 2002, Bolivia in 2003. Were the United States and the world to join together in acknowledging the Court of Rome as the ultimate tribunal for such cases, we could go a long way toward assuring that the most heinous crimes against humanity are punished. This would make it much easier for nations like ours to extradite dangerous criminals and larcenous ex-leaders that are wanted abroad.

Clamping down on the Rio Grande after 9/11 did some good for both the United States and Mexico on fighting drugs and crime, but it was not without cost. Hundreds of billions of dollars' worth of legitimate cargo crosses back and forth every year between the United States and Mexico, the most lucrative border trade on the planet. But freight that once took twenty minutes to cross now takes an hour and a half. In the months after September 11, it was worse, as perishable items like broccoli and lettuce rotted in freight cars and truck beds halted along the border.

September 11 also exacted a human cost. Americans who hated Latinos, immigrants, and dark-skinned foreigners now had a pretext for acting out their xenophobia. Suddenly Latins, Asians, Indians, African Americans—just about anybody with black hair, olive skin, a dark mustache, or a foreign accent—were stopped by airport security guards who profiled them as Arabs. From L.A. to London, radio airwaves and TV talk shows swelled with fear and hate, demanding that the politicians crack down on immigration. Send tanks to the Rio Grande, they said, build a wall, "secure our borders."

The Mexican consulates responded by issuing identification cards called *matrículas consulares* to our undocumented immigrants in the United States, Canada, and abroad. This consular ID does not protect an immigrant from deportation, but the *matrícula* at least aids security by proving to authorities exactly who our immigrants really are—that they are honest Mexican citizens in good standing at home, and not terrorists. The *matrículas* were controversial in the United States; even today Bank of America is pilloried by the xenophobes in the United States for accepting our consular IDs as the basis for issuing credit cards. But the *matrículas* enable our workers to earn housing, health care, bank accounts, and insurance—and to deal with the police as law-abiding members of society, instead of criminals.

Clamping down on the border, of course, did not reduce the demand for drugs in the United States. But it had the unintended effect of increasing drug abuse in Mexico. When the cartels were unable to get their poison into the United States, they "liquidated their inventory" inside our borders, spawning a larger consumer market for drugs among our young people. The *narcotraficantes* did what Coca-Cola used to do to expand the market for soft drinks: They gave away free samples at shopping malls and soccer games, selling their oversupply on the cheap to a whole new generation of Mexican youth.

Here the newfound affluence of the Mexican middle class hurt us, as kids used the buying power of our stronger peso to sample this exotic, dangerous lifestyle. Mexico's burgeoning appetite for recreational drugs also came home for Christmas and Easter from the United States—ironically, too many immigrant youths were learning bad habits from their peers in East L.A. Along with the many good things Mexico learned from the United States—democracy, job skills, better sanitation, education, productivity—it also imported some negative aspects of the modern American lifestyle, from violent video games and misogynistic hip-hop lyrics to more serious problems like drug abuse and gang violence.

I tell you these things not to excuse my government's failures to deal with security issues or to blame Mexico's crime problem on the United States. Mexico has its own long history of corruption, violence, and lawlessness to blame for this epidemic. But I want you to have a complete picture of the special challenges our country faces on crime and drugs. It was certainly my biggest disappointment as president. We struggled valiantly; many good law-enforcement officials risked and gave their lives in the battle. Ultimately my government performed insufficiently in this area, and the buck stops here.

Again we come to the delicate balance in a new democracy between peace and security, between the rule of law and human freedom. I liken it to horseback riding, where you must carefully pull on one rein, then the other, in order to keep the horse heading down the path. My critics would say that I gave society too much rein altogether, and they may be right. But I agree with the experts who hold that the best law enforcement is the "internal police officer" inside every citizen. Until each person polices his or her own behavior within their own hearts, no amount of police activity outside will ever keep us safe.

In Mexico all too often, our citizens justify stealing because they are poor. They say that bribery is acceptable, because that's the way things work. Even murder is justified, because the killer was under the influence of alcohol. In Mexico our people too often say, "She takes a little bit from the till, because her children need food," or "I killed him because I was drunk." Our job is not just to enforce the laws on the streets but also to instill the rule of law in people's hearts. When our citizens begin to think of themselves as free owners of a society where they have a stake in Mexico's future—only then will they take responsibility for the discipline that goes with that privilege.

This is a common challenge for new democracies. The old order, as dysfunctional and corrupt as it was, is no longer in place. The sudden burst of freedom is blamed for every crime. Under iron rule of the Communists in the Soviet Union, apartheid in South Africa, or the military dictatorship of Suharto in Indonesia, the streets of Moscow and Johannesburg and Jakarta were indeed much safer than they are today; one of the things about a police state is that there is always a cop on the corner. Certainly the "nostalgia effect" has led some fledgling democracies to abandon freedom and return to authoritarian regimes—a trend often fueled by the rise of crime.

Also, we cannot discount the effect of a suddenly free press. For the first time, citizens of a new democracy see uncensored television and newspaper photos of the bloody crimes that were going on all along under the old regime but never before made it into the government-sanitized news coverage.

By 2006 headlines and TV reports had made crime a major political football, north and south. It played a major role in the Mexican presidential race and dominated the immigration debate in the United States, where Mexico bashing became a favorite sport of U.S. congressional elections.

In Mexico the PRI's candidate, Roberto Madrazo, a throwback to the old dinosaur wing of the former ruling party, cultivated a tough-guy image. He saturated the airwaves with slick TV ads produced by his spin doctors, showing the tall, fit former Tabasco governor jogging down country lanes, pumping his fists through the air like a boxer training for a match. With the dapper gray suits and hoarse voice that reminds one of a movie gangster, Madrazo harped on the crime issue. Early on, common wisdom was that the PAN would fall if my approval numbers did not improve. Pundits predicted that if López Obrador's radicalism scared the Mexican people, the PRI would retake Los Pinos.

Within the PAN, three Fox cabinet ministers dueled in a series of open primaries. The early frontrunner was my interior minister, Santiago Creel, who bore the brunt of public disappointment in the lack of sufficient results on crime. He had also been in charge of negotiating with Congress, so he was pilloried for not having won approval of bills to liberalize the economy. Alberto Cárdenas, my environment secretary and former Jalisco governor, was a formidable contender. Then there was the energetic, outspoken Felipe Calderón, a forty-three-year-old rising star who had been PAN party chairman, a leader in Congress, and my secretary of energy. Felipe made fighting crime and creating jobs the cornerstones of his campaign. He upset Creel in one primary election after the other and swept to a surprise victory for the nomination.

Felipe's upset put to rest any possibility that the opposition could logically accuse me of resurrecting the *dedazo*. A brilliant and outspoken advocate for hard-core *panistas* who had often been critical of my presidency, Calderón had resigned from my cabinet after only eight months in protest of our administration's direction. By barring members of my cabinet from running for president while on the job, I forced them to choose between staying in government and resigning to devote full-time to the campaign. It backfired with Felipe, who criticized Creel and me sharply for our government's attitude. I respected this independence in Felipe, who named his own autobiography *El Hijo Desobediente*—a subtle reminder to Mexicans that Calderón had rebelled against the Fox administration and was very much his own man. Felipe won the primaries by promising to take the PAN back to its roots and be a more aggressive agent of change—more Fox than Fox.

An articulate and skillful debater who spoke fluently without notes, Calderón used clever props in his televised debates, displaying white cards with key campaign themes like LIFE SENTENCES FOR DRUG DEALERS. Felipe had assembled a bright young team of PAN mavericks—the smart, good-looking thirty-two-year-old congressman Juan Camilo Mouriño, who became Calderón's presidential chief of staff; automotive businessman and former PAN finance chief Gerardo Ruiz; former Fox cabinet members like our human services secretary Josefina Vásquez, my old comrade-in-arms and tourism secretary Rodolfo Elizondo; congressman and polling expert Juan Molinar; my brainy chief economic adviser, Dr. Eduardo Sojo, now Mexico's secretary of the economy; and a whole array of bright young advisers like Cesar Nava, Alejandra Soto, Ernesto Cordero, and Max Cortázar.

These sharp youngsters staged their own "yuppie revolution" within the party. Gathering with Starbucks coffee in hand early each morning, the PAN presidential nominee's team plotted out a carefully honed strategy to take advantage of the results our administration had delivered—like housing, health care, education, cleaning up corruption, restoring economic stability, and building democracy. But they differentiated Calderón sharply from my presidency's shortcomings on crime, employment, and the reforms we had been unable to lobby through Congress. Felipe put his brand on the law-and-order issue early, and stressed his experience as a professional politician—with the not-so-subtle message that the intellectual *panista* Calderón would be much better than the clumsy outsider Fox at negotiating with Congress to get things done.

Thus Calderón and his team positioned themselves perfectly to take advantage of any rebound in my popularity—while assuring the public that Felipe Calderón would be better than Vicente Fox in the areas where my government had been less successful.

At Los Pinos we stayed within the strict limits of the law, which forbade the president from mentioning the presidential candidates or parties: I could not even encourage citizens to vote. Soon federal regulators curbed my ability even to speak about the successes of our administration. Ironically, democracy reforms had empowered the Federal Electoral Institute, the IFE, not only to regulate what the candidates could say and do in their advertising but also to set limits on what I as president could say or not say in my own speeches, TV messages, and press conferences. I was sanctioned for infractions as mild as touting the results of a health-care program for immigrants while traveling in rural Washington State. The IFE slapped me down for saying things like, "Mexico is on the right path to the future." In fact, all three political parties had ads yanked off the air by the IFE, who considered various commercials too negative, unfair, or inaccurate.

Even though I was sidelined by the IFE rules, our new-style 2005 State of the Union Address, the accompanying Informe TV messages about our progress on social issues, and the slowly improving economy all helped reverse the decline in my job-approval ratings. We stopped feuding with AMLO and started contrasting how far we had come. This resulted in a dramatic turnaround in my own popularity.

My approval ratings had dipped below the 50 percent mark after the drubbing we'd taken during the AMLO *desafuero* fight. But, over time, voters began to feel that I had done the right thing by erring on the side of democracy. By the spring of 2006, when an IFE "gag order" silenced me for the rest of the election period, my favorability ratings had headed back toward the 70 percent peak that I would reach before leaving the presidency.

López Obrador is more a gifted amateur than a professional politician. AMLO had little understanding of the modern paraphernalia of polls, focus groups, and advertising. But he was a talented and passionate orator. Something happens to Andrés Manuel when he gets in the *Zócalo*: He loses all his bearings, like a mad bull in the ring. Frustrated by my rise in the polls, angry about my comments about Hugo Chávez and my speeches calling for Mexico to stay on the path of democracy, he finally lost his temper. Like an angry *toro,* Andrés Manuel charged. In his own version of Black Tuesday, AMLO mounted the podium and lost the presidency.

Red in the face, hair askew, Andrés Manuel shouted hoarsely that Fox should "Shut up, *¡chachalaca!*"—using a rude Mexican term calling me a noisy tropical bird. In that one moment he evoked Mexico's worst fears of a Hugo Chávez, who had called me a "puppy" and George Bush a "donkey." Imagine, while Bill Clinton was defending the results of his administration during the Gore-Bush election of 2000, that George Bush or John McCain had shouted that Bill Clinton should "shut up, you loud-mouthed pig!"

AMLO was trying to relive his moment of victory in the *desafuero,* when it had been good politics for him to position himself as the anti-Fox. But the Vicente Fox of 2005 was in the doldrums; by 2006, I was leaving office on a high note, with poll numbers near 70 percent and some credit for the rebounding economy, democracy, a balanced budget, and significant social changes that touched people's lives. Calderón's team reacted swiftly to AMLO's tirade, crafting a brilliant commercial that in best political-ad fashion repeated Andrés Manuel's ugly outburst—"Shut up, *¡chachalaca!* Shut up, *¡chachalaca!*" The PAN's commercials linked AMLO to similar outbursts from Hugo Chávez, using footage of the Venezuelan generalissimo as he reviewed goose-stepping soldiers, interspersed with scenes of economic crisis and mob rule in Caracas.

It was a chillingly effective view of what life in Mexico would be like under a Chávez-style ranter like Andrés Manuel López Obrador. The portrait it painted of AMLO as *un peligro para México*—"a danger to Mexico"—was unassailably accurate. After all, this was López Obrador in his own words.

Eventually the IFE made the Calderón campaign withdraw the commercial, saying it was too incendiary for calm political debate. But the damage was done. Mexicans had seen AMLO for the intolerant demagogue he might be as president, silencing a popular, democratically elected president by shouting me down in the streets.

Then AMLO compounded his error by arrogantly refusing to attend the first debate against Calderón and Madrazo. Andrés Manuel's negatives soared. Calderón, with his obvious intellect and poised delivery, trounced the old-school PRI politician Madrazo in the debate—the PRI nominee's script-bound delivery and gangster image would eventually drop his party to a distant third place. When Madrazo tried to make an issue of crime, Calderón zinged back that it was Madrazo's corrupt PRI that had given rise to the cartels in the first place. Despite the huge improvements that young, reform-minded governors and local leaders had made in the former ruling party, the choice of the dinosaur Madrazo killed the PRI as a brand in presidential politics in 2006. Madrazo would end up with just 17 percent of the vote in the presidential election, which reduced the PRI to the smallest bloc of votes in Congress—this in a country the Revolutionary Institutional Party had run from top to bottom just six years before. As the clock ticked down to election day, AMLO and Felipe Calderón were neck and neck in the polls. On July 2, 2006, less than half a percentage point would determine the winner.

CHAPTER 21

WALLS OF FEAR, DREAMS OF HOPE

SADLY FOR MEXICO, 2006 was an election year in the United States, too. Now maddeningly intertwined, the issues of terrorism, crime, drugs, security, and the war in Iraq continued to haunt our hopes for immigration reform in Washington. Despite our differences, George Bush and I had talked one-on-one about the upcoming election year as early as November 2005, at the same summit where we stood side by side to defend free trade against Hugo Chávez and Argentina's President Kirchner.

"We're going to push hard for a bill next session," Bush promised, despite the precarious position he faced in Congress. But he was candid about the problems within Republican ranks on Capitol Hill, where the right wing that controlled the U.S. House was bitterly opposed to any bill that allowed immigrants to earn legal status.

"We're in good shape in the Senate. I think we can get a guest-worker bill there," he said. But Bush explained that GOP House members, worried about reelection amid growing public unease over Iraq, fiercely opposed allowing Mexican guest workers in on temporary visas. "The hard-right conservatives in my party just won't move on a guest-worker bill unless we couple it with security measures to tighten control of the border."

Outside, antiglobal rioters threw Molotov cocktails at police and hanged Bush in effigy. Inside, the beleaguered globalist president outlined the White House game plan on immigration. "I want you to be prepared, Vicente, because I know it won't be popular in Mexico," he said tersely. "We are going to have to pass enforcement-only measures first and step up security on the border, before we can even talk to Congress about a guest-worker bill. And . . . ah, Vicente . . ." He paused, obviously uncomfortable. "My people on the Hill tell me that next month the House may vote to build a wall along the Rio Grande."

Congressman Duncan Hunter, now a 2008 U.S. presidential candidate, had filed the bill in his Armed Services Committee in early November. In December, before adjourning for the 2005–2006 holiday season, the U.S. House shocked the world by passing its shameful proposal to build a seven hundred-mile wall along the U.S.-Mexico border, at an initial cost of more than $3 billion.

This was silly, on several levels. First, there were the practical absurdities of the project. The border is nearly two thousand miles long, so a fence of seven hundred miles would hardly keep immigrants out of the United States. (If they wanted to, immigrants could probably figure out how to go *around* it.) The wall's cost estimates now exceed $6 billion and may go over $10 billion—this at a time when the United States is at war halfway around the world, its federal budget deeper in the red than ever before in U.S. history.

Former Israeli chief of staff and national security chief Uzi Dayan of Israel took one look at the plan and laughed. "Don't do it," he told the Americans flatly. "It will not work." Israel, the most security-conscious, militarized state in the world, is building a defense barrier to keep the Palestinians on their side of the West Bank, but it has served only to antagonize and radicalize the people on the other side. Palestinians still enter Israel. The only difference is that now, incensed by the barrier, they have veered even further left to elect the radical Hamas faction to lead them.

We worried that America's new Berlin Wall would do the same. López Obrador and the radical left in Mexico seized on the wall and Bush's subsequent ordering of National Guard troops to the Rio Grande, citing the immigration crackdown as evidence that Fox's policy of "cozying up to the gringos" as "Bush's lapdog" had failed Mexico. The idea of building an American Berlin Wall gave ammunition to Hugo Chávez and his allies, who pointed to the wall as a symbol of U.S. hatred for Latin America. All around the world, people saw the border wall as a monument to the indifference of Bush's wealthy United States to the plight of the poor and downtrodden of "have-not" countries.

I spoke out vehemently against the project, calling it "shameful." We even considered going to the site of the proposed wall, making a dramatic speech like Ronald Reagan in Berlin, when he said, "Mr. Gorbachev, tear down this wall!" But cooler heads prevailed. In early 2006, George Bush called me personally to ask that I not lobby the issue in the United States. "Let me carry the ball on this," Bush said. "You're a foreign head of state, and you coming here to talk about the wall will just inflame the people who don't like Mexico."

Even after Congress passed the fence portion of the bill in early 2006, we were quietly assured by our allies in Washington that the wall might never be built. "Once we figure out what this is going to cost, even the right-wingers will quietly abandon the idea," one Republican congressional leader told our diplomats. "We can't pay for a hot war in Iraq and a Cold War with Mexico."

I still believe this to be true. U.S. taxpayers might balk at the insane cost of the wall, and wiser leaders may someday recognize the negative message that fortifying the border sends to the world at large and to Latinos at home. With the Democrats having taken control of Congress and a pro-reform president in the White House, I hope that Washington may yet defund the wall project and pass a dream five years in the making—a guest-worker program like the earlier plan outlined in the McCain-Kennedy bill.

Such legislation would allow entry only to those temporary workers who can prove they have jobs waiting—jobs that their employers cannot fill inside the United States. It also required that immigrants already in the United States go through a lengthy, serious, and costly process if they want to get on a path to citizenship. This sort of bill would keep many workers home in Mexico to find work in our economy, allowing them to obtain guest-worker permits only when temporary jobs are available in the north.

Politicians are nationalists in election years; usually they become internationalists only after they are safely reelected. But in 2006 global thinkers like John McCain led fearlessly on the immigration issue, even at their political peril. Rabid Mexico haters like Colorado Congressman and 2008 presidential candidate Tom Tancredo, Arizona Congressman J. D. Hayworth and talk-show fixture Pat Buchanan fumed on the airwaves. On the Democratic side, Senator Kennedy and Speaker of the House Nancy Pelosi faced down the anti-immigrant contingent from blue-collar union states, arguing the issue as a matter of civil rights and equal treatment for poor working people who were being treated as second-class citizens.

In the Senate many pro-business, pro-family Republicans backed immigration reform, both on economic grounds and as a matter of moral principle. Hispanics also were an important constituency. Latino values of hard work, family, and faith make Hispanics potential Republicans; leaders like Senator Mel Martinez, national GOP chairman, argued forcefully for reform. Republicans could not afford to lose this massive voting bloc—as Pete Wilson had done with Proposition 187 in California, utterly destroying the GOP in California until the election of Governor Arnold Schwarzenegger, who had a majority of Latino voters.

For Democrats, too, immigration reform was a matter of both principle and politics. Bush had done better with Latinos than had previous Republicans, gaining record percentages of Hispanic voters to win the Texas governorship and two presidential campaigns. Democrats wanted an issue to bring Hispanics home. As Latino voting strength grows and the U.S. population swings to the South and Southwest, the descendants of Mexican immigrants have become a core Democratic constituency.

By the spring of 2006, the experts in Washington and Mexico City agreed: It was time for me to accept a backlogged list of invitations to visit the American West. I went to visit friendly governors like Republican Jon Huntsman of Utah, governor of that reddest of red states but a strong backer of humane treatment for immigrants. I had also been asked to pay a call on Democratic governor Christine Gregoire of Washington, a passionate advocate of educating Mexican American children in the Pacific Northwest, where apples would rot on the trees without the labor of our *paisanos*. Then there was Governor Schwarzenegger, an immigrant himself: Arnold had been a tireless friend of Mexico, popular with Mexican Americans in his state. At risk to his own standing with right-wingers, the former action star was brave enough to ask me to address his legislature at the front lines of the Great American Immigration Debate.

Our plane landed in Sacramento after a successful whirlwind tour through the West, where I had spent the previous two days. I met with the leaders of Utah's Mormon Church hierarchy, where a suprising number of Republican officials spoke beautiful Spanish—many Mormons have done mission work in Latin America, retaining a gift for our language and a lifelong sympathy for our people. Seattle's globalist business community gave me a standing ovation: Mexico purchases the airplanes of Boeing, uses the computer software of Microsoft, provides the coffee sold at Starbucks, buys products retailed at Seattle-based Costco. Among the apple orchards, I met with Oregon's Governor Ted Kulongoski, who hailed the importance of immigrants to the agriculture and manufacturing industries of the Pacific Northwest. As the wheels of the *Benito Juárez* bumped down on a hot, sunny runway in Sacramento and taxied to where Arnold and his wife, Maria Shriver, waited at the head of the red carpet, the pilot's radio crackled with the electrifying news: The United States Senate had passed the McCain-Kennedy bill.

Though we knew the more conservative House might vote it down, this was a historic leap forward. A guest-worker bill had passed the GOP-controlled Senate and had the backing of a conservative Republican U.S. president. As I entered the capitol dome to speak to California lawmakers, I saw that the issue had gotten the public's attention: Right-wing Republican lawmakers staged a walkout on the floor of the legislature. Maria Shriver explained the maneuver to Marta in the House galleries, where Maria sat with my first lady and the four Schwarzenegger children. "I never take them out of school for anything, ever," Maria whispered emphatically. "But I wanted them to see this. President Fox is a hero of democracy, and this is a moment in history."

I was touched to hear Maria talk about her passion for Mexico later that evening as we sat in the backyard of the governor's mansion. The speech had gone well: I had a new, more finely tuned message on immigration for this trip, carefully calibrated by my advisers in the Foreign Ministry to meet the tense U.S. political climate. I had toned down my pre-Christmas attacks on the "shameful" Berlin Wall as a "disgrace" to American values. I did not reiterate our opposition to President Bush's decision to order the National Guard to the Rio Grande, stressing instead that "we recognize the right of the U.S. to secure its borders." I talked about the need, now that Mexico was a democracy, for our two countries to work together for security and prosperity on both sides of the border. I focused almost exclusively on the good results that freedom had brought to Mexico: the first economic stability we had known in a century; progress on housing, education, health care, and poverty. And I had extolled that day's Senate victory, which gave the United States and Mexico a historic opportunity to work more closely together—as business partners, neighbors, and friends.

On Arnold's back patio that evening, a powerhouse group of California business leaders—wine growers and technology entrepreneurs, Hollywood producers and financiers—came one by one to our little table beside the vine-strewn trellis to emphasize their support and congratulate us on the passage of McCain-Kennedy. Arnold lit a cigar and poured some good Napa pinot noir. The pop star Clay Aiken of *American Idol* fame crooned for the crowd. Maria Shriver put a microphone in Marta's hand and cajoled her into serenading us with "Bésame Mucho." But in the distance, over the back wall of the governor's patio, we could hear the faint and distant chant of the Minutemen in their camouflage fatigues and Uncle Sam outfits. *"Fox go home!"* they chanted. *"No more Mexicans! Fox go home!"*

I DID. Demonstrators were shouting there, too. The Distrito Federal, or D.F., as we call Mexico City, is a city of protest. Rarely a day goes by when D.F.'s Paseo de la Reforma or the downtown *Zócalo* is not jammed with *manifestaciones:* striking teachers, protesting miners, leftist street agitators, indigenous-rights activists, handicapped-rights activists, outraged pet owners, or dispossessed soccer fans, snarling up traffic to the fury of taxi drivers—who respond by going on strike.

I welcomed the freedom of our people to protest. I love the example of Charles de Gaulle, who became president after France had endured the occupation of the Nazis. One day after the war, an aide rushed into President de Gaulle's office in the Élysée Palace and said, "The students are protesting, *Monsieur le President*!"

"So?" de Gaulle said coolly. "Students always protest."

"But they are protesting *you*!" the aide remonstrated.

"Good," the president replied. "Then France must truly be free."

Mexico's democracy was like de Gaulle's description of his own country: "How can anyone govern a nation with two hundred forty-six different kinds of cheese?" But in Oaxaca things grew more serious. A teachers' strike against an unexceptional but democratically elected PRI governor in that poor southern state had escalated into violence and civil unrest. Even though two thirds of the population told pollsters that they disapproved of the governor's administration and wanted him to resign, there was little the federal government could do. Oaxaca's PRI governor had been elected in a free election with a significant majority. Unless he was found guilty of a crime or the violence spread to present a danger to the nation, we could hardly send in the Mexican army to put down the strikers or to remove a freely elected governor, no matter what we thought of him.

It was devastating to the thriving tourist trade of colonial Oaxaca, one of the most beautiful mountain cities of the Mexican interior. The international media made it look as if Mexico teetered on the edge of rebellion—though a visitor could walk through the heart of Oaxaca's chapels, cafés, and ruins at the height of the strike and order an ice cream in the *zócalo* without fear of violence.

On May 3 of that year, in the village of San Salvador Atenco outside Mexico City, local state police of the state of Mexico got into an altercation with sixty flower vendors at the local Texcoco market, shattering the calm of a peaceful spring morning in the town where rioters had blocked the building of a new international airport in 2002. The dispute flared quickly out of control. The National Human Rights Commission would later charge that hundreds of citizens were rousted from their homes, beaten, arrested without cause, and loaded into trucks; police were alleged to have sexually abused women they arrested; at least one youth may have been killed in the violence, when a tear-gas canister allegedly struck a fourteen-year-old boy in the chest.

Critics charged that it was the State of Mexico's own Abu Ghraib. My government ordered an investigation, which Mexico's Supreme Court launched last year. We sent in federal officials to restore peace to the troubled village and worked with the local PRI state governor to make sure that this sort of brutality would not happen again. But it was a black mark on our country's enormous progress on human rights under democracy, and I continue to take it as a personal challenge. In fact, the presidential library we are building now at the Centro Fox in Rancho San Cristóbal will include exhibits of all the evidence of the riots at Atenco, with every page of records, evidence, and photographs for future scholars, investigators, and prosecutors to scour. Latin America cannot have democracy without the freedom of citizens to protest peacefully. And we cannot criticize the human-rights abuses of Cuba's Castro or Iraq's Hussein—even the treatment of our immigrants at the border, or U.S. detainment of prisoners without trial at Guantánamo Bay—unless our own hands are clean.

LIKE DE GAULLE'S FRANCE, now Mexico was truly free. Whether our country would remain that way lay at stake in the 2006 presidential election. As the clock ticked down to July 2, López Obrador seemed determined to give up his once-commanding lead. By May 2006, Felipe Calderón was deadlocked with AMLO in the polls. In the second debate, AMLO reluctantly showed up; he was obviously uncomfortable, shifting from one foot to another, rambling vague promises. His performance contrasted poorly to Calderón's articulate mastery of public policy. People watched bespectacled, earnest young Felipe on television and said, "*There's* our president."

My friendship with George Bush continued to serve both countries well. That winter there had been widespread reports of a Mexican army incursion into Texas near El Paso, where ten men in the uniforms of Mexican soldiers allegedly attacked U.S. law-enforcement officers. The story made its way into the congressional debate on immigration, as senators and congressman demanded White House reprisals against this Mexican "invasion" of U.S. territory. I called George immediately on the hot line. "George, this did *not* happen" I said firmly. "We have investigated this from top to bottom, and I am telling you, this simply did not happen." President Bush took me at my word. "Vicente, if you tell me this is how it happened, I believe you." And that was the end of it. This is what it is for presidents to be good neighbors and good friends.

The Mexican army had entered U.S. territory for the first time since Pancho Villa's raids—on September 8, 2005, in the wake of Hurricane Katrina. We had monitored the hurricane's devastation carefully from Mexico City, fearing that it could strike farther down the Gulf of Mexico. When the scope of the disaster in New Orleans and Mississippi's Gulf Coast became clear, I called President Bush and asked for permission to send ships of the Mexican navy from Tampico bearing 250 tons of food and a massive store of relief supplies to New Orleans. We dispatched aid workers to the Houston Astrodome to help the hurricane victims who had fled and sent a team of crack epidemiologists specialized in mosquito-borne diseases common after floods. I also got permission from the White House to send an army relief convoy across the border at Laredo.

Many people think of Mexico only as a poor country that needs the help of its neighbors. But perhaps because we do not send our army to fight overseas wars, Mexico's armed forces have extraordinary resources for disaster preparedness. Living as we do amid hurricanes, earthquakes, volcanoes, tornadoes, floods, and epidemics, our navy has the ability to deliver vast quantities of water, sandbags, food, and relief supplies at a moment's notice. Our army had the medics, trucks, bulldozers, and logistical capability to reconstruct Veracruz after Hurricane Stan and the outskirts of Mexico City after the eruption of Popocatéptl. Several weeks after Katrina destroyed one of the great U.S. cities, leaving millions homeless and destitute along the Gulf Coast, Hurricane Wilma utterly devastated Cancún and Cozumel. Within twelve months we had repaired the damage, and today the beaches of Yucatán are more gorgeous than ever, the residents back on their feet, the elegant hotels of the Mayan Riviera fully occupied.

So on September 8, 2005, a convoy of 167 Mexican soldiers crossed the U.S.-Mexico border for the first time in peace, bearing food, water, and supplies to aid the hurricane victims sheltering at Kelly Air Force base in San Antonio. There, African American refugees from New Orleans and homeless white southerners in gimme caps hugged Mexican soldiers in army green. Above their heads fluttered the eagle-and-serpent flag of Mexico, alongside U.S. flags of red, white, and blue.

More than four hundred Mexicans died crossing that border last year. They died of thirst, mostly, suffering dehydration or exposure in the unexpected cold and aridity of the Arizona desert. The human-smuggling *coyotes* to whom they have sold their souls do not prepare them for the reality of the conditions. These *coyotes* are criminals, but the people who die in the desert are not. They are sons and daughters, mothers and fathers. They are pioneers, like the brave people who built your country and mine, crossing deserts in search of a dream.

Our sin was greater, mine and George Bush's, because in Mexico we have failed to provide them the jobs they needed to survive while, in the United States, businesses in the world's richest economy held out the promise of opportunity, then officers with guns arrest those who come in hope. For decades both governments chased them, cheated them, beat them, abandoned and ignored them, leaving many to die in the desert.

My administration was criticized for giving out what the media called "happy boxes," first-aid kits with maps, bottled water, food, bandages—and yes, even condoms—to those determined to cross. But this was unfair. We did not encourage immigrants to leave—quite the opposite: We spent millions on advertising in the poorest immigrant-sending regions of southern and central Mexico and along our northern border, urging prospective immigrants to stay home in the new democracy. We told them that they could find jobs in the *maquiladoras* and factories spawned by the NAFTA trade; offered them low-interest loans to buy a home, scholarship payments to help keep their children in school, health insurance to care for their families. No president working to build prosperity wants to lose his hardest-working citizens to a wealthy neighbor.

But when you are a poor country living next door to a nation sixteen times richer, where parents can make ten times more to feed their children and these workers can send home $23 billion a year to people they love, there will be immigration. Until we create more jobs and the United States reforms its laws, we can only do our very best to make sure that no one dies from it.

Back in 2006, when the Republicans controlled both houses of Congress, the right wing was more powerful in the House than the Senate. The nature of congressional districting was that key GOP House leaders had been elected by conservative voters in Republican primaries, where immigration was for many a right-wing litmus test. Some of the loudest voices on the House side were border-state congressmen like J. D. Hayworth of Arizona. As the Congress moved toward adjournment for the 2006 campaign season, the right-wingers convinced the House leadership to make "securing our borders" a last-ditch rallying cry for Republicans seeking to hold on to Congress against public protest versus the war in Iraq, disgraced former majority leader Tom DeLay, the prosecution of lobbyist Jack Abramoff, and the page scandal involving Florida congressman Mark Foley. The U.S. House voted down the Senate's McCain-Kennedy guest-worker reforms, substituting a tough enforcement-only bill calling for that seven hundred-mile wall along the border, stiffer penalties on employers who hire undocumented immigrants, and new laws to make undocumented immigration a felony. Hard-liners even proposed that 12 million workers be deported back to Mexico, an astonishing act of economic madness. If it had been enacted, the original House proposal would have shut down the financial markets of the United States and brought American business to a halt overnight.

In the end, of course, Republicans went down to defeat in 2006, in both the House and the Senate. J. D. Hayworth is no longer a congressman. Tom DeLay's House seat is now held by a Democrat. The men of hate brought their party to disaster, despite the politicians' trick of wrapping themselves in the flag. Supporters of comprehensive immigration reform were vindicated: Exit polls of U.S. voters in the November congressional elections reported that 57 percent favored a guest-worker program with Mexico.

Our own elections in July 2006 were the closest in Mexico's history—not as close as the Bush-Gore election, but just as dramatic. In 2000, the United States had thirty-six days of protests and court rulings about the Florida count; in 2006, Mexicans waited almost twice as long for the courts to recheck the outcome, a process that went on for nearly three months after the July 2 election. But in Mexico's case the outcome was much more clear-cut: Felipe Calderón had won the popular vote by less than a percentage point over Andrés Manuel López Obrador, earning 243,934 more votes than AMLO.

It was a rainy night in Mexico City on July 2. The helicopters swept their spotlights ceaselessly through the downpour. There were no riots or disturbances; the mood was tense but peaceful. Careful not to repeat the mysterious "computer errors" of the old regime in 1988, the IFE cautiously released all the returns in real time on the Internet, as they were processed simultaneously by computers under the watchful eyes of all five political parties.

By midnight it was clear to all but AMLO's camp that Felipe Calderón had won a narrow upset. Andrés Manuel took to the *Zócalo* to declare himself the victor, saying he just "knew" that he had won. Nine of ten national exit polls and the IFE's official count, certified by impartial observers from all over the world, showed the PAN candidate in the lead. But López Obrador evinced little interest in the actual count: AMLO said he represented the spirit of the people and planned to rule Mexico regardless of the results the electoral authorities reported.

For more than two months, AMLO's supporters thronged the streets and clogged the major arteries of the nation's capital. At first Andrés Manuel's rallies drew hundreds of thousands of citizens to the *zócalo* in protest, then tens of thousands, then hundreds; fewer and fewer marched as the weeks wore on and more evidence came to light that Felipe Calderón had won the election. At one point AMLO stormed into court and showed the international press corps a videotape that he said "proved" that the government had rigged the election by stuffing ballots into "pregnant" boxes. As the press reported the next day, examination of the tape showed that the IFE authorities had in fact simply moved to the correct box a handful of congressional ballots that had been misplaced; all the observers present at the polling place—including López Obrador's PRD representative—had approved the move.

Many of my advisers—security officials and cabinet members, PAN leaders and well-meaning friends, expert legal scholars, Los Pinos aides worried about weakening the presidency—urged that I move in the police or the army to open the capital's streets. AMLO's protests practically shut down the Paseo de la Reforma during that long, hot summer, frazzling tempers among the citizens and hurting the tourist economy. It was ridiculous, really—a handful of protesters in virtually empty tents down the Paseo de la Reforma, Andrés Manuel's encampment looked like nothing more than an abandoned flea market by August and September. Every few hundred meters sat a few paid PRD henchmen cooking tamales on a hot plate or flipping through an issue of Mexican *Playboy*, chatting on their cell phones as millions fumed in the traffic. A few feet away, the city's hotels, shops, and restaurants sat empty, the employees laid off.

In Oaxaca, things grew more violent—a shooting or two every week, bombs set off by far-left radicals. But at AMLO's Mexico City protests, no one was getting physically hurt. Perhaps in my youth I might have agreed with my security advisers and sent in uniformed men to enforce the law with riot guns and tear gas. But I believe that the greatest strength of a democratic president is *patience*—as the old Chinse proverb holds, "Patience is power." At each step in the seemingly endless drama of AMLO's *complots,* conspiracies, and crises, I chose peace over violence, democracy over order—the avoidance of conflict over the impulse to action.

History will be the ultimate judge. Certainly my critics said that Fox had lost control of the situation. The media howled that mob rule was bringing the country to its knees. The critical point came on September 16, our Independence Day, when the president traditionally reprises Father Hidalgo's famous Grito de la Independencia from Mexico City's *Zócalo*. To avoid confrontation with AMLO's protesters, I broke tradition and gave my speech in my home state of Guanajuato at the cathedral of Dolores Hidalgo, where the great priest had given his original cry of independence. Again my detractors said I was being weak, but Mexico celebrated its freedom in peace.

The next flashpoint came with the State of the Union Address, the Informe, which the president traditionally delivers from the rostrum of the congressional palace of San Lázaro. Leftist lawmakers of Andrés Manuel's PRD blocked the entrance and seized the podium, refusing to let me speak. So for the first time in memory, Mexico's president went to the front door like Martin Luther nailing his ninety-five theses to the church door in Wittenberg. I handed in my speech in writing, complying with the literal requirements of our Constitution, then went back to Los Pinos and gave my speech on television. The media made hay with this. The PRD exulted in their victory on the congressional dais. PAN stalwarts complained that I had retreated and should have shoved my way to the congressional podium, the way we did in 1988. The PRI reminded everyone that this sort of thing never happened when *they* ran the country. But, given our history of revolutionary bloodshed, the Mexican people value serenity. Citizens gave me high marks in the polls for my handling of the protests, while AMLO's stock plummeted. Quite simply, we fed López Obrador enough rope to hang himself.

Andrés Manuel took to the *Zócalo,* where he had been living in a tent. On November 20, Mexico's Revolution Day holiday, he stood in the main square before a dwinding group of fans, many of them paid to attend. They milled around the *Zócalo,* eating fried corn on the cob and cheering at designated intervals. On the makeshift platform, his face puffy, his flowing shock of salt-and-pepper hair flying in the air, López Obrador donned a green, white, and red sash of his own design and declared himself the nation's "legitimate president." He introduced his own "alternative cabinet" and asked the mob to approve them by acclamation. AMLO promised a parallel government for which he would collect his own taxes and make his own laws. Finally the "president of the *Zócalo*" had his wish: a government where AMLO called all the shots. I have not heard whether any taxpayers have chipped in.

The public understood the wisdom of our commitment to peace, patience, and the institutions of democracy. In the end we simply let Andrés Manuel López Obrador wear out his welcome. By the time the courts ruled that the IFE's election process had been fair and accurate, naming Felipe Calderón the uncontested winner of the presidential election, nearly 70 percent of the Mexican people expressed a positive view of my presidency. Less than 13 percent approved of Andrés Manuel López Obrador.

Felipe Calderón is off to a fast start. Within the first hundred days, his government had extradited fifteen top cartel leaders to the United States and arrested dozens more in Tijuana, Oaxaca, and Sinaloa. In a recent drug bust in Mexico City, the government impounded more than $200 million in cash from the swank villa of a naturalized Chinese immigrant who had risen to head one of Mexico's most ruthless drug gangs. President Calderón has announced his intention to build out our health-insurance program to include every citizen of Mexico and expand our housing program to put more new families in their first homes. Reaching a quick budget compromise with reform-minded members of the PRI and PRD in Congress, the Calderón administration has increased the nation's education budget, expanding scholarship payments to keep three hundred thousand more kids in school. President Calderón has pledged to continue the fiscal discipline that has produced the longest period of economic stability and the strongest peso in memory. In his first hundred days in office, his government has put new energy into creating 116,000 new jobs to help keep our people at home, where they belong. He and his bright, enthusiastic team are focusing their enormous talents on two areas where we still have the furthest to go—attacking crime and reducing poverty. With a foundation of democracy and a talented team of cabinet members and political advisers, this brilliant young man will lead Mexico into the twenty-first century as the most successful president in our nation's history.

Mexico's best days are just ahead. We are a democracy now, proud and strong. Of course we have our problems, as do so many countries around the world. I am headed to some of those hard places now, to do my best to help.

It wasn't long until I escaped my rocking chair at Rancho San Cristóbal. The fissured vertebra from my disagreement with that two-hundred-pound bull is nearly healed—really, it was too small a bull for a grown man even to mention, more of a child's pet, very embarrassing to a vaquero.

As I travel the world now, I see that conditions have never been so ripe for our revolution of hope. For example, on immigration, my friends in the United States tell me that they have not given up hope for reform; that Congress may yet pass a guest-worker bill, if not during the Bush presidency, then after 2008. I hope that this book will help.

IMMIGRATION IS a no-win issue for politicians. Pro-reform Republicans circle warily around their conservative base in red states; Democrats do the same in blue states, where many working-class voters blame Mexicans for the loss of jobs. Today's leaders know what is morally right for people who are being treated as second-class citizens and what is economically best for America's future. The question is: Do they have the courage to stand up for what is right? Will they be guided by what Lincoln called "the better angels of our nature"?

No cause is closer to God's will than the spiritual imperative that we love all people, treat others as we would be treated, and give every human being equal rights and equal dignity. Anti-immigrant groups can stack up all the polls and economic statistics they like, but in my gut I believe that the United States must seize this chance to lead, so that American idealism does not trickle away in the sands of Iraq. If George W. Bush fails, the opportunity for a presidency on a moral high note will pass to another. John McCain, Barack Obama, Hillary Clinton, Rudy Giuliani, John Edwards, Bill Richardson, Fred Thompson—the world watches and waits, hoping that the United States elects a leader with the courage, vision, and character to restore the original promise of the American dream.

THIS DREAM of the Americas is symbolized by the Statue of Liberty, not a Berlin Wall along the border. It is a vision of global democracy, worthy of the architects of Bretton Woods and the Marshall Plan, not a war plan for America to become the world's judge, jury, and policeman. To date, the United States has lost more than three thousand soldiers and spent more than $500 billion in Iraq. More than sixty thousand innocent civilians have been killed in that country since the war began.

A United States freed of such a burden could focus its attention on the Americas. Such a spiritually renewed beacon of freedom could join with Mexico and Canada to lift up our hemisphere and the world with a mighty economic Union of the Americas.

Certainly this is controversial, a former president of Mexico pushing to unite North America. "Fox," the isolationists will say, "who are you to tell

America how to defend its borders? The last thing that our rich, safe, peaceful, stable superpower would do is to join our economy with poor, violent, corrupt Mexico. Instead we should build that wall to protect the American dream from people like you."

But think globally for a moment: Will prosperity work if it is only for the rich? If the world is flat and we are all connected by globalism, as Thomas Friedman tells us, the American dream cannot flourish inside a walled compound. Who will be allowed inside these walls, and who will be shut out? The Einsteins? The Bells? Won't the walls keep *out* the workers you need for your industries? The innovators you need for your technologies? The customers you need for your products?

And what about security, Iraq, terrorism, personal freedom? The world cannot be a global democracy if one superpower has the only vote that counts. Will the First World ever be safe if the only citizens who matter are those born inside its walls?

Surely all the world's people are human beings under the eyes of God. Surely they deserve the promise of the Americas: peace and freedom, democracy and prosperity. And just as surely, if the wealthy nations of the world decide that this dream is only for those lucky enough to live within the walls of a Fortress America, the poor locked outside will not forever suffer in their shadows.

America has always been about freedom. This is not just democracy and the right to vote, but *personal* freedom—the right to move and work and learn, to be whatever you want to be. It is *economic* freedom—to migrate freely to jobs and trade freely in open markets. America also depends on *intellectual* freedom—to express, create, invent, debate, innovate, and expand. The American way of life simply cannot exist in a Fortress America. Even if you could build a wall two thousand miles long on the Rio Grande, it will not protect the wealthy people inside, any more than the walled haciendas of Spanish conquistadores could survive the hungry dreams of my immigrant grandfather, who was willing to trade his sweat for our little piece of heaven here at Rancho San Cristóbal.

If our own history teaches us anything, it is that we cannot live forever with a wealthy few inside the walls and the masses locked outside, poor and hungry. We learned this in my own country in 2000, when our peaceful revolution stormed the walls of the longest-running dictatorship of the twentieth century. For years they told us that Mexico needed the walls of isolation and authority to *protect* us—to shield the poor from exploitation by the rich United States, to defend farmers against cheap competition from abroad, to guard the rich from the criminals—to protect the whole lot of us from student agitators, Communists, and dangerous troublemakers like Vicente Fox.

The irony, of course, is that walls of fear don't protect the poor, the rich, or the middle class—*they just keep us apart,* so that those with jobs to give can't offer them to the poor who need them. The razor wire at the guarded border, the government agent tapping your phones—these do not protect you from any threat. They *are* the threat. There are no walls high enough and no soldiers vigilant enough to keep out the poor, to jam the transmission of new ideas, to deny the hopes of people willing to work for a better life. Consider this irony of the border wall: It would cost billions upon billions of dollars, a fraction of which, invested in a revolving fund, would create hundreds of thousands of jobs inside Mexico to keep our immigrants at home, in the land they love. The only jobs the border wall will create, of course, are for construction workers along the Rio Grande. And who will they hire to build this wall, if not Mexican immigrants?

THE AMERICA we love will never crown the Statue of Liberty with barbed wire. You cannot abandon us to fear, just when we are seeing the light of hope. We admire your principles too much for you to lose heart in them now. My answer to fear is hope: a new American Revolution of unity, generosity, and love to unite our hemisphere. Contrary to the words of Robert Frost, good fences do not always make good neighbors. In a global economy, the best way to build a clean, prosperous neighborhood in our hemisphere is to help the neighbors to build a better house next door.

With Castroism fading from Cuba, the only real threats to our hemisphere's future are Hugo Chávez and his allies, from Bolivia and Ecuador to Iran. But Hugo Chávez is more uniform than general, more bluff than bother. The Americas would be wise to wait him out—and spend that time building a house of free-market economics, human progress, and social justice so strong that every nation of Latin America will want to come inside. Given his head, Hugo will wear out his welcome in the world as quickly as AMLO did in the traffic of Mexico City. Hugo is primarily a danger to his own people in Venezuela. When the price of oil drops and the money runs out, he will no longer be able to intrigue with Evo Morales in Bolivia or Mahmoud Ahmadinejad in Iran; Chávez will be too busy scrambling to cover Venezuela's debts. I suspect that someday he will join the other ex-dictators in exile in Europe or Miami, dodging extradition warrants.

The key for the United States is not to go off by itself to attack a populist like Chávez; this will only turn him into a martyr for a developing world estranged by the war in Iraq and by the gap between rich nations and poor. The clear way forward for the United States is to form a true economic union with Mexico and Canada. Soon like-minded, free-market democracies to the south, like Chile and Costa Rica, would join. Someday this Union of the Americas might include a Brazil after Lula, an Argentina after Kirchner, a Cuba after Castro. If that seems far-fetched, just think how preposterous it would have been thirty years ago to dream of Poland's joining NATO.

The key is for us to come together as nations to fight poverty instead of fighting wars. We should build schools and hospitals instead of building walls. Rather than spending billions on walls and wars, we could launch a revolving fund like the Marshall Plan to lift up the people of our own hemisphere. The last thing the United States and the wealthy nations of the world need is a resentful, poor, explosive Latin America. The best thing for America is to make its neighborhood a calm, wealthy, prosperous haven of democracy in a dangerous world.

In 1835 the definitive foreign visitor to the United States, the French writer Alexis de Tocqueville, marveled at the prosperity, opportunity, and human values he found there. He is often quoted as having said, "America is great because it is good. If America ever ceases to be good, America will cease to be great."

This is brand U.S.A.: the goodness of America. And the day America no longer stands for this goodness—the day the United States turns out the torch on the Statue of Liberty and replaces it with the searchlight of the guard tower, the day that the visionary America of the Marshall Plan becomes the Fortress America of the Minutemen—on that day America will cease to be good and will no longer be great.

I WENT to Nigeria for one day last weekend. I was in Texas, Oklahoma, Ohio, and Nevada last week. I will be in Canada tomorrow. In the age of high-speed travel and the Internet, we cannot wall ourselves off from the global economy, any more than our ancestors could ignore the chance to "make the Americas." Nor can we remain indifferent to the global divide between rich and poor, any more than our ancestors could remain indifferent to the evils of religious persecution, poverty, slavery, and tyranny that drove them out of their Old Worlds and into ours. Even then, in a time when each journey took forty-five days in the bowels of ships from Santander to Veracruz, our grandfathers knew that the future was here in the New World. Surely now that Rancho San Cristóbal is only the click of a computer key from Lagos, Toledo, Dallas, and Ottawa, that land of opportunity is here still, waiting to be discovered, ready for a revolution of hope.

This revolution is to be found not in the politics of George Bush or Vicente Fox, Barack Obama or Hillary Clinton, John McCain or Felipe Calderón but inside our own hearts. Just as democracy will not come to Iraq until its people free themselves from ancient hatreds, a closer union will not come to the Americas until we free ourselves of fear. We must liberate our souls from the envy and hatred that makes us build walls where we should build bridges. Where today we close doors, we should open hearts.

This is why I take exception to those who say that the leaders of government should not express religious faith. Why not allow the hand of God to guide our actions? We have seen what happens when leaders are guided by greed and power, politics and polls. We should not be afraid, each of us, to ask from time to time how the teachings of our youth—Christian or Muslim, from a Catholic priest or a wise mother—might apply to the great questions facing our societies.

What would God think of His people building a wall between them to keep the rich on one side, in isolated splendor, and the poor on the other side, in desperation and misery? What would Father Schiefler, the Jesuit priest who urged us to be people for others, advise the leaders of Mexico to do today? Would he tell us to wash our hands of the poor and exile them northward—or to roll up our sleeves and build an economic union to make their futures as bright in Mexico as they are in the United States? On Iraq, would our faith dictate that the nations that stood for peace now sit back, watch the United States dragged deeper into the morass, and call it "George Bush's war"? Or can we act together through the United Nations, to bring that troubled region back to peace?

I slept well as president, and I still do today. This is perhaps because, for a Catholic-educated farm boy, things have always seemed pretty clear to me. I am a native son of Mexico, with the blood of an American farmer, Spanish grocers, a French soldier, and an indigenous peasant coursing through my veins. In my heart are the examples of a compassionate mother and a hardworking father; in my head are the lessons pounded into me by Jesuit priests and business-school professors. This life has taught me that all the things we want for this world—peace and prosperity, democracy and security—cannot be forced on people at the point of a gun. Freedom must come from within.

So this will be the next chapter of my life: on the road again, riding off with Marta on my favorite horse, Dos de Julio. But we're not riding off into the sunset. We are headed your way, to sell our dreams.

Since leaving office we have broken ground on the Centro Fox here at Rancho San Cristóbal, burrowing under the foundations of the old walls of the former hacienda. Where once I dug for bandit treasure with my campesino friends, now we have built the foundation of a new academic center, presidential library, and think tank. Marta and I haven taken a firsthand look at the useful "afterlives" of Bill Clinton, Jimmy Carter, George H. W. Bush, Nelson Mandela (and soon of Tony Blair). They have proved that retirement is for old people. Instead these ex-leaders are still people "in a hurry"—fighting poverty and AIDS in Africa, preventing election fraud, raising funds for tsunami relief. Their postpresidential success teaches me that even a guy with a few gray hairs and a bad back can still build houses, feed children, and change lives.

From the Centro Fox, Marta and I have enlisted the help and advice of the Clintons, the Carters, and other former heads of state like Chile's Ricardo Lagos and Brazil's Fernando Henrique Cardoso as we expand the Vamos Mexico foundation to fight poverty worldwide. I plan to keep on working for global democracy, peace, and social justice at our think tank. We can show how the microcredit revolution of Dr. Yunus and the socially conscious market policies of the thoughtful center can do more for those less fortunate than all the rhetoric of populists who prey on the ignorant and cheat the poor.

In recent weeks Marta and I have been to France and the Dominican Republic to meet with the leaders of center-right movements for social democracy, to Nevada to talk with businessmen about protecting the environment, to the Kennedy Center in Washington to address women about gender equity, to dozens of universities and conferences across the continent to share our democratic experience, to Nigeria to learn more about poverty reduction and talk about healing our global divide.

But I write these final words here at Rancho San Cristóbal, with a classic Mexican invitation to you: *Nuestra casa es tu casa*—"Our house is your house." Please come to visit us at the Centro Fox, where we can work miracles together—with love.

In order to move mountains, first we must move souls. This is our challenge. This is how we become men and women for others. This is our revolution of hope.

INDEX

PHOTO CREDITS

Insert page 1 *top*, pages 2–5, page 6 *top and middle*, page 7, page 8 *top*, and page 16 *top*: Vicente Fox personal collection

Insert page 1 *bottom*: *El Mundo Illustrado*, 1905

Insert page 6 *bottom*: *El Universal*, 1988

Insert page 8 *bottom left and bottom right*, pages 9–15, and page 16 *bottom*: Presidency Web page, © Creative Commons Mexico